D1615742

Art and Responsibility

Art and Responsibility

A phenomenology of the diverging paths of
Rosenzweig and Heidegger

Jules Simon

continuum

The Continuum International Publishing Group
80 Maiden Lane, New York, NY 10038
The Tower Building, 11 York Road, London SE1 7NX

www.continuumbooks.com

Library of Congress Cataloging-in-Publication Data
A catalog record for this book is available from the Library of Congess.

ISBN: HB: 978-1-4411-0952-1

Typeset by Pindar NZ, Auckland, New Zealand
Printed and bound in the United States of America

to Kate, my beloved

Contents

Contents ix

Contents

PREFACE

Nothing can compare with the feeling of fulfillment at having completed, after many long years, a difficult book project. But what those many years also mean is that I have much to be thankful for and many to thank. The generous support and guidance that I received from others enabled me not only to bring this book to publication, but also to dare to write this kind of book in the first place. Writing philosophy is the most difficult of disciplines since to express oneself philosophically means embarking on an unpredictable path of deconstructing and reconstructing one's very sense of well-being and questioning one's frameworks for meaning. In my case, almost from the very beginning of my self-imposed exile as an intellectual, I was guided by my mentor and friend Norbert Samuelson. I owe much to him, beginning with his demanding work ethic and including his philosophical acuity and wise guidance. There are countless passages in the following pages that echo with his wise insights. I am also thankful to Bob Gibbs for encouraging me to think Heidegger's thoughts along with Rosenzweig's at the very beginning of this project. At various stages of preparing the manuscript, I received support from Rheinhold Meyer, Edith Wyschogrod, Bernhard Casper, Friedrich-Wilhelm von Hermann, and David Hall. I subjected many of my undergraduate and graduate students at the University of Texas at El Paso to reading and trying to understand unfinished portions of the manuscript, an onerous task for which I thank them, in general. Institutionally, I thank the University of Texas at El Paso for its financial support of my scholarship and members of the Department of Philosophy for enabling me to explore these ideas in various seminars and colloquia. I am grateful for the support that I received from The Fulbright Program for providing me with the resources to begin writing about Rosenzweig, Hegel, and Heidegger in Tübingen and also to the German Academic Exchange Service, with the Leo Baeck Institute of New York, for enabling me to continue work on this project by supporting me during a Summer Semester at Freiburg University. Finally, I am especially grateful to Haaris Naqvi of Continuum for his enthusiastic support and for kindly indulging my requests for more and more words.

In ways too numerous to account for, my children — Rebekah, Josiah, and

Jared — grew up with this book and provided countless occasions for me to test ideas from it for their intelligibility. In particular, Josiah has provided tangible and inestimable support having read and critically commented upon parts of the manuscript. Indeed, he became so involved that he decided to become a Rosenzweig scholar himself and is writing on Rosenzweig's philosophy of history. Finally, this book would not be what it is without my wife Kate who has been my constant companion, beloved dialogue partner, and lover these many years. She has intimately shared with me the great suffering and the deep joy that this book has brought to our lives. I end my prefatory words, which are just as much conclusions, by offering to her in deepest gratitude and respect what she treasures most — from my heart and my lips to hers, a kiss.

INTRODUCTION

Art and responsibility: two distinctly human phenomena, but also two distinct phenomena that humans have tended to hold apart from each other. Can we think these two phenomena together? Should we? Do our artistic acts have ethically normative implications? What are the aesthetics of our ethical actions? Are aesthetics necessarily political or apolitical? The same can be — or should be — asked of ethical relations.

In the first decades of the twentieth century, two German philosophers — Franz Rosenzweig and Martin Heidegger — separately developed philosophies of art that present diverging and yet concurrent claims that indicate how intimately our ethical choices are inextricably bound up with our aesthetic and communal lives. Their philosophical works are dense and inordinately complex, respectively reflecting their deep immersion in the philosophical life-world of their common generation, namely, the socio-political and intellectual milieu of post-Bismarckian Weimar, Germany. Moreover, both philosophers chose to publish their works and to publically engage in teaching, which indicates their commitments to influencing their life-world. As a phenomenological enterprise, my task in this book is to identify, elaborate, and then evaluatively compare the essential normative elements that constitute the philosophical guidelines of their respective works.

A phenomenology of diverging paths

In considering their philosophies, I proceed phenomenologically and do not attempt to historically chronicle nor psychoanalytically determine the sources or after-effects of their written works. That is another kind of scholarship. On the one hand, this makes my task somewhat easier since I do not intend to duplicate the fine work already done of situating Rosenzweig and Heidegger in the stream of reconstructed causal relations that is the tool-in-trade of intellectual historians.[1] On the other hand, my task is more demanding since I exercise a phenomenological critique of their philosophies, with special attention paid to the underlying ethical threads, in order to build my account of their divergence. As Kwame Appiah notes in a recent work, *Experiments in Ethics*, and with no small measure of ironic self-referential deference, the phenomenon of offering a most likely account has been the *modus operandi* for philosophers since well before we ever began to self-consciously reflect on how we go about crafting our works in this occasionally hallowed but more often embattled profession of philosophy.[2] In this regard, Heidegger's confession in the opening pages of *Being and Time* about his own phenomenological orientation is instructive. He informs us that while he proceeds phenomenologically, he does so quite otherwise than his mentor Husserl. He develops the lines of his hermeneutic theory and fundamental ontology out of sources such as Schleiermacher and Dilthey while nonetheless arguing that, for example, in *Basic Problems in Phenomenology*, phenomenology as a task is fundamentally the most recent version of scientific philosophy.

Rosenzweig's work has often been characterized as intractable — a hybrid of Hegelian dialectics and Nietzschean anti-metaphysics as well as being metalogically structured by Cohenian mathematics and yet infused with Goethe's poetic German sensibility. But because Rosenzweig also fashioned his philosophical narrative by creating a mosaic wrought from normative, literary, and sociological vignettes, his work — at least his major work, *The Star of Redemption* — could also be said to fall into the realm of descriptive, essence-oriented phenomenology itself. Indirect evidence supporting this position is the oft-cited declaration by Emanuel Levinas in *Totality and Infinity* that Rosenzweig's work was too often present in his own to be cited with regularity, keeping in mind the obvious fact that Levinas's dissertation was an important phenomenological interpretation of Husserl's theory of intuition.[3] That Levinas was deeply affected by, and strove to overcome Heidegger's ontological/hermeneutical version of phenomenology further supports my interpretation of *The Star of Redemption* along the lines of divergence from Heidegger's phenomenological path that I sketch out in the following chapters.

Both Rosenzweig's and Heidegger's key works reveal their deep rootedness in the socio-political conditions of their day. For example, from his many essays and the huge corpus of letters that he left behind, it is obvious that Rosenzweig was deeply affected by events surrounding World War I, including his having enthusiastically enlisted to serve in the German army and his subsequent disenchantment with Germany's role as protagonist in that war. As he himself notes in his first major published work, *Hegel and the State*, he would not have written the same book after the war that was begun before the war.[4] Since he died in 1929 of amyotrophic lateral sclerosis before the Nazis came to power in 1933, his further involvement in what became the fascist course of German socio-political history was curtailed, as a Jewish intellectual and vis à vis the attempt by the Nazis to exterminate European Jews and Jewish influence upon the course of world events.

Heidegger, on the other hand, was just as clearly not disenchanted by the course of the World War I but instead maintained his patriotic faithfulness to the Fatherland into and beyond World War II.[5] In ethical fairness to the complexity of his personal development, however, I should point out that Heidegger did distance himself during World War II from his earlier advocacy of the Nazi's ascendancy and political agenda in what has been referred to by Heidegger himself and others as his "turn."[6] But despite the much-vaunted claims about his controversial "turn" — some of which I will discuss below — he lost his official teaching position at Freiburg University following the War precisely because of his earlier, willing support of the Nazi socio-political agenda, his ongoing membership in the Nazi Party, and his role as Party functionary as Rector of Freiburg University from 1933 to 1934.[7] Recounting such historical and political instances matters since they serve as the historical and horizonal prelude for the reflections in this book on the ethical and aesthetic commitments that characterize these two philosophers.

But given the methodological constraints already indicated, namely, that I proceed phenomenologically and not with the tools of an intellectual historian, I do not provide a simple or straightforward accounting of this or that chain of historical happenstances. Rather, my intent is more narrowly defined in how I proceed to initially frame what Werner Marx has identified as a "phenomenological ethics" and that, as I appropriate that approach, has been taken up in various ways by Emmanuel Levinas, Hans Jonas, Hannah Arendt, Edith Wyschogrod, Robert Gibbs, Robert Bernasconi, Walter Benjamin, and others.[8] Each of these authors aligns themselves, without explicitly enunciating their position, in what I have come to regard as the quintessential characteristic of phenomenological ethics that was pioneered in a positive way by Rosenzweig and negatively by Heidegger; namely, the mode of indirect intuitive guidance that has normative consequences. Although not directly overlapping in a biographical narrative, both philosophers provide strong accounts of how their philosophies resist the echoes of that famous Hegelian dictum at the end of the Preface to his *Philosophy of Right*, that "The owl of Minerva spreads its wings only with the falling of dusk." What Hegel meant was that philosophy only is able to understand reality after the event and cannot predict how reality ought to be. Respectively, Rosenzweig's and Heidegger's direct involvements in the political and cultural events of Germany resulted from their particular ethical commitments that led to their divergent but indirect involvements in political life, turnings that implicate their attempts to normatively effect ethical choices through inscribing well-defined and differentiated aesthetic orientations in social practices. This complicated thesis is what I propose is their resistance to the spreading wingspan of Hegel's "owl of Minerva." In other words, I contend that Rosenzweig's disillusionment with World War I and Heidegger's withdrawal from an administrative role of leadership at Freiburg University, and thus from his public role in the Nazi Party, are clear signs that both philosophers "turned" in response to their historical conditions, turning away from their own earlier work and political engagements to phenomenological analyses of art and language. The key to my thesis, however, is my contention that in

their respective turnings, Rosenzweig was more acutely sensitive to the indirect
ethical implications of his position whereas Heidegger engaged in a more direct
and thus instrumental manipulation of those very same ethical implications.
Maintaining and defending either one of these positions is difficult enough, so
it should be apparent that the interpretive path that I provide in the following
chapters is treacherous because of both textual limitations and the vast wealth
of primary and secondary sources related to these two philosophers. In what
follows, I attempt a preliminary overview of that path.

There is no possibility of real and effective critique without setting out real
and tangible differences, differences that often have tragic socio-political consequences. Others have already made the case for understanding Rosenzweig
and Heidegger as either much closer or much further from each other than I do,
beginning with Else Freund's famous first study that argues for a convergence,
and Karl Löwith's famous essay from 1942, "Heidegger und Rosenzweig:
Ein Nachtrag zu *Sein und Zeit*," that argues for both a strong divergence
and linkage, precisely on the issue of theology.[9] The most recent attempt to
historically link the works of Rosenzweig and Heidegger in their German
intellectual milieu is the work done by Peter Gordon who argues for a strong
convergence in the philosophies of Rosenzweig and Heidegger precisely on
the level of an understanding of their respective commitments to existential
philosophy. He claims that the political and aesthetic dimensions of their
works are inessential for understanding their more fundamental convergence,
relying for his contention upon a brief, cryptic article Rosenzweig wrote at the
end of his life, comparing his own work (Rosenzweig's) with his necessarily
uninformed — because it was superficial and incomplete — understanding of
Heidegger's philosophy as an existentialist.[10]

Rather than attempting to situate the works of these two philosophers
on that horizon of intellectual history, I draw from direct readings of their
primary works, intending especially to trace the ethical implications of their
philosophies of art. Gordon considers Rosenzweig and Heidegger "philosophical partisans" who have an "unlikely kinship"[11] and "intellectual affiliations
that cut across all of the apparent divisions of political life."[12] More troubling,
he claims that the "chief task of [his] book is to situate Rosenzweig alongside
Heidegger in this unusual intellectual horizon."[13] That horizon is something
Gordon calls philosophical expressionism, which he argues is based on a
resemblance between "Rosenzweig's category of redemption . . . [and] . . . what
Heidegger later called authenticity."[14] In the chapters that follow, I present a
radically different reading that locates Rosenzweig's category of redemption
and Heidegger's concept of authenticity in the horizontal parameters of what
I have been calling phenomenological ethics.

Prior to Gordon's work, the most recently celebrated argument for relating
Rosenzweig with Heidegger was that found in Emil Fackenheim's *To Mend
the World* where he condemns Heidegger for his silence on the Holocaust

and reconstructs a possible response by Rosenzweig: "Yet it is Heidegger's thought that cannot confront the Holocaust; and it is Rosenzweig's thought that — had the thinker lived long enough — would have found a confrontation with the *Ereignis* inescapable.[15] However, Emmanuel Levinas's philosophical critique of Heidegger is a critique that was also inspired by Levinas's reading of Rosenzweig and that is arguably the most far-reaching because the most ethically and intellectually sensitive to Heidegger's own phenomenological approach. Additionally, and for my own purposes, the major works that Levinas produced also serve as extended responses to the phenomenology of Heidegger, providing a powerful, ethical phenomenological alternative to Heidegger's phenomenology of existence out of Levinas's direct studies with Husserl and Heidegger.[16] While I do not explicitly highlight that critique here, it certainly serves as an implicit ground for this work as well as providing a horizon for further development. What distinguishes my approach from Levinas's in this current book is that, while I also proceed exegetically and phenomenologically I explicitly highlight the ethical moments of divergence of Heidegger from Rosenzweig through analyzing their respective philosophies of art. For Gordon, it could be argued that his self-limitation in restricting his conclusions about Rosenzweig's philosophy to a novel interpretation of the beginning of Rosenzweig's *The Star of Redemption*, is what leads him to strongly align Rosenzweig with Heidegger as an existentialist expressionist. With typical self-deprecation, Rosenzweig may have associated such self-limitation as the kind of misreading that he himself welcomed upon learning that either no-one was reading his book or simply could not get past the opening passages. In comparing his book to other so-called philosophical masterpieces, he noted: "The only time that it is certainly rewarding to read a philosophy book is when one either misunderstands the beginning or understands it falsely."[17] Indeed, if we simply want to take Rosenzweig's word at face value, as Gordon argues that we should, we could also look at Rosenzweig's statements that outright rejected any association with claims of "authenticity." For example, shortly after his self-reflective bemusing about the lack and/or failure of his readers to understand *The Star of Redemption*, he ironically undercuts the language of authenticity by noting that his venture into the domain of phenomenology can be grouped in with the general characterization of all philosophy as that activity which asks after the concept of essence (*Wesen*).[18] That is indeed the case for philosophies grounded in commitments to ontology.

Philosophies of history

Rosenzweig's first major work, a biographical interpretation of Hegel's philosophy of history, emerged from his doctoral studies with the historian Friedrich Meinecke and was published in 1920 as *Hegel und der Staat*.[19] That work

remains a seminal interpretation of Hegel's development of a political theory of
the state by way of recounting the development of Hegel's intellectual biography
and of his development of the concept of the interrelatedness of the individual
and their social framework, that is, their national situatedness as determined
by a concept that Hegel called the "will." In important ways, Rosenzweig's
work contributed to the ongoing assessment of Hegel's philosophy as it was
embedded in German intellectual history and philosophically contributed
to the ongoing success of those very traditions. Its specific contribution and
continued relevance is as a hermeneutic that reconstructs the psychologically
determined, genetic development of Hegel's system as the idealist expression
of an unrealized fulfillment of the willful longing of the German people for
self-determination. However, as I have already noted, Rosenzweig's apology
in the preface that he appended to *Hegel und der Staat*, that he would not
have written the same text post-World War I, is based on his hard-won disillusionment about the hoped-for successful fulfillment of a Hegelian dialectic
based on violent conflict. That fulfillment failed since any hopes for the victory
of a liberal, democratic state were dashed in the militaristic conclusions of
Bismarckian-Wilhelmian imperialism. Perhaps because of his own training as a
historian, Gordon's best analytical work of Rosenzweig's development appears
in his chapter assessing the place of *Hegel and the State* for his thesis about
the existentiality of Rosenzweig's thought. He notes that, following Dilthey's
Lebensphilosophie in rejecting Hegel's "eclipse of the individual," Rosenzweig
went on to reject as well his understanding of Hegel's dialectic as resulting in a
drama of metaphysical reconciliation rather than social redemption.[20] Gordon
notes that ". . . the abandonment of dialectics allowed for a deepened appreciation of finitude, propelling Rosenzweig away from Hegel and toward Nietzsche
as the "first" philosopher of subjectivity. Given this new perspective, it is not
surprising that the *Star of Redemption* regards the sheer fact of mortality as
Hegel's defeat."[21] However, that is simply not the case since Rosenzweig contends with Hegel's Idealist aesthetics in significant and determinative ways in
the early parts of *The Star of Redemption* and provides a well-developed social
theory in the latter parts of the text as a distinct political alternative to Hegel's
philosophy of the nation-state. It is also simply not the case that Rosenzweig
adopts in any significant, metaphysical way a position that can be reduced to
the "sheer fact of mortality" as a riposte to Hegel's formidable "philosophy
of the All." Indeed, Gordon is correct in his judgment about the heretofore
disjunction of *Hegel and the State* from *The Star of Redemption* maintained
by most scholars in assessments of Rosenzweig's work. However, I question
Gordon's reduction of the interrelation of those works to a Heideggerian
circumlocution of "the nonrelational and nontransferable experience of possible death" as that "conceptual instrument for exposing the falsity of idealist
totalization."[22] Rather, based on what I argue is a more balanced reading of *The
Star of Redemption*, what Rosenzweig thought that post-war conditions called

for was socio-political resistance in the form of the development of exilic communal alternatives that would emerge from the religious and everyday cultural practices of ordinary, albeit highly educated, and socio-politically engaged people. But precisely because of the a-political character of the ritual structures of daily life, Rosenzweig thought that they could provide political resistance — but a resistance that depended upon a transformation of social culture and thus of the aesthetic choices of those peoples. However, and unfortunately, as the history of Nazi–Jewish relations played out, Rosenzweig's role in promoting such a choice of political marginality (and not a-politicism!) became part of a great tragedy. From the start of this book, I should point out that I am well aware that it is necessary but insufficient to develop independent, communal bodies capable of political critique. In fact, we need to continue to do so. But post-Holocaust, and faced with ongoing instances of other genocides, it has become apparent that we must also become more vigilant and directly engaged *in* the political process without compromising our ethical commitments. With some careful reconstruction, I contend that within Rosenzweig's work itself there resides that which can still provide guidance in constructing such ethically informed political alternatives.

However, during the last decades of the second half of the twentieth century, many intellectuals turned to Heidegger to provide just such a guiding framework for political critique, a turning that — given Heidegger's political affiliations — is at least puzzling but even more so, problematic.[23] In 1927, Heidegger published what was and remains his seminal work, *Being and Time*, with which he was able to secure a position in the German university system and that, arguably, serves as the foundation for all of his later philosophical contributions. The publication of *Being and Time* directly resulted from his study with Husserl in the field of phenomenology and remains within that field, especially in how Heidegger anticipated the decisive constructions of what Husserl eventually developed as the conceptual constellation of the "lived world" as a means to present his problematic ideas on inter-subjectivity and the flux of our perceptive relationships with the world of "things."[24] But Heidegger significantly and clearly departs from Husserl's agenda by undermining any attempt to situate philosophy as a positivist scientific enterprise by turning from phenomenology as the study of the logical structures of consciousness to his presentation of phenomenology as the elaboration of the ontological and existential analytic of the structures of Da-sein. This move was presaged by the development in the history of philosophy known as the philosophy of history, a development begun by Hegel, taken up by scholars such as Dilthey and Simmel, and attended to in different ways by both Rosenzweig and Heidegger, each respectively beginning new chapters in the history of philosophy as differing ways of performing philosophies of history with far-reaching ethical consequences.[25]

Outline of this text

I divide this text into two main divisions: the first on Rosenzweig, the second on Heidegger. I begin by interpreting Rosenzweig's work for both historical and thematic reasons. Although Rosenzweig and Heidegger belong to the same generation of classically educated, German intellectuals, Rosenzweig's writing and publication of his major works, *Hegel and the State* and *The Star of Redemption*, were published several years before Heidegger's first major work, *Being and Time*. Additionally, since Rosenzweig died in 1929, he truly belongs to that generation of intellectuals of the first third of the twentieth century, neither influenced by Nazism and the Holocaust nor by the political emergence of the modern state of Israel. Heidegger, however, lived through those turbulent and often violent events, including the onset of the domination of world-politics by a capitalist America and a communist Soviet Union, and continued writing and teaching, and thus directly influencing many thousands of other students and intellectuals until his death in 1976.

Rosenzweig's "turn" to philosophy, art, and the ethical

The Star of Redemption presents a challenge to the sorts of traditional systems of rationality that have dominated Western political and social life, from their Greek inception with the Ionian pre-Socratics to their culmination in, for Rosenzweig, the generative sickness of Hegel's dialectical philosophy.[26] Thus, in order to take up this challenge, in Chapter 1 I present my reading of Rosenzweig's diagnosis of what he intimates is an allergic, generative sickness. For Rosenzweig, the history of humanity, narratively presented as the history of philosophy, has unfolded as an endemic system of rationality, proleptically alleviated by neo-Kantian revisions such as Hermann Cohen's, and definitively undermined by the philosophical–ethical standpoints established by Arthur Schopenhauer, Søren Kierkegaard, and Friedrich Nietzsche. Including these signifiers early on in his text indicates Rosenzweig's intent to "cure" that sickness — that results in desperate solipsism or destructive nihilism — by engaging readers through the dynamic of his text as a preparatory impetus for extra-textual enactments of an aesthetically induced ethical imperative. He highlights that imperative path to ethical health by ending his Introduction to the text with three philosophical references: (1) Schelling's *Weltalter*, in order to set the tone for his later development of a temporally and aesthetically significant revelation; (2) Hermann Cohen's *Logik der Reinen Erkenntnis*, whose mathematics Rosenzweig uses as an organon for thought in constructing the calculi of the elements, god world human; and (3) an integration of Kant's rational–ethical metaphysics in order to maintain philosophical accountability, that is, in order to retain the high standards of formal communication achieved by Kant.[27]

Because he prioritized *the ethical* through developing an a-political cultural aesthetic, iterated in the very writing and reading of his text, Rosenzweig was able to mount an attack on the educational thought structures that led to totalitarian political and social systems dominating European, but especially German, universities at the end of the nineteenth and the beginning of the twentieth centuries. Understanding the ongoing relevance of his "attack" remains one of the compelling motives for continuing to recommend his book today. At that time, his immediate experience of such structures was enlivened by his participation in The Freiburger Circle, which he helped form with Siegfried A. Kaeler and Viktor von Weizsacker to study Hegel's philosophy of history. While Rosenzweig remained a critical, political liberal as a student, Kaeler became a faithful political conservative.[28] For Rosenzweig, such conservative, educational structures validated a universal and dialectical historical process that eventually and inevitably resulted in the oppositional violence and human destruction of The Great War that engulfed Europe in the first decades of the twentieth century. Although relatively marginal — from a pragmatically quantitative perspective — a vital consequence of Rosenzweig's critique is the breach in conservative ideological tendencies that is made possible and, while not explicit, has been employed against the totalizing forms of Marxist versions of an Hegelian totality of a progressive, dialectical–material political system or National Socialist totalizing forms of political organization. These adaptations of Rosenzweig's seminal work can be traced in the trajectories of Walter Benjamin's and Emmanuel Levinas's socio-theoretical works, to name just two examples, both of whom had read and were influenced by Rosenzweig.[29] Additionally, that Rosenzweig worked in and through community structures such as the *Freies Judisches Lehrhaus* in Frankfurt is a concrete indication of his attempt to forge alternative forms of educational praxes on the ground — in his neighborhood — and for his time. Clearly, Rosenzweig's influence was limited, but that may have had as much to do with the destruction of European Jewry as Rosenzweig's early death on the brink of that destruction. At the beginning of the twenty-first century, that influence seems to be markedly increasing given the rise in interest in his work in general and, specifically, the institution of the International Rosenzweig Society in Kassel, Germany in March, 2004, and the appearance of the *Rosenzweig Yearbook* associated with that Society.[30]

Given Rosenzweig's horizons, I form my own stance from the context of select social issues, such as twentieth century fascism and the phenomenon of Jewish diaspora existence, rather than from the kind of socio-political analysis that is abstractly removed from concrete, historical praxes Rosenzweig himself applied in his earlier writings.[31] Instead, as I note in Chapter 1, Rosenzweig begins his text by taking us on a Faustian journey to defiantly know and experience all, via a descent into what he refers to as the depths of the nothing of our knowledge; more precisely, a descent into the three nothings of our presuppositions that we positively know something empirically concrete related to the conceptual structures "god world human," which he calls the elements. The reason Rosenzweig begins the way he does is that in order to attack the totalizing systematic claims to absolute comprehensiveness, such as Hegel's, one needs to posit an unassimilable point of difference. Rosenzweig accomplishes that by presenting us with an aesthetic re-narration of the hypothetical starting points for what constitutes any act of thinking whatsoever.

Focusing on those starting points in Chapter 1, I interpret how we are initially moved by Rosenzweig's philosophical-aesthetic performance to take up the threads of human intellectual productions, an interpretation that moves from thinking about death in the first pages of *The Star of Redemption* and Rosenzweig's challenge to the totalizing agenda of Western philosophy to his development of a peculiar narrative form of philosophizing as his response to that agenda. I emphasize the aesthetic quality of Rosenzweig's construction and the accompaniment of Nietzsche and Goethe throughout his text by reading his work as it is initially prefigured by the guiding and masking metaphor of a Mephistopheles-like persona. In Chapter 2 I present a reading of how Rosenzweig contests conventional theories of epistemology and thus philosophies of history with his method of narrative philosophizing. He does so by way of transforming traditional epistemological theorizing that I read through correlating his method with some of the innovative breakthroughs that emerged from chaos-complexity theories of the last quarter of the twentieth century. In this chapter, I align Rosenzweig's work with complementary research being done by contemporary scientists and mathematicians in their attempts to understand how complex systems behave, systems that include almost every possible instance of dynamic behavior that we find in the universe, such as individual biological systems, human brains, hearts, economic and political systems, and any other type of open system that involves positive and negative feedback and is capable of evolving. The importance for making this link has to do with my interpretation of Rosenzweig's exploration about the limited possibilities of the principle of prediction, that is, of the comprehensive claims of the project of science in general. This is important for what I say about Rosenzweig's recognition of the ambiguous and unpredictable ethicality of relationships, namely, that any genuine relationship based on dialogue entails a radical element of unpredictability and thus openness to the absolute alterity of the other and my own inability to totalize that other in my pre-existing categories of determination. This could extend to issues such as how to account for the dynamism of evolving social organizations, artificial intelligence, and the role of personal decision-making, agency and autonomy with respect to social justice. But that would be another chapter in another book.

In this book, I then proceed in Chapter 3 with my interpretation of Rosenzweig's narrative philosophy in the cultural form that it assumes as *midrash* by following a thread of the ethical contours in his analysis of what constitutes any possible aesthetic engagement at all as that occurs with an other in revelatory acts of love. Finally, Part I culminates in Chapter 4 when I take up that ethical thread as it continues in the social theory that Rosenzweig presents as Part III of *The Star*. That theory and the threads that knot it together form his proposal in the final pages of his text for redemptively enacting ritual performances in communal lives of faith and trust with others. Such redemptive affirmation affirms and thereby renews the uniquely different traditions of existing communities while encouraging responsible interactions of individual members of those gatherings both intra-, and inter-community. As I correlate the ethical effectivity of Rosenzweig's *The Star of Redemption* with Heidegger's work, it should become clear how his textual constructions mirror the ethical content, enacted as a philosophical–aesthetic performance, in the way that those constructions exemplify an application of the ethical explications of his aesthetic theories within that very text.

Heidegger's "turn" from politics . . .

Rosenzweig and Heidegger both "turn" to art and language as responses to contemporary political events, but differ significantly in their attempts to affect, through their respective philosophies of art, the course of human history. Rosenzweig's response took form with his textual construction of a multi-dimensional object of art, which also refers to a natural object — a star: the *Magen David* — that, even more significantly, also stands for the evolving cultural and thus historical formations of specific communities — Jewish, Christian, and Muslim — set in terms of their dynamic relationships with each other and other peoples of the world. Heidegger has no such figure at his disposal and, for all of the attention paid to the significance of his "turn" and for the attention that he pays to elaborating the structures of being-in-the-world, relatively few images of objects — real or ideal — are evoked for his readers upon which to focus. However, while we are provided with a few references to material objects, such as Van Gogh's "Peasant Shoes" or the Greek temple, which occupies a centering role in *The Origin of the Work of Art*, Heidegger decisively turns our attention to poetry, as Rosenzweig also does at the core of *The Star of Redemption*. In both cases, we are presented with dialectics of identity and difference. While Rosenzweig chose to provide an interpretive *midrash* on a selection of biblical texts to further his speech–acts approach set in the dynamic of "othering" that occurs in love relationships, Heidegger chose to focus primarily on interpreting the poetry of Hölderlin as the quintessential German expression of the impulse towards polis and self-identity. For both philosophers, poetry is that art form which serves to found a people, and since, again for both philosophers, the destiny of a people depends on a particular work of art, particular poems serve to establish respective peoples with either an ontologically or ethically determined destiny. For Heidegger, it was Hölderlin's poem on the Ister; for Rosenzweig, it was the pagan Song of Songs with its ambiguous authorship. Indeed, one of the fundamental points of divergence separating Heidegger and Rosenzweig arises in the way that Heidegger interprets the work of the poet's creation of the work of art as subservient to the theme of establishing a people ontologically destined to a certain kind of ethos in the polis, while Rosenzweig chose the quintessential poem of love that has so strongly and deeply resonated throughout the history of "Western" civilization. For Heidegger, submitting to the dictates of the ethos of the polis indicated in its place by the poet — for Germans, the Ister (or Rhine) and Hölderlin — prepares that people for a certain way of being-in-the-world. That way of being-in-the-world is then prepared by Heidegger — in his work as the interpretive philosopher — through *Being and Time* and *The Origin of the Work of Art*, and becomes the way that establishes the right political relationship of Da-sein to Being and other beings. Heidegger eventually presents that elaboration as the conflict of earth and world, which becomes the revision of Hölderlin's fourfold (*Gevierte*) into earth, sky, Da-sein, and the gods, an elaborated way that awaits its justification and verification with the return of the right political leader.

While Rosenzweig's ethically intended (although ontologically indeterminate) philosophy of art develops over the course of his relatively short but productive life, because of the way that it is concentrated in *The Star of Redemption* I draw primarily from an exegesis of that work for the first part of my thesis. However, that sort of textual singularity is not privileged in the case with Heidegger since we need to have read *Being and Time* in order to best interpret the philosophy of art that Heidegger then develops in *The Origin of the Work of Art* after his "turn." And we need to have read both of those works to be able to further interpret his analyses of Hölderlin's poetry from the mid-1930s. Finally, we must work through Heidegger's philosophy of art in order to come to terms with what he has to say in his later philosophy about "The History of Being" and the "*Ereignis*" in order to assess what his philosophy of art means for the political positions that he took during the Nazi years. Thus, while his method remains phenomenological, that is, remains faithful to the methodology that he establishes in *Being and Time*, we none the less must read more of his texts in order to come to a judgment about the ethical consequences of his philosophy of art. Therefore, in the final three chapters of this text I present a reading of Heidegger's development of a philosophy of art out of *Being and Time* set against the here-undeveloped background of his political engagement in the Nazi party.[32] I develop that focus by reading through several of his works, specifically: Chapter 5 presents my reading of *Being and Time*; Chapter 6 my reading of "The Origin of the Work of Art;" and Chapter 7 my experimental engagement with other contemporary interlocutors who contend with Heidegger's interpretations of Hölderlin's poetry.

. . . To art and language

Continuing to set the context for my argument, in Chapter 6, I explicate how in *The Origin of the Work of Art* we again take up the "hammer" from *Being and Time* but now transformed from a mere tool in a constellation that includes the hammer as tool in a mediate position between the generic or "natural" thing and the work of art. While the "natural" thing is that which is unworked-upon, the tool is that which is worked-upon and retains a connection to thingliness, while the work of art is that which stands in some way alone. In the first part of the book, I introduce this character of "standing alone" in my interpretation of Rosenzweig's way of handling works of art. But Heidegger's move from the workshop of *Being and Time* to a more diversified world that includes things and "independent" art-works is no simple matter of phenomenological description of some arbitrary state of affairs to another. Rather, what is included in constructing such a "world" and moving his readers along is also the establishment of an overriding structure that houses the origin of meaningful existence. But discovering such an *origin* entails already having been prepared by already having experienced the kind of authentic/inauthentic choices established through the hermeneutic of disclosure presented in *Being and Time*. One must already have been reminded about the existential structures of one's temporal, historical existence and how that existence is itself embedded in the ontological structures of being-in-the-world, of one's determination by the they-self and of Da-sein-with. After being reminded about these ontological structures, however, we move with Heidegger to the necessity of discovering the political destiny of a people, which is only possible through coming to terms with the work of art as it is relationally situated in and guides the very understanding of the being-in-the-world of Da-sein as an aesthetically grounded and ethically oriented, politically destined people. In discovering the ground and orientation that destines a people, we then learn what decisions should be made for the sake of maintaining not only the authentic existence of a people, but what decisions are made to establish a "holy," independent, existence. In fact, despite his earlier disavowal of an onto-theology, Heidegger uses just such an onto-theological framework, in such a way as to ground the political, poetical and philosophical choices that he contends co-determine the appropriating *ek-static* event of being as presence-of-the-world.[33] Such a grounding, however, must be established by way of the opening of the presencing act of the work of art. An analysis of that work is what I do in Chapter 6 of this book.

With the naming of Hölderlin, and with Hölderlin's diagnosis of the sickness of the modern age (i.e. the flight of the gods, that we have forgotten our origin and what endures), we have two of the essential cornerstones of Heidegger's so-called "turn" to art and language, namely, a combining of the philosophical and poetic traditions of Greece and Germany in such a way that they valorize the elements of Heidegger's philosophical project. As I explicate in more detail in Chapter 7, that project consisted of resituating the work of poetry as founding works of art that decisively determine not merely the existential direction of an individual, but of the German people. Because for Heidegger the place that is near the origin is, in fact, Germany, as that people to whom the right poet gives shape, the great poet is Hölderlin. Moreover, Hölderlin is *the* definitive poet who acts as the stream from which the German people are set their task to fulfill their ownmost historical destiny of leading the modern world out of the age of decline by, in part, remembering the acts of the gods who founded authentic community. But here we have a problem, and that problem is that Hölderlin is a poet, and only a poet. As such, the enormous social burden of having to secure the very redemption of a fallen work that Heidegger locates with Hölderlin seems to be beyond even the powers of the mythical figures of Hercules or Jesus Christ. In closing this Introduction, I would like to draw attention to that problem by referring back to both *The Origin of the Work of Art* and the different way that Rosenzweig's concept of redemption diverges from Heidegger's phenomenological task, a parting of the ways that I elaborate at the end of Chapter 7 and in my concluding Final Words.

Messianism and politics

Heidegger also establishes in *The Origin of the Work of Art* the possibility of the festival that occurs in defining the region of the holy. Such a definition sets the place of the temple as that from which the gods are encountered and are set in relation with Da-sein, that is, are set in relation with the people who define that very region (*Bezirk*). With the advent of Hölderlin, and most pointedly with Heidegger's later interpretations of Hölderlin's poetry, Heidegger was already in retreat (*in Entrückung*) from his active engagement in the political process from which he could envision a radical change, that is, at the start of his "turn" or, more specifically, at the beginning of his reflections on *The Origin of the Work of Art*.[34] Rather than continue to engage in what he apparently thought to be a losing battle for influencing the direction and goals of the Nationalsozialistische Deutsche Arbeiterparte (NDSAP,) Heidegger moved into a waiting mode.[35] That waiting mode entailed turning from direct political engagement to what he thought were the possibilities of more deeply guiding the destiny of the peoples of the world, namely, to philosophy and poetry. And this meant turning to the work of Hölderlin.

With his early interpretations of Hölderlin, Heidegger introduced the "threefold" — the poet, philosopher, and the politician. That introduction was at the beginning of his "turn" to publicize his lectures on what he considered the "beginnings" or "origin" of the political as such, namely, the setting into motion of an aesthetic process of political change made possible by the gift of the poet, Hölderlin, translated by the philosopher, Heidegger, and which could be taught to the politician, Hitler. It was the role of the politician, then, to make the new beginning accessible to the people, a role for which Heidegger, as the interpreting philosopher, found himself best suited. As events unfolded with the demise of the NDSAP, however, Heidegger came to the begrudging realization that the greatness of the party did not in fact or in deed measure up to the work of the poet and the philosopher. And so the counsel of the philosopher had to change. And so it did. For the last decades of his life, instead of decisive political engagement, Heidegger worked out a theory of the "history of being," which rested on a teaching of *Gelassenheit* — of a "letting be" — that he read in Hölderlin's poetry. Such a philosophy of "letting be" is, of course, likewise to be found already lurking in the details of *Being and Time*, but only in a rereading of the text that is just as violent as the initial robbery for which it originally calls. In the end, Heidegger turns merely to preparation, turning his disciples inward to their ownmost destiny in order to wait for the coming god.

Rosenzweig, on the other hand, provides a messianic aesthetic that does not merely wait for the coming god, but continues to act in shaping history by maintaining an aesthetically formed community life based on communal festivals, such as Pesach and the Feast of Booths, which not only work to provide temporary structures, dwellings, for the meal itself, but — in turning simultaneously inward and outward — celebrates the love and growth of family and communities of diversity while leaving a door open and a place at the table for the wandering stranger, the unaccounted-for other.

Notes

1   cf. Gordon 2005 and Pollock 2009.
2   See Appiah 2008: 17: "When modern philosophers, whether Analytic or Continental, need a story, what usually matters isn't whether it *is* true but whether it *could be* true." He means logical or metaphysical and not psychological or historical.
3   See Levinas 1969: 14.
4   See HS: XII.
5   See Sluga 1995, esp. 7ff. where Sluga canvases "The Philosophical Field" to assess Heidegger's political involvement.
6   Fackenheim points out that since Heidegger did not utter any condemnation of Nazi policy towards the Jews either before or after the war, he remains an ethical failure primarily because he "endorsed in advance the Führer's actions as German "reality" and "law," . . . deliberately and *with the weight of his philosophy behind it*." See Fackenheim 1994: 168–9.
7   See Wolin 1992: 3 ff.
8   cf. Levinas 1969; Wyschogrod 2000; Gibbs 1992; and Marx 1992.
9   See Karl Löwith 1942: 53–77. For a recent analysis of Löwith's position, see

Düttman 2000: 6–10. Also, see Freund 1929, 1979 for the first serious attempt at aligning these two philosophers.

10 See Gordon 2005: 313 where he argues for a "strong resemblance" but also cf. Rosenzweig's own brief and cryptic remarks (upon which Gordon places great weight) in "Vertauschte Fronten" in GS3: 235–7.

11 Gordon: xxiv.

12 Ibid: xxv.

13 Ibid: xxviii.

14 Ibid: xxix.

15 Fackenheim 1994: 320, and previously, Karl Löwith 1953 points up what Heidegger calls the "circular structure of understanding." All interpretative understanding is pre-structured by virtue of the interpreter's purpose, preconception, and slant or prospect on what he interprets. Because of this pre-structure [*Vor-Struktur*] the circularity of interpretation is a necessity that cannot be overcome.

16 See Levinas 1969 in general, but especially Levinas 2000, Chapter 2 (42ff.), for his departure from Heidegger's theme of language as the way in which Being becomes as a process of temporalization. Levinas agrees with Heidegger that logos gathers in Being making it accessible, but diverges from Heidegger in arguing that a gap exists in the lapse of time between lived immediacy and its representation that is not able to be taken up by logos. The lapse becomes a challenge to language as such and like transcendence falls outside the realm of Being understood as process — it is "otherwise than being." Levinas's critique of Heidegger is a critique of Heidegger's philosophy of language and not his ontology, as such.

17 See "Das Neue Denken," in GS3: 142ff.

18 See Gordon 2005: 143 ff. See also footnote #79 in Chapter 1 for his distinction between a philosophy of authenticity and a narrating philosophy.

19 See Rosenzweig HS; his dedication reads: "Friedrich Meinecke: in thankful honor."

20 Gordon 2005: 111.

21 Ibid: 112.

22 Ibid: 113.

23 See, for instance, "Post-metaphysical Politics: Heidegger and Democracy," in Dallmayr 1993: 49–76, for a reading of Heidegger's philosophy as anti-ideological, based on an interpretation of Heidegger's philosophy of reticence and *Gelassenheit* as a mode of questioning democratic "popular sovereignty" through its reliance on ideological formations out of a traditional, unquestioning metaphysics.

24 Dermot Moran takes into account the many detractors of Heidegger's work, but as the second most important phenomenologist after Husserl, notes that "Any fair assessment of Heidegger's contribution must recognize that it changed the shape of twentieth-century philosophy." See Moran 2000: 193.

25 And both go through Dilthey's "critique of historical reason" and division of human endeavors into the "hard" sciences and the "social" sciences and his work in analyzing how individuals, institutions, cultures, and communities are "carriers of history" and for how they produce or generate meaning and value. See Dilthey 2002, especially "Drafts for a Critique of Historical Reason": 203ff.

26   See BGK/USH.

27   See GS2, 21–4; also Schelling 1967: 195–344; and Hermann Cohen 1977.

28   See my remarks on their relationship in my encyclopedia article, "The Life of
     Franz Rosenzweig," in Simon 2000b.

29   See my "Benjamin's Feast of Booths" in Simon 2003, for indications of the seminal
     influence of Rosenzweig's philosophy for Benjamin. Robert Gibbs also argues
     for a Marxist denouement of Rosenzweig's social philosophy as it is worked out
     through Levinas in his chapter "Marx and Levinas" in Gibbs 1992: 229–54.

30   As of this writing, four yearbooks have appeared: http://www.verlag-alber.de/
     jahrbuecher/uebersicht_html?k_onl_struktur=1375127 (accessed 16 November
     2010).

31   What I have in mind is the hermeneutic approach developed by Dilthey with
     which Rosenzweig was familiar. See Dilthey 2010, esp. "Lived Experience and
     Autobiography": 213ff.

32   For a well-argued thesis on the relationship of Heidegger's positions on education
     and technology with his political choices and his so-called onto-theology, see
     Thomson 2005.

33   See HW: 55; PLT: 67; and specifically my comments in Chapter 6, pp. 188 and
     212.

34   "*In Entrückung*" could mean "in retreat" but also "enraptured." The timetable is
     adequately enough worked out in two essays, the first "The Greatness of the Work
     of Art" by Robert Bernasconi, and the second "Heidegger's Freiburg Version of
     the Origin of the Work of Art" by François Dastur. See Risser 1999: 95–142.

35   In his biography of Heidegger, Safranski assesses Heidegger's departure from the
     office of Rektorat as what could only have been a crisis of disillusion and as a
     turn from political discourse to philosophical logic: "*Die Wendung von der Politik
     zurück zum* Geist *kündigt sich schon an in der Vorlesung des Sommersemesters
     1934.*" See Safranski 1994: 316–17.

CHAPTER 1

THE MASK OF MEPHISTOPHELES

In this chapter I provide a guided reading of Part I of Rosenzweig's *The Star of Redemption*.[1] I do not comprehensively take into account the many alternative readings of Rosenzweig's presentation and treatment of what he calls the "Elements," which serve Rosenzweig's readers as the cornerstones for his systematic construction of his configuration of reality. Instead, I explore that part of his account that has specifically to do with how he grounds the development of his aesthetic theory in an epistemologically oriented philosophy of history. I hope to make clear by the end of this chapter Rosenzweig's implicit contention that to know anything at all entails a retelling of the stories that one has received from the intellectual traditions within which one finds herself at any time in her life. In general, that is, methodologically, this is one of the results of broadly interpreting Rosenzweig's work within a stream of phenomenological ethics that has to do with the forming and retelling of ethical narratives. But in particular, this means that while starting points are not arbitrary — we are unavoidably determined both with what is at hand in our environment and the hermeneutic tools provided to us by our predecessors — we nonetheless begin our philosophical journeys with the self-reflective recognition that our first steps must necessarily be self-critical ones, steps towards a better understanding of how we know the world, speak of and from the world, and interact within self-replicating biological groups as interdependent subjects. This is, in part, what is meant by a "re"-telling. The very first steps of retelling, however, also entail that we become critically aware of just who has been acting to guide us along in the "tellings" that we receive and what, more precisely, the roles are that we have been assigned to play and the masks that we have come to don.

Following Rosenzweig's guidance, this process takes the form of unmasking the kinds of languages that have come to define us in our intellectual and cultural developments, implying — of course — an initial general grasp on the mask we already wear. Hence, in the following exegeses (the work of unmasking) I consider how Rosenzweig analyzes the development of our practices of self-reflective analysis by way of a philosophy of language that he calls speech-thinking (*Sprachdenken*) that he sets forth as a mathematics-based, symbolic logic based on Rosenzweig's understanding of Cohen's development of an alternative form of mathematical logic that employs mathematical infinitesimals. He applies Cohen's logic of infinitesimals as a way of distinguishing between what Levinas later developed — possibly influenced by Rosenzweig — as the incongruity between "the saying" and "the said." It is a phenomenology of language that distinguishes between language as a function of relating human speakers *a posteriori*, and of presenting the limits of formal linguistic analysis — a phenomenology of language practices that distinguishes between spoken language and positivist forms of deductive logic.

At the end of the "Introduction" to *The Star of Redemption*, Rosenzweig proposes that our attempts to think by making "positive" epistemological judgments leave us with practically nothing, attempts that result in the possibility of negating traditional scientific methodologies. Instead, Rosenzweig proposes to conceive of thinking as a negative, meta-activity with hypothetical starting points. He sets into motion a variation of a Husserlian eidetic reduction — the kind of negative suspension involved in establishing an *epoché* — in order to focus upon how we initiate any thinking process whatsoever. However, Rosenzweig also claims that we have *given* starting points, given as the historical results of human, philosophical inquiry; results, moreover, that respectively imply their own limitations.[2] In other words, determining what "thinking" means entails questioning our own way of thinking as it is the result of historically established patterns of thinking. That means that the only way to begin without beginning arbitrarily is *in media res*, namely, in the middle of things. This particular starting point further entails beginning by analyzing our speaking and thinking patterns, a philosophy of language that Rosenzweig calls speech-thinking (*Sprachdenken*).[3] Husserl would call this phenomenology.

Rosenzweig, however, embodies his questioning of those established patterns of speech-thinking by taking us on a Faustian journey into the underworld, guiding us to explore our inner life and the origins of our thinking processes. That journey of exploration already initiates his philosophy of art because Rosenzweig implies that in order to come to any determination about what it means to speak about the knowledge of our historically material condition in the world and our ethical relations with others like us, we must turn to the art of our actions as a material expression, and understand the extent to which our actions work as art. But art is bound up with ways of knowing the world and so Rosenzweig ends his Introduction to *The Star of Redemption* with the following quote from Goethe's *Faust*:

> The Nothing of our knowledge is no single Nothing, but rather a triple Nothing. Thus, it contains in itself the promise of definability. And therefore we can hope, like Faust, to again find the "All" that we have to dismember in this Nothing, this threefold Nothing of knowledge. "Descend then! I could also say: ascend!"[4]

With this pronouncement, Rosenzweig initiates an epistemological discourse on what he calls the elements — god world human — by beginning with the claim that we know nothing about each element, a "nothing," however, that is not universal and general as is the Hegelian Nothing but, rather, consists of three particular "nothings" and is thus plural by definition. While Rosenzweig points to the "promise of definability" subsequent to his dismemberment of the "All," because of the possibility of determining the absolute limits of each with respect to an other that is not itself, there is nonetheless a twofold danger inherent in dismembering the theoretical Hegelian All. The danger is that if we are not able to rationally account for all of the possible permutations of reality or to control those permutations, we could be reduced to insignificance in either a totally fragmented or a totally determined world. We are not so capable. Thus, the obvious question becomes: what difference does any single human act or series of acts make in a universe that is utterly fragmented and disconnected or so totally determined that any act whatsoever is already only a consequence of a logically determined causal or teleological chain? Rosenzweig suggests that we should *hope* for an eventual reconstruction of the individual, isolated members into an "All" that is other than the first, implying that such a reconstruction would entail a revaluation of thinking which is a responsible, and therefore ethically meaningful act of thinking. By the end of Chapter 4 in this book, the reader should be better able to judge, at least preliminarily, the plausibility of such a hope. By the end of this book, in balancing Rosenzweig's account against Heidegger's, the reader should be in an even better position to judge competing claims for how we should proceed in prioritizing our ethical and cultural choices.

For Rosenzweig, each one of the three Nothings is initially a way of referring to one of the three elements as a hypothetical principle. Other philosophers besides Hegel, such as Plotinus or Spinoza, attempted to comprehend the All as *Wirklichkeit*, or what is actual, with the goal of determining what we should do in and with that comprehended reality. Rosenzweig begins with the assumption that an examination of how we think about what reality is and how it functions conditions our actions in and with that reality. That is, Rosenzweig presents an initial assumption as valid, which he will later disprove but which entails that if we know the first principle that serves as a unifying and guiding source for what we experience of reality then, based on rational deductions from that principle, we can logically determine the course of events and determine our individual role relative to that total course of events. In other words, "knowing" also entails that we would know what we should do.[5] Rosenzweig's presentation of how and what we think about the elements of reality, what we provisionally know (but only provisionally), was his way of undermining traditional philosophical attempts to establish the origins of knowledge, origins that serve to determine what we should do as a deduction from one of many possible arbitrarily stipulated first principles. But just thinking about reality does not constitute reality; since the activity of thinking is just that, namely, a thinking about some hypothetical particular about which we at first know nothing, or rather, practically nothing. Rosenzweig speculates that we not only begin thinking by *not knowing* precisely what the elements (or principles) are, but that there are just three of them. That there are three of them is not arbitrary since that number is determined by the historical context for our thinking, namely, the elements referred to are those three indefinites that have been traditional starting points in the history of both Eastern and Western philosophies. However, the new thinking that Rosenzweig proposes as an instrument to guide us in our quest for actual, positive knowledge of those elements entails not only taking up the historically traditional results of philosophy — the Hegelian method of thinking is, after all, a methodological process of negation — but also serves as an introduction to the notion that the objects of thinking are particular, Cohenian infinitesimal kinds of nothings.[6]

As I noted earlier, Rosenzweig concludes his Introduction with a quote from Goethe's *Faust*, from Mephistopheles, who is the "spirit who always negates," and who commands that Faust learn about his own art but only after Faust agrees to sell his soul to the devil. The references to Faust are significant because, although Rosenzweig deals with *Faust* as a model of modern tragedy explicitly only in Part II, Book 3 where the topic is redemption and community and specifically as an elaboration of the dramatic relationship of humans in community with the world, the figure of Faust serves as a key motif for Part I because of how it prefigures the structure of the meta-ethical self that Rosenzweig develops in Book 3. In fact, the German word "Faust" translates into the English word for "fist," which signifies the kind of defiance and self-centered negation of the value of any knowledge or experience outside of that which the self itself creates, which is the essential core of that which constitutes the self in its self-identity.[7]

All of Part I, however, is dictated by what Rosenzweig undertakes as a negative kind of thinking and so, as our guide, Rosenzweig assumes the negating voice and omniscient authority of Mephistopheles, while we assume the role of the ardently longing, and insatiable Faust. We are the ones seeking to understand reality and our role therein, and therefore we are commanded to descend or ascend having made a pact with our guide by trusting him with our time and clearing a space for him in our lives. Thus we follow. At the point of the command to "Descend!" in Goethe's drama, the epicurean desires of Faust to know and experience everything have already been sated by the multicolored pleasures at hand in his present life. But to have drunk deeply from the cup of earthly sensuality is not enough for Faust; he desires more (as presumably we also do), namely, to know the roots of the organic and creative forces of nature. He craves understanding.

Rosenzweig sends us to the realm of the "Mothers," which is the realm of "emptiness" and is without "place or time." Furthermore, it is the realm of "loneliness" (*Einsamkeit* — "at-one-ness") where Faust and we, the readers, must go to "learn emptiness" and how to live alone and, by implication, how to be at-one with ourselves. Moreover, alluding to the aesthetic condition of the task set out for us, Faust is promised that in visiting that realm he will "increase (his) art as a force," an increase that we also (hopefully) experience. Hence, learning about this realm of emptiness means learning something about oneself in some kind of *separation* or *alienation* from "reality," which means experiencing an aesthetic dimension of life.

According to German and Scandinavian folklore, the Mothers are three spirits who represent the original creative forces of the universe,[8] and in Faust the Mothers assume various structures and are situated on a tripod (*Dreifuß*). The elements Rosenzweig constructs likewise assume various structures and number three and could also be situated on a kind of a tripod; but in Rosenzweig's case the literary tripod would literally be the three Books of Part I of his text. By extension, each element corresponds to one of the three major Parts that make up the entire text, which, as a whole, would act as a contemporary interpretation of that myth. Following this motif in the direction of the inner development of each element, Rosenzweig indicates the variety of the structures of reality by presenting the way that the ancient Greeks, with their mythical gods of Olympus, and the Asian philosophies, with their Nirvana and Tao, have understood reality.[9] But for Rosenzweig, any understanding of reality has to also take into account modern, philosophical epistemology and so he echoes Faust's saying to Mephistopheles: "In your Nothing (*Nichts*) I hope to find the All." This is the Nothing which Rosenzweig refers to above in triplicate, namely, the Nothing of knowledge with which we begin our journey and which is threefold, with three vectors. Hoping to "find the All" expresses a hope for ultimate meaningfulness and directionality. Mephistopheles goes on to reply: "Descend then! I could also say ascend! / It is all the same. Flee to the creations / In the images of the detached realm." We are also ordered to descend to the "detached realm" and experience an aesthetically induced separation in order to abstract from (to bracket in negation!) our usual ways of thinking. For Rosenzweig, this is the activity of historically informed self-reflection. And like Faust, we also go via negation in order to find out about the origin of things and the initiation of our acts. Thus we descend into a realm of abstract hypotheticals.[10] Our stations along the way in the text, however, are structured by what Rosenzweig calls the metasciences that are built on a foundation of mathematical logic learned from Hermann Cohen and colored by Rosenzweig's selective readings of aesthetic productions from antiquity.

I. *A mathematic-based symbolic logic*

In presenting his theory about what constitutes any thinking activity at all, Rosenzweig employs the formal structure of a set of fundamental propositions based on a mathematical equation of the form "$a = b$," where "a" and "b" stand for a range of variable terms, while "$=$" stands for the function that holds between those terms. Although Rosenzweig does not spell out the genealogy of his logic, by means of his formulations we are able to consider an *irrational* dimension of "reality" through applying the differential calculus of infinitesimals developed by Hermann Cohen. Employing a nuanced proto-version of complexity theory, the mathematical–symbolic logic of Part I is relative to a grammatical logic of the dynamics of speech–acts that are aesthetically embodied through his philosophy of art in Part II. Both of those Parts then provide the building blocks for the more complex conceptual developments in Part III of *The Star* where the geometric image of a radiating and vibrant Star of David — with striking similarity of both structure and function to a Koch Curve of fractal science — aesthetically parallels, and yet transcends the mathematical/logical/algebraic processes of Part I and the philosophy of language and phenomenology of art of Part II.[11]

In our Faustian journey from the Nothings of our knowledge about the constellation of "god world human," Rosenzweig does not seek to subordinate one concept to another but to phenomenologically delineate each one as it is in and for itself. Accordingly, he claims to determine each element in its "absolute factuality" (*Tatsächlichkeit*), and therefore directly in its "positivity" (*Positvität*).[12] As a foundational movement for depicting reality, the differential movement of each element from nothing (*Nichts*) to its own something (*Etwas*) models the dynamic development of a universe which consists of contingent concrete particulars set on similar but never identical courses of their own development. Because this logic occurs early on in his text, the reader is encouraged to entertain a pluralistic conception of the universe as opposed to a monolithic one that has as its object of study a class of particular Nothings as opposed to one general Nothing. On historical grounds, however, the three particulars in this image of reality are the elements that establish the context for taking up the history of philosophy as Rosenzweig narrates it, namely, the three particular elements that are each on their own way from Nothing to Something. These particular Nothings are the Somethings of which historically conditioned branches of philosophy have claimed to possess complete knowledge, namely, "positive" knowledge of god, world, or human, while others have denied that knowledge of these Somethings is at all even possible. Rosenzweig intentionally begins with these three particular concrete negations of knowledge, each denoted as a particular Nothing, because each of them serves as a starting point for a presentation of one of three distinct hypothetical elements. To summarize, Rosenzweig uses a metascientific mode of logical construction initiated by his denotation of each element as a specific, indefinite Nothing, that then moves through an act of negation — that is, through an act of judgment — to finally arrive at a conception of that element as that which is involved in a dynamic process of becoming its own defined Something.

Taken from another perspective, Rosenzweig begins by setting up a context that consists of these starting points of the three Nothings of knowledge and induces the structures of the three elements that constitute the philosophical groundwork for his new thinking. But the process is even more complex because each of these three elements — god, world, human — serve as infintesimal, empirical starting points for a philosophy of history as respective founding principles of the three epochs which Rosenzweig distinguishes as having constituted succeeding historical epochs of humanity: Antiquity, the Middle Ages, and Modernity. Even more demanding, each one of the three sections in Part I of the text corresponds as a metascience to a negative thought structure that results from one of the representative thought structures that corresponds to the results of the negation of the positive science of the respective historical epochs: metaphysics negates the science of physics which corresponds to the results of Antiquity; metalogic negates the science of logic which corresponds to the results of the Middle Ages; and meta-ethics negates the science of ethics which corresponds to the results of Modernity. In brief, Rosenzweig's claim is that historical epochs should be characterized according to representative bodies of philosophical thought that take for their starting point traditional rationalist principles, namely, principles that entail that we can know something about the respective element which corresponds to each epoch but that end in doubting that we can obtain positive knowledge about the element under primary consideration. However, Rosenzweig asks us to doubt even the doubt of the representative thinkers of those epochs, in effect negating the authority of their knowledge claims. In other words, whereas these former thinkers began with "positive' but ungrounded knowledge and conclude that knowledge is not possible, namely, a thinking process that rationally moves from Something to Nothing, Rosenzweig begins with their results, particular irrational Nothings, which he negates in order to arrive at positive "Somethings" of knowledge about each of these particular Nothings. The historical figures whose "results" Rosenzweig negates are the philosophers Maimonides, Descartes, and Kant, and whose concerns were to reductively conceptualize, respectively, the concepts: god, world, and human.

II. *The god: metaphysics as negation of negative theology*

Maimonides's negative theology introduced doubt about the knowledge of god that is the starting point for the metascience which Rosenzweig labels metaphysics and that deals with a negation of the kind of philosophical "physics" that is traditionally denoted metaphysics. Briefly, Maimonides's negative theology proceeds from the assumption that no predicates or descriptive terms can be applied to god unless those terms are used in some way that does not constitute "normal" usage or are understood to be negative.[13] In other words, all statements about god, if true, are statements made to determine what god is not. Furthermore, attributes provide ethical imperatives — if god is good, we must strive to be good; and that hatred is not ascribed to god entails that we ought to avoid hatred.[14]

a. *The irrational, empirical starting point*

Rosenzweig considers god as an object for thinking by restricting our attention
to centering on a particular problem, a particular Nothing of our knowledge
about some as-yet-undefined entity. Drawing on Cohen's asymptotic calculus
to structure his conceptual construction, we move from nothing to something,
from 0 to 1, or from the initial, particular Nothing of our knowledge of god
towards a Something — towards what Rosenzweig terms the "the actuality of
god" (*die Wirklichkeit Gottes*).

According to Rosenzweig, the concept of god is to us at first a nothing;
however, that concept of god can be thought as a mental movement from a
particular nothing called god, as its *own* nothing, which is involved in a process
of becoming that particular's *own* something. But Rosenzweig uses language in
a novel way such that this something is not to be confused with a conventional
understanding of the word "something" because we are not seeking just any
something; we are seeking the "something" of god. What can be expressed
minimally about this seeking is that god is *not* the initial nothing with which
we begin. By beginning with a denial of nothing, it appears that there are two
ways to continue the task of defining this particular nothing called god, which
depends on analyzing the structures of thinking in itself. One way of thinking
is that of "affirmation" (*Bejahung*) of the initial negation of the posited nothing
of god, what Rosenzweig refers to as the "not-nothing" (*Nichtnichts*) or "the-
sought-after" (*das Gesuchten*: the something). This is also what Kant means
by an infinite judgment, namely, that an affirmation is the result of a double
negation.[15] The other way is that of "denial" (*Verneinung*) and refers to that
which is presupposed, namely, the nothing. This latter point is that with which
we begin talk about god. However, these two ways are and remain different,
and consequently result in different logico-linguistic points of arrival: a "Yes"
(*Ja*) and a "No" (*Nein*).

The two arrival points in this process of defining the concept of god reveal
a twofold structure of the something, and likewise, a twofold relationship
to the original nothing. The Yes applies to the not-nothing, or the double
negation, which is actually an affirmation, while the No applies to the simple
negation, or the nothing. Furthermore, as with every affirmation that occurs
through a denial, the Yes posits an infinity (the Kantian infinite judgment) and
as a something, stands in relation to nothing as its in-dweller (*Anwohner*).
The No as denial, on the other hand, posits that which is finite, limited, and
defined, and stands in relation to the nothing as that-which-escapes-from (*der
Entronnener*). For Rosenzweig, the former, the arc of the Yes path, refers to
the infinite fullness of god as something that is not nothing, while taking the
path of the latter, the arc of the no path, means referring to the something of
god as that which "breaks the prison of the nothing," or as the "event of this
liberation from the nothing." This process of breaking-free occurs, nonetheless,

only within what is hypothetically conceived to be god. There is no relationship to anything outside of the domain of god. Nonetheless, the yes refers to what god "is," and has to do with "essence" (*Wesen*) and the "origin" (*Ursprung*), while the no refers to what god "does," and has to do with "act" (*Tat*) and the beginning. Taken in conjunction, since both ways refer with equal weight to god, what it means for god to "be" is that god freely "acts."

b. *Formulating metaphysics*

Rosenzweig depicts the dynamics of how we conceptualize "that god acts" on the model of an algebraic equation of the type "y = x" where the signs "y" and "x" are variables which are substituted with alternate specifications in the elemental proposition, and "=" represents the asymptotic function that holds between those specifications. Moreover, the structure is similarly modeled syntactically in grammatical categories of subject and predicate, where "y" takes the subject place and "x" the "content of the expression," or predicate place. This syntactic modeling is significant because of Rosenzweig's parallel appeal to his reader's aesthetic sensibility that I discuss below.

According to Rosenzweig's logic of negation, briefly outlined above, "the Yes is the Beginning" and complements the condition that the "No is [also] in the beginning."[16] Hence, the Yes is the affirmation of the not-nothing or how one thinks the infinity of god. Furthermore, the power of the Yes represents the "unlimited possibilities of reality" and is the primal word (*Urwort*) of language. But since language is made up of sentences, this means that the primal word has also to do with sentence structure. Although the Yes is not itself a sentence part, it is one of the three primal words, the others being "No" and "And" (*Und*), and all three constitute the logical substructure we use when we form or utter any sentence whatsoever. Consequently, the Yes is that which "first makes possible any kind of sentence-forming words at all." The Yes is the "Amen" or affirmation that both "gives every word in the sentence its right to exist," and, as the "first Yes in god, establishes the divine essence for all infinity."[17]

Moreover, this Yes refers simply to the original, positive One that Rosenzweig denotes as the primal determination; it is the pure "Thus" (*So*). This Thus becomes a "Thus and not otherwise" (*So und nicht anders*) when the "Other" emerges vis à vis the original One. According to Rosenzweig:

> It is only through this transition to multiplicity that the determination becomes the denial. And as the primal-determination happens in the Yes, so the primal-positing (*Ursetzung*), the positing of the original subject, happens in the No; every individual positing (*Setzung*) of a subject is simply for itself a groundless position, but the original positing, which lies before all individual [positing], the

pre-supposition (*Voraus-setzung*), is denial, namely that of the Nothing; every individual subject is simply "other," namely, other than the Nothing.[18]

The complex logic in this passage results from Rosenzweig's conceptualizing the element god with both symbolic logic and grammatical categories in a two-tier platform of both mathematics and aesthetics, which is also the case in his conceptualizations of the other elements: world and human. He attempts to hold fast to the mental constructions built up on the "way to the completion of god" in "well-known logical-mathematical symbols" but with awareness of the aesthetic character of symbolic presentation. Indeed, Rosenzweig's logic is not a straightforward rehashing of the mind-numbing three-step dance of standard syllogistic logic. Rather, his constructions become labyrinthine because of some original insights that direct the course of his exposition and that are also compressed within the passage just quoted.

The discussion focuses on the priority of affirmation. Rosenzweig employs the mathematical function of an affirmation of a double negation to denote the origination of god's nature, but with the disclaimer that simple denial is its presupposition, and is thus the *actual* starting point. Hence, even though affirmation may be the primal determination, it is groundless, whereas "simple denial" is a primal positing that logically positions the proposition in its correct semantic order needed to depict Rosenzweig's syntactical reconstruction of the semantics involved in linguistically expressing a concept that is meant to allude to the process involved in thinking the "nature" of god. In other words, the actual Thus of affirmation does not become situated without the implied "other" of denial because, in fact, each and any subject can only be one subject insofar as it is *not* any other subject. And thinking Thus means that even though the Thus may come first in the expressed affirmation, in terms of conceiving god's *physis*, the Yes stands on the right side of the equation, which signifies its order in the underlying metalogical equation. Returning to the language of algebraic equations, Rosenzweig designates the symbol "A" for god's nature, which signifies "simple, infinite, affirmed being" (*Sein*). In the beginning we only think of god in terms of a hypothetical thought construct, which is why we start with a Yes and the infinite, unlimited possibilities allowed in a hypothetical thought construct, as such. But then we restrict the possibilities by negating other finite possibilities and posit a concrete place for action with the construction of a whole sentence, thus hypothetically allowing for a grammatical depiction as an analogue for the concrete activity of god, depicted symbolically by Rosenzweig with actual, constructed syntactic equations that operate with the "language" of mathematical logic.

According to that logic, if the divine nature corresponds to the primal-word Yes, divine freedom corresponds to the primal-word No. Rosenzweig calls the affirmation of the Not-nothing god's infinite essence, which entails that the finite is that which the Nothing is, since that is what is "left over" (*das Nichts als ein Endliches zurückgeblieben*). The Nothing is identified as finite because it is, in fact, the Nothing which is the particular starting-point of thinking about god; it is the concretely empirical place of the posing of the problem. In this sense, it is directed at itself as an "other." This "other" then breaks out of the Nothing in an original act of self-denial and takes form as a free, original No. Analogically, the Nothing of god itself denies itself, and is thus denoted as the No of god; consequently, it is not an essence, since it contains no Yes — it is a pure No, understood as an act of "pure" negation. It is directed to everything that is "other" in god, the No to everything that is not the self of god but is other than god. Thus, as that which is directed towards all other that is not god it becomes divine freedom. This is the act and movement in god whose structure is finite but is nonetheless an always-new infinity (as act) breaking out of its finite source (as a negation of all finite others). For this reason it is also inexhaustible power (*unerschöpfliche Macht*), because of the way it flows out of an inexhaustible source (*Quelle*). Moreover, it is not the freedom *of* god — as subject, because that would entail a relationship of god to something outside of god — as object, but is rather entirely self-enclosed intra-subjective activity. Consequently, divine freedom is symbolically depicted on the left hand side of the underlying equational scheme, and is specified by "A =." This denotes the fact that divine freedom has to do with the "original No," and is a directional activity with unlimited power to negate everything that is not itself. Regarding its directionality, Rosenzweig has in mind that it is like a mathematical vector[19] but, since this freedom is limitless, it is also characterized as arbitrary (*Willkür*).

However, both ways — double negation and simple negation — are ways to think the inner dynamic of the hypothetical element called god. Hence, insofar as divine freedom is directed towards the unmoved being of divine essence (as a vector), its active power is "restricted" (*gehemmt*) in that its movement is hardened into a "thusness" (*Sosein*). Because divine freedom is so hardened, it functions as power and arbitrariness in Rosenzweig's equation, whereas divine essence functions as divine compulsion and fate (*Muß und Schicksal*). What physically emerges in depicting this logical transition from infinite movement to fixed essence — as a movement from freedom to fate — is a vision of the divine countenance (*Antlitz*). Rosenzweig symbolically depicts a transition that he analogically correlates to the vitality (*Lebendigkeit*) of god.

Rosenzweig deepens the theoretical layers of his hypothetical construction, intimating the possibilities of its linguistic substantiation, by noting that what confirms (*be-stätigt*) and sets fast (*festge-legt*) the two is what similarly occurs in any sentence construction and is thus akin to standard synthetic propositional logic. By placing words in a sentence-whole (*Satzganze*), the interdependence of the parts that emerges is brought to light. In fact, it is the primal-word "And' which presupposes both of the other two primal words: "And" signifies the binding together of two words comprising the minimal requirements for a sentence. Thus, what ultimately brings a sentence together can be understood in terms of the normative Yes *And* No of any discourse built on "grammar" of propositional logic:

> The sentence itself first occurs (*kommt erst zu-stande*), it first arises (*ent-steht*) thereby, in the way that the situative (*er-örternde*), definitive (*fest-legende*) No seeks to overpower the con-firmative Yes (*be-stätigende Ja*). The sentence, even the smallest sentence part — where language is isolated, the word; where it coalesces in the union of two words; where it inflects in the union of stem and inflectional ending of a word — presupposes Yes and No, Thus and Not-otherwise.[20]

The primal-word "And' presupposes both Yes and No with its connective power, and is likewise the final key holding together the vitality of the figure of god being constructed by Rosenzweig; that is, propositional logic elicits for us a *sense* of vitality in the figure being constructed. Rosenzweig's construction functions in this way because it simultaneously supports the visible structures we recognize in constructing any sentence whatsoever — the *logos* of any language — and the rationality of language as such.

This final area of knowledge about the self-contained logic that is used to depict the inner dynamic at work as an analogy to the nature of god is symbolized by Rosenzweig with the apparently tautological equation "A = A," which indicates the "pure originality and inner-self-satisfaction" of god (*reine Ursprünglichkeit und Insichselbstbefriedigtheit*). Its simple appearance of tautological self-identity gives no indication of either directional movement outward or of the source of the individual signs. Thus, god's nature, or *physis*, is conceived as self-enclosed, with no connection to either the world or to humans, concealing its inner dynamic. God is conceived metaphysically — as that which is beyond the physis. In other words, talk about god's *physis* is not talk about what god "really" is, but rather is a metaactivity. What engages us even further in Rosenzweig's depiction of the figure of god, however, is his recourse to parallel structures in intuitive syntactical constructions without which constructions of semantic meaning would not be possible. The self-enclosed sentence as the barest unit of meaning serves, in the early part of Rosenzweig's work, as a metaphor for the hypothetical construction of the element god, which is symbolized in mathematical language but that is physically embodied through the work of imagination in art.

c. *Where are the mythical gods of Olympia?*

First formal aesthetic excursus
For Rosenzweig, the mythical gods of Antiquity are still living and, in fact, especially *in fact*, immortal: "Death lies under them. They have not conquered it, but death does not approach them." In fact, death has a separate realm: the

Underworld, with its own god from Olympus, Hades, ruling it; albeit by tyrannical fiat from Zeus. Moreover, the gods of Antiquity have dominion in their realm and are living gods, but are not gods of the living because, as Rosenzweig maintains, such a condition entails an "actual stepping out of themselves" whereas the gods of Olympus live among themselves and hold death away from themselves. This has consequences for Rosenzweig's theory of nature, since there is no supernatural realm apart from the gods; they are "as humans have hypostasized them, forces of nature where nature is nothing other than the particular natures of the gods."[21] There can be no separate realm of nature, since all natural phenomena are *aufgehoben* (taken up and appropriated) in the divine sphere. Accordingly, "The world of the gods always remains a world for itself, even if it encompasses the entire world; the encompassed world is then nothing for itself to which the god must enter into a relation, but rather [it is] entirely closed off from him. Thus, god is here without world," or it is a "world without gods."[22]

Rosenzweig introduces the first of three formal principles of his aesthetic theory in what he calls the "Aesthetic Foundation Concept: Outer Form." The *outer form* is the sensual appeal of the external figure, that is, what is *visibly perceived*: architecture, sculpture, the human body, and figures on a stage. The as-yet undeveloped aesthetic experience which Rosenzweig works with in this part of his theory comes from Kant's epistemological argument that humans experience things in the world through spatio-temporal forms of intuition and apprehension, but also that each experiencable thing is externally perceivably experiencable precisely because of its own inner movement.[23] However, in true Kantian form, the thing-in-itself, although having its own constitution, can never be fully known with certainty, an axiom that serves as a foundation for what Rosenzweig calls the "wealth of the contradictions of life." Thus, centuries before Kant's Critical Philosophy, the perspective of the art of Antiquity, with its "self-containedness of the mythical world" and its association with myth, serves as the source of *all art*, which operates under the law of outer form, inner form, and content. Drawing further on Kant's aesthetic theory (at least at this level of his development of aesthetic form),[24] Rosenzweig postulates that for art to be counted as art, it has to be self-contained and without consideration for any other outside itself, independent of any *higher laws* and *free* from *lower duties*. Accordingly, a "tremor of the mythical" emerges from each work of art even if it is veiled in the clothes of our everydayness and even if the content of the work is "need and tears," there has to remain that breath of detached liveliness of the unencumbered "easy life" of the gods around the work. That liveliness is phenomenally expressed in the externally visible and perceivable form and serves as the foundation for what Rosenzweig calls the "threefold mystery of the beautiful."[25] That "threefold mystery" is the threefold relatedness of art as a form of communication that Rosenzweig presents in Part I as the conjunctive counterpart to the pre-linguistic structures of math.

In the "Twilight/Dawn of the Gods," Rosenzweig proposes that our concept of god, as such, could change and that we are not determined to hold one version or another.[26] In fact, he introduces the idea that a turn (or change) in our concept of god is possible: "If God should ever emerge out of the hitherto attained liveliness and become the living god of life, then the result which was earned thus far on the way from Nothing must itself become a Nothing, a departure point." Such a departure would be a primary source with which Rosenzweig posits the possibility of a conversion of the simply living to the life-producing concept of god, helping us along by pointing out how such a conception already emerged in Antiquity but only resulted, then, in the esoteric mystery religions and the thoughts of great philosophers. The problem with both of these phenomena is that the movement in each is always only a movement from human acts of loving and striving toward a god, with the disallowance that god could ever suffer the passion of love (*Leidenschaft der Liebe*).[27] This would always end up in one form or another of apotheosis or gnosis and could never be a free gift that would awaken the love of the human.[28] Awakening anybody self-evidently requires a physical self-presencing of one to another, which is not possible in the myth of the independent gods of Olympus. This is a critical point for my overall thesis since the possibility for such face-to-face self-presencing to occur is one of the critical, ethical points where Rosenzweig and Heidegger diverge.

Such presencing could only happen "from face to face, from named person to named person,"[29] as Rosenzweig stresses, and such a gap could only be closed by the "inextinguishability of the proper name."[30] What is most characteristic of the myths of Antiquity is that all particularities of human or world are consumed in the desire for god, in the divine fire of apotheosis. The gods of Antiquity are monistic and never able to extend beyond the self-secluded constitution of their own nature — unable to give or to love, such gods remain metaphysical, beyond sensuality. But what kind of art presents a relation based on non-sensuality? From his extensive correspondences, Rosenzweig's awareness of developments in the European art milieu at the beginning of the twentieth century — especially abstract Modernism, provide ample indications of how that intellectual climate in art is expressed through both the structure and content of his text.[31]

III. *The world: metalogic as negation of negative cosmology*

a. *Doubting Descartes*

For Rosenzweig, the world is the most self-evident object of knowledge. As he notes, however, Descartes' methodical doubt negates any knowledge of the world; accordingly, there is nothing in the world that is beyond question.[32]

Rosenzweig's metalogic begins by recalling this historical negation. But the actual goal of Descartes' systematic doubt was to deny any attempt to found science on probability, in favor of science being founded on absolute certainty. Hence, Descartes' use of the geometrical method can best be understood as an attempt to devise a method of discovery that is analytic and heuristic and not deductive and synthetic as in Spinoza's case. Rosenzweig rejects the very starting point of this method since what follows Descartes' doubt of all is the first indubitable proposition which halts all doubt: the *cogito ergo sum* of the *res cogitans*; an analytic that actually collapses into merely the *cogito* of the proposition. With an ironic twist, Rosenzweig negates Descartes' methodically applied universal doubt in favor of a doubting/negating, which is practical and instrumental, following Descartes' own heuristic lead but transforming the order of application. Rosenzweig harnesses negation to relative, practical, and specific applications such that doubt, or negation, is at the clear and distinct service of the doubter's analytic, and serves as a *means* in a systematic quest for positive "truths," and not as some abstractly hypothetical starting point for an arbitrary method. What Rosenzweig rejects is Descartes' attempt to achieve certainty of knowledge by setting doubt over against the presupposition of the "one and all" universe (or universal). By claiming to accept only clear and distinct ideas to ground such certainty (and what could be more clear and distinct than the existence of one's self as a thinking thing?), Descartes thought that he had the problem solved. But Rosenzweig rejects Descartes' method precisely because of how science can only provide hypothetical doubts from which belief about the facticity of the world arbitrarily "springs" into an unconditional Something of knowledge of the world. We start from our experience of the world *as* it is conditioned by our hypothetical presuppositions theoretically constructed about the world. Descartes' geometrical method, based as it is on the doubting thinking of the thinker, does not go far enough. Even the doubt of the thinker must be questioned.

According to Rosenzweig, Descartes' substance, the *res cogitans*, is an unacceptable starting point because of how Descartes defined it in terms of the argument from the *cogito*, that is, grounding existence by recourse to the groundlessness of a thinking subject. Rather than serve as a ground for any kind of empirical substance that would secure knowledge of the world, such a starting point is more translucent in its immateriality than the doubt it is supposed to silence. Such a superficial dualism presupposes that there are only two attributes that determine how we think about reality; namely, thought and extension. Thus, all properties of physical things are *ways* of being extended, of "thinking things" *ways* of thinking. It is clear, though, that the *ways* of extension are merely unexamined *ways* of thinking themselves. Furthermore, in order to "prove" the existence of an external, contingent physical world, Descartes has to proceed from the contents of his own consciousness, which entails the initial corollary step of proving the existence of god, the idea of which necessitates thinking of god as perfect, purely rational, and intellectual. In such a Cartesian metaphysical system, questions of detail are relegated to the realm of mere technical or practical difficulties that are already solved in principle beforehand. Since we already know the answers to all the questions, the only aspect worth awe and wonder is the Creative Source of physical happenings and of the self that is ultimately the monistic Creative Source. In such a universe, there can be no spontaneous newness; there is never anything new under the sun.

Moreover, the problem of Faustian striving after ever-more experience, which Rosenzweig uses to suggest the universal problem of how we humans acquire knowledge, is dealt with by an appeal to "explain the truths which can be deduced from things so ordinary as to be known to all of us," a presupposition which putatively enables one to discover all other truths. What Descartes' method does not even take into account, however, is Aristotle's dictum that it is predictable that the unpredictable will occur.[33] Indeed, Descartes' doubt results in a polar universality, the universal doubt posited by the cogito set over against the universal All, likewise posited by the cogito, and is also rejected by Rosenzweig with his insistence on three starting points and the unavoidable inviolability of human existence.[34]

The way of negating how we know the world that Rosenzweig negates is that of the universal doubt of Descartes. We know nothing about the world in the sense that the Nothing we know is the particular Nothing of our knowledge about the world and is not the absolute doubt about the universal All. What is affirmed is a particular, concrete doubt, or negation, as a "means" (*Mittel*), and not as the "purpose" or "end" (*Zweck*) of thinking. Thus, according to Rosenzweig, by beginning with, and fastening onto, this particular Nothing, we again "sink into the depths of the positive," or the empirical, as with thinking the concept of god above.

b. *Formulating the metalogic*

In conceptualizing the element world, Rosenzweig posits three components that can be visualized via the symbolic formula "$B = A$," which, similarly to conceptualizing god, corresponds to a specification of the signs in the equation $y = x$. The components are: "worldly order" (*weltliche Ordnung*), "worldly fullness" (*weltliche Fülle*), and "actuality of the world" (*Wirklichkeit der Welt*). On one level, this is an instance of the way Rosenzweig has woven structures of self-similarity into his work. However, he also makes clear that the element world is not identical with the elements god or human; thinking each element entails the projection of a different pattern of thought.

In contrast to the infinite resting essence of god, the world's infinity, its affirmative Not-nothing, is characterized as "full of structure," which entails inexhaustibly and constantly giving birth to a fullness of ever-new aspects, or faces (*Gesichte*). What it means to be "full of structure" is that the world demonstrates an inner "worldly order." The infinite affirmation of the Not-nothing of the world shows the infinite applicability of this worldly order to everything in the world. Hence, the Yes of the initial double negation grounds and stands for the essence of world as *logos* as the law of this applicability, which is applicable "always and everywhere" (*Überall und Immer*). The *logos*, as the essence of the world, is universally and necessarily applicable in the sense that categories of thinking are always and everywhere applicable to what is in the world. However, the *logos* itself is not of the world but occurs in thinking abstractly about the world. And since the *logos* is what characterizes thinking, the "*logos* is the essence of the world."[35]

Worldly order is symbolized by "= A" which represents the "passive attractive power" of the universal characterized as "that-which-is-to-be-applied" (*das Anwendbare*). In the sense that *physis* is the essence of god, *logos* stands for the intelligibility of the world, and even though a thinking-about-anything-whatsoever-in-the-world is itself not in the world, it is universally applicable to the world (*Allgemeingültig-keit*). Thus, the science of the *logos* of the world is a metalogic — a *logoi*, or logic, which is "meta"-world, or simply defined as not-world. Just as in set theory, thinking *about* the world does not necessarily belong to that set which constitutes all that is *of* the world.[36]

On the other hand, what is "in" the world is the particular Nothing of the world. This is the second component of the world, "worldly fullness," which is specified by the symbol B because it represents that which is a particular other. This corresponds to negation of the world as a No, and like the No of divine freedom, breaks out of the "prison of Nothing," but with "ever-new contractions of production and birth." The world gives birth to the fullness of ever-new particular aspects, or faces. Each new birth is the birth of a uniquely new particular that negates the universality of the Nothing of the world. As Rosenzweig points out, what is disconcerting about talking about the world in terms of universality, as *logos*, is that the world is precisely not Absolute Spirit (*Geist*).[37] It is filled with an actual and infinite variety of states, arts, families, etc. This is already an implication by Rosenzweig of a kind of chaos of particulars that is not subsumable under the category of Absolute Reason that is implicit at the beginning and explicit at the end of Hegel's logic.

The third component, the "actuality of the world," signifies the conjunctive functioning of the previous two components and is thus symbolized by the completed formula B = A. The logic of such a construction entails that each particular is drawn into its own universal, that is, the particular becomes increasingly dominated by its own universal until a certain moment when the "blind eyes of the particular are opened," and it becomes "conscious of its direction towards the universal."[38] At that moment (the German word for moment is "*Augenblick*," which literally means the instantaneous opening of an eye)[39] the particular is transformed into an individual, and the universal into the species, which is defined and constituted by that particular set of individuals. The relationship of particular to universal is consummated through a process of the universal working on the individual until it has become an "individualized universal" (*ein individualisiertes Allgemeines*) within the limits of its own species.

In other words, the particular is not *Aufgehoben*, as the reconciliation of opposites, into the general principle of Hegelian idealism. Hegelian logic entails that the one-and-all universal form penetrates and forms the already-existing inert particulars with its one-and-the-same form. Rosenzweig's formula, in contrast, maintains dissimilarity of content, whereas the formula for idealism, A = B, asserts identity, since the universal is that which fills the particulars by "externally" overpowering them, and thus universalizing them into instances of "universal" individuals. In Rosenzweig's metalogical world-view, there is no ultimate meltdown, or overpowering, of an individual in its species. In contrast, the formal structuring activity is inner-worldly and allows for a plurality of species, of units of specific individuals distinct from each other, to constitute the world as that which comes together as associations of various species, peoples, states, etc.[40] This relationship of the individual to the species is evident in every classificatory phase of the biosphere, from the lowest levels of plant life to that of the relationship of the individual human being with the larger social community. Ordinarily, the relationship is defined by the natural and social sciences, but it is depicted for us by Rosenzweig in metalogical terms in order to bridge the gap between concept and thing. According to Rosenzweig, this is a problem nexus that neither Plato nor Aristotle resolved with satisfaction.[41] With Kant however, the problem of epistemology is correctly located in how we understand the structures of the cognizing "I." But that discussion must wait until we consider the specific role that art plays with respect to presenting the element world.

c. *The sleeping, plastic world*

The world as plastic cosmos depends on the philosopher herself bearing the metalogical world system, a system, moreover, which is foundationally multidimensional. This means that from any given single point in the system, relational threads can be traced to any other point — a correlational coherence system of truth — but the whole itself and the unity of these countless relations is the "personal, lived and philosophized standpoint of the philosopher,"[42] at least for Rosenzweig, through Schopenhauer, Kierkegaard, and Nietzsche.

More than any other phenomenon, the unity achieved by the standpoint philosopher depends upon the degree of clarity of vision that she achieves of an interconnected world whole. Again, by contrast, the primitive traditions

of India and China disallow the vision necessary to perceive the interconnectedness of the world; in the case of India, flight from the world leaves it
in darkness; in the case of China, submersion in the world results in a "night
where all cows are black." As this phrase indicates, Rosenzweig utilizes Hegel's
famous condemnation of Schelling's version of Idealist philosophy by applying
Hegel's condemnation to criticize Asian philosophy of religion. By contrast,
only the Greeks, as the "people of discoverers," have been able to lead the
way to clarity of vision of the connection between figure and background.
However, the resolution of that relationship, of the overarching connection
of, say, the city Athens with its namesake, Athena as the goddess of wisdom,
is a problematic resolution since there really is no "overarching connection."
Instead, the Greek Polis, Rosenzweig's reference for the "plastic world," has
no need of connecting to any structure outside of itself since its very constitution is such that, as figure, it represents the second fundamental law of all
art, namely, *closedness in itself*. There is a connection "of every part with the
whole, of every detail [of the work] with all other details" in that connectedness
to the whole. Rosenzweig stresses, however, that such connectedness is not
relational but is, rather, a "connection that is irreducible to a logical unity and
yet is uniform throughout; no part is mediated through another part; rather,
each is adapted [i.e. inserted] immediately into the whole."[43] While the first
law of art forms the ground of "the idea of the beautiful" and the realm of
the beautiful, this second law forms the ground of the particular law of the
artwork and, above all, of the "individual beautiful thing, of the beautiful
figure (*Gestalt*) — Hellas."[44] Etymologically, the word *Gestalt* has to do with
that which is externally outermost, as that which is created to be seen by an
other. It is closely connected to the German verbs *gestellen*, which means "to
place [something someplace]," and *gestalten*, which means to construct or
form something. Thus, Hellas stands for the created thing of beauty, that which
human hands have placed and formed amongst themselves to demonstrate their
own inviolable coherence in a certain place. The dialectical consequence is that
every *other* outside of that *Gestalt* — for the Greeks — is barbarous.

But such a world remains *just* a self-enclosed *Gestalt*, a figure infinitely rich
within and ever-renewed and clarified as it rests within itself, but weak and
poor from without. There is no relation from figure to figure, from statue to
statue or temple to temple, since each is enclosed within itself and dictated by
its own inner laws of self-satisfaction to itself. If there is an existing god/dess in
the temple, s/he remains enclosed within and ineffectual for the working of the
world, and thus, as macrocosm, is invisible. If there is an existing human, as
long as s/he remains merely a protagorean "measure set against the world from
outside and not a moving force within it," then the world, as microcosm, is deaf
to the existence of the human. And the world remains blind and deaf as long as
there is no shining god and no speaking human. As long as the world remains
"enclosed within its own self-groundedness, inspired with its own spirit, in the

fullness of its own splendor," it remains meta-logical, and asleep.[45] While the cities, statues and temples, which represent the plastic arts of the Greek world may be filled with an inner form that relates each individual part to the other, there is no living relation from city-state to city-state, no connection from one god's temple to the next, and no word spoken from statue to statue or even a glance from one to the other.

IV. *The human self: meta-ethics as the modern method*

a. *Kant's soul-less negative psychology*

Rosenzweig analyzes the process of human self-formation. The self defiantly and freely roots itself in its own character by means of a twofold function: first, securing itself against an ontological meltdown in any kind of Hegelian social structure; and then, establishing a basis to develop a kind of autonomous self that is necessary for Rosenzweig's Jewish/Kantian ethical framework. The human element is the last of the three elements that we are *given* insofar as these particular Nothings of our knowledge of each element correspond respectively to the three major epochs that epitomize our humanly constructed world-views historically based on those nodal points (as principles). As already noted, Rosenzweig avoids merely repeating the logic of previous thinkers by developing a series of meta-inquiries, which enables him to radically question any system that purports to include all inquiry, that would result in excluding any real difference. However, the meta-ethical inquiry is not simply one among others; rather, it is the most critical because it characterizes the modern period within whose parameters we find ourselves. In fact, it assumes a more significant place in Rosenzweig's work than either speculative metaphysics or the natural sciences of metalogic and thus orients my own thesis.

This third major epoch is highlighted by the critical philosophy of Kant whose negative psychology sets limits on the knowledge we can have about the cognizing All, because, significantly, it is also the volitive All. From Kant we learn more clearly that how I think is bound up with how and what I desire. For Rosenzweig, Kant's philosophy resulted in bringing the most self-evident of all entities, the "I," into question. But Kant also instructs us that we can only cognize something about the "cognizing I" (*erkennende Ich*) in relation to cognition, that is, to the fruits of that cognizing I. Moreover, Kant's morality entails that our actions and responsibilities remain hidden from us. In other words, Kant does not allow for any relation to the self as it is innately "in itself" but only in relation to that which it produces. According to Rosenzweig, this is the kind of "negative psychology," which has produced an entire century of "psychology without soul." Hence, Rosenzweig negates Kant's negation of the possibility of knowledge as constituent in the formation of human self-identity because, as with Maimonides and Descartes, Kant simply had the wrong starting point.

Kant's idealist epistemology and ethics depend on positing an *a priori* principle, the "moral law," as a universal standard. As with Descartes's methodical doubt, the regulative nature of Kant's Categorical Imperative, the centerpiece of his theory of his moral law, leaves its application to actual examples open. For both philosophers, the details are dealt with as the need arises since, in Kant's case, one only needs to have the universalizable moral law and the practical application follows. Consequently, Kant's application of the categories he "discovered" is, like Descartes' philosophy, analytic and heuristic, or regulative. This inevitably leads to a problem of self-accountability and ethical responsibility in particular instances.[46] Rosenzweig goes even further and questions the claims to the universality of such an idealist philosophy.

Indeed, Rosenzweig's critique of Kant's philosophy shows how it is not only necessary to disclose the limits of philosophy, it is also necessary to reveal the content of belief. Such a disclosure entails pointing out, again and again, that the self-evidence of knowledge is only apparent, and that it is at its roots shackled with an absurdity. But this is a peculiar kind of absurdity because saying that all knowledge presupposes an *absurdum* is not the same as saying that all knowledge is ultimately absurd, and that our quest for knowledge is reduced to the futility of language games or a meaningless waiting for Godot. On the contrary, the point is that only after it is shown that knowledge is not so clear and simple (*ein-fach*) can the space be cleared for belief to take that rejected *simpliciter* and itself become simple. In other words, what it means to know something is to know that that something is not monolithically deducible from some first principle, that is, either generated from the dialectic of Being or as the necessary product of the automatic application of the categories through our faculties of intuition, as Kant attempted to demonstrate in *The Critique of Pure Reason*. To more closely approximate this simplicity, Rosenzweig uses Hermann Cohen's theory of infinitesimals in order to develop a logic that moves us beyond, by extending, traditional logic. It is beyond traditional first-order predicate logic because it includes irrationals. It extends that logic because of Kant's insistence on the possible synthetic nature of the *a priori*. Recall that Rosenzweig's concern for truth entails determining that what is true is not simply a matter of judging the truth and falsity of propositions. Rather, his approach is more holistic and context-oriented, which rigorously takes into account the historical origins and empirical accountability of our presuppositions, first premises and goals of our actions. It is more phenomenological in its concern for determining intentionalities and motivations. Consequently, only after the relationship of belief to knowledge is ascertained can the normative nature of ethical activity be introduced. If belief is bracketed out of what it means for human beings to know, as Kant does, or simply identified with knowledge, as Hegel does, then accounting for the motivations and goals of human activity becomes problematic.

Rosenzweig initially sets the terms for discussing the relationship of belief to knowledge in the traditional setting of an inherited conceptual structure, in this case, the traditional proofs for the existence of god or for knowing the world with absolute certainty. And when we refer to the complex of conceptual structures we call "human" (*Mensch*) we are confronted with an irrational element that is as methodologically unprovable (*unbeweisbar*) as god and the world are. As soon as "knowledge" attempts to "prove" the existence, certainty, or facticity of any one of them, it necessarily loses itself in the "absurd" realm of the Nothing. This Nothing of the proving knowledge (*des beweisenden Wissens*) or the Nothing of the proving (*Nichts des Beweisens*) is the "0" coordinate from which we move asymptotically, or differentially, to the "fact' coordinate, the "1," which, because of its unmovable factuality, grounds the space within which knowledge moves and exists. Again, we move from the unprovable Nothing of knowledge to the Something or factuality of the fact which subsequently "grounds" positive knowledge.

b. *Formulating meta-ethics*

As with the elements god and world, three components constitute the formulaic picture of the human element. They are: "human own-ness" (*menschliche Eigenheit*), which is freedom; "human will" (*menschliche Wille*), which is defiance; and "independence of the human" (*Unabhängigkeit des Menschen*), which is the self. Continuing to weave in a logic of self-similarity (which is not the technical structure of the self but, rather, an underlying logic), Rosenzweig uses the equation $x = y$ as the propositional form to hypothesize the dynamical structure of the human element. Given the methodological similarities, the human element is nonetheless, and precisely, neither god nor world. However, it does share certain similarities of content and form with both of these other elements.

The human element is that figure alluded to in the opening paragraphs of Rosenzweig's text which is not only constituted by its temporality (*Vergänglichsein ist sein Wesen*) but also as an everlasting essence (*immerwährendes Wesen*). However, as everlasting, the human element is constituted as neither immortal and unconditioned as god, nor universal and necessary as the world. Its permanent essence is posited as distinctiveness (*Besonderheit*), but a distinctiveness that, in this case, is differentiated from that of the world's. In the world's case, "the structure of the world perfects itself in the individual and the species . . . [as] . . . the individual's penetration into the species" where the relationship of the individual to the whole, when one thinks of the structural processes of the world, is that of the individual to its species and, thereby, to its genus.[47] However, Rosenzweig distinguishes human distinctiveness from the world distinctiveness because of the identity of its form with the idea of god. That formal identity, however, is likewise distinguished because of human worldliness, or our finitude.

Human freedom, designated as free will, is what characterizes the human because it is finite, as opposed to god's infinite freedom, and momentary in its manifestation as is worldly phenomena. So, in contrast to the former, it is specified B, and not A =, but likewise, in contrast to the latter, it is a B =, but not just B since it is not satisfied with its mere existence — it is directional and strives for holistic completion. In the world's case, the directional process is symbolized as an = A, where the universal "draws" the distinctive to it. The movement in the case of the human element, on the other hand, expresses the human's dissatisfaction with its mere existence, because, by definition, it has freedom, and freedom in this sense means that the human thinks, creates, and is created in the image of god.[48] Like god, it has vitality and is characterized as a living self, and, thus, must become the "And," which signifies that it is more than merely volition (directional) or existence (just B). Again like god, it wants its own essence, but unlike god, whose divine essence is compulsion (*Müssen*) and fate (*Schicksal*), it wants its *own* finite essence. In this case, the And signifies the continuation of the process of defining the human element as a process from the unconditionality of free will, recognizing its finiteness (and not power as god), to defiant will (*trotzigen Willen*):

> Defiance, the proud "Yet" (*stolze Dennoch*), is to the human what power, the sublime "Thus" (*das erhabene Also*), is to God. The claim of defiance is as sovereign as the privilege of power. The abstraction of free will takes shape as defiance.[49]

As god and the world were considered "in-themselves," so the self has no relation to either of them in terms of its own developmental process. Rosenzweig presents what constitutes the inner movement of the human element in such terms that how a human relates to "outer" things is necessarily excluded in order for the human to attain independence. Hence, the primary symbol remains the same B, but becomes a transformed B. In other words, this latter B is the same as the original B but has undergone a process of inner transformation designated as the process of the transformation of defiance. Defiance runs its course until it is felt, that is, until it can no longer be ignored, to the point where the human has to claim this defiance as its own. This point is defined as the "existence of own-ness," (*Existenz der Eigenheit*), which becomes determinative as the core constituent factor for simply being human. What it means to be determinative is that this own-ness (peculiarity) of distinctive defiance that uniquely differentiates each human being does not allow itself to be dissolved in a universal "Nothing" or Being. Formulated otherwise, it is a point of blind existing factuality that comes to lie in the path of free will, a factuality

Rosenzweig calls "character." Whereas the will (*der Wille*) of an individual is annihilated in its peculiarity in the process intrinsic to the world structure, the particular B being absorbed by the universal A, it is not, as defiance, annihilated in character. Ultimately, there can be no enduring distinctiveness in the world-process. The very logic of the world-process disallows this possibility, because every distinctive part is inevitably drawn to and defined by its specific genus, which is the universal. For the human, on the other hand, its process is characterized by a defiance that finds its *content* in character. Furthermore, the self is the And of defiance coupled with character, that is, its content is understood as the process of its development:

> defiance remains defiance, it remains formally unconditioned but it takes on character as content: defiance defies up to the point of character. That is the self-consciousness of the human, or more briefly said: that is the self. The self is that which, in this primal concept of the (movement of) free-will towards peculiarity/owness, originates from the "and" of "defiance" and "character."[50]

In other words, the self is rooted (*Verwurzelung*) in character and not, as in the case of the world, in an individuality determined in its development of completion toward and in its species. Rather, the self is self-enclosed precisely *because* it is rooted in character, which is the corollary of its peculiarity. In contrast, were the human, as self, rooted in individuality as personality, it would play out the role fatally assigned to it as one role next to another in the many-voiced symphony of humanity. But this is not the case. The self is unique and *incomparable*, unlike the personality of the world-process that is always one among many and merely an abstraction of the group. The critical distinction is that, unlike individuality or personality, the "self is not a part (*Anteil*), not a type case (*Unterfall*)," which can be classified according to this or that category applicable to some social-scientific formula based merely on, say, class or economic determinative forces. The self cannot be "given up" for any common social good or cause since there is no one *there* to *give* anything to; the self is alone: "The self is not able to be given up — to whom could it be given? There is for (the self) no-one there to whom something could be 'given'; it is alone; it is not one of the 'human-children'; it is Adam, the human (it)self."[51] Hence, with deft parallelism, Rosenzweig supports his negative assertion with the metalogic previously established. He is careful to note, however, that such support is not essential to ground his metaethical argument. On the contrary, the idea is a new one. It can be alluded to with the help of metalogic, but it is in fact capable of being comprehended merely in terms of the metaethical argument. In other words, it is not necessarily developed *only* by means of the metalogic; otherwise, Rosenzweig's argument is self-defeating, namely, each element could be reduced to an interchangeable part in the one, universal logic. The "self" is not a product of the generative birth and death peculiar to every biological species, that is, it is not merely an offspring. Rather, the self is set apart, in isolation as it were, just as Adam in the biblical story is set apart and created alone.

However, in terms of Rosenzweig's dynamic logic, ethical personality, as it is normally construed in terms of personality and relationships, is such that:

> Many predications are possible about personality, as many as about individuality. As individual predications they all follow the scheme B = A, the scheme in which all the predications about the world and its parts are conceptualized. Personality is always defined as an individual in relation to other individuals and to a universal. There are no derivative predications about the self, only the one, original B = B.[52]

Further, Rosenzweig's method of tripartite, yet parallel, development of the elements entails that, like god, the equation for human has the same sign for the subject and predicate positions in the logic equation. As distinctive individual, the B appears on the left hand side of the equation and is denoted as subject, as all individuality is. Rosenzweig develops such assignments in the section "Logic of the world as metalogic."[53] However, following the inner activity denoted by the formal development of the element god, the form is parallel to that of god's, but the content is different. The self and god demonstrate activity of form versus passivity of content. If there is a confrontation between god and the human, it occurs on the issue of finitude versus infinitude. As the equations demonstrate, god's self-sufficiency is signified as A = A, while the self's is B = B. Rosenzweig sums up the parallelism of his constructs by noting that, "the total contradictoriness of content (*Gegensatzlichkeit des Inhalts*), together with an equally total identity of form (*Gleichheit der Form*), is equally evident in the finished equation as it was in the equation in the making."[54] Unlike the world, the human element, analogically Adam, is really made in the image of god (*nach Gottes Ebenbild geschaffen*) whereas the world, as B = A, is not.

As was already briefly indicated, the right hand side also uses the same symbol B as the predicate assertion of the distinctive individual statement. The distinctive (*Besondere*) develops its distinctiveness (*Besonderheit*), literally its separateness-from, "by allowing itself to become the subject (*Gegenstand*) of predicates." What this means is that the entity itself is what undergoes its own peculiar, inner development, and thus is not capable of being made the object of predication, since it is also the active subject of its own predication. As an aside, this logic is other than Leibniz's calculus-based logic.

Rosenzweig maintains further that this development happens in the way that it does so because the underivative nature of the self entails renunciation of the development and presentation of the distinctiveness of the distinctive under consideration (*es verzichtet auf die Entwicklung und Darstellung*). The *structure* of the equation is B = B, which, together with the asserted meanings of the denoted symbols, namely, B = as free will becoming defiant will in the process of assuming its own distinctive B (right hand side of the equation) as its own character, constitutes the mathematico-logical way of referring to the element *Self*. In such a scheme, the particular "makes itself into the predicate content (*Aussageinhalt*) for something other." Only character, and not individuality, is capable of doing this as that "predication (*Aussage*) which *defines* free will more closely."[55] In other words, the predicate defines the subject as that which becomes ever-more and only itself, whereas in individuality the universal A draws and defines the distinctive B. Hence, in the case of the self, the confluence of the terms as they are defined in their conjunctive connection, of the B = (defiant will) and the B (character), results in a concentration into the structure (*Gestalt*) of the self. As already mentioned above, the human, as self, is "created in the image" of god, because of its equivalence (*Gleichheit*) of form, but it also stands in contrast to god, because of its opposition of content (*Gegensätzlichkeit des Inhalts*). Both are self-enclosed and display inwardly directed development perceptually modeled for us in the equation as a directed movement from left to right, similar to that of a vector. However, the unbridgeable difference is that the one, god, is infinite while the other, human as self, is finite.

In respect to world, on the other hand, the human element is both a part of and yet separate from its sphere. This can also be seen in the form and function of the equations. Both the human and the world elements use the same symbol B to represent distinctive individuality. However, the predicate elements are opposite: the B for the human, and A for the world denote their difference in form.

For Rosenzweig's model of the metasciences to work, Kant's insight, namely, that the human is a "citizen of two worlds," has to be qualified, as Rosenzweig himself notes.[56] The problem lies in identifying the human sphere as "a world" and not allowing either "the world" or "the human" spheres to have their own separate determinations. Rosenzweig clearly differentiates the three spheres by presenting the formal parallelism of god and the human on the one hand and the formal difference of the human and the world on the other hand, while affirming a parallelism of content (*inhaltlichen*) between the human and the world elements. This holds because even though both the world and the human elements predicate an opposite "factor," which completes the process of their development (A as universal category in the case of the world and B as character in the case of the human), the predications are made about the same entity (*ein Gleiches*) in both cases, namely, B as subject.

c. *Defiantly tragic heroes*

Summarizing the previous analysis: as part of the world, the human is a finite particular and its particularity entails that, unlike other world particulars such as rocks or sheep, it has both a free will and its own inner development of identity — as a free will defiantly becoming its own character.[57] Moreover, one only becomes conscious of oneself in the process of defiance: "That is the self-consciousness of the human, or briefly: That is the self. The self is that which originates in this encroachment of the free will upon peculiarity, as the And from defiance and character."[58] As rooted in character, it is closed within itself, which Rosenzweig illustrates by reminding us of his role as Mephistopheles: "yet you remain ever what you are." He closes his description of the structure of the self with a rhetorical question regarding the relation of the self to the whole: the self is not a part, not a categorical type and thus, "the self can not be given up: to whom?"[59] The self only takes from the world all that it touches to make it its ownmost.

In terms of his formal aesthetics, Rosenzweig does not lose sight for long of Goethe's Faust, as he includes a lengthy section entitled Heroic Ethos within which he discusses differences between personality as individuality and the relationship of ethos to the self: "the self is the lonely human in the hardest sense of the word. The *political animal* is the personality." He continues with a phenomenological description of the self by drawing on Heraclitus' reference to the *daimon*: the self is *born* on a particular day, namely, as *daimon*.[60] As blind, dumb and self-enclosed, the *daimon*, the ethos of the self, assaults the human wearing the "mask of eros" and accompanies him from then on until it lays down the mask and reveals himself as "thanatos." The *curriculum vitae* of the self is determined from the death of the individual in the moment of sexual mating, the awakening of desire and the inception of the formation of ever-increasing defiant individualizations concretizing into the self as peculiar-defiant character, until the moment of death when the development is complete and the self is most defiantly self-secluded and hardened, and most tragically alone. Consequently, contends Rosenzweig, the less the individual, the more the self: "There is no greater loneliness than in the eyes of a dying one, and there is no more defiant, proud isolation than that which is painted on the paralyzed countenance of the dead one."[61] As he notes, this is the development which Goethe displays in Faust: "he has already forfeited his rich individuality at the beginning of the Second Part and just on that account appears in the Final Act as a character of the fullest hardness and highest defiance, even truly as *self*: a true picture of the ages of the human."[62] The significance of this passage is that Rosenzweig has likewise led us on a journey from the opening in Act One, at the end of the Introduction when, wearing the mask of Mephistopheles he guides us into the underworld holding the key of Nothing. In order to follow through, like Faust, we must agree to sell our souls to Rosenzweig/Mephistopheles and trust that he will deliver. And if, like Faust, we have followed through on the journey, we are likewise stripped of our own wealth of individuality and are left with the prospect of living out the rest of our ethos developing in our own particular characters by reclaiming the earth from the wild sea in splendid, but blind, and lonely isolation.

What does it mean to say that the self has an ethos? It means that every relational category of ethical distinction — lover, friend, family, nation, genus — the entire moral world — are all mere material to widen and deepen the possessive nature of self-identity. The whole world is its presupposition and thus belongs to it as its ownmost possession without, in return, the self having to obey the laws of the world. And such a *Gestalt* is likewise best found in Greek Antiquity, where genus in the form of the polis was actively at work. On that historical backdrop, the self took shape as *Gestalt*, not only with the Sophists, who made the human the "measure of all things" but with the Greek "impetus of visibility," that is, with the heroes of Greek Attic tragedy.[63]

Rosenzweig's first exemplar, however, is clearly not Greek, but is Sumerian, from the Tigris–Euphrates Valley, from the cradle of civilization — Gilgamesh. His purpose in signifying Gilgamesh as exemplary seems to be three-fold: first, it is used to provide a typological model to verify his argument; second, he uses it to demonstrate how one *experiences* the fear of one's own death in one's living life, namely through the death of a friend; and finally, that exemplars of primal life experiences do not all originate from one cultural root — there is more to the origins of human history than the Greeks alone are capable of transmitting. Through the death of his friend Antos, Gilgamesh is thrown into silence and his entire existence is tested by this encounter with death through his friend. As his own death is glimpsed in the death of his friend, Gilgamesh is tested by the inescapable reality of his own mortality that becomes the ruling event of his life and leads him into the sphere of silence, the silence of his own self.

This silence is the sign of both the greatness and the weakness of the self; its greatness is that such non-relational silence allows for particular self-development, that is, learning one's own art (with the help of Mephistopheles and Nothing); but its weakness is precisely its silence and inability to communicate with any other self. This weakness is most clearly demonstrated in a joyless and fruitless life. Attic Tragedy dealt with this kind of speech by developing the art form of drama to present silence represented most clearly by Aescheylus' tragedies. With such characters as Agamemnon or Prometheus, the protagonist is silent for long periods of time and is only supported by the chorus that develops the content of the tragic situation. But the real tragedy is the defiantly isolated self, beyond all situations and therefore unable to change, by itself. Sophoclean and Euripidean heroes, although speaking, do not speak *with* each other but merely *at* each other, carrying on mutual monological debates. The only kind of exchange is the musical one between the chorus and the lyrical monologue of the hero. As Rosenzweig points out, with the help of Aristotle, such an art form is *dia-noetic*, that is, an opposition moderated through rationality.[64]

Thus, this defiant self-modeled in Greek myth — with only rational oppositions at its disposal — is buried in itself and cannot express itself in speech, for to do so it would cease being self since what constitutes self is the aloneness of non-relational speechlessness. It is important to note that as such a defiant self, the will is solely directed towards maintaining its own isolation and not, as in modern tragedy, directed to breaking and directing the will of the other. The two examples Rosenzweig provides are love scenes from Aescheylus' *Phaedrus* and Shakespeare's *Romeo and Juliet*. For *Phaedrus*, the unrequited feeling is appropriate for Greek Antiquity, while Juliet's fortunes and misfortunes are reciprocally augmented and thus can be only modern. Romeo and Juliet each contribute to the development of the other in mutual dialogical events. But, perhaps more important, because the self exemplified in Greek tragedy lacks bridges and connection, there is no possibility for an understanding of what occurs to him. What moves him from an *other* perspective is responding to the change in tone from another singer, or an unexpected challenge from a neighbor, or from a god. Tragic heroic figures, unlike Job, are puzzled by the actions of god(s) and cannot pose Job-like questions; they relinquish them to the poets to pose.

This reduction of tragic drama to the paralysis of the heroic figure and to blind speechlessness is the image Rosenzweig leaves us with as representative of the poetic attempts by the Greeks to depict the self. There is only apparent resolution in the work as a whole that rests ultimately on the final demise of the hero. The very definition of the tragic nature of the hero entails that the hero remain closed within himself until the very end, unable to relate to any external event. But by holding on to such a self, the self never really dies since death is only a cessation of temporal individuality. As heroic, the silence of the self echoes immortally into eternity. The echo sounds through the generations of human history until today because immortality is the final, enduring constitution of the self — the self defiantly wants to be its self forever. Since it is cut off from all relations, the self consciously seeks eternity as a way to perpetuate its own mode of identity as self-possession; but, in fact, its immortality is merely a *not-being-able-to-die*, which leads to various theories of the transcendental psyche and eventually to the opposition of body and soul.[65]

Rosenzweig claims that in order for us to overcome this facile opposition and to save the soul from its ghostly fate, the lonely self needs to become a soul with a different sense, namely, a speaking soul. The key is art, but more specifically, the artist. As already noted with respect to the elements god and world, there is a speech of the unspoken: the mythical grounds the realm of the beautiful in the "excluding self-containedness" of outer form; the plastic grounds beautiful things in the self-containedness of inner form; and so the tragic grounds the "wordless understanding" through the "eloquent silence of the self."[66] And only through such groundings can art attain reality. What emerges with the tragic self is content (*Gehalt*), as that which holds between artist and spectator. Content is what the artist creates which, understood on the content-ual basis of being a living human, enables her to create a bridge between herself as artist and the rest of the world. It is this act of transferring the work, as content, from the private sphere of creative origination to the public sphere, which forms connections of common understanding between living humans. It is not the world that the artist communicates, because that is common to all through each individual's particular standpoint. Rather, the artist communicates equality (*das Gleiche*) of humanity that, however, is not what is common with each individual's relations with the world. What the artist does is simply to *present for visibility* to others the self as human, which is ordained to silence in order to awaken the self in every other who sees this figure. But there is no speaking communication because the presentation is accomplished through stimulating "fear and compassion" (*Furcht und Mitleid*), as Aristotle first noted in his own analysis of the cathartic experience in tragic art; namely, the spectator is awoken to their own self and immediately directs their attention to their own self-identity. However, although all of these souls are awoken to selfhood they nonetheless remain speechless and do not form a community; rather, they remain a collection of unmoved, rigid selves. Indeed, what is created is a common content such that, while the selves cannot come to each other, a common sound sounds out of each of them — the sound of the "feeling of their own self."[67] At this level of art, although no bridges are formed what does significantly occur is a transfer of the same *feeling* for the human self from one isolated self to another isolated self.

It is a world of silent, rational agreement but with no *actual* working effects, no living connections and, thus, no love or birth. The possibility that is structured by this form of art, however, emerges in that every moment and now every standpoint is capable of becoming vitalized for a moment at a time. It is like a room full of flickering lights with no sound disturbing the scene, because only in the interior of each isolated self, can one *feel* the other in one's self. Art effects this feeling of the unity of humanity which, says Rosenzweig, is the pre-speech of common understanding and which is a prerequisite for "actual human speech" (*wirklichen Mencshensprache*).[68] Although the tragic self does not speak, it is seen and on this perceptive basis, common understanding can be formed. Art in itself indeed creates threads from human to human but they are momentary ones that "run only for moments, only for the short moment of the immediate *glance* (*Shauen*) and only at the place of the glance."[69] However, just because the self is perceived does not bring it to life, since the process of being perceived merely enables the awakening of other selves to selfhood. Instead, art creates the ground upon which selves can be awoken but can never become a plurality of selves. This latter negative condition is the case because each self that is awoken through the effects of art remains ever rooted in the illusory world of art.

But what this kind of art does do, contends Rosenzweig, is to sound the "magic flute" of common humanity. It is limited, though, to a sound that each self hears with its own self since the isolated self can never hear the sound of another self. It is limited because if hearing such other soundings occurred, we would already be in the realm of what Rosenzweig refers to as a relation of souls. Instead, the defiantly isolated self is not capable of tracing the human *as* human in any other, because there is no other for the self. Produced under such conditions, the self is walled in and its field of vision is limited to its own self-inspection, that is, all the world, insofar as there is world, is there only as "its own possession."[70] Any *other*, ceases to be *other* because s/he has to be relegated to the visible space of self-willed, self-enclosure (*eigensinnigen Selbst*). Hence, all ethical orders of the world are likewise delimited to the possessive claims of the self's ownmost ethos (*zum eignen Ethos*) because the self "is only capable of reducing all foreign others to its own and can only see its own."[71] This is the status of the self being master of its own house, its own ethos and is that which Rosenzweig defines as meta-ethical, because it is beyond ethical relations.

V. *Art and the new philosophy*

Rosenzweig rejects attempts to *think* the All as objective, claiming that such attempts should be reinterpreted as *Weltanschauungen* whereby an individual *reacts* to how both theology and philosophy are mutual dimensions in a combinatory reaction which he names an "eternal paradox."[72] The untenability of such a multidimensionality finds its most extreme expression in Nietzsche's aphoristic utterances as exemplary of the new kind of standpoint philosopher, that is, as the only kind of philosophizing possible Hegel post-mortem. Defiantly willing one's own standpoint has the consequence of resulting in a paradox, which, if pursued to its own end, can only be resolved in insanity; it is insanity because it is absolutely subjective, non-objective and non-verifiable. Reading Rosenzweig, we engage with our own subjective development in the text itself and intuit our own extra-textual development by way of considering his text as a work of art. It is art, in part, in the way that it is presented as objectively other than me. Analogously and inner-textually Rosenzweig argues that philosophy needs revelation as the relational content of theology precisely as a guarantee of objectivity because, as subjects, we necessarily are faced with "the given."[73] Theology, however, needs philosophy for the sake of subjectivity, namely, to keep it honest, in the sense that as thinking humans we respond to epistemological demands by not grounding the certainty of what we think on the old model of a threatening authority but on the new model of an experiential, relationally bound existence. But how are we to grasp that boundedness if not conceptually?

Instead of merely conceptual elements, such as those exemplified in Part I of *The Star*, theology deals with what is concretely at-hand, with historically contingent "at-hand actualities." Hence, instead of the concept of reality, theology presents us with the concept of creation as a narrative form of philosophizing that can then adequately draw upon the resources of philosophy as a precondition for what theology presents as revelation. Namely, "philosophy as creation" presents us with a "created content" as prophetic activity that necessarily precedes theology whose "content as revelation" *miraculously* fulfills the promised sign (*Zeichen*) of philosophy. Miracle, then, returns to its originary capacity to excite wonder and awe, which previously had been co-opted within the history of philosophy as its privileged possession. The created content that miracle reveals is that which is already self-evident to humans as their "common humanity." What all good art does is to awaken the awareness in each individual of the common thought of humanity as those finite beings caught up with self-appropriating acts that contribute to forming their ownmost identities. This common thought of humanity is the *ground* upon which and out of which the "actual commonality of speech" grows.[74]

However, thinking is not a *speaking*. Rather, it is the "secret ground of speaking" and its primal words are not actual words but promises of actual words.[75] Rosenzweig uses the word *Verheißung* for promises, which has the verbal root of *heißen* that has roots in *sich bewegen* which means to set into movement.[76] What this means for Rosenzweig's work is that what philosophy and philosophy as creation-thinking provides for us is a promise of speech-movements (*Sprachdenken* or speech–acts), which are fulfilled in revelatory events of actual speech. And art-events accomplish not only the promising activity but are irreplaceably instrumental in delivering on the promise. The actual words of speech *need* firm ground beneath their feet in order to *heißen* — call, signify, command — at all, and art provides this necessary ground for initiating movement. What art does, correlative with the forms of math and symbolic logic, is to make elements of reality perceivable, that is, visible, which then receive their standing orders (they become *verständlich* — which refers to both *understanding* and to *having a standing*) in the actual application of their forms in human relations with each other. In fact, a human can only become aware of their being human in the first place through engagingly and committedly speaking with another human. For Rosenzweig, speech is the "morning gift of the creator to humans" and the "emblem which makes a human human," since, we are told, "the human [only] became human as he spoke."[77]

But there is clearly an empirical problem with maintaining such a standpoint, namely, there is no common language or *Esperanto* that unequivocally unites all humans in a common undertaking. In fact, what characterizes the peoples of our linguistically diversified world is precisely that we struggle to understand each other and so frequently fall into such grievous misunderstandings that there is never a time that is free from some kind of war or injustice in our human relations. While Rosenzweig says is that there could be an "ideal of complete understanding,"[78] and that what characterizes actual language is that it both unites and divides us, implying that we have to work at creating common understandings. Such work has to be carried out via "engagingly and committed" relations, the kind of relations that only occur, however, through creative, revelatory, and redemptive works of art.

Es folgt aber jede Lebensform und ihr Rhythmus aus den Geboten, die das Leben Schaffender bestimmen. Walter Benjamin[79]

Notes

1 Throughout my book, but especially in this chapter, I frequently provide the original German words or phrases "in text" to facilitate a clearer understanding of Rosenzweig's ideas. The translations from German to English are mine throughout the book, unless otherwise noted.

2 See Levinas 1973. As one of Husserl's most important disciples, Levinas recognized the fundamental importance of "intuition" for Husserl with this his first and still seminal book. It remains, arguably, one of the best commentaries on *Ideen I*, where Levinas criticizes the primacy of theoretical consciousness and the "existential" meaning of the reduction. Levinas argues that Husserl does not take into account "memory" and thus the "historicity of consciousness" fully enough (or at all). Namely, that humans have a very specific way of "being their past" and thus living their objective, or intersubjective, intentionality. For Husserl, his retention of the "possibility" of an a-historical, self-sufficient egology or sphere of consciousness is problematic if we take *Sinngebung* seriously. The connection to Rosenzweig is not self-evident but can be constructed through Rosenzweig's choices in reconstructing the remembered accounts of our history as embedded in the threefold web of personal development (Part I of *The Star*), intersubjective relations (Part II), and the educational structures of communities (Part III).

3 Rosenzweig refers to the term "*Sprachdenken*" in the essay he wrote after *The Star of Redemption*, "Das Neue Denken," in GS3, 151ff. The difference between what Rosenzweig calls the "Old Thinking" and the "New Thinking," that is, between logical and grammatical thinking, is that the latter takes into account "the need for the other" and "takes time seriously." The latter kind of thinking also always entails a speaking to a particular someone and a thinking for a particular someone during a particular time and never merely to a "universal" ear or mouth.

4 GS2: 21; SR: 24.

5 There are various forms of such a deductive-based ethics. Two of the most obvious are Spinoza's and Kant's. See Spinoza 1992, esp. propositions 16 and 42 in Part V, for Spinoza's idea that the intellectual love of God, or blessedness, entails the consequence that we keep our lusts in check. See also Kant 1989, esp. sections 422–31 for the categorical imperative.

6 This is the point that Rosenzweig alludes to in the Introduction, stating that Cohen was the first to understand that mathematics was an "organ of thinking" while working on infinitesimals in his differential calculus (GS2: 23). See also Norbert

Samuelson's discussion of Cohen's mathematics as a methodological "organ" for Rosenzweig's philosophy in Samuelson 1989: 165–73.

7   The etymological root of Faust can be traced to sixteenth-century Germanic use for the "right of the stronger," or an even earlier usage meaning "battle of two" (*Zweikampf*). See Etymylogisches 1993: 329.

8   In the Norse version, the Mothers are named Norns who function as the Fates who spin and weave the web of life: Urth as past; Verthandi as present; and Skuld as future. Besides prophesying his own overarching temporal structure — creation/past, revelation/present, redemption/future — Rosenzweig explicitly refers to this realm again in the "Transition" section of the *Stern* as a movement from that "orgiastic confusion of the possible" (or chaos) to a reality of order, clarity and certainty (see GS2: 95; SR: 84).

9   GS2: 38–40; SR: 35–7.

10 Ibid: 28; 26.

11 The analysis of Rosenzweig's indedtedness to Cohen and Cohen's mathematics is, at least in Rosenzweig scholarship, by now well known. I am indebted to Norbert Samuelson for his work in making these connections and for first raising the remarkable observations that Rosenzweig's *Star* could be understood on the basis of fractal mathematics, specifically the "imaging of the Koch curve." He details this correlation in his comprehensive study guide on Rosenzweig's *Star*. See Samuelson 1999: 213, 215, 274.

12 GS2: 25; SR: 23.

13 Maimonides's views on anthropomorphism are well known and significantly determine his ethical philosophy. See, for example, *Mishnah Torah* Book I, Chapter 1, Section 9, cited from Maimonides 1963: 57–9. Also, see Norbert Samuelson 1991: 69–76.

14 Although not central to my own argument, related to Rosenzweig's concern for ethics is how Maimonides's philosophy serves as the starting point for Rosenzweig's philosophical theology, which begins with creation. As is clear from the *Mishnah Torah* (see Maimonides 1972) and *The Guide of the Perplexed*, Maimonides's chief concern in recommending theological community is the just ordering of social relations. See the *Mishnah Torah*, I, 4, 13: "For the knowledge of these things gives primarily composure to the mind. They are the precious boon bestowed by *God*, to promote social well-being . . ." Also see Maimonides 1963, Part III, Chapter 27 for ethical proscriptions on being healthy and forming appropriate political associations and Chapter 31 for his teaching that all 613 commandments "are bound up with three things: opinions, moral qualities, and political civic actions."

15 See Samuelson, Norbert, "The Concept of 'Nichts' in Rosenzweig's 'Star of Redemption,'" in Schmied-Kowarzik 1988b: 647.

16 GS2: 28; SR: 26. As Rosenzweig notes; this is not a Nothing as a dark ground as in Schelling's philosophy; nor is it some kind of a mystical starting point as in Eckhart's or Boehm's mystical theology. Neither is it any kind of a "place." Rather it is just the starting point of knowledge. This clearly serves to distance my interpretation from several other Rosenzweig scholars who understand Schelling's late philosophy as determinative for Rosenzweig's system. cf. Mosès

1992: 39ff; Schmied-Kowarzik 1991: 51ff; and Gibbs 1992: 40–4, where he argues for Rosenzweig's indebtedness to his reading of Schelling's book, *Weltalter*, for structuring his inherently narratable series of eternities. According to Gibbs: "Rosenzweig's major constructive impulse in *The Star of Redemption* is directly dependent on Schelling's *Weltalter*." See also GS2: 44.

17 GS2: 29; SR: 27.
18 Ibid.
19 A vector has a defined magnitude and direction and, if counterposed by a vector with the same magnitude but opposite direction, both are cancelled out. This is important for Rosenzweig's hypothetical element "god" since it is constructed with one vector and no opposing force and is thus "positive." See Spiegel 2009.
20 GS2: 35; SR: 32.
21 GS2: 36.
22 Ibid: 37.
23 See Immanuel Kant 1965: 201–8 for the "Anticipations of Perception" section, where Kant discusses the anticipation of the intensive magnitude (or degree) of sensation which influences our sense.
24 See Kant 1951: 28–9. Kant's argument proceeds along the lines of developing the conditions of "a singular judgment of experience" which entails a dependency on a particular "empirical representation and [that] cannot be bound up *a priori* with any concept."
25 GS2: 41.
26 The German *Dämerung* which Rosenzweig uses, recalls Nietzsche's own ambivalent use of the term in *Dämmerung des Idols* that can mean either twilight or dawn and actually refers to the perceptual transition from dark to light or light to dark.
27 GS2: 42.
28 Ibid: 43.
29 Ibid.
30 Ibid.
31 See Batnitzky 2009: 20, for a fine argument about Rosenzweig's embrace of representational art and its place in religious community, contra Jewish traditional teaching about images and idolatry: "For Rosenzweig, images themselves are not intrinsically problematic or shameful."
32 René Descartes. See "Rules for the Guidance of Our Native Powers" Rule IV (Regulae ad directionem ingenii, 1629) in Descartes 1958: 19f.: for reference to a "Universal Mathematics . . . as a general science which . . . can extend to all things." Also, the collapse of world and *god* in the "res cogitans" follows the logic that because I think, the world exists (Meditation IV: 217). Further, because I can and do think *god*, and *god* possesses all perfection by definition, which includes existence, *god* exists (Meditation V: 225).
33 See Aristotle's discussion of spontaneity and change for reference to knowledge of the "coming to be and the passing away" of "every kind of physical change" in *Physics*, Bk. II: Ch.3–Ch.6 (194: 20–198: 10) in Aristotle 1941. There, spontaneity and chance are causes of effects which occur, however, *incidentally* and as posterior to intelligence and nature. In a discussion on this point, Norbert

Samuelson communicated to me (26 February 1993), "That there will always be unpredictability in the concrete is a consequence of the fact that all particulars are contingent somethings that Aristotle schematizes in his judgment that only what is material is particular and the material is not reducible to the formal."

34   Else Freund's thesis on philosophy of existence is problematic as is Eva Rosenstock's thesis about death because the introduction was an appendage and Roseznweig has more at stake than a simple thesis about the priority of existence, i.e. he ends talking about truth and justice, for example. Goertz's focus on Hegel's experience is also problematic because there is an obvious Kantian and Jewish orientation in Rosenzweig's work. Stephan Mosès's and Schmied-Kowarzik's theses about Schelling's influence (which Robert Gibbs echoes, but with a significant and appropriate emphasis on speech) is likewise problematic since Schelling is more of an instigation rather than central to either Rosenzweig's total structure or final orientation from and towards art.

35   GS2: 45; SR: 42.

36   Set theory, in its formalized, axiomatic form as with Cantor's set (1880s), was turned on its head by the insights about self-reference with "Russell's paradox" or "Grelling's paradox." For a popular, germane discussions of such paradoxes, see Amir Aczel 2000; and Hofstadter 1980: 20ff.

37   GS2: 48; SR: 45.

38   Ibid. 52; 48.

39   The *Augenblick* is also the *moment* of revelation, which Rosenzweig prophetically prepares us for more fully accepting by building the word into thinking the World process. This is another indication of the artistic "attention to detail" characteristic of this work.

40   GS2: 52; SR: 48.

41   Ibid. Rosenzweig's criticism is that neither Plato nor Aristotle teaches what is entailed in an "active" relation between the thing and the concept: "The idea rests. The phenomenon moves itself towards it. This appears to be exactly the metalogic relation."

42   GS2: 57.

43   Ibid: 66.

44   Ibid.

45   Ibid.

46   For example, before the 1961 Jerusalem court, Adolf Eichmann invoked Kant's categorical imperative, asserting that he was merely doing his duty, for duty's sake, and that the "maxim" of his acting was, in fact, to make through his own will and acting the Führer's will into universal law. See Fackenheim 1994: 270ff.

47   GS2: 48; SR: 45.

48   Ibid.

49   GS2: 73; SR: 67.

50   Ibid.

51   Ibid, 74; 68:

52   Ibid.

53   Ibid: 54; 50.

54   Ibid: 74; 69.

55 Ibid: 75; 69.
56 GS2, in the section on Metaethics, Part I, Book 3.
57 GS2: 73.
58 Ibid.
59 In Rosenzweig's translation work with Buber, Rosenzweig rejects Buber's sug-
    gestions that woman was created by *God* to be a *Gegen-teil* or *andre Teil* or
    andre Hälfte for man. Rosenzweig replies: "*Widerpart geht ganz und gar nicht;
    das kratzt einenem ja die Augen aus. ihm zur Gänze? ihm zur Ergänzung? seine
    Hälfte? geht alles nicht. Am ehesten wohl: ihm zur Seite.*" Quoted from, Bauer
    1992: 403.
60 GS2: 77.
61 Ibid: 78.
62 Ibid.
63 Ibid: 80.
64 See Aristotle 1941, "Poetics": 1455ff.
65 This point, about *not being able to die* is appropriated by Levinas in how he
    distinguishes the phenomenon of the *il y a* from Heidegger's concept of the *es
    gibt*. See Edith Wyschogrod's analysis of this important distinction in Wyschogrod
    2000: 8–10, 69–70.
66 GS2: 87.
67 Ibid: 88.
68 Ibid.
69 Ibid: 89.
70 Ibid.
71 Ibid.
72 Ibid: 116.
73 Ibid: 118.
74 Ibid: 121.
75 Ibid.
76 Etymylogisches 1993: 526.
77 GS2: 122.
78 Ibid: 123.
79 See Benjamin *Illuminationen: Ausgwählte Schriften 1*. Frankfurt a.M. Suhrkamp,
    1977: 20.

CHAPTER 2

RENEWING NARRATIONS OR CHAOS IN CREATION

When in 1990 Ian Stewart, a popular British physicist, responded to the new science of chaos by bringing up Einstein's old question, *Does God Play Dice?*[1] his answer, that randomness occurs even within closed, deterministic systems, led me to question what role the phenomenology of chaos plays in Rosenzweig's philosophy of art. Put otherwise, my question became: what role does both the phenomenon of chaos, as a reference to "actual" randomness, and the kind of science of chaos now called complexity theory play in Rosenzweig's "turn" to a philosophy of language and art?[2] As I have already noted in Chapter 1 (Section III b), Rosenzweig conceptualizes particularity by way of a generally accepted concept of "chaos." That conceptualization occurs in what he establishes as an epistemological account of how humans know at all, an accounting that is based on a peculiar form of narrativity. That is, Rosenzweig's phenomenological account-giving is peculiar in the way that he retells the history of philosophy as that scientific activity that takes shape through narrations of the emergence of competing-yet-complementary elemental perspectives on what it means to be ontologically engaged in the meta-sciences. Those are: metaphysics as the metascience of knowing at all, metalogic as the metascience of knowing the physics of the world, and meta-ethics for that science that corresponds to a revision of psychology for recognizing the human self as that knowing, self-reflexive agent whose way of being is to know and act with and within the world.

But even more striking in Rosenzweig's epistemology is how he includes an abiding indeterminate moment denoted by the term "chaos" as part of the process, an inclusion that only becomes clear in the further development of his philosophy of art. I specifically consider that development in this and the next two chapters, covering what Rosenzweig noted were the specifically aesthetic sections of *The Star of Redemption* in Parts II and III of his text. For reasons that will become clear in my own interpretation, that moment must remain indeterminate as part *of his* ongoing story in order for his work to take on the ethical signification that I contend is at the core of his work. Indeed, Rosenzweig contributes to this with his version of an ethically significant narration of the development of human ways of knowing alongside many other traditions, Hegel's own totalizing philosophy of history notwithstanding. The difference is that for most other accounts, the ethical consequences are determined by the inherent determinism of each of the respective accounts. For millennia, narratives about the origins of the world coming from philosophers, theologians and poets have almost always and invariably included a concept of chaos. Paradoxically, the invariable is that a concept of chaos was used in order to develop a determining concept of order that would regulate all possible instances of indefinable particularities. For example, in the Genesis account we are told about a god brooding over chaos, referred to as "waste and void" (*tohu va vohu*) or the primeval waters, dispelled through the formation of an ordered, hierarchical world. In Hesiod's *Theogony*, chaos is the primeval emptiness of the universe that somehow begets darkness and night, a pairing that then in its turn begets air and light, leading to the production of the rest of the universe. Somehow, chaos is forgotten as the primeval source in the rush to produce an assuring account of controlled origins.[3] Aristotle identified chaos with space that could be accounted for in terms of causal relations,[4] while the Stoics saw chaos as an original formless mass in which all is disorder and confusion from which the maker of the cosmos, the ordering agent, produces the elements as forms of determinate being, order and harmony.[5] By contrast, Rosenzweig's schema entails a concept of chaos that helps to better understand the renewal capacities of the world and implies that any story about how the world works that neglects chaos as part of the process is a flawed conceptual construct. What is significant about the difference in Rosenzweig's account of how chaos works in his story of the dynamics of the relational streams of reality is in how closely it parallels contemporary accounts in physics and mathematics. In other words, the strength of Rosenzweig's account is in how it plays over several dimensions of the stories that we tell each other about our competing and contradictory experiences in and with the world. Rosenzweig calls this creation.

I. *Rosenzweig's creation story as: "chaos in creation"*

Werner Heisenberg, one of the Copenhagen physicists who revolutionized the discourse on quantum mechanics, maintained that it is necessary to focus on the distinction between the conceptual framework used to discuss empirical "facts" of reality and the discussion of the facts themselves which are structured by that framework. His emphasis on the roles of discourse and frames of reference in scientific method — of the inextricable involvement of the observer with the observed, led him to postulate "Uncertainty-Relations." His physics definitively undermined the validity of classical determinism and Newtonian mechanics by restricting the predictability and definability of the position, time, velocity, and energy of sub-atomic, micro-particles.[6] Nearly 40 years earlier than Heisenberg, Rosenzweig contended that considering the philosophical presuppositions involved in the linguistic and logical structures that constitute Hegel's Idealist framework would undermine the determinism of Hegel's dialectical rationalism, problematizing the ethics of his ontology as well. The logical problem that Hegel's philosophical system presents was the problem of the determinism of speech patterns and cultural productions, a form of social determinism similar to problems that were addressed not only by physicists such as Heisenberg, but also by mathematicians in the late nineteenth and early twentieth century who were working on problems in set theory, such as Georg Cantor.[7] And while Rosenzweig does not reduce Hegel's philosophy to the formulaic perambulations of a mathematical framework, his critique of Hegel's rational, dialectical system can none the less be understood in precisely those kinds of metadiscourse terms. Since Rosenzweig does not examine either the epistemological or the mathematical/scientific validity of Hegel's philosophy, I follow Rosenzweig's lead by highlighting what I consider to be his most important challenge, namely his presentation of an aesthetic theory that is ethically charged.

Rosenzweig confronts Hegel's philosophy with what he calls "creation-thinking," a way of thinking that permeates the entirety of his reflections on aesthetics. I contend that this adoption of a storyline from the traditions of Western theology is an aesthetic way of thinking that conditions Rosenzweig's metadiscourse and is what he called his narrating-philosophy. This new, alternative way of philosophizing is best approached from the relative standpoints that we ourselves assume in our own revisionary adoptions of traditional storylines. It is also another way of saying that Rosenzweig's philosophizing work is like a work of art in the way that he indirectly presented that as the thesis of his text, namely, as a narratively depicted story of reality with chaos as an integral part of the story. The success of such a narrative does not depend on the execution and explanation of the various parts of the story, which would make it a classical and mechanical variation on the modern scientific method. Rather, the success depends more on the extent to which the contextual conditions of story-teller and story-listener are taken into account. Furthermore, such an approach provides the possible conditions for undercutting the kinds of determinism involved in totalitarian claims of a scientific epistemology about the putative role of an impartial or absolute observer. This would challenge the tacit assumption that knowing it all includes knowing ahead of time any possible outcome of any given event and ignoring the inextricable role that the observer or storyteller plays in any discourse with a possible, unknowable respondent.

Although complexity theory in its earliest form as the science of chaos arose several decades after Rosenzweig's lifetime,[8] consider the following outline of the narrative developed by Rosenzweig through the first part of *The Star*. In Part I Rosenzweig describes the dynamic processes of the elements originating as historical exemplars specifying how those processes were actually presented in forming the storyline for the history of philosophy and the arts of Antiquity. The mathematical formula for the world, introduced by Rosenzweig to represent the process of development of that element, postulates that the process of world activity, considered in itself, is $B = A$. The signs "A" and "B" stand for the particularity "B" as it becomes an individual with respect to its inclusion

in the set of its own universal species denoted by the symbol "A." The "="
sign stands for the Aristotelian notion of the process whereby the individual
is drawn by the universal to its completion or is overpowered by the subject
as it hardens into its universal category. Where the old story is the story of a
metaphysics of substance, of "A = B," that is, of a universal "substance" — "A"
— generating a plethora of self-same particulars — "B"s, Rosenzweig revises
the story based on a process of "self-revealing emergence" of the world, which
he sets in opposition to a self-creation of the world, *sui generis*.

Rosenzweig may have taken his cue from the work he did interpreting
Hegel's *Philosophy of Right*, when he recast the status of the relationship of god
to world from that of a logical emergence in an ongoing developmental process
to prioritize the act of self-determination, thus presenting a story of creation
that results from the willful actions of a determining agent.[9] By describing the
process in traditional terms as a relationship of creator to creation, Rosenzweig
correlates the process of the ongoing emergence of particulars in the world
to one of artist to artwork. What it means to be created, then, means to be
involved in a process of self-formation, a process conceptualized in an account
of the world's initial status as some particular but initially undefined infinitesimal nothing moving to a more concretely visible and apprehensibly identifiable
something, and configured as world by its own willful non-engagement with
any other entity. The first moment of the world's act of self-configuration is
its transformation, understood as a conversion (*Umkehrung*), of its enduring
essence from its structure as universal species (as "A") to a profusion of
chaotic particulars. This is the story of a created world, namely, the species
as that which produces, or births, many individuals (many "B"s), and these
individuals are what become transformed from enduring essence to that which
is momentary, finite and unenduring. Through this process of the ongoing birth
of a plurality of individuals, the world as individual itself (as "B = A") becomes
that which is "in-all-times renewed" and yet remains an enduring essence:

> It is an essence which at every moment originates anew with the whole content
> of the distinctive (*Besondere*) which it includes. It is an essence which includes all
> distinctiveness and yet is itself universal, which recognizes itself as a whole with
> every moment. It is: existence (*Da-sein*).[10]

What it means to be distinctive is to be counted as a chaotic particular, willfully
involved in a process of creative self-transformation that negates all others.
But since the particular originates as distinctive individual out of the universal
essence, it does so by retaining the very character of essence itself, and thus
endowed can be counted as an existing particular individual.

Moreover, the world is "universal" but it is not "always and everywhere"
because it is constituted as particularity and so must continually become new
in order to continually contain this concrete particularity called *existence*. As

such a renewal, the world can only be apprehended as occurring, or as existing, by considering it as the stream of the instantiations of particulars and, withal, as a particular that occurs only for the moment. In other words, for the world to become what the world is, the world must undergo an ongoing process of transformation from ever-new particulars, or existents, that crystallize to form a completion in death as a denial of life. Upon completion of this specific form — the form of ephemeral denial of enduring life — new particulars emerge, constantly denying the stability of the world and yet ever-becoming that stability again, and so on. For example, the sexual maturity of human individuals is the stage of the completion of a particular form that represents stability and endurance of the species, the central tenet of Darwinian science. But from a Rosenzweigian perspective of including the moment of chaos in interpreting the process, the Darwinian account fails because it neglects that part of the mating process when a human denies their very own self-identity in order to serve the needs of another in sexual union, a moment that constitutes the creative process that births a uniquely new particular individual. The newly birthed particular human being begins as practically nothing — absolutely non-identical to either of its co-creators. This is the case since both individuals had to respond to the "chaos" of the other, denying their own self-identical endurance in order to affirm the other, thus enabling another particular to emerge and, in its own differential process to become its own definable something.

On another level of his narrative, Rosenzweig introduces the theological concept of providence to refer to the denial of the stability of the world and to descriptively capture the process of emerging particularities. His peculiar presentation of what he calls providence enables him to further differentiate what he calls the process of "revelation" as distinct from the process of creation. To do so, he contrasts his account with the Hegelian account of actuality as a process of the phenomenal appearance of individuals in a necessary, dialectical unfolding of Spirit. The limitation of that account is due to its very necessity as a process of unfolding that is dictated by the all-encompassing conditions of a totalizing concept, namely, the *Begriff*. The term *Begriff* stands for that process of actualization by which the process itself appropriates or "grasps" all.[11] By contrast, for Rosenzweig, the world's ongoing relationship to god, as created creature to creator — the relationship of providence — has to occur as denial because the

> divine grasp of existence does not occur in creation, which took place once and for all. Rather, it is a momentary grasp, a providence which, though universal, renews itself with every smallest distinctive moment for the whole of existence in such a way that God "day by day" renews the work of the beginning.[12]

Rosenzweig explicates what he means by this renewal of creation by turning to linguistic structures, specifically analyzing the transition from mathematical symbolic logic to a discourse based on the laws of grammatical distinctions. Humans are not quite like other beings populating the rest of the world: we think, desire, speak, love, and hope. Unlike Hegel (and other German Idealists) who reduces the difference of human being from other beings to thinking as such, Rosenzweig names this other insight of dissimilarity, "creature consciousness," a phrase that he uses to develop the specific meaning of human distinctiveness. Humans are not merely part of the cycle of *"enstehen und vergehen,"* of coming into and going out of existence. Rather, what differentiates humans has to do precisely with our capacity for aesthetic presentation; namely, that humans speak in different ways and create works of art that "speak" from one human to others, and is a dynamic process of "human" communication that reveals ordering principles. Those revelations affirm the unconquerability of our sensuality — of the chaotic dimension in nature, and thus are ultimately ethical in how they function. I explicate this puzzling claim in what follows.

As I noted in the previous chapter, Rosenzweig considers mathematics to be a language of the silent pre-world.[13] However, Rosenzweig also claims that art is another form of silent language, created by humans in order to bridge the logical substructures of how we understand our world as the actuality of how we live our world. The move from the silence of mathematics to the silences of art and grammar is determinative for Rosenzweig because, by moving from the "dead" form of mathematics — a language that can never refer to speech — to grammar — a language that uses both symbolic formulations and refers directly to the phenomenon of speaking — we are able to entertain a phenomenology of spoken language, as Rosenzweig does in Part II, Book 2. He contends that humans need to more adequately represent the sense of the fluidity of reality and the relationships of emerging concrete particulars, which is a science of living sounds or word forms, through a grammar of language. Accordingly, as there are rules of logic, namely, premises, deductions, inferences, and conclusions, Rosenzweig maintains that there are also laws of grammar which result from investigating the emergence of hearable root-words from the silent source-words. The source-words are "Yes, No, And" and are assigned in Rosenzweig's "negative" thinking as those corresponding variables in a differential calculus that corresponds to the model of the hypothetical structures of the pre-world. Rosenzweig also contends that those hypothetical structures correspond to how anyone thinks at all about any one of the three primary elements of reality: god world human. But by integrating the "logic"' of grammar into a story of creation, Rosenzweig claims that we can better understand how words work and how and why they occupy the space that they do in the sentences composed of them. In short, the grammar of words and sentences can be related to the emergence of particulars in creation as a way of accounting for the renewal of the unconquerable and anarchic dimension of chaos. Words are related to creation because what we say about creation, that is, about the world, also has to do with things and the space that they occupy. The sensual nature of words, both written and spoken, makes them the special case of being both thing-like — having to do with world-space — and, in some way, temporal and ephemeral, that is, speech as essentially chaotic. But in order to catch the sense that chaos plays in our speech–acts, we must begin with sentences, not words.

To illustrate his point, Rosenzweig analyzes the syntax and semantics of the adjective (*Eigenshaftswort*) as the grammatical analogy for the particular nothings of creation. He moves from an indefinite adjective to the noun as the *carrier* of adjectives, to the necessity of considering the pronoun "this." The underlying logic is deductive, that is, to understand anything in particular we must first be given and then understand something in general. Such is the sentence. The importance of the indefinite pronoun "this" in syntactic struc-tures is that it functions as an indefinite pointer to the *fact that* a "something" should be sought as a concrete, definite referent. Rosenzweig may have drawn directly from Hegel's discussion of the "this" in "Sense and Self-certainty" from the *Phenomenology of Spirit* for the basic lineaments of his syntactical map.[14] What is just as determinative for his syntactical map, is that a "here" is also implied in the process of conceiving the "this" which consequently allows for *space* to be posited as the universal condition under which the thing, so far only an undefined "something," is to be sought. Hence, given the initial evaluative affirmation of the adjectival attribute we are led by logical inference to consider the noun and then the pronoun, which consequently points us to space as the dimension of objectivity and "thinghood" where things are located.[15]

But getting from the adjective to something more substantial is what becomes crucial for Rosenzweig's storyline, because of the apparent problem that in any thought construction a particular, individual adjective is merely one of many, indicating an unacknowledged plurality at work in our speech–acts. In the context of the set of language practices as a whole, however, we have more than just sentences composed of variable parts since noting that adjectives function as chaotic particulars is not the end of the grammar lesson. Indeed, adjectives become definite — defined — through the simple affixation of the definite article: "fixed by the definite article, the adjective is a definite, affirmed thing in the endless space of cognition or creation."[16] In order to carry his grammar "story" a step further, Rosenzweig correlates this syntactical arrangement as a semantic analogue to creation, such that the adjective "comes to rest" as grammatical object in the sentence and stands "free and affirmed" just as created creation stands in an objective relationship "free and affirmed" to the creator.[17]

We are reminded, however, that reality is conceived not merely as objectivity but principally, and in fact radically, as movement. This can also be depicted by way of grammatical structures, in the way that the copula *is* is inherent in every indicative construction. What this means is that every affirmative utterance entails an object and the verbal movement, in the presupposed form of *being*, from one pole in what becomes a sentential utterance to the other. Hence, the process involved in our speech–acts themselves is seen to be the ground of reality. But, as Rosenzweig further explicates, even process can be understood as objective or thing-like. As a Husserlian would likewise concur, the constructed world, like the sentence, like a work of art, is thing-like because it consists of thing-like mental objects or "objective" things that become mental objects. It is not, however, one objective thing, but rather it consists of a multiplicity of particular things that depend for their particular identities on their relative orientation in "mental" space, as Rosenzweig analogically demonstrates with his grammar of sentential speech–acts. The conceptual move that we are encouraged to make entails accepting the implication that the unity of objectivity of the world, like our sentential utterances, is none other than space.[18]

In other words, Rosenzweig narrates a philosophical story for the "being-there" of the world, for its "hereness" which he calls creation. But how do we get to the regenerative process of its becoming, what he calls, "new with every morning," a process that must, by definition, entail chaos in order to count as new? Rosenzweig claims that space is not what is created at first because, from his grammatical perspective, its presuppositional condition is the adjectival indicator "this." But in the general indicative phrase "this here," the "this" is logically prior to the spatial determinant "here." The world, notes Rosenzweig, is "totally, in its primal origin, the fullness of the this," which is expressed by means of adjectival words. According to Rosenzweig, another way of describing this fullness is to call it chaos. "This chaos" is what he calls the "firstling" of creation and is the perpetual renewal of creation's existence. In fact, the world is not created until this existence, this chaos, is itself first called into existence. Existence, in its universality and all-fastening formfulness, remains the immediate, created ground, the "beginning," out of which the ever-new births of the fullness shoots forth.[19] No chaos, no creation, no world.

The world can be fullness, or chaos, because it is there, because it is a "given" for us — it is given or, as Rosenzweig notes, it is "created." The fullness, or chaos, is its transitory appearance as particular existents, which is the first statement about its existence. The ethical significance of Rosenzweig's grammatical analogy is that the very existence of the world corresponds to the root-word of creation, the "*Urja*" or the "*Ja!*" that he interprets as an affirmative and evaluative "*Gut!*" uttered in judgment upon completion of a creation. It is an estimational judgment that is logically before the fullness, the chaos, of adjective-words. And thus, according to Rosenzweig's linguistic narrative of creation, "chaos is in creation not before it; the beginning is — in the beginning," which is the act of creation.[20]

II. *Theory of art*

As I noted in the previous chapter, at the end of each of the three books of Part I Rosenzweig presents three formal principles of aesthetics that guide us through his philosophy of art, namely: outer form, inner form, and content. Each of those principles corresponds to not only different kinds of art but to different kinds of life experiences. Those three are: epic/narrative, lyrical/poetic, and dramatic/performative. Additionally, each Book of Part II ends with Rosenzweig's exposition of a section of biblical text as a demonstration of the art which the text and our reading of it comprises. Besides integrating readings of biblical texts as exemplars, Rosenzweig focuses our attention on reflexively rethinking about art itself in terms of the application he develops to that point in his own work. In Part I the perspective developed is epistemological, as Rosenzweig opposes his philosophical "absolute empiricism" to the Idealist thinking and aesthetics, which has reigned from Plato to Hegel.[21] In Part II, Rosenzweig develops an alternative aesthetics based on his philosophy of language, some of which has already been referred to in this chapter. That perspective moves us from his philosophy of the written word to a *midrash* on the dialogically spoken words of song, a necessary move done in order to more adequately present what is involved in ethically responding to a radically other being. The next movement is to the dimension of performative language, aesthetically enacted and embodied in actual communities, in order to form identifiable and enduring communities that are not only distinct in themselves but are composed of diverse individuals. The art form is communal because it is based on ritual and liturgy as well as all of the other art forms: written and spoken speech, song, poetry, dance, and architecture. Ultimately, Rosenzweig draws us into his movement, away from unhealthy and unethical Idealist-thinking and towards the speech–acts of a revelation-thinking, which entail the related dimensions of creation, revelation, and a redemptive messianic politics.

III. *Critique of generation in Idealist aesthetics*

Rosenzweig's criticism of Idealist aesthetics is based on his aversion to the prescriptions recommended by Idealist philosophers that we should only think about the world in which we live in terms of a deductive logic that presupposes both a rationally defined source and a rationally defined goal. Rosenzweig explicitly targets not only Plato and Hegel but also, by implication, Schelling. As I noted in the previous chapter, Rosenzweig implicates Schelling in his critique, a position I take that goes against most of the conventional scholarship which aligns him clearly with Schelling, especially with Schelling's later philosophy.[22] Rosenzweig surely drew on Schelling's tripartite conceptualization of history and his project of orienting our understanding of historical development, of past present future, according to the theological categories of creation, revelation, and redemption. However, just as much as the other German Idealists, Schelling's philosophy is marked by his propensity to reduce all of our experiences to categories emanating from a process of thinking generated from an ideal source. While it is true that Schelling famously mounted one of the first attacks against Hegelian philosophy, it is also true that Schelling was as much committed to systematic philosophy as Hegel was. And Rosenzweig was well aware of Schelling's systematic work since, in the archival work he did for his dissertation on Hegel's philosophy, he discovered a handwritten outline, "The Oldest System of German Idealism," with which he argued that Schelling was actually the author of a work hitherto attributed to Hegel, viz. an outline of a unified system of Idealist philosophy. [23]

Additionally, consider Schelling's introductory remarks to the "Stuttgart Seminars," first delivered in the Autumn of 1809 between the composition of *Treatise on the Essence of Human Freedom* (1809) and *Ages of the World* (begun in 1810):

> If the system that we wish to uncover shall indeed be the system of the cosmos, (1) it must intrinsically rest on a principle that supports itself, a principle that consists in and through itself and that is reproduced in each part of the whole; (2) it must not exclude anything (e.g.) nature, nor must it unilaterally subordinate or suppress anything; (3) furthermore it requires a method of development and progression to ensure that no essential link has been omitted."[24]

Rosenzweig's critique of all systematic, Idealist thinking is that such thinking is based on a principle of generation, whereby a succession of particulars identical to the original generator is produced, with the built-in teleological goal of an ordered cosmos. In Schelling's case, the generating principle is the ongoing production of the identifying of non-identical principles, e.g. the Real and the Ideal, in what he calls a doubling (*Doublirung*) of the initial unity, whose ultimate goal is the exclusion of non-being as evil. However, the final redemption that Schelling has in mind is ultimately very Christian: God becoming man and then everything, i.e. nature, becoming God the Father. At the end of the "Stuttgart Seminars," Schelling concludes:

> . . . if indeed there still obtain three periods, they must be placed in a successive hierarchy: (a) the period of God as he has become man (and, perhaps, still a particular dominion of worlds of nature and spirit, though without separation); (b) the dominion of spirit; (c) finally everything is transformed unto our Father . . . This last period within the last is that of the entirely perfect fulfillment — that is, of the complete becoming man of God — the one where the infinite will have become finite without therefore suffering in its infinitude.[25]

By contrast, Rosenzweig's concept of creation entails neither an ordering connection between world and creator nor the supposition of an ultimately ordered cosmos, except for the *fact* of the act of creation. Creation is, by definition, anarchic since, as an event, it is not set in a previously ordered horizon determined by this or that principle. Whereas in the Idealist tradition, precisely in order to circumvent the concept of creation and to provide an ordering connection, all Idealist philosophers resort in one way or another to a concept of generation that leaves no gaps in its logical development. Rosenzweig notes about Idealist philosophers that, for them, "Generation should accomplish the same as creation; it should give to the plastic, objective world, the world as Antiquity saw it, the point from which its multiplicity closes together and orders itself in unity."[26]

This would be their ultimately unifying Archimedean point. Creation-thinking achieves such a unifying point with the concept of the creator whose only relation to the world, however, is that of having created it. Hence, the world retains its separate elemental character, namely, its pictureability (*Bildhaftigkeit*) and the plastic self-containedness already elaborated in Antiquity. The significant departure for Rosenzweig is that by hypothesizing a concept of god that is not so inextricably bound up in managing the laws of the world, the world is therefore not chained to a causal determinism that would undermine the basic insights of standard empirical philosophy.[27]

Rosenzweig challenges the contention that the thought of generation is capable of achieving the same objective level as the thought of creation, namely, the same level of self-containedness. While the thought of generation does provide an Archimedean fixed point, denoted as the generator, the difference between that and Rosenzweig's concept of a creator is that in the former there is supposed to be a rationally graspable connection between the unit point and that which is to be unified. The wedge that Rosenzweig drives in to disclose the weakness of such a connection is his observation about the necessity of comparability (*Vergleichbarkeit*) and proportionality between the generation and what is generated. As with creation, god is presupposed in idealist logic as the generator since god can function as unconditional source for the existence of the world: as "unconditional condition, un-originated origin."[28] This means that, unlike the self-referential exclusivity of the elements that Rosenzweig posits for his model, for Idealist philosophy the elements must, necessarily and ultimately, be comparable in terms of identity in order to be posited in a rational thought structure as such. And the elements are such rational thought structures.

In his analysis of propositional logic in Part II, Book 1, Rosenzweig argues that the Idealist logic of generation, in order to be rationally comparable to the world, has to change the order of the formula which stands for the world to $A = B$ instead of $B = A$. This change is needed because in Idealism the world is taken as a whole at first and then particulars stream down out of that whole in an emanation (*Hernieder-strömen*) with ever-new emanations of the *same* form of that original whole. In other words, every new stream that pours forth is a copy of the prototypical divine origin, of the divine totality; each is a re-origination of its origin. The problem with this model arises in the conclusion that entails ordering the terms of the proposition in such a way as to merely mimic the original starting point. Whereas the particular is informed by the universal in the equation B = A, that which denotes metalogic and is the elemental basis for the created world in Rosenzweig's creation theory, in generation-emanation theory, the equation A = B entails that the universal emanates, or generates, ever-new particulars like-unto-itself in apparent chaotic dispersion and profusion. Since the predicate term is presupposed by the subject, namely "A" presupposes "B," the emanation-thought presupposes the chaos of the generated particulars without accounting for the order or their disorder. According to Rosenzweig, "The doctrine of emanation can not do without the thought of primal-chaos," that then has to be brought into rational order by subsuming the particulars into the universal.[29]

The confused particulars of chaos in emanation theory roughly correspond to Aristotle's "matter" (*hyle*) which undergoes "generation" through the universalizing-ordering principle of the continual act of the primal generator. Rosenzweig's critique of that model is that in the later development of emanation theory found in Idealism, namely the generation found in German Idealists such as Hegel and Schelling, even god must be an object of rational thought since god must be able to be cognized and set in a framework of comparability to that which is emanated. Hence, from its "origin" in the doctrine of emanation, god becomes the "content" of the conceiving process of an entailment determined by the Idealist principle that everything that is is cognizable, the Parmenidean identity of being and thinking revisited. But since the world cannot be its own origin, it needs an origin for itself which is not itself. By exclusion, the only other candidate is the *self* which, as pure subject in the cabinet of Idealism, has had various names: the "I" for Fichte, the "subject" for Schelling, the "transcendental unity of apperception" for Kant, or "Spirit" for Hegel — any one of which the self assumes (*annimmt*) when it appropriates (*übernehmen*) the generating function of the generator ("A = A" not "B = B!"). Further, its task is likewise only fulfilled when the world is in the form of comparability and thus is "produced" in the form of "A = B." Thus, the world is "the same" as the self, namely, as subject it is denoted as "A" while the production produced is "B," otherwise simply denoted as "not-I" (*nicht-Ich*). This means that the subjectivity ("A") of things fulfills itself in particularity ("B") as objectivity ("A = B").[30]

Rosenzweig contends that an Idealist's logic of identity reduces the key terms — nothing, being, and chaos — to members in a class whose functional relation to each other is merely that of tautological repetition where nothing different is being said. In other words, it is trivial. Rosenzweig's creation thought, on the other hand, accounts for chaos because "chaos" is the first-created fullness of the particular which "bubbles forth" into the given universal vessels of creation. Chaos is neither presupposed nor reducible to the terms being and nothing, but retains its own peculiar "identity" and functions as an ever-integral part of the creation story that helps to characterize the ongoing world process.

Again, what remains problematic from the Rosenzweigian perspective that I have been constructing is that there is no place for any actual irrationality in the world process for Idealist thinkers. This is the case since irrationality is defined merely as chaos in the traditional sense of the term as a nothing, which is presupposed and avoided as such.[31] Since it is by definition irrational, it can have no place in a totally rational system; chaos can *not* be. Given an Idealist framework, the human subject merely uses the world as a *bridge* to return to cognition of their own thinking, which entails the elimination of the actual world as such, especially one that includes chaos as a constituent function of its process. In a framework conceptualized in terms of creation, however, the world is radically other and behaves according to its own laws which are other than those of the cognizing self. Rosenzweig figures this difference into our comparisons for us with the two distinct formulas for human, B = B, and world, B = A. In that logical narrative, the human, as self, has the peculiar characteristic of bifurcation, since it shares both the "factual" content (*Gehalt*) of the world and the self-contained form of god. Whereas, again by contrast, for the Idealists the factuality of the three elements are thrown into the "universal strudel of destruction" and thus indifferentiation.

IV. *Ascending from underground to the Garden of Life*

In Part II of *The Star of Redemption* Rosenzweig combines two powerful images to make his point about the connections of art to knowledge, linguistic structures and reality that provides important insights for the thread of ethical considerations that I pursue in this book. The images are those of the cave found in Plato's *Republic* and the tree of life from the creation account in Genesis, images translated by Rosenzweig into his narrative of a chaos-determined fruition of language. In the Garden scenes found in Part II, Book 1 of *The Star*, images of light and darkness, growth and nourishment, are intertwined with, yet differentiated from, the phenomenon of language:

> Although language is rooted in the primal-words in the subterranean grounds of being, it already shoots upward into the light of terrestrial life in the root-words, and in this light blooms forth in colored multiplicity. It is, therefore, a growth in the midst of all growing life, from which it is nourished as that life nourishes from it! Language is differentiated from all this life because it does not move itself freely and arbitrarily above the surface, but rather stretches down roots in the dark grounds below life.[32]

In other words, language — as a kind of living and growing "art" form — and life can mutually nourish each other because language is rooted in earthy-metaphysical grounds, an image of grounding used to express the formative function in what Rosenzweig refers to as speech-thinking or speech–acts. Rosenzweig's philosophy of language — as his philosophy of art — entails that our speech is rooted in grounds that can be logically analyzed but only fully realized in the actual expressions of a thinking that is bound up with speaking performances. By contrast, an Idealist philosophy of language wants to remain in the subterranean grounds of logical analysis — disconnected from art and lived reality — and pull all of the over-world down into its under-world realm, a logic of reduction that transforms the living, multicolored multiplicity into a one-dimensional realm of shadowy, lifeless formulas. Having been to the cave, the philosopher *qua* philosopher has *seen* the elemental reality, but his advice is to return to the cave and thus manipulate others in naive simplicity that is the self-same play of shadows of merely logical relations.

However, remaining in the realm of conceptual shadows — of merely logical relations — brought Idealists to the recognition that they were losing the feeling of living existence with which they had attempted to ground and conceptualize the connections of reality.[33] Hence, since Idealism was "sunk-down in the under- and pre-world shadow realm of logic, it sought to hold open an access to the over-world."[34] In order to move us into another level of his narrative, Rosenzweig moves from "tree of life" imagery to "Garden of Paradise" imagery, carrying along the distinction between those who trust in what he calls the visible confirmation of god's creative power, that is, speech-thinking, and those unbelievers in this creative-power who have left paradise of their own accord and trusted in themselves alone, that is, those who have turned to philosophy alone. Since the latter no longer trust in language they need a substitution; they need another supposition to account for, to mediate, and to confirm the dynamics of reality. Moreover, according to Idealist conditions, this substitution would have to be a human garden, a human paradise in which humans themselves plant the structures, but which retains the character of arising unconsciously. In short, it must be a garden with signs that the work is directed to a purpose and yet at the same time it must be a garden that has arisen without purpose, a variation of the Kantian purposeless purpose from his *Critique of Judgment*.[35] Such direction is achieved by the simultaneous rejection of the limitations of human particularity and of speech-thinking in favor of an apotheosis of art while, by contrast, Rosenzweig would wed human particularity with its mode of expression as speech-thinking and as art.

The point is that it is a matter of trust the way one handles or talks about what occurs in the relations that hold between observer and observed. Plato, Plotinus, and Augustine, or even Kant in his analyses in *The Critique of Judgment*, reflected on that relation in terms that indicated that they were referring to "the living beauty of the work of God."[36] For Idealists, however, the object observed has become "beautiful art" to the observer, merely representing "the actual-that-can-be-sighted." Having seen the living reality, Idealists, at the very entrance to life, resorted instead to various theories of recollection to insure that the "blood of reality" continues to circulate in the remainder of its shadow-life.[37] But the kind of artificial figures which the art revered by Idealists produces can be trusted still, not only since they are human productions, but also because of the unconscious way in which they arose. What this process of arising unconsciously entails is that the unquestionable nature of their existence depends on the way they appear "like a piece of nature," which enables an Idealist to see — and therefore honor — art in correspondence with a revelation, that is, corresponding to a vision of reality. But for Rosenzweig, this vision of reality is apparently the problem with Idealists since it precisely favors the artificiality of merely a "vision" of reality rather than the natural beauty of the living art of language.

Based on its presumption that there is a "common root" to the reality of the All, Idealist philosophers *believe* that the art-product alone is the visible figure of that root and, consequently, the justification of its process. But why is such a justification necessary? Rosenzweig postulates that it is necessary to quiet the doubts of one's conscience about the ordering of reality: "When doubt overcomes him about the admissability of its method of the 'panlogistic' pure generator, he only needs to look at the art-work, produced by spirit and yet also part of natural reality, in order to again obtain a good *conscience*."[38] The art-work has its roots in the colorless night of pre-world spirit, the realm of shadows etc., and is yet *there* in full bloom in the meadow of existence. This is then the "confirmation of the method of thinking" that serves as its "organon" preferred by Idealists.[39] It provides the "visible" proof of an "absolute" verification of certainty that one's roots are drinking from "the" reality of the All and therefore quells the doubts that dwell at the root of all philosophical undertakings. Indeed, it seems to be the very "common root," guessed at by Kant, and is the "visible appearance of an absolute" that has ethical significance and thus ultimate justification.[40]

V. *Trust, the holistic author, and art as language*[41]

The apotheosis of art associated with an Idealist aesthetics results in the kind of ethical problem that, from a Rosenzweigian perspective, crystallizes as a matter of trust. In turning to art for its ultimate verification, Idealists relied on trusting the primacy of their own human word in itself, rather than as an answer to what he calls the word of god, and what I take to be the word of an other as such. What this means is that the Idealist trusts only in the human work that comes from themselves and that can be visibly verified through observation and experimentation, by themselves and for themselves. Moreover, instead of believing in the "speech of the soul, which is a self-revelation of human innerness that encompasses, supports, and completes all other self-expression," an Idealist trusts merely in art in itself, in one torn-off limb of humanity.[42] But for Rosenzweig, what it means to become fully human is precisely to become "ensouled," which I take to be an ethical process in the way that becoming ensouled transcends and transforms the isolated, meta-ethical self. In an aside clearly aimed at moving us beyond Nietzsche, adopting Rosenzweig's stance means accepting that a human life is not, in essence, a work of art, although without that limb humans would be crippled. Without art a human would still remain human, whereas without the spoken word of language, which testifies to a human's soul, a human ceases being fully human. Utilizing again the language of creation, art is a product but a product that does not stand alone, individuated and self-defined. Rather, a work of art signifies as well and in its function of signifying, we are instructed to think of art as one of the pre-revelatory ways of expressing the reality of the pre-world, the world of the elements. As signification, art becomes an historical analogy of that pre-world and should best be understood as the appropriate vehicle to express the elements of a pre-world as they are, before what Rosenzweig calls the miracle of revelation. Art signifies as a concrete, visible, and plastic testimony to such a pre-world by actually expressing the diverse forms of the elements of that world through the embodiment of historical analogies, namely, as lived cosmogonies, theogonies, and psychogonies.[43] In terms of art as language, art is what is already spoken, a "said" reality, which is set in contrast to the living, streaming reality of actual language, namely, what Rosezweig calls the language of revelation.

As I noted at the end of the last chapter, Rosenzweig's narrative depends on his assertion that "there is only one language,"[44] by which he means that the conception of language as an art form (or style) does not constitute a reduction which would or could explain the origins of the world in creation:

> Were the reality of the artwork also language here, it would be language next to language, and indeed there can be many languages, but only one language (which is speech). As "spoken," however, it stands in the midst of all other actualities, inseparable, necessary for their completion, member amongst its members and, as such, recognizable. As such recognizable, but not, as Idealism would like, to engage in its total reality the relationship of the world to its origin and to measure all else on this relationship. Rather, in the thought of creation we only grasp a part, only the beginning of the artwork. Life is richer than the world and its becoming . . .[45]

The point is that as language is more than its individual structures, it is also the case that art is too rich to be completely cognized merely out of, and in relation to, the concept of creation or the initiatory expressive dimension of language.

This is a complicated issue because, on the one hand, we only grasp the idea of the initial formation involved in the intention and expression of an artwork, or of its creation, as such, but not the effects of its becoming or its life-course, that is, one does not conceive the whole by isolating and analyzing atomistic parts, which includes isolating the creative origin of a work of art from its life-work, as it were. On the other hand, following Rosenzweig's narrative from Book 1 to Book 2 in Part II of *The Star of Redemption*, we find his entire analysis modified by the context of the holistic dimension introduced by the aesthetic concept of revelation. Revelation itself is part of a greater whole of which creation is the beginning and redemption the end, but it is not creation itself. And the fact that art is just a part, that is, is just a beginning, means that the most that we can account for is its origin in the sense of an intentional purpose. But the question remains, since it is a part, what is it a part of? Addressing the question of where the artwork comes from discloses an insight about its purpose which has to do with its effects. But, just what are its effects? Rosenzweig notes that, as creation is only the beginning in the framework of world-time, so *creation of an artwork is only* its beginning. There is also its formative conception and the hoped-for present effect it works on the viewer. In Rosenzweig's theological, and thus aesthetic terms, the present effect is also the revelatory effect and that has to do with language.[46]

To complicate matters even more, Rosenzweig notes that the *spoken* artwork is only an analogy of the independent value of language as it occurs in drama or poetry. In terms of the process of its origination from thought to spoken reality, however, an artwork shares the same formal mechanics of its relationship that transpires in the mental activity of one realm, the pre-world, and the conversion of that activity into recognizable entities in the real world. Both activities presuppose an inner conversion of the pre-world elements and their emergence as various art-objects or art-forms in individual, analyzable pieces into the realm of observable reality. Whereas the essential elements of reality for Rosenzweig are "god world human," those of the aesthetic dimension are the corresponding categories of Antiquity which constitute the pre-aesthetic world, "mythic god, plastic world, and tragic human." For Rosenzweig, those mythic elements are actually "artworks" that were produced in the epoch of Antiquity but not cognized as such.

Rosenzweig makes a point of distinguishing between "spoken language" and "the living, streaming actuality of actual speech."[47] His point is that we only grasp the initial idea of formation involved in the intention and expression, but not the actual effects of its becoming, that is, its completion in the other, the viewer. In short, we only "see" the beginning — in creation — but not the life of the work. That entails revelation. Another way of articulating this issue is to note that we do not "get" the whole by isolating the parts in some kind of atomistic analytic act, but only in relation and in process is it possible to intuit the inner conversions of the "elements"' from the dark and shadowed pre-world of their origin to the colorful and vibrantly connective "world." Only in the revelatory "saying" of actual, living, streaming language is "human content" able to be expressed by way of the beautiful "artwork." What is "exposed" or freely brought out in the "life-day of the work of art," that is, in building up a work of art, are individuals — a kingdom of details — that emerge from a pre-aesthetic totality in an historical procession from the "ground-concepts" to an aesthetically rich actuality — god-as-mythic, world-as-plastic, human-as-tragic.[48]

VI. *Genius*

The sections on genius, poet and artist in *The Star* connect Rosenzweig's theoretical discourse with his practical demonstration, especially with how he presents Scripture as the authored "word of god"; that is, Rosenzweig presents us with a picture of a genius as a creative author, a description that could just as well apply to the biblical creation story that narrates a "creation" authored by an extra-ordinary genius, god. To begin with, Rosenzweig tells us that the creation of the artwork happens in the author, using the word "*Urheber*" for author.[49] In using such a word, Rosenzweig wants us to think of the activity of the genius-as-author in terms of one who draws something up or out of an already existing reservoir, out of the past, since one of the etymological roots of *Urheber* means to raise out of the primal depths. The work of art is raised out of the primal pre-reflective and pre-linguistic depths of the particular author revealing the created work as a process of bringing something forth that is already there. Hence, creation of the artwork happens not so much as an act of remembrance breaks out of the author, as with Plato and other Idealists. Rather, the creation, as such, is an unconscious activity of becoming which presupposes the status of the author already having become someone who is capable of bringing forth a work. This is what Rosenzweig calls being-already-created.

He also points out that the happening of the work of art in its relation to the viewer depends on the viewer for its completion, a completion which is measured by its degree of actual liveliness. This provides an important part in Rosenzweig's theory for the role of art as cultural and political phenomenon. As one of the criteria for measuring the actual effectiveness of a work of art, the liveliness is that aspect of the work that is capable of arousing the feeling of common humanity in others, that is, liveliness presupposes that there is another human other than myself who, through that work, awakens me by way of the feeling of liveliness to my own humanity. That feeling that is awoken then initiates a process within the viewer(s), which leads to the formation of self-identity through instigating a process of self-reflexivity based, at first, on the formation of a perceived sense of commonality. That commonality is that the other is like me, a commonality, however, that is in the next instance negated in order to allow for one's own self-affirmation. As I will indicate later in the Heidegger section of this text, similar acts of recognizing commonality that are then negated for the sake of the integrity of one's own identity not only occur but remain as one of the characteristics which distinguish Heidegger's ideas about self-identity from Rosenzwieg's.

In order to better elucidate his ideas about this matter of self-identity, Rosenzweig turns to an ideal case, namely, the case of the genius and the "eruptive" act by which someone becomes marked as a genius by an evaluating public.[50] The issue of the "genius" is not new with Rosenzweig, but instead indicates his roots in the German Idealist preoccupation with using such a term to categorize extraordinary works of human artistry. Kant's analysis of genius in his *Critique of Judgment* comes to mind as a possible source for Rosenzweig's play on the formulation of genius.[51] Rosenzweig begins phenomenologically by pointing out our general assumption that we think that geniuses are born geniuses and therefore that the heavens have destined only an elite, pre-determined few in a process of natural selection to designate as geniuses. Rosenzweig broadens this birthocratic Platonic/Aristotelian limitation of the criteria for who counts as a genius by shifting our attention from the category of personality to what he had earlier described as the self. If geniuses were *born* to inevitably become geniuses then the category of personality would provide the criteria to determine who is or is not a genius. But for Rosenzweig, personality is simply that determination of a human being which results from cultural and environmental determinations and not genetic heritage. Indeed, Rosenzweig maintains that the category of genius is tied to the category of self and to become a self is open to almost everyone: "Miracle-children have just as much, or just as little, chance to become a genius *as any other human.*"[52] Rosenzweig's point is that just as a self "suddenly surprises someone one day," so genius "surprises someone one day." What is common between the genius and every other self is that both presuppose a pre-existing totality of human being whereas what differentiates the genius from every other self is that the genius, drawing on his/her "complex of in-genius characteristics," which constitute its ownmost self, is able to draw from within him-/her-self and set free a work.[53] Being able to *draw from within* and to *set free* a work is what constitutes the difference and not personality as such, a distinction that sets him clearly against Hegel as well.[54]

As an author, the genius is that one who can draw from within herself and set free what is withdrawn, and because the process of drawing-from-within-and-setting-free is analogous to the process of self-formation, it is therefore the very process that best demonstrates the whole course of life, a demonstration that holds not only for the self but for Rosenzweig's text itself. This latter claim is the case because, contrary to Rosenzweig's own assertions about the stand-alone character of each of the three Parts of the text, as a work there is another level of inner coherence that binds the parts together and which can be traced (with a bit of diligence) if the work itself is handled as a work of art and judged according to the very categories Rosenzweig himself provides. This has to do with my interpretation about the role that chaos plays within the work, that is, that the work demonstrates a wholeness that calls for an ever-renewing chaotic birth of interpretations itself, just as any particular other "birthed' in actuality does. While Rosenzweig opens up the definition of genius/author to include every human being capable of becoming self, he restricts members of that set to those who are capable of "increasing and completing oneself within oneself."[55] What this means is that the genius is able to "begin a new beginning" just as the genius, with respect to personality and self, is the beginning of a new phase of one's life. Moreover, the true genius has to become a poet, as opposed to being an artist — since every genius is an artist but not every artist is a genius,[56] which means that the genius has to have access to an "inner manifoldness, a world of creations, of imaginative insights and thoughts which . . . harmoniously strive towards each other in simply being with one another." Rosenzweig calls this harmonious inner striving of co-existing thoughts "family resemblances," a concept that connects his ideas about art with the ethical relationship of dialogue, developed later in Part II and instrumental in his social theory of responsibility which he develops in Part III. This supports, as well, my own thesis about the coherence of the text as a whole, that the "family resemblance" holds for each of the respective Parts of *The Star* in how each part stands in relation to each other providing interconnectedness of the work as a whole. It is simply not possible to take any one point within the text as definitive for determining the rest of the text — philosophy, theology or sociology; but rather, each provides a perspective of self-similarity to the other points while nonetheless remaining markedly different from the others. Moreover, Rosenzweig notes that unless one is capable of inexhaustibly producing new creations out of this "covenant" of family relations, then one is a "crippled" genius. It seems that the life of the genius, although open to everyone, is actually very demanding and complex.

Keeping with the line of family relations, Rosenzweig maintains that a teaching of the work of art presents us with an analogical picture of creation in terms of a systematic family tree, anticipating his later analysis of the dynamics of speech in Book 2, Part II. Art cannot be the organon of speech because it is that which is already spoken or expressed.[57] The reason that it cannot be the organon of speech is because art is a single concept or limb of the human — albeit a very significant one — which is semi-independent like the limb of a tree, whereas a teaching about speech can only be accomplished in tabular form. In short, speech is always and only analyzable "*a fortiori*," namely, ordered and categorized after the fact of having been spoken. Speech is experiential and dynamic, and every attempt at ordering all of its potential permutations with the peculiarity of each of its individual moments-in-process is utterly impossible. What we do have, however, are recorded events of speech–acts, namely, those occurrences of speech–acts/events, which have already happened with complete originality. But even the categories that are brought in as a formal apparatus to order and make sense of those events do not — and indeed cannot — be identical with it. This means that every attempt at ordering the actual occurrence is itself another instance of the process and can only correspond to (*ent-sprechend*), or literally speak-from, the original. In a series of historical events, every occurrence is totally different every time because it takes place in a constantly changing, relative-dynamic time/space universe, which itself must then be interpretively accommodated to a new reality.[58] Hence, symbols are composed to denote the elements that constitute a tabular ordering of speech-events and which appear as identity terms for the original, unpredictable reality itself. Additionally, it is the relation that holds between those elements that functioned implicitly in algebraic formulations and can then be identified as the course that holds between any two of them at any given time. For Rosenzweig, the elements of Part I: god world human, are the elements of the course of reality that is the subject of Part II — as content, while language is that organon we use to describe the course or passage-of-the-world-day as form. And for us, narrative art is that form that the description assumes.

Hence, Rosenzweig does not so much negate or reject art or mathematics, which would then be submitting to the inexorable appropriation of a dialectical logic; rather, he proceeds phenomenologically by asserting that there is a transformation of those silent languages from a kind of logical atomism whose power is the analysis of the individual point, to a story which descriptively reveals that which is believed to be the entire course. The hypothetical and isolated elements are withdrawn from within the author and assembled to form a philosophical/theological/sociological narrative that makes ethical and thus corresponding sense. The "corresponding" only applies, however, given the establishment of an ethical relation, and ethical relations depend on establishing relations of believing trust. In Rosenzweig's words: "We describe the course in which we believe, with the words in which we trust."[59] But which words should we trust? Which do we believe in and where do such words come from? In order to address those questions we have to ask: what does Rosenzweig mean by trust?

The sense of trust that Rosenzweig has in mind has to do with that which we trust because it is familiar; namely, we trust because we are accustomed to using something based on faith in its reliability. As we will see later, this very notion of reliability is very close to what Heidegger will propose as essential to what happens in the origination of a work of art as well.[60] Rosenzweig tells us that it is necessary to trust language, which is easy because of its utter familiarity:

(language) is in us and around us, and there is nothing else which comes to us from "without" (*außen*) in the way that it re-sounds (*widertönt*) out of our "inner" (*Innen*) to the "outer" (*Außen*). The word is the same as it becomes heard and as it is spoken.[61]

In other words, the underlying logic is neither a coherence nor a correspondence theory of truth but rather a re-soundence theory, which provides a cornerstone for Rosenzweig's philosophy of language. Language is that phenomenon which bridges interiority and exteriority such that, what we hear from the other is what we *intuitively* say from our own hearts. That means that even though the inner-structural processes for constructing the elements "god world human" can be and should continue to be differentiated, Rosenzweig asserts that the "word of god and the word of the human are the same" — they resound. Accordingly, drawing on what is closest to his own heart, Rosenzweig claims that what human beings hear in their heart and take to be their own human language is "the word which comes out of the mouth of god." For Rosenzweig, this means that the words found in the Bible and the art-form that he uses to translate those words into a language that is relevant now — *midrash* — are the same.

VII. *Renewing the story of creation*

Using a *midrash* in order to bridge the earlier grammatical analysis of the structures of thinking about the elements with the actual story itself, Rosenzweig begins his interpretation with the one-term sentence "good" which, he claims, runs through almost the whole chapter of Genesis (*Bereshit*). This one-term sentence stands for both the results of philosophical activity and for the concrete, evaluative affirmation of creative work activity. A judgment is verbalized with the term "good," but only after the expression of the narrative form indicated by "God created," a declarative that is characterized by the past tense of the verbal form. The syntactical form of analysis used by Rosenzweig is informed by the mathematical logic of the element "god," with the term "god" holding the syntactical place of subject, that "'freely' releases the predicate to calm objectivity," an iteration of the thinking process that now returns from its earlier presentation that, according to my analysis, first appeared in Rosenzweig's hypothetical conceptualization of the moment of the expression of "freedom" that characterized the element of god in Part I of *The Star*. However, with the historically later *midrash*, that moment is no longer merely an inner logical moment inherent in the independent *physis* of our thinking about god but, rather, is the negatively inverted moment of an experienced expression called creation, which is the logical negation or limitation of that freedom resulting in the positive, material work called "world." Utilizing Rosenzweig's speech–act analyses that we worked through in Part I and Book 1 of Part II, we are in the position to accept the logical claims of referentiality that Rosenzweig makes about narrative speech — that it necessarily refers to *having been* and therefore refers to what *was* created or already given. In other words, narrative speech can only ever refer to what is already there, to what has already been experienced.

As interpreters of this kind of speech that refers to the temporal past, we are urged by the form of the narrative speech–act itself to search for what is most primordial and originary and thus to ask: what then is already there? What is already there are created things; in a sense, we find ourselves already in the midst of things. But what are these primal, originary things in the creation narrative? At first, heaven and earth, but then all of the other natural objects that we commonly find in the world, such as plants and animals. However, in the creation narrative, as in any narrative form of speech, god as subject is the only term set in the accusative case in the speech–act, whereas the things are nominatively defined, that is, they necessarily occur in the nominative case by the affixation of definite articles. With definite articles affixed, the Creation story situates the nominatively defined things in their respective species for the whole of worldly and heavenly things, since each individual thing begins its self-development in indefinite anonymity denoted earlier by its initial affixation with an indefinite article. Moreover, the definite article provides a syntactical indication that what is at stake in the initial act of creation is creation of *space*, that is, a conceptual space is provided for us to think about the interrelatedness of all things, even the sun and moon, which are subsumed under the totality of creation. But it is only with the reference to chaos and the origination of the world of things that the story introduces the possibility of a real plurality where an element of ongoing unsubsumable originality is built into the very process of organic creativity itself and thus into the ground of ethical relationships as well.

Notes

1 See Stewart 1990. The interdisciplinary applications that this new science has — Stewart refers to chaos as "fact" and not "theory," ranges from meteorology, ecology, and biology to neurology and economic forecasts; discerning order in the turbulence of chaos is revealing new ways to look at subjects as diverse as cardiac arrythmia and accounting for memory production in the way synapses are formed in our brains, to modeling the probability factor in an idealized toss of a coin.

2 See Johnson 2009: 39–66, for an eminently readable overview of Chaos Theory and its place in the interdisciplinary phenomenon of contemporary complexity science.

3 See Hesiod 1973.

4 See Aristotle 1941, esp. "Physics" IV, I.

5 See Epictetus 1940: 240.

6 See Heisenberg 1958. For a less technical presentation, of his physics, see Heisenberg 1989.

7   See, for example, the discussion of Georg Cantor's contribution to set theory in Aczel 2000. On the complex relationship of Rosenzweig to Hegel's "system" as such, see Pollock 2009. My own thesis was formulated prior to Pollock's work and any attempt to definitively address his exhaustive study would not do it justice. Preliminarily, though, my initial reading tells me that his thesis runs strongly counter to mine.

8   See Johnson 2009; Gleick 1987; and Stewart 1990.

9   See Hegel 1970, esp. sections 34ff. in the Introduction for the difficulties in distinguishing between objective and subjective and the action of free will. The analysis is set in the context of determining the development of Abstract Right, from the phenomenon of subjective freedom to its translation into objective property.

10 GS2: 134.

11 Again, given Rosenzweig's earlier, comprehensive and groundbreaking work on Hegel's *Philosophy of Right*, it is safe to say that he could have been referring to Hegel's elaboration of the role of *Begriff* in the formation of the state, in connection with the function that the Idea plays. See Rosenzweig HS, Zweiten Bandes: 103ff.

12 GS2: 135.

13 Because it operates with equal and unequal signs and brings basic concepts, such as essence, to presentation ("Darstellung") — literally, a "placing-there" for cognition.

14 Which leads, of course, to a discussion of intuition in Hegel. See Hegel 1977, esp. Sections 91–104, 58–63.

15 GS2: 142; SR: 127.

16 Ibid: 143; 129.

17 Ibid. The German word Rosenzweig uses to characterize this condition is "Gegenstand," which literally means that-which-stands-over-against an implied or specified other. Rosenzweig constructs a mental bridge from the actuality of the grammatical distinctions to those of relations which hold in thinking about creation: It (the object) now "stands" *there* on its own feet over-"against" a supposed creator, a definite, affirmed thing in the infinite space of cognition or of creation.

18 Ibid, 146; SR: 132. As I mentioned in my Introduction, Rosenzweig's work displays several characteristics of Husserlian phenomenology, as this instance of his development of speech–acts demonstrates. The connection with Husserl's analysis of distinctions between the noema as a mental object and the noetic process should be self-evident to those familiar with Husserl's phenomenology. See Husserl 1931: 235–328.

19 Ibid: 148; 134.

20 Ibid.

21 See GS3, "The New Thinking": 161, where Rosenzweig claims his method is an absolute empiricism, an "absoluter Empirismus."

22 See Pöggler, "Rosenzweig und Hegel," in Schmied-Kowarzik 1988b: 839–853, where he claims that in turning from the path of professional historian to that of a philosopher in the 1920s, "Rosenzweig wird dort immer noch von Hegel und Schelling oder doch von deren Jugendfreund Hölderlin begleitet." See also

Schmied Kowarzik's extended treatment of this connection in Schmied-Kowarzik 1991 and his essay "Vom Totalexperiment des Glaubens. Kritisches zur positiven Philosophie Schellings und Rosenzweigs" in Schmied-Kowarzik 1988a: 771–774. Robert Gibbs also recognizes the importance of Schelling for Rosenzweig in Gibbs 1992, claiming that "Rosenzweig's major constructive impulse in *The Star of Redemption* is directly dependent on Schelling's *Weltalter*": 44. But Anna Bauer points out how Schelling never completed his system and does not draw on either dialogue or speech as Rosenzweig does. See Anna Bauer, "Rosenzweig's Sprachdenken" in Schmied-Kowarzik 1988b: 903–912.

23 See Rosenzweig's "Die älteste Systemprogramm des deutschen Idealismus," in GS3: 3–42.

24 See Schelling's "Stuttgart Seminars" in Schelling 1994: 198.

25 Ibid: 243.

26 GS2: 149; SR: 135.

27 See Rosenzweig's thoughts on empiricism in "Das neue Denken" in GS3. Also see Gibbs 1992 for his argument that Rosenzweig's theological sociology presents a theory of redemption as social action that "is an empiricism of the future — that we can make society conform to these concepts, and so redeem the world": 128. See also Samuelson 1999: 60 for his judgment that Rosenzweig would restrict all variants of philosophy, including empiricism as a modern form of Atomism, to his general critique of traditional philosophy at its philosophical best, i.e. as idealist philosophy. However, in his logic of creation, Rosenzweig maintains a firm link to the empiricist tradition by citing Bacon in order to express the empiricist principle that the future is absolutely unlike the present and cannot give us knowledge of what is actual or of actuality: "Gar die Zukunft gilt als absolute ungeeignet 'unfruchtbar' für die Erkenntnis des Wirklichen." (GS2: 146; SR: 132).

28 GS: 150; SR: 135.

29 Ibid: 151; SR: 136.

30 Ibid: 152–3; SR: 137–8.

31 Ibid: 153; SR: 138.

32 GS2: 162; SR: 146. See also Hegel 1955, esp. Georg Lukác's excellent introductory essay in Band 2: 589.

33 Which is why Schelling was concerned with grounding his philosophy in a vitalism of nature, against what he saw was Spinoza's mechanical determinism. See Schelling 1975: 40ff.

34 GS2: 162; SR: 146.

35 Kant 1951: 78.

36 GS2: 163; SR: 147. Again, the critical point is the breakdown in the relationship of the percipient and the "percipi" (that which is perceived), which leads to an unsatisfactory theory of knowledge because of an inability to adequately account for the multidimensionality of reality.

37 This is a "Platonic" theory about which Kierkegaard also had some reservations. See Kierkegaard 1941: 184: "The recollection-principle belongs to speculative philosophy, and recollection is immanence, and speculatively and eternally there is no paradox. But the difficulty is that no human being is speculative philosophy . . ."

38 GS2: 163; SR: 147. (My emphasis.)

39 Ibid.

40 On Kant and the common root as the source for the nothings of our knowledge, see
    GS2: 24; SR: 21: "Mindestens das 'Ding an sich,' und der 'intelligible Charakter'
    bezeichnen zwei getrennte Nichtse des Wissens, nach unsrer Terminologie
    das metalogische und das metaethische. Und die dunklen Worte, mit denen er
    gelegentlich von der gehemnisvollen 'Wurzel' beider spricht, suchen wohl auch
    dem metaphysischen Nichts des Wissens einen festen Punkt zu ertasten."

41 The sense of "holism" I develop in the following pages is quite other than what
    Gordon means by holism as a category for identifying the works of Rosenzweig
    and Heidegger.

42 GS2: 163; SR: 147.

43 See GS2: 98; SR: 90 for Rosenzweig's use of "Theogonie, Psychogonie,
    Kosmogonie" as the pre-histories, in the sense of philosophically structured
    stories, to re-tell the origins of the so-called sciences of the elements.

44 "Es gibt nur eine Sprache"; see GS4$_1$: 3ff. The context is a discussion of the task
    of translating and Rosenzweig's conception of the translator as a spatio-temporal
    activity: "Der Übersetzer macht sich zum Sprachohr der fremden Stimme, die er
    über den Abgrund des Raums oder der Zeit vernehmlich macht." And the task of
    the translator is to then, through the application of the universal "speech-spirit
    of his [own] language (allgemeinen Sprachgeists seiner Sprache), *renew* language
    through the estranged human other, through the estranged other language. Such
    a renewal is possible because all foreign language is "embryonically contained"
    (keimhaft enthlaten) in every human speech (alles menschliche Sprechen). Michael
    Brocke, in Kassel, Germany, December, 1986 at the "Internationale Franz
    Rosenzweig-Konferenz," (unpublished presentation) argued that such a renewal
    of language is at the heart of the conflict Rosenzweig had with Gershom Scholem
    about Rosenzweig's translation of "original sources," principally Judah HaLevi's
    poems but, and perhaps even more importantly, the Bible. For an extended discus-
    sion of Rosenzweig's translation theory in the context of universal languages, see
    Galli 1995: 360–99.

45 GS2: 164, 147.

46 Ibid.

47 Ibid.: "*gesprochene Sprache*" and "*der lebendig strömenden Wirklichkeit der
    wirklichen Sprache.*" cf. The distinction between *le dit* and *le dire* in Levinas 2000:
    5–7, 37–8.

48 GS2: 165; SR: 148.

49 Ibid.

50 As I noted in the Introduction, Heidegger specifically rejects that an artwork, as
    great and authentic, originates from a genius. This point is elucidated in Chapter
    6 below.

51 See Kant 1951: 150–64.

52 GS2: 165; SR: 148. (My italics.)

53 Ibid: 166; 149.

54 The distinct divergence from attributing genius to personality may also indicate
    Rosenzweig contesting, again, Hegel's phenomenology of social ethics articulated

in *The Philosophy of Right*. In sections on "Abstract Right" Hegel claims that self-determination in any society has its origins in the stipulation of personality as "'the' defining human characteristic, which then leads to his theory of property rights, etc. See Hegel 1970: 115–23.

55 GS2: 166; SR: 149.

56 Rosenzweig provides us with a pair of examples to differentiate between poet and artist: Flaubert as mere artist versus Balzac as poet, and Huch as artist versus Lagerlöf as poet. The difference is that in the case of Flaubert and Huch, their artistry consists in their attempts to retell history *realistically* in some kind of mirroring effect. Balzac and Lagerlöf, on the other hand, create new adventures and comedies to depict social extant but also possible social relations. Additionally, Rosenzweig provides gendered pairs, Balzac and Flaubert are both male, Lagerlöf (who was the first woman to ever be awarded the Nobel Prize for Literature, 1909) and Huch are both female.

57 In referring to the term "organon" we are reminded of Aristotle's collection of logical treatises, esp. his categories, and his contention that speech is the organon for the logic of the categories and that, therefore, his ten categories of rational logic are the essential structures of actual speech. These categories are: substance, quantity, quality, relation, place, time, position, state, action, affection. See Aristotle 1941: 7ff.

58 For a related analysis of this process, see Samuelson 1999, 116–122. Samuelson focuses on Rosenzweig's move from the formalism of mathematics to the laws of grammar and universal necessity of root-words. As I note in the following lines, this move sets the stage, so to speak, for Rosenzweig to present a language-based description of the interrelation of the elements of reality.

59 GS2: 167; SR: 150.

60 See below, Chapter 6.

61 GS2: 167; SR: 150.

CHAPTER 3

ROSENZWEIG'S *MIDRASH* AS PHILOSOPHY
OF LANGUAGE

I. *Knowledge, interpretation, and ethics*

Rosenzweig refers to Book 2 of Part II of *The Star of Redemption* as the "heart-piece" of his book not only because of its locative centrality, but also because, in terms of content, it is in those pages that he deals with the founding and orienting phenomenon of what he calls the event of revelation in how it occurs as a love relation. It is also where we are presented with a phenomenology of the structure of how any present event occurs as temporal at all. Briefly: where Part I of *The Star* presents a phenomenology of the temporal past, Part II of the *The Star* — specifically Book 2 — presents a phenomenology of dialogue and the temporal present. In the next chapter, I discuss the way that Rosenzweig also presents a phenomenology of community and the temporal future, including a phenomenology of messianic expectation.

Prior to this explicitly "revelation" section of his work, the components of Rosenzweig's speech-analytic *midrash* were forged in the aesthetic/philosophical "realm of the Mothers" referred to in Chapter 1. These components are coupled with Rosenzweig's critique of German *Geisteswissenschaft*, that is, his critique of the nineteenth-century historicism framed in the guise of a history of the spirit of human achievement.[1] Such a critique is presciently similar to Heidegger's attack on Herder's influential attempt at describing an evolution of the spirit(s) of humanity.[2] In Rosenzweig's case, however, the components of the critique that are brought to bear on the text are taken up not merely as common tools lying ready-to-hand (as would be the case with Heidegger). Rather, they are taken up as tools forged for this specific interpretive purpose of reading and translating "then" a specific text written from his perspective in the past, in order that it resounds for a "tomorrow" that could only uniquely originate from how the factuality of that past was renewed by how it was dealt with in the present. Despite the apparent similarities with Heidegger's hermeneutic method, Rosenzweig's *midrashic* method does not accord with his ontological and existential analytic of Da-sein, in contrast with Peter Gordon's assertions. This is so because Rosenzweig's dialogical structure and content have ethical signification, evident throughout his entire work. Where Heidegger's hermeneutic institutes a turn away from the ontology and metaphysical categories of traditional philosophy, he none the less operates in the language of an ontology of being that returns to and reiterates some of the most basic characteristic traits of that Western philosophical tradition he attempted to subvert, as evident in the opening sections of *Being and Time*. By contrast, Rosenzweig's philosophy of language, although never explicitly articulated, is based on a complex analysis of speech-thinking refracted through an ethical lens that introduces a radically new way of dealing with texts, the world and other humans.

Considered phenomenologically, Rosenzweig's divergence from Heidegger becomes evident in how each respectively deals with the idea of god in their works. Rosenzweig explicitly draws on an historically determined concept of god not only because of the narrative sources from which he draws inspiration and guidance but also in order to plot a course that includes both an ethical and a pluralistic guide for community life. Consequently, Rosenzweig chooses the Bible as a source text because, as I intimated in the previous chapter, he considers that text to be an exemplary work of art that includes an idea of god that originated in a context of trust and that entails a commitment to building communities of human responsibility and interdependency. For Rosenzweig, the Bible, like other community founding texts, is that sort of text that continues to provide a trustworthy source for experiencing how the constituent elements of reality — world human god, eventuate as revelatory experiences out of a textually based interpretive community. But even given that epistemological and metaphysical primal experience, the matter of trust is what differentiates this particular founding text from others.

That Rosenzweig begins his own reworking of the elements "world human god" by considering them as three nothings of knowledge that are order-less with respect to each other, indicates that he recognizes how much we know about any one of them, namely, practically nothing. But in his hands, they do not remain in the gray realm of disorder, in the realm of the indeterminate sphere of the "perhaps." Rather, he reorders them through the lens of biblical texts, thereby renewing the philosophical important questions of "how" and "what" we know of reality, conditioned by the threefold temporal apprehension of any textual reading whatsoever. For Rosenzweig, making sense of our historical condition as humans living in interrelated communities with each other entails that we address ultimate questions about the meaning of our lives, namely, how we have originated and use the idea of god and world and how we identify ourselves as humans through the textual traditions of the language communities within which we find ourselves embodied and interacting with others. For Rosenzweig, that means taking into account an interpretation of foundational texts of those communities in the context of their historical and ethical spectrums.

The character of a text being-past, of having been created, means reading it for its structural coherence as it is already there and attending to its already established history of interpretation. The work of interpreting the historical determinations of such contextual coherence is initially accomplished by reading that text in its "objectifying narrative form of the past," namely, its having already occurred in such a place and at such a time. This initial form of textual critique was initiated by Spinoza as a form of historical apprehension that questions an orthodox, literal application of a text. Such an orthodox, traditional reading of the text entails that the text should be read in such a way that it could be applied prescriptively to current and future human actions in precisely the form as it is received — as perfect and timeless, and thus that it should command obedient submission and adherence to its absolutely binding dictates. However, Rosenzweig relied on a stream of exegesis from the Jewish tradition that maintained that any interpretive act, as a past event, must rely on not only *scientific*, or analytic, kinds of *peshat* analysis but must situate any *peshat* within a *midrashic* and thus historical framework.[3] In other words, form-critical analysis is secondary to historical, literary, ethical-political readings.

Addressing the present context of interpreting a text, addressing how one practically ought to respond to a current political, social, or life event via the resources of the traditions of a particular community, is the hermeneutic function of *midrash*. With *midrash*, the inclination to delete or emend a text to account for its apparent irregularities is suppressed; rather, the text is allowed to speak for itself in order that its own particularly unique resources can be drawn upon. In other words, Rosenzweig does not engage in the merely historicizing activity of a "Science of Judaism"[4] or, on the other hand, in some early form of a-historical analytic philosophy. Rather, the present value of the text is enunciated through the active application of the philosophical method he uses, namely, that method which takes seriously objective reality (as nature, world, or immediately given phenomena) and otherness from the one who is actually reading/speaking. What occurs is a radical and dynamic interchange of the members currently involved in the relation. Not only is the text reinterpreted, thereby receiving a new dimension through the new reading, but the interpreter is also transformed by the act of interpreting the text in the face of the demands of a current event. But the more important ethical supposition is the transference of that kind of interchange to inter-human activity. For instance, I can imagine myself faced with a stranger who may have something to say that is as unpredictably unique and necessary for their own fulfillment as a human being that is other than what I may have to prescriptively say out of the dictates of my own needs. Indeed, while I may indeed need that particular other who faces me, it could very likely be the case that that other may need my own particular response as a response that is open to their demand with even more urgency. As I will elaborate in the following pages, Rosenzweig describes this propensity to be open to the demands of the other in terms of the bond of lover and beloved. In another but related context, Walter Benjamin might describe the condition for such an event with the word "aura" — that binding and compelling experience that occurs when I have the sensation that, in glancing at someone I get the feeling of being gazed upon in return, of being held in careful and attentive consideration.

But even the future dimension is built into both the content of the text at hand, the applied method, and the ethical extension. We are directed from simple, free affirmation asked of us in directly apprehending a text in the present to the prophecy implied in the biblical text and explicated in Rosenzweig's words. These words make sense to us because of our common heritage (Hebrew, Greek, and European) and our having been recently instructed in the art of applying the tools of Rosenzweig's peculiar kind of philosophical analysis, that is, an analysis that directs us to attend to the dynamic structures of systematic predictability and chaotic unpredictability in speech-thinking. The importance of the future is the fact that each of us, as organically spiritual beings, is involved in a process of becoming more fully who we are and can individually be, but nonetheless remain incomplete, as individuals and as a species. We remain incomplete as long as each and every other human being has not been reached by the language and fullness of the revelatory experience of love; of not merely being considered and held in regard but of having someone attend to my needs and desires, and to mine alone. This imperative of what I call *attending justice* is one of the most critical implications in Rosenzweig's philosophy and, as we shall see, the omission of such language from Heidegger's philosophy puts the two contemporaries on radically divergent paths.

In order to demonstrate the need to refer to different kinds of texts to meet the demands of different situations and different domains of language, in Book 1 of Part II Rosenzweig analyzes the opening verses of the first book of Genesis (*Bereshit*). He analyzes the narratives of creation, with their temporally past and spatial coordinates, and the place in that narrative of the self-exclusivity of the elements and of human beings. The peculiar aesthetic form of that narrative is epic, its grammar is indicative, and its key words are *knowledge and faith* and its culminating thesis is the phenomenon of death. Ethically, such a domain deals with the formation of individual identity, namely, with the monological "I." He analyzes the biblical Song of Songs (*Shir Ha Sharim*) in Book 2 of Part II in order to narrate the event of revelation, with its focus on the present, temporality as such, and the relational and non-relational aspects of reality that specifically determine the foundations of human ethics. Its peculiar aesthetic form is the lyrical poem-song, its grammar is imperative, and its key words are *faith and love* and it is ordered around the phenomenon of relationship as such. Ethically, this domain presents the reader with various structures of occurring relations that take the dialogical form of an "I and you." The final domain is highlighted by considering the hymns of praise in the Psalms, especially Psalm 115, and has to do with redemption, the future, eternality, and social structures and activities of communities. Its peculiar aesthetic forms are drama and song, its grammar is dative, and its key word is *hope*. Ethically, this level deals with broader social structures represented by the challenge of the stranger as neighbor, namely, that one who stands outside the circle of family and loved ones who is nonetheless called to join in and become a member of a community. Addressing the anonymous neighbor is a further response to the demands of *justice*, namely, that each and every human being should — by being personally attended to — have the opportunity to live a more vital and meaningful life. As an ethical task, loving an other and providing them with the opportunity to respond and develop as a unique, particularized individual dissolves the homogenizing and reifying hold that the world has on an individual and is therefore an act of redemption, an attending justice.

But how are we to conceive that moment when a third is sought to join in with an initial community of two? What are the concrete steps that must be taken? For Rosenzweig, the first steps take the form of engaging in *midrashic* analysis presented as a way to interpretively address such questions. As previously mentioned, the particular *midrash* chosen by Rosenzweig is based on the ancient biblical text, *Shir ha Sharim*. His *midrash* inspired by this biblical text focuses on the transformative, revelatory drive of love that occurs in the way that one loves another, and that eventually includes another other — the third, and is a process that is based on the occurrence of an interchange of speech–acts. To begin with, Rosenzweig considers the naming of god as an instance for encountering the other and attesting to the ongoing process of factually situating that other as an essential part of one's reality. According to such an instantiation, we attest to the factuality of the other through speaking about and with that other, which in turn leads to orienting our own existence differently in the face of that other. Getting to know the other with epistemic and sensual certainty as other than me, but in an ongoing determinative relation with me, is accomplished through the process of loving the other, a process that entails a denial of the self that was formed in the originating negations of the metaethical, autonomous self. This act of negation takes the form of a denial of one's original self-affirmation (accomplished already through a double act of negation) that is a transformation of the negation of one's meta-ethical negation of others, to the humble acceptance of one's relational status with that other. Briefly, I voluntarily limit my own self-affirmation in order to listen to and attend to the needs of that other in the moment that the other calls to me. The ethical consequences are a rejection of meta-ethical self-concentration and absorption in favor of ethical responsibility to and for the other. One is awakened from the tragic introversion of the speechless self, by being called by the other, as one awakens an other through directly addressing her by making and responding to imperatives of love. Such speech–acts of love reveal a renewal of one's life and point to an ideal asymptotic and ultimately messianic goal of the completion of each and every human in a just society. I will deal with why this attending justice is also a messianic goal in the next chapter in order to be able to focus on the development of *midrashic* analysis in this chapter.

Midrash does not begin with analysis. Rather, as a kind of art-form in itself, it begins with a direct experience out of which we wrestle, or induce, conceptual meaning. The beginning of Rosenzweig's formal consideration of the term we use to describe the "experience of" (that is, the "wrestled-out of") conceptual meaning, is a particular sentence that, according to Rosenzweig, has universal application, namely: *Love is as strong as death*. Found in one of the oldest and one of the most pagan of biblical texts, namely, *Shir ha Sharim*, this particular sentence immediately situates us in a defined, particular context, namely, that of universally pagan human conditions set within the cultural language-world of the Bible. By choosing such a starting point for his *midrash*, Rosenzweig implies that we humans begin with our experiences in the actual, relational world of particular non-denominational human communities, a condition of a kind of faithlessness that has been taken up and distorted by a variety of faith communities. But without any direct reference to such historical faith communities, such as Jewish or Christian communities, Rosenzweig begins with the sentence, *love is as strong as death*, with the intention of demonstrating, through a particularly Jewish *midrashic* activity, that this archetypal, secular love song is the quintessential work of art to which we can turn in order to best understand the dynamics of a love relationship, namely, the love relationship as it occurs in itself. This makes phenomenological sense as well, because the dynamics of a human-to-human love relationships best serve to reveal not only what he presents as the paradigmatic function of a god–human relation for any understanding of the actuality of human-to-human relations in general.[5] In order to grasp the importance of that demonstration for his aesthetic and ethical stance, it is necessary to explore some of the details of Rosenzweig's *midrash*.

II. *The analogy of love as ethical dialogue*

As is clear from the statement, "Love is *as* strong *as* death," Rosenzweig begins his *midrashic* task by comparing two concepts on the level of analogy, namely, the concepts of love and death. There are two respects in which Rosenzweig uses analogy as an analytical tool to disclose the similar and dissimilar structures of the two experiences of love and death in reference to the experience of the earth-bound souls of a man and woman: (a) as a paradigmatic analogy to the love of god and the human; and (b) as applied to the aesthetic/theological categories of creation, revelation, and redemption and their respective temporal horizons of past, present, and future. For the *midrashic* interpretation, the aesthetic continuum of creation-revelation-redemption is analogously equivalent to the temporal complex past-present-future, and we are encouraged to bridge the gap between concept and reality, that is, the gap from speech-thinking to speech–acts. But to complicate matters, the very artificiality of Rosenzweig's preferred art form — his *midrashic* model with its theological vocabulary — is the interpretive device used to engage and transform other humans in their secularly insulated realities. The enactment of a philosophy of art proceeds by way of an aesthetic performance that intertwines with the theory in which we have already been educated (Part I and Book 1 of Part II) and anticipates that which is to come (Part III and Book 3 of Part II).

The analogies of the relations god–human to human–human and to woman–man are just as important as the continuum because, as Rosenzweig claims, the event of love that the revelatory love poem re-sounds is more than analogy. As a speech–act, the revelatory event that occurs in a relationship of love expressed by *Shir ha Sharim* expresses that transformative process by which humans convert themselves into other than what they are: "Revelation is to the soul the lived experience of a present which although it rests on the existence of the past, it does not dwell therein, rather it walks [changes, converts, turns — *wandeln*] in the light of the divine countenance."[6] The point of using a term such as "*wandeln*" signifies that an empirical effectiveness holds in the kind of transformative experience of love that happens as the dialogical relationship that Rosenzweig depicts in his theological construal of this work of art. The transformation accomplished in the relation, a transformation called revelation, transforms the individual involved by impelling her to turn to her neighbor in love simply because she is there, now. Rosenzweig again refers to this text at the very end of *The Star* after the reader has learned more about how Rosenzweig understands the communal ramifications of the ethical imperative to love one's neighbor. In the central parts of his text where he is theoretically concerned with aesthetics, he makes a bold claim for the medium of art to initiate such a transformation, although it takes an actual speech–act beyond art — from one human to another — to ultimately accomplish change in the world.[7] According to this theory of art, just as each of the individual details of a work of art is *ensouled* with life by an artist, each individual human being in the community of all humans is "analogously" ensouled through various speech–acts of love of a human who has already been loved to the next human who happens along in her life.

The ethical task that Rosenzweig envisions consists of publicizing to a wider audience of others the good effect that an ethically "demanding and responding" relationship of love can have. This effect is at first conditioned by the event that in the closed circle of being loved each member remains limited to their own voice, just as each detail in a work of art has its own time and place of occurrence in the production and perception of any whole work of art. But the demands of the relationship of the individuals in a love relation-ship, and of the details in a perceived work of art, lead to a "self-opening-up of that-which-is-closed." Through concentrated and attentive concern for the individual, a movement occurs from the silence of negation and repression of that individual to an observable and vital sounded expression — from one detail to another. What happens is the occurrence of a "self-denial of a merely silent essential being through a sounded (made open or public) word."[8] But the transformation is likewise an imperative of *attending in justice* in turning to the unknown other, who is still isolated and defiant, in an act of love that draws that anonymous other into the community of known believers (or lovers), that is, into a community of souls. In other words, Rosenzweig addresses the demands of the structure and role of a total community as part of a historically effective process. The collective kind of community that he has in mind is one that embraces each particular individual in their particularity as self but which nonetheless overthrows the death of individuality by calling each individual to become a soul by joining in a unitive song of hoped-for eternal peace. The Hobbesian war of individuals, also entailed by the logic of Hegel's dialectic, is overcome by affirming each human's own separate identity and answering her needs, yet calling each of them — in their own turn, through the particular constraints of the language practices of a historically determined dialogue, to stand in a community of responsible and concerned relationships with and for each other.

At issue is how the relationship between the lover and the beloved develops. Even though the loving-one loves solely the beloved only in this singular moment with the greatest measure, the lover experiences with each new day merely that part (just that *Stück* — that *passage*) of life which he loves, and which is not ever loved so much as one loves that other today: "every today love loves the beloved a little better."[9] Rosenzweig names this process *Steigerung*, and means by that a kind of progressive climbing as a process that takes the form of a transcendence that reveals what is both certain and enduring in the transitoriness of a love relationship. In contrast to the moment of *sinking* into the realm of the Mothers (referred to above and at the end of his Introduction), with the revelatory relation of love one is able to transcendently rise from one loving moment to the next with the confidence of having positively engaged with an other and thus having effected actual — and enduring — change in the world.[10] Indeed, this progressive movement begins with the former process of sinking into the realm of the Mothers as highly abstract and conceptual in nature, which changes into the regular intensified gradation of the process of *Steigerung* that takes the form of something concrete and particular coming into enduring existence. *Steigerung*, as an elevating transcendence — a raising of the particular out of the anonymity of the individual–genus relationship, connotes that which stands out from the rest because of the strength of the connection that is forged in the moment.[11] What Rosenzweig has in mind is the forging of a form of relationship defined by such German nouns as *Bestand*, *Beständigkeit*, and *Treue* as well as the verb *bestehen*, which entails "withstanding a test.'[12] To summarize, this concretizing structural process constitutes the enduring formation of actual human communities that consist of particular individuals standing in ongoing and transformative relationships with each other.

One of the consequences of such a model for enacting ethical dialogue is that it is only in the authentic demand to love that one encounters the "I" of one's dialogue-partner. In fact, the other is only able to emerge in their other-ness in the mutual interchange of denying oneself in being-open to desiring this particular other, a denial that is made possible by recognizing the tragic isolation that was the case in having rejected, or negated, just this very other. The result of such a voluntary self-denial — a negation of the rejection of that other — is an increased level of mutual trust between the two who stand in dialogue, a mutual trust which should then lead to the process of *Steigerung*, or of affirmatively sustaining the growth of one another as a qualified means for helping each other achieve more complete and fulfilling lives. The mediation is qualified for the sake of resisting an ethics of crassly exploiting the other as merely the means or self-serving or self-aggrandizing ends. The process of voluntary self-denial and *Steigerung* is finalized in the narrative by categoriz-ing the enunciation as a "saying of the Eternal" (*Spruch des Ewigen*), which crystallizes Rosenzweig's speech-thinking/speech–act treatment of revelation into a receptive focus. The verbal enunciation by the prophet of the "saying of the Eternal," which Rosenzweig also translates as the "saying of God,"[13] prepares the listener by leading her to the reception of a speech-claim — a speech-judgment — by an other whose applied validity is unlimited because this judgment is a judgment of the *Eternal*. However, it is not entirely clear why such speech-claims should be applicable to "all" based on their original recep-tion from the "eternal." It might be clearer if the origin were the "universal" (*Allgemein*), which would encompass every one in its universality. But then that would be a return to a Hegelian ontology of ethics.

I suggest that Rosenzweig's use of the ambiguous phrase "speech of the eternal" can be universally applicable not because it is a once-and-for-all revelatory event, which would make it a tyrannical form of fatalistic necessity. Rather, the necessity and universality of the claim is based on the condition that in order for that which occurs within the relation to be effective it has to be made known or made public. The actual spokenness of the speaking is emphasized such that in order for any love relation to be designated as a revelatory one — one that opens something to the world in a new and effec-tive way — everything that occurs within the limits of that relation must be sounded word. The occurrences must be empirically and sensually sounded; otherwise, like any other expression that cannot be sounded it would fall into the category of pre-world, that is, algebraic–symbolic language or, post-world, geometrically structured, figurative-ritual language. Accordingly, in the mutual interchange of a love relationship the beloved soul answers the love-demand of the lover with a love-confession, in German, a *Liebesgeständnis*. Literally, the loved one *stands* by her love in a durative speech–act, which is an act of

signifying as testifying to the presence of the other, as other. It will become clear
in later chapters that this is not the same kind of standing-as-appropriating
that is found in a Heideggarian relation of Da-sein to *its* other. Rather, the
ultimate significance of conditioning the relationship on the sounded word is
that it enables us to move beyond the limits of art to what can be considered
the larger domain of truth or reality which occurs in the broad range of our
inter-human and worldly activities.

In preparing us for this more expansive domain of social theory, Rosenzweig
further develops the complexity of the relationship along the already established lines of recognition and duration. Initially, the soul testifies by confessing
its love for the other in a twofold form: (a) as *Geständnis*, where the soul
"stands" by, or to, its faith in the other; and (b) as *Bekenntnis* or *Bekennen*,
which denotes a "saying-of"' or acknowledgment. Both words generally mean
confession, but reconstructing Rosenzweig's analysis, the actual process of
confessing occurs in two stages that correspond correlatively to the differences
in meaning of these two words. Moreover, the way the soul receives god's
commandment to love is reflected in how these two major speech–acts are
constituted in the process of self-development.[14] The first, as *Geständnis*, falls
under the heading of "Shame" for Rosenzweig which has to do with expressing
the two-fold self-recognition by the soul of: (a) not having loved in the past,
that is, not being adequately prepared to be open for another; and (b) a desire,
which thus already points to the future, that is, a desire to continue loving
in the present. As already noted, to "continue" is understood in the sense of
something coming into existence by remaining standing.[15] However, since it is
ongoing, ever-present, and momentary, the lover's love can never be a *congealing* admission of love, which is what Rosenzweig understands as something
standing or lasting.[16] For example, a poem lasts and physically stands on its
own because it congeals as part of this sensual world as an objective thing,
whereas present acts last in a more important but elusive way by counting in
the human balance of who we are in terms of what we have done. There is a
durability in acts of love that are publicly verbalized: they come into existence
and have a history of effects in the between of individualized human beings.
For the beloved: "Her love is born once, as that which remains and is constant;
so she is allowed to *stand to it*, she is allowed to confess it."[17] Note again the
play on staying, constancy, standing, endurance, and confession as words that
evoke a quality of empirically enduring existing. The beloved's love is also of
the present, but is other than that of the lover's: she is concerned with duration.
For Rosenzweig, *speaking* is what signifies the duration itself, but not just
any kind of speaking. Rosenzweig contends that confessional speech reveals a
future-directedness of the present and a groundedness in the past, that is, our
speech–acts condition the temporal parameters of our reality, in terms of the
possibilities of our effective working, in terms of actually affecting and being
affected and thus producing reality.[18]

Consequently, by standing-up to the actual effects of her responsibility to and with the other in the present, the soul transforms the ephemeral present into an experience of temporality that will endure; it will endure because it is already directed towards the future with the promise of effectiveness-to-come. As opposed to the dark and gloomy coveredness of the past, the future — with its promise of a continuing "*Steigerung*" relationship, the presently experienced event of revelatory love appears bright and light. Hence, the beloved *wants* to continue in the light of her present condition, namely, as the one who is *singled out and attended to*, desired, and be-loved in a love relationship. Moreover, because she wants to, she wills to continue — desire triggers volition. With hope in her heart inflamed by desire for the other, the beloved's love assumes the characteristic structure of "faithfulness to constance," and thus only occurs with "reference to the future."[19] The beloved soul desires to remain faithful to the other who loves her — to god, that is, to his or her human lover. She desires to remain faithful because, by assuming responsibility she experiences temporal and spatial orientation through being attended to (as *attending justice*) and by directing her own attention to the other, in her turn, with her ability to respond to that other.

Rosenzweig's *midrash* explores just this phenomenon of "attending to" by exposing the turning point where the soul turns from a state of detached self-concern to one of engaging other-concern. Having been attentively addressed by one who loves her, the soul becomes consciously aware that standing in the light of a love relationship is much better than her previous state. Making a comparative judgment, the soul becomes ashamed of her past darkness and closedness as well as her past inability to break out of her self-enclosed circle all by herself.[20] This judgment leads to the monological declaration by the soul that "I have sinned, in the past."

The importance of the interior monologue is that it establishes a ground fact that serves as that *upon which* the beloved can stand (*stehen*) and confess (*ge-stehen*) that I *was* a sinner. Note again that the verbal act of confessing is associated with the physical stance of standing — the speech–act serves to localize and temporalize the speaker. On the one hand, this speech–act still does not fully meet the *present* demand of god's love-command (or the command of the lover), which is momentary and in the *present*, and thus requires a *presently existing* relation. But on the other hand, the first level acknowledgment opens the way for the second-level acknowledgment of present responsibility to emerge as something currently existing with the verbalized acknowledgment that "I *am* sinning, *now*."

With such an acknowledgment of one's temporally present existence, the fact that the soul *was* a sinner, that is, was only concerned with herself, is done away with. In other words, with the acknowledgment of present responsibility — that one stands in a determined, and thus determining and ordering way to the demands of an other — the disorder (which means lack of responsible relation or determined orientation; that is, indeterminacy) of the past is recognized for what it is, namely, as past and done. By acknowledging my "lack" as a failure in the current demands of a situation of responsibility, I am better able to order my role in the current state of the relationship by systematically understanding and then categorizing the events of my past experience. In other words, when the present is temporally related to the past through connecting current events with past experiences, responsibility can be ordered through processes such as orienting, directing, and determining. Thus, the beloved is *grounded* in the groundless love of the lover, and can begin to freely orient herself to act according to the particular temporal and spatial parameters within which she finds herself.[21]

And indeed, the freely orienting transformation is such that the soul now loves, and *acts*, by *speaking* in another way than she had done in the past. She now loves in the way she has experienced love, namely, with the determined and determining certainty of a speech–act, impelled by an other and with a transcendence of concern for her own self-centeredness. She is now free to love her neighbor in this turn from self-concern to other-concern, in the way god — or another human lover — loves her, namely, as an other. No longer merely concerned with one's own self, the soul can now immediately relate with an other. Her twofold confession/acknowledgment of her past/present status is none other than the soul's own admission of love. Such is the process which the soul enacts in order to liberate herself from the imprisoning "chains of shame," which results in complete, trustful submission to the openness of a love relationship. This peculiar kind of submission initially takes form on a cognitive level by way of an interior dialogue but, as submission becomes conversion, is then translated into a freedom to act, that is, a freedom to openly turn to the face of the other, to *speak*. It is a movement from the isolation of speech-thinking to the social engagement of speech–acting.

III. *The grammar of particularity*

What this means for ethics is that our speech–acts are dictated by, and thus dictate, our language as that determinatively occurs in love relations with other humans. It is determinative because such speech–acts also then dictate the way that we order reality. Consequently, such language events should, and often do, make a difference for the ethical character of our relationships. Statements and propositional logic correspond to the event-orientation of speaking in past-tense categories in a level of discourse that corresponds to the ordering of creation (the things of the world) framed in the logic of categories and species. These expressions of propositional logic deal with objects "simpliciter" and objectivities, and thus are expressed sententially by the object-directed accusative case. However, when we come to the dialogue form that characterizes the actual speaking experiences of an I and a You, the appropriate grammatical form shifts to the imperative. As Rosenzweig notes, it is only in the command form, which structures the interplay of the love relationship dialogue, that the rigidity of the object-like, third person pronouns of creation (he-she-it) is broken.

This is a peculiar kind of *breaking*, however. The movement is not one of displacement and discarding, as might be the case in a grammar based on the appropriating dialectic of a Hegelian kind of logic. Rather, the forms of creation are fulfilled in the relation I–You as an imperative of revelation out of which the I–You relation grew. The I, as subject of experience, is not a thing under things, as in creation, but is determined to be radically individual, that is, so chaotically individual that it is not capable of being classified as merely one other thing among many other things of the same species. In other words, it is singular, which, as such, does not follow the logic of indefinite and definite articles; rather, it is an "individual without species/category." In place of the article distinctions, the proper name emerges as constituting "immediate determination" of the particular individual. Grammatically, the designation of the individual, and the disruption of the objective, can then be sententially expressed by moving attention from the object of the sentence, viz., from the accusative case, to the singular subject of the sentence, viz., the nominative case.

As "singular subject" the individual has her "own category," and thus has no place in the world in the moment of the event(s). Rather, she "carries around [her] here and now with [her]self" such that "wherever [she] is, is a middle point, and where [she] opens [her] mouth, is a beginning."[22] As singular, the subject of experience, then, is the individual in the utterly simplest way, meant either as god or as the human who, in creation, was created as the first individual in the "likeness of god." Rosenzweig does not mean this likeness as literal reproduction, however, since he uses the German phrase *Ehrenbild Gottes*, which means more like an honorary image of god, or an image honoring god. The more important grammatical point, though, is the move from grammatical analysis to speech–act analysis in the way that the singularity, in contrast to reified objectification, is applied to both the first and second persons, namely, either to I or You. With the call by one individual to the other using their own name (which *is* the word of revelation), a "breech is made in the rigid wall of thingness." The ethical significance of this new speech-endowed state of affairs is that whatever (or whoever) has her own name can no longer be a thing, "no longer be at everyone's disposal" as a mere member of a species or category: the spatio-temporal categories that dictate world order are disrupted, the objectivity is broken through the expressed singularity of this unique individual as someone concretely distinguished from the commonality of all others by being designated by her own name.

However, how do "community" and "word" grow out of speaking the name of god or anyone's particular name? Rosenzweig answers by asserting that by verbally confessing-acknowledging the name *in belief* leads to the realization that names are not the wooden emptiness attributed to verbal activity by unbelievers.[23] Rather, the activity of naming is one of "word and fire," and that what it means "to name" is to speak by naming in the sense of designating. This means to confess in the sentence form: "I believe in him" (*Ich glaub ihn*). The logic of the grammar of revelatory speaking leads us to consider the structures inherent in the active assertion of oneself and of my placing trust in an other, of engaging in active, effective, and effecting relationships with a plurality of others beginning from this first speech–act of love.

The problem with both Hegelian Idealist logic and, as we shall see below, a Heideggarian ontological logic, has to do with the ethical orientations that underlie their respective metaphysical suppositions. Rosenzweig argues that Hegel's logic does not allow us to take into account how our human speech–acts condition our interhuman relationships, through not revealing, as Levinas would later also contend, both our destitution and desire in the face of the other. I contend that such an inadequacy is also the case with Heidegger, who diverges as much as Hegel does from Rosenzweig at this critical, ethical juncture. For Hegel (and other Idealists), an underlying metaphysics of substance leads to an apotheosis of art and of placing trust in merely human products and not the producer herself.

Although the ethical ambiguity of Heidegger's position is not as obvious as Hegel's — since Heidegger deconstructs Descartes' metaphysical dualism grounded on the *res cogitans* and *res extensa* in Sections 19–21 of *Being and Time*,[24] it is nonetheless indefensible on this point since the question about the destiny of Da-sein begins and ends with the anonymity of the peculiarly self-referential construct. How Da-sein comes to "know" itself is as an anonymous 'self' and not through some form of human-to-human relational dialogue. Rather, the fundamental concern that is at the core of Da-sein's restive *Angst* is its concern for its constitutional inability to master the Being of beings, which is revealed in the light of "beings" as they remain "things" (*Seiende*) situated in the horizon of the limited possibilities of any Da-sein's ethos of appropriation. As Heidegger's later philosophy of art unfolds out of this beginning, we find ourselves on a path determined by the necessary structures of an ontology of self-referential subjectivity, such that not only an individual Da-sein, but an individual People itself determines its ownmost destiny.

If, by constrast, we follow Rosenzweig's argument for regarding humans holistically with ethical determinations based on inter-human relations, the phenomenon of art, and the artist as such, can only ever be a *part* of being human and by extension any individual artwork can never fully represent reality. Rosenzweig further notes that each human, face to face with any other human, is demanded to think and to act and, insofar as one *does* do so, such an act is only done out of one's total humanity. Rosenzweig calls this philosophy of action speech-thinking which leads to an ethical philosophy of speech–acts. Again, in anticipating what I say about Heidegger below, his claim that art is *the* happening of truth and history because of the way that art discloses the strife relationship of the human with the things of the world, takes shape as a resolute conviction about the descriptive and prescriptive character of our inter-human role in the world that needs to be measured by what Rosenzweig says about the purpose of art.

IV. *The purpose of art: the holistic human*

For Rosenzweig, the artist remains somehow inhuman because she is called to do what humans in general are not called to do, namely, to create a work of art. An artist is called to create what is not natural and to effect something which is removed from the stream of reality, to create something that is without direct precedence and consequence in reality.[25] Adopting such a philosophy of art resists reducing philosophy to such reductionist teachings as determinism and consequentialism, teachings that tend to feed malignant social tumors such as prejudice, racism, and sexism. Therefore, an important task for the artist is to responsibly deal with reality when she takes up her categorial terms, such that by reducing the elements of reality to categories (as concepts) she reveals the indices of the *partial* character of the elements (god world human) and how each stands in relation to the other and not somehow solidifying their status as this or that source for a kind of totalitarian or authoritarian justification. By extension, this task of the artist also holds for any ethical relationship characterized by the form of attending justice, namely, that sort of attention that is directed through the work of art to reveal the artificial character of the work. This is a revelation that thereby awakens the other to awareness of their own self; but even beyond that, to demand of "their own self" the initiation of a response to various levels of relationships. Because of the demand to point out the categorial character of everything that is empirical, while being empirical itself, art "represents" the tendency to be valid *only* for that isolated, separated "whatever" to which it applies. Again, this restricted validation appears quite different to that aspect of Heidegger's theory that art which purports to disclose the materiality of a *thing* and the fundamental (and thus universal) strife of earth and world — the strife of Da-sein with other Da-seins and with the gods. For Rosenzweig, reality is both chaotically contingent and relational, and so he contends that art is necessarily limited in its function to represent reality.

However, that is not his final position since he also contends that art is the only *necessary* empirical half-reality. I alluded to this position earlier and the complete quote is worth citing. Art is limited but none the less necessary because:

If there were no artists, then humanity would be crippled; because then they would be missing the pre-revelation language, through the existence of which alone revelation has the possibility of entering into time as historical revelation and, once there, to indicate what has been from primal time (*uran*) onwards.[26]

Humanity would be crippled because it is precisely as art that revelation is expressed as revelation of both temporally durative and spatially plastic "creation."

But even more importantly, we need art in order for the event of revelation that occurs in a relation to retain its character as disclosure of what was signified. What becomes signified is an *ethical act* of understanding that, through the taking place of the phenomenon of art provides for the possibility of the forming of a self-conscious awareness of one's responsibility for and to an other. But in order for such a self-awareness to occur we also need to learn the context for how art best happens. For Rosenzweig, the revelatory disclosing act of art is only possible in the face of an other human which entails learning to speak with each other as fully human. Learning to speak with others in such a way is possible because as creatures of a creation having already occurred we can become aware of ourselves as individuals of an already existing species. That means that, as humans, we already know how to speak but only in fragmented fashion, because "that which is within was still inexpressible."[27] However, "art, as language of this otherwise inexpressible" allows for the expression of the inexpressible, because speech is always there from the primal depths of creation, from "*uran*." It assumes a precedence over art for Rosenzweig insofar as it enables "the speech-miracle of revelation to [become] the sign of divine creation and, therefore, to [become] authentic miracle."[28] And while this heavily theological terminology veils Rosenzweig's intent, it also serves to point out an important point about the way that humans relate to the world as such, namely, that the extent to which we effectively talk about and refer to *things* in the world corresponds to the extent to which we are aware of our historically situated orientation in the space–time continuum that Rosenzweig calls the courses of reality: creation-revelation-redemption. This is the art-inflected awareness that only becomes possible by way of inter-human speech–acts. This means that, following Rosenzweig's *midrash*, the artist must then sacrifice part of her humanity for the sake of bringing to the world an awakening of the meaningful sensual sense (*Sinn*) of being human amongst humans. Such an embodied sacrifice is the necessary ground for the emergence of the consciousness of just such a series that constitutes the acts that occur which in their turn constitute the courses of reality. Those courses ground our humanity in a creation as past, the revelation of our relational responsibilities in the present, and an expressed demand to direct our individual acts of responsibility toward creating a community of justice in the future. As a way of dealing with both things and people in the world, art not only instigates us to speak, but instigates us to attend to others more closely. And to the extent that we become aware of the origins of such instigated speech–acts is the extent to which those who experience certain forms of art become aware of the horizon that is more ethical, a world of humans on their way to becoming more critically and sensitively responsible to others.

Rosenzweig's *midrash* is just this sort of art form, namely, one that enlivens our sense for the "present" give-and-take character of our ethically determined and determining experience with others. And while it is as unusual to think of art as an experience that can elicit a sense for ethical relations, it is just as unusual to think of *midrash* as art. As an ancient Jewish form of responding to contemporary social relations, the practice of *midrash* occupied an empirically verifiable role of forming the identity of those communities that read their foundation (sacred) scripts together with their attempts to respond to their social conditions. In the next chapter I turn to Rosenzweig's application of this *midrashic art form* to interpret the biblical Song of Songs, a move in the development of his messianic aesthetic.

V. *Accomplishing the aesthetics of ensouling*

In Rosenzweig's formal aesthetic categories, the concept of revelation has less to do with the elements as "stuff" than with how the elements, especially elements-as-humans, relate. In other words, Rosenzweig's choice, like Levinas' after him, is to prioritize ethics over ontology, which means that, reading Rosenzweig through Levinas, a Rosenzweigian aesthetics provides the grounds for an epistemology that is derived from an already established ethical relationship. Standing in an ethical relationship with another means that the "breech in thingness" has been already effected, and that concern for one's referent converts from an anonymous concern for the third person objective (it/he/she), to a personal concern for the one I address as you and who addresses me in return.[29] Indeed, the aesthetic categories themselves, as revelatory-relational concepts, have to do not with breadth of "content," defined as *Inhalt*, which would have to do with creation, but rather with the evaluative intensity of content defined as *Gehalt*.[30] While *Inhalt* connotes that which is contained in something else, as liquid is contained in a vessel, *Gehalt* connotes that which is earned and experienced, and only thus held. Hence, because of its association with the evaluative–intensive kind of "content," Rosenzweig describes the event of revelation as a process of en-souling.[31] Unlike creation, the revelatory event of ensouling is not one of a "setting-free-from" but, rather, one that takes the form of a wrestling-out-of the pre-aesthetic wholeness. Such a process contrasts with the epistemological method established in the hypothetical element "god" where the distinction is made between modes of thinking determined as a "staying-at-home" versus a "running-away-from."[32] In view of the pre-enacted wholeness of the conceptual vision, Rosenzweig maintains that "the pre-aesthetic whole has to sacrifice itself for the sake of aesthetic ensoulment." In the *midrash* that he performs with *The*

Star, such a sacrificial act is similar to that of god as lover forgetting (it)self by intending towards the other as beloved "object." A relationship of "tension" occurs, of *attentive intention*. Any lover who turns out of her or himself and attends to the other bestows priority on that other, thus "ensouling" the other with an intensity of value, of "holding" the other in consideration along the lines of a Benjaminian auratic relationship. But for Rosenzweig, this is not merely a subject–object, dialectical process; rather, it is one in which both subjects — lover and beloved — stand in immediate relation to the whole of their cohering relationship, just differently.[33] What was previously mere *stuff* or *content* as *Inhalt* becomes ensouled content with particular value as *Gehalt*. In other words (that is, in words from other parts of Rosenzweig's text), the revelatory process is a way of talking about how those involved in relating to one another from their respectively isolated and relatively differentiated status as individually created object-things, can be translated into a differentiating process of particular subjects endowed with value — so endowed because each is loved/named/identified in and for her/himself.

But are we not again faced with some variation of the Hegelian three-step dialectic, namely, from the logic that moves us from a general sense of being through the nothing of negation to individualized being, that is, from Sein to Nichts to Da-sein? No: as opposed to a dialectical logic, the initial "stuff" corresponds to a Cohenian infinitesimal nothing, initially designated as non-relational *Inhalt* on its differential way to becoming its own something, valorized as *Gehalt* because of having gone through the process of intending relational attention — establishing the ground for the phenomenon of *attending justice*. In order to bridge the gap, rather than relying on a moment of logical synthesis, Rosenzweig presents the author-as-artist involved in a differential process as that one who sacrifices part of her own humanity for the sake of addressing the other (object-become-subject), thus bringing the individual detail to ensouled life with attentive love. Significantly, Rosenzweig's model of ensouling entails that in each fragmented experience of the process one nonetheless draws on the wholeness of the human:

> It is quite clear, that this ensouling of the stuff, this becoming of the quantitative content to qualitative content does not come from the human as author, rather, it comes from the whole human, in whom the author himself could first originate (*enstehen*).[34]

The author does not lose herself in her work whereas the self, as "manifold totality," forfeits its "wholeness and closedness" and through the self-negating act of self-forgetting, sinks into the "sleeping" stuff until it awakens with life. Dead *Inhalt* becomes enlivened *Gehalt*.

The genius, however, is too "constricted" (*verengt*) to be *able* to love in such a way. Even though the genius *conceives* the work, the work only awakens and *comes to life* in the "love of the human (him)self."[35] The genius of the author is that which conceives a creation (a creature), but it is also that impulse to ever-renew the process of opening the human heart, a process that ensouls the whole work with life. This is what Rosenzweig means by the wholeness of the human. But what exactly is this ensouling process? To ensoul an other, the author, as lover, has to diligently submerge herself in each and every individual detail — in every *Einzelheit*, in every single one of the whole; that is, the author invests herself in that single individual that stands silent and still over against her in order to invest it (or him or her) with the enlivening, ensouling attended-to-tension called life. In doing so, the individual work receives "diligence" via such "rounding" (*rundende*), "love-full" (*liebvolle*), "work of self-forgetting" (*Arbeit des selbstvergessenen*).[36] Just as the artist works passionately with her heart, so the lover "works" with the individual beloved, and so I draw the other out of their own seclusion of self-concern. What Rosenzweig means by "rounding" is the self-forgetting "rounding" that occurs in a kiss of love that rounds the other out of the hiddenness of their tragic seclusion into the possibility of a healthy wholeness, the healthiness of a whole soul.

With such attentive intention, the individual work is brought to life — the work, or beloved, is attended to *as if* it alone existed. The beloved, or detail of the work, is attentively and intentively chosen from out of the many others, bringing her to life. And such diligent attention rewards the artist as well by "bringing (her) to consciousness of (her)self." However, it is not the fullness of her creations but the individual, love-filled figure which awakens the artist to consciousness of her own existence. Creativity is genius and is *self-creation*, but only with artistry occurs self-revelation, namely, conscious knowledge of one's own self as an existing, sentient being that occurs because of the demand to respond to the work. However, the totality of the conception of the work is only realized in the execution of the details, such that love is only complete when each moment, and thus each and every single individual, is enlivened with love. Indeed, this process of completing the work, as the *leading-out* or *singling-out* of the individual aspects, akin to what Husserl describes as the unifying process of whole to parts as "founded acts,"[37] is the precondition for the realization of the whole. In other words, each individual must be ensouled before the entire work can attain completion, thus disclosing for us the importance which Rosenzweig places on attending to details and attending to the chaos of unique and empirically unpredictable individuals.

According to Rosenzweig, the artistic event of creation gave us the presupposition of a whole that projects, via an aesthetic vision, to a plenitude of chaotic particulars. Revelation gives us the same presupposed whole that projects, however, to a plenitude of content-endowed, and thus "ensouled," individuals. Redemption, however, projects from the ensouled individuals to a broad totality of all particulars in a content-ensouled connection as an aesthetically portrayed ideal of what a finished or completed condition might be. While the projected completion is an ideal expectation, that very expectation has relevance only insofar as the immediate sensual effect that a work instigates, its empirically aesthetic character, itself becomes part of life and is set into the process of changing the greater course of the world. That change only happens insofar as an art work aesthetically affects the public audience, furthering Rosenzweig's teaching on art as that sort of activity that directs the artist and the audience away from the experience of art into life. In other words, the mask of the artist — which is the work of art — is not the face of one's neighbor.

VI. *Applying the* midrash: *from art to the ethical*

I understand Rosenzweig's *midrash* on the Song of Songs to be his exemplification of a textual interpretation where the sensual and over-sensual sense of the embodied-in-ritual poem coincides in such a way that reality is transformed through this particular work of art. In the case of this poem, the utterly pagan Song of Songs, Rosenzweig interprets how the bridegroom referred to in the poem is in reality a shepherd and imagining to himself what it feels like to be a king. In this case, the bridegroom–shepherd–king interpretation embodies the process of our own over-sensual and overlapping and thus aesthetically altering process of the sensual texture of our reading. Reading is sensual and effective insofar as it works changes on an extant reality, on us and our extant realities, just as the *midrash* that is Rosenzweig's text itself does. Indeed, what we learn is that this more-than-human dimension of the love dialogue in the "Song of Songs" depends on the very phenomenon of a speech–act as a fusion of sensual utterance with supersensual communication of meaning:

> Since she [love] speaks — and she must speak, because there really is no other speaking-out-from-itself than the speech of love — therefore, since she speaks, she already becomes more-than-human; because the sensuality of the word is full to the brim with its divine super-sense; love is, as speech itself, sensual-supersensual.[38]

In other words, in the actual, physically sensual uttering of the words of speech occurs an experience of how we reference a *beyond* of the presently occurring experience of reality. In the dialogue of love in the Song of Songs, a limit is encountered which separates the one and the other — the man from the woman — indicated by referring to the model presenting the absolute transcendence of god from the human. It is the limit, margin, or "border" (*Rand*), where the connection and division of the one from the other takes place. It is an absolute division because there is no identification of the one with the other, as there would be in a Hegelian dialectic. But what also occurs is the experience of connection, experienced as the relation and through the relation that occurs by means of the very sensual physicality of a speech that ever-recurs as a desire to transgress the very limits that separate one from the other, the desire for absolute connection in order to unite the two in an immanence of wholeness. The brim or "margin" of the word is that which overflows with "other" meanings such that the orienting relevance of the one for the other occurs in how one calls, responds to, is attentive to, or exercises responsibility for the other — in a chaotic plethora of the spilling-over of speech. Such an experience of brimming over with speech is the over-sensual meaning itself that flows over the limit and transgresses the apparently infinitely abysmal border that divides the one from the other. That abysmal division, or border, initially occurs as the separation of the lover from the beloved, but under the demands of desire in the revelatory speech–act of love, the speech–act occurs as the sensually spoken word that endows the event itself with over-sensual, transcendent meaning. Not only does an actual relation between the two formerly isolated selves happen through the speech–acts of love, but the sensually charged phenomenon of actually speaking and responding, as an event in itself, discloses the "divinely" over-sensual transcendent meaning that reorients each of the two immanently "held" in such a relationship, and thereby altering each one of those involved in the process. But what does it mean to be "held" in such an immanental way with reference to some sort of transcendent meaning? And towards what are each of them reoriented?

According to Rosenzweig, in order for the language of love, expressed through poems such as the Song of Songs, to approach such an immanental "holding" entails that the love language of comparison used by lovers in their descriptions of each other, the language of analogy, has to be more than merely ornamental. To love *is* to analogize, to compare, to find eternity in transience — to find in ever-new and unexpected ways the over-sensual in the sensual. For William Blake, it is to "Find eternity in a moment." For Husserl, it is the kind of experience that accounts for "the infinitude of particularizations of the same universal."[39] For Rosenzweig, the event of love does appear to be transitory and thus merely illusory, but that apparently illusory appearance is its very truth: "That appearance is as necessary as this truth; love as love is not able to appear over-transitory [as eternity or duration]; but in the mirror of this appearance love itself immediately mirrors the truth."[40] While appearance is the illusion of truth in an art phenomenon such as Impressionism, Rosenzweig asserts the opposite, namely, that it is precisely with the threads of appearances that we weave the fabric of truth. Said otherwise, what it means for appearances to immediately "mirror" the truth parallels what Rosenzweig says in an earlier section of *The Star* about truth "resounding" as iterations of certain depth structures at various levels of reality.[41] In this case, the ideal structures enacted and embodied in the ritual play that occur in the give and take of the speech–acts of love, actually transform those involved to the extent that the reality outside the closed circle of their relationship can be consequently affected.

What Rosenzweig means by "truth" is that which constitutes the content of the dialogue of love.[42] The activity that is speech, which binds lover and beloved together is the self-revealing, self-forgetting interchange of imperative demand and responsive fulfillment. Moreover, those speech–acts which bind a man and woman in the imperatives and responses of love are referred to as the pattern-setting speech of a god–human relationship, of the fusing of immanent sense and transcendent super-sense.

In Rosenzweig's *midrash*, the beloved initiates another love-action in the way that she has learned to love from the lover, namely, through re-membrance as a unique way of putting together again that which originally transpired in the earlier experience of revelatory love. This acting on her remembrance enables her to break through the limit of the personal into the public domain, empowered with the dictum: "As he loves you, so [should] you love."[43] Rosenzweig interprets this sentence as a speech–act, whereby such an utterance has the double value of being able to provide the initial occasion for comparative recall that then becomes an imperative for prescriptive action. On Rosenzweig's reading, the analogical "*Wie*" (translated, "as" or "how") opens the sentence and evokes the memory of an objective experience, indicated by the use of the third person objective pronoun "he." With the use of the present form of the verb, "he loves," however, (*Er liebt*) the sentence also evokes the present nature of the comparative experience. Moreover, the form of the sentence fragment is highly individualized, and thus is flexible enough to apply to the unique way in which each reader addressed through the text may have experienced a love relationship. Finally, the resolution of the sentence carries the prescriptive form, "so you should" with the present verb form of "love," coupled with the outward, public-facing, word for the familiar "you" (*Du*) occupying the sentence conclusion, thus encouraging an ongoing concern for the next "you." Such an imperative command is thus an ethical prescription that holds universally, but only in the sense that the demand to love another is a demand to love that other who is not identical to me, in the similar but not identical way as I have been loved by one who has not "appropriated" me for his ownmost (Heideggarian) ethos. In other words, I love another in such a non-possessive way that the other is liberated to love the next tragically isolated one who comes along who desires, and thus needs to be loved.

Summarizing Rosenzweig's *midrashic* interpretation: the beloved moves from out of the closed circle of two-aloneness and revelatory love, from the closed circle of that family that produces autonomous individuals, to incrementally build communities step by loving step in the world. This gradual, incremental process occurs by liberating other individuals from their identity forming self-reflexivity and necessarily self-defiant ontological seclusion from that very world. Building on his presentation of the multi-layered dimensions of the dialogical experience of love relationships, Rosenzweig turns to the significance of love relations for broader social relations and community formations. He turns our attention to how the practices of textual interpretation that are now woven throughout our inter-human relationships determine, as well, the essential structures of interrelation that characterize Jewish, Christian, and secular (pagan) communities. The significant new development that Rosenzweig adds to our reading practices is that of ritual. He takes us from the phenomenon of textual interpretations as an aesthetic activity called *midrash* to other aesthetic performances such as community-forming rituals such as Passover (*Pesach*) and the Festival of Booths (*Sukkot*). This latter Jewish festival commemorates the ongoing condition of exile as the time of wandering over the space of the earth, directed to the ideal of eventual rest when the fullness of communication and the Eros of love relations will take place. Meanwhile, though, for Rosenzweig, humans remain essentially restless, with the work of transforming the others of the world into loving ones who are still outstanding. Hence, those who have experienced love are directed — are commanded! — to also love by testifying to the rest of the world about the empirically verifiable effects of love. Those effects have to do with inspiring phenomena such as the dialogue of speech–acts, the formation of love relationships, and igniting the passion to love one's neighbor, one neighbor at a time. For Rosenzweig, the underlying concept that works to cohere those "ignited" loves in the "work" of love is the traditional ideal of those communities that the one god of love alone is god.[44]

Notes

1 cf. Rosenzweig's critique from "The New Thinking" and my treatment of that as "Response to Myriam Bienenstock" with regard to her essay, "Recalling the Past in Rosenzweig's *Star of Redemption*," in Anckaert 2004.

2 See Bambach 1995: 222, 269. The similarity is that in Heidegger's attack on the theory of a meaningful progressive evolution of history he implicates Hegel, Humboldt, Ranke, Rickert, and Meinecke as well. These are seminal figures for Rosenzweig's rejection of historicism as well, especially Hegel and his former mentor, Meinecke.

3 Peshat: a traditionally Jewish method of interpreting textual material that is primarily systematic, used in disciplines such as linguistics, philology, and grammar. See Edward L. Greenstein, "Medieval Bible Commentaries," in Holtz 1984: 217–257.

4 The "Science of Judaism" is the Jewish equivalent of the German "Geisteswissenschaft" referred to above. For a representative example of Rosenzweig's attitude towards this "Science" and Jewish education in general (as well as the phenomenon of Western "Reform" and its impact on training a new rabbinate), see his open letter to H. Cohen, "Zeit Ists . . ." in GS3: 473ff. Rosenzweig criticizes the "scientific production" of the "Science of 'Judaism'" as just another instance of the presuppositions inherent in accepting a "century of the Protestant treatment of the 'Old Testament'." In other words, Rosenzweig

accentuates the need to recognize that the various disciplines of "science" need to be carefully scrutinized for their distortion by the agenda of the Christian world and modern Christianity. It is a re-turn towards a study of the sources (eines Heranführens an Quellen) with a renewed sense of Jewish community (i.e. "Nicht judenschaftliche, sondern jüdischgeistige Organisationen").

5   He is also able to highlight the relation of pagan and believer because of the situatedness of this secular love poem in a collection of "divine" texts.

6   GS2: 174; SR: 156.

7   The importance of the work of art to mediate the initial encounter is that through the mediation of an object, the possibility of doing violence to the other, by laying one's hands on the other, is obviated. The work of art is used to initiate the contact which, after establishing familiarity, can become a tender caress as an expression of desire for the sake of the other (in a Levinasian sense, despite Levinas).

8   GS2: 179; SR: 160.

9   Ibid: 181; SR: 163.

10   See Chapter 3, above, for the discussion of the "Mothers" and the significance of descending and ascending. Prior to the experience of a *relationship*, of love, we remain without orientation in the dark of mere monological reason, categorized by Rosenzweig as the metaphysical realm of thinking about thinking, i.e. the realm of dead objectivity.

11   As I note below in Chapter 5, this process is similar to the phenomenology of authenticity to inauthenticity, of *Da-sein* to *das Man* (or the They) in Heidegger's ontological structures. This can also be compared to Husserl's *epoché*, that is, the movement of intentionality that brackets or parenthesizes the particular object of regard.

12   Bestand: existence, duration; stability; certitude; strength of a unit Beständigkeit: continuance; permanence; stability; faithfulness die Treue: fidelity, faithfulness; constancy, sincerity, honesty bestehen: how one withstands a test or a fight; how one "stands" through a process, i.e. whether one faithfully stays on and "sticks with it" or whether one runs away. It has to do with constancy/duration/certainty and the strength and certainty of one's values.

13   A common phrase in German, "Spruch" means a "saying."

14   GS2: 198; SR: 179.

15   In German, a *Stehendes*.

16   Congealing has to do with how Rosenzweig understands "Dichtung," which means poem. "Dichten" would seem to mean, on Rosenzweig's interpretation, to poeticize in such a way as to draw meaning and sense together in formative relationships and groupings which, because they have been so *drawn together* tend to *make sense* and *endure*.

17   GS2: 199; SR: 179. The italics are my own. The quote in German is: "Ihre Liebe ist, einmal geboren, ein Stehendes, Stetes; so darf sie zu ihr stehen, darf sie gestehen."

18   The play in Rosenzweig's German has to do with the etymological root of the word for reality, *Wirklichkeit*, in the verb *wirken*, which has the sense of effectively working.

19   See 2 Sam. 12.13 and Ps. 51.6.

20 That is, with her own defiant will. Also, note (from GS2: 227; SR: 203) that such a recognition corresponds to the beloved's confession of her "darkness" (as self-enclosedness) in the Song of Songs. It is a darkness, however, that is also determined to be beautiful and seductive (lieblich), because it suggests an unknown pleasure within, like the "tents of Kedar" or the "curtains of Solomon."

21 That is, she is *momentarily* separated (transcended) from her past. See GS2: 203; SR: 181.

22 GS2: 208; SR: 187.

23 GS2: 209; SR: 188: "Of empty shells and smoke (Schall und Rauch)."

24 See Heidegger, SZ, 89–101.

25 See Kant 1951: 1501–51: for his description of the work of the artist as unassimilable, i.e. the unique work of art is created originally, not imitated mechanically: "We thus see (1) that genius is the *talent* for producing that for which no definite rule can be given; it is not a mere aptitude for what can be learned by a rule. Hence *originality* must be its first property. (2) But since it also can produce original nonsense, its products must be models. i.e., *exemplary*, and they consequently ought not to spring from imitation, but must serve as a standard or rule of judgment for others. (3) It cannot describe or indicate scientifically how it brings about its products, but it gives the rule just as nature does."

26 GS2: 212; SR: 190.

27 Ibid: 213; 191.

28 Ibid.

29 Such an address and counter-address is not unlike what Walter Benjamin in another context refers to as "aura," namely, that "Derivation of aura as the projection of a human social experience onto nature: the gaze is returned." See Walter Benjamin, "Central Park" in Benjamin 2003: 173.

30 GS2: 212; SR: 190.

31 Ibid and see GS2: 213ff; SR: 190ff. for distinguishing between "Inhalt" and "Gehalt." At the end, Rosenzweig depicts the Star of Redemption whose "content of Judaism" (Gehalt des Judentums) flames forth with the truth of the oneness of God." See GS2: 457; SR: 411.

32 See the concepts *"Anwohner des Nichts"* versus the *"Entronnener"* at GS2: 26; SR: 24.

33 As an aside, recall the analysis of the respective emergence of the "Yes" and "No" from the Nothing above in the section on metaphysics in Chapter 3 for an analysis of the logic of "wrestled out conceptual meaning." This is a *re-soundence* of that process on another, more complex, level. In terms of chaos theory, the application can be compared to that of a scaling of structures of similarity with self-recursivity. The success of Rosenzweig's project depends in no small measure on the way these sort of anti-dialectical structures permeate his text.

34 GS2: 214; SR: 192.

35 Ibid.

36 GS2: 215–217; SR: 192–194.

37 See Husserl 1980: 1521–56: "§48. Charakteristik der kategorialen Akte als fundierte Akte." But the whole chapter, "Sinnliche und kategoriale Anschauungen"

is germane to Rosenzweig's work in this section, especially what Husserl has to say about *Erfüllungen* of *Bedeutungsformen*.

38   GS2: 224; SR: 221.
39   In the context of how Husserl accounts for determining the universality of a set of particular members in how concepts are formed in relations of comparison. From such considerations, Husserl leads us towards reflections on the relationship of actual particulars to a horizon of infinitely extended possibilities, as "the pure being of the universal." See Husserl 1999: 2862–87.
40   GS2: 224; SR: 201.
41   GS2: 122; SR: 109. By now, this should be a familiar theme in my text. Rosenzweig first refers to "resounding" in the transition section between Parts I and II when he defines the role of the silent language of math (or formal logic) as the common foundation which re-sounds in the spoken speech of "real words."
42   Compare this with what I have to say below about Heidegger's notion of truth as the happening of conflict in the work of art. See Chapters 5 and 6.
43   GS2: 228; SR: 204.
44   GS2: 364; SR: 327.

CHAPTER 4

THE MESSIANIC AESTHETIC

In this chapter, I continue to trace the ethical implications of Rosenzweig's philosophy of art but now for what those implications mean for constructing a socio-political theory out of the threads already drawn from his work. This moves us beyond a philosophy of *Existenz* to a provocative social theory that provides guidelines for developing alternative modes of communal relations other than those that exist today. Those existing modes are founded on a warrant of violence that is justified by claims of absolute independence and that holds for most current forms of national sovereignty.[1]

I. *Partners in immanence*

While passages on the concept of "Revelation" function as the heart of Rosenzweig's *The Star of Redemption*, Book 3 of Part II, passages on the concept of "Redemption" extend Rosenzweig's phenomenology of interpersonal love relations to a social theory that presents a prescriptive kind of thought structure at work in community formations. By entering into those structures we are moved from considering the dynamics involved in forming a private and exclusionary ethical bond with a unique other into reflecting on the possibilities of public structures in a system of social justice that includes both intra-, and inter-community relations. Rosenzweig presents those structures as involving a tension that holds between a proleptic anticipation of a completed work, that is, a complete whole of a relation, and a sense of wholeness that, paradoxically, necessarily remains incomplete. Said otherwise, I personally experience an embodied sense of wholeness in how the artful "drama" of events unfolds over the course of what seems to be my completed, singular life. However, through being singled out and loved and then loving an other in my turn, the singularity of my isolated, individual human existence is revealed to contingently depend on what Rosenzweig refers to as a *sinnlich–übersinnlich* event of a love relation. The double-entendre in German of *sinnlich–übersinnlich* is such that, on the one hand, we are at first inclined to think of a sensual/trans-sensual distinction, that is, of an empirically determined and physically embodied experience that moves us beyond physical embodiment as such and into a conceptual or spiritual realm of experience. But on the other hand, another common connotation of *Sinn* in German is "meaning," which entails that *sinnlich–übersinnlich* can also lead us to think in terms of beginning with a fixed sort of meaning-structure and then, at the same time, opening up to an unexpected meaning structure that is not determined by the systematic constraints of the initial meaning structure. This is the connotation of the *über-* in *übersinnlich*, which carries us beyond the initial framework in such a way that I am set into an unpredictable and indeterminate chain of events. That chain is intrinsically open and not able to be completed; if it were actually able to be fully completed, if we could experience absolute fulfillment, then that would be the end of time and the end of our world. But according to my understanding of Roseznweig's work, we can and must envision the ideal of such a fulfillment. In aesthetic terms, Rosenzweig presents the tension involved in a love relation in terms that include what I have suggested can be a chaotic dimension of patterned unpredictability, that is, as the empirically contingent and essentially ephemeral relationship of a lover and beloved that is always blind and unsusceptible to the visionary categories canonically reified out of the history of philosophy. What this means is that if I reveal myself to an other in the kind of relation that Rosenzweig characterizes as love, then I necessarily remain at risk and vulnerable, unable to determine or predict the actual course of events of that relationship. However, while I lose a sense of stable predictability, I gain the fullness of vitally experiencing the range of sorrows and joys that only becomes possible through remaining vulnerable in engaging in the risky relation of loving others. Only by accruing these sorts of actual "fulfillments" can the world move closer to a redeemed state where humans and other beings live enduringly "full" and thus satisfying lives with each other. Such extensions of the work of love relationships form the core of Rosenzweig's social theory.

If the next moment in the event of love in such a relationship was able to be predicted, that would reduce that moment to merely a utilitarian means for calculating a fixed propositional state of affairs. Rather, the tragic and sovereign seclusion of the autonomy of singular aloneness is broken into and interrupted as I am called by the other to respond to her particular and unforeseeable desires, while simultaneously desiring that particular other beyond the static categories of any possible comprehension. Precisely because of the openness to and attraction towards an unaccountable other, the relationship itself takes on a character of open-ended wholeness, as each member in the relationship — the lover and the beloved — stand face-to-face and then embrace in a kiss in order to enclose their "covenant" of trust with each other. The kiss, as sensual contraction, is also the next step in building a relationship of trust with that particular other that provides the basis for community formation. Such formations would not make any sense, however, unless our actual organic and existential conditions were taken into account. In fact, love can be *as* strong *as* death only because acts of love join formerly isolated and tragically singular individuals into enlivened and colorfully comparative relationships of passionate movement towards, for, and with each other. Through being called by and responding to each other's personal name the complex process of intertwining personal histories begins as does the process of ordering more closely and ascertaining more concretely the unaccountability of the other. But Rosenzweig notes at the end of Part II, Book 2 that the union "ends" with a cry, a cry of prayer and of hope and utter longing that such a relation will continue, that is, that it will endure beyond its fragmentary character. Such a cry happens because the experience is the experience of an immediate and sensual/trans-sensual being-at-one-ness with the other, a union that must necessarily remain incomplete. For lack of better words, the experience is of transcendence *in* immanence, of a taste of infinity in the very finite experience of transitoriness and ephemerality, which is also an intimation of the full actualization of ecstatic satisfaction.

The cry occurs as a yearning for a public commitment and completion that would signify the publicly visible formation of an enduring bond of relationship. For Rosenzweig, such an enduring bond takes the form of publically committing to a marriage that includes the possibility of rearing children, and is thus directed towards the future. However, that Rosenzweig relies on the Song of Songs to carry his intention of building on the pagan, non-denominational element of an utterly sexual and sensual love poem means that he roots an ethical relation in the phenomenon of a direct encounter that is openly available to anyone, any pair, anywhere and at anytime. We speak words of love to each other in just this way of a love song, played out between humans for thousands of years in poems such as the Song of Songs. But it is only the Song of Songs that Rosenzweig trusts because, he claims, these are words that were previously sung in his community by others as immemorial witnesses to the efficacy of just those words sung with just that harmony, with just that rhythm, and with just those lyrically intended meanings. Indeed, the Song of Songs is one text in a body of traditional texts that comprise the Torah, a set of texts that testify to the historical verity, and thus to a certain kind of predictable stability of an institutional, communal way of life that has love and ethics at the core of its relational praxes. Adopting such a song means learning to sing along, but in such a way that the words that we use are both determined and yet indeterminate since our *own* love song to an other relies both on the comparatives available to us in just this love song *but also* on our own inimitable lived experience. The important difference is that our song is primarily and necessarily dictated by an actual other whose organic face, skin, eyes, body, experience, and spirit appears otherwise than this or that universal "model" of pre-existing relationships. Because of its multi-valent roots in both an utterly pagan context (its affirmation of our organic roots) and its appropriation in the body of texts of the Jewish and Christian peoples, the Song of Songs exemplifies the phenomenon of a multi-textual tradition, of a tradition with texts calling for other responses, other texts, and other voices. Drawing on such a multi-textual, multi-voiced tradition, Rosenzweig turns to another textual voice from that tradition within a greater community of texts and voices, the Book of Psalms, in order to direct our attention to how, in at least this tradition, the welcoming of the other occurs as an act of redeeming the world.

Unfortunately, given the intractable tendency of humans to prefer and defend their own kind, to form identities over against any other who is dissimilar by way of violating their very otherness, we have to search for alternative means that may be provided for redeeming an apparently hopeless world. At least one of those possibilities could be Rosenzweig's alternative. But in a world governed by the *Realpolitik* of recycling and dialectically reincarnating violence from one generation to the next, is the alternative provided by Rosenzweig — pre-Holocaust — capable of adequately addressing the claims made by several contemporary scholars that the twentieth century has been "the century of genocide?"[2] Such difficult but important questions can only be addressed by facing what some postmodern intellectuals (such as Jean-François Lyotard) have done by challenging historically conditioned forms of narrative and the subsequent fragmentation of modern communities.[3] For us this takes on the specific form of exploring the relationship of myth and history out of Rosenzweig's political context. That is, taking seriously the criticism that adopting a form of social ethics out of an aesthetically applied theory such as Rosenzweig's, results in fleeing the political cauldron of historical developments to, somehow, to hide within the confines of Jewish community life so as not to have to deal with the challenges that confront us in choosing one political path over another. Such criticisms are superficial assessments of Rosenzweig's social ethics that caricature his meta-historical approach as ahistorical, an approach that is much more closely aligned with a Benjaminian philosophy of history than, say, a Cohenian approach.[4] Structuring one's daily life through the rituals of the meaning-endowments of a faith community that resists an absolute commitment to any particular political ideology, a commitment that entails signing on to the social contract that one may have to give up one's life violently defending one's country in a military conflict, for example, rules out the possibility of retaining any sort of ongoing critical *differand* to existing political systems. This was precisely what happened in the case of the totalitarian policies of the Nazis. As Hannah Arendt argues in *The Origins of Totalitarianism*, the primary principle animating modern fascist political systems that are totalitarian is their inability to allow for any element that is other than the dominant and domineering ideology.[5]

But an even more important question that emerges, given a Rosenzweigian version of a social order, has to do with the ability of any social system that presupposes a legal structure based on preserving the stability of its own autopoietic existence, namely: can it at all allow for actual dissent and difference? This is the case that Niklas Luhmann made in the middle of the twentieth century in *Law as Social System*.[6] Luhmann's complex argument depends to a large degree on accepting the relatively straightforward thesis that systems incline towards preserving themselves in an organic analogy to biological homeostasis. Rosenzweig's position, by contrast, inclines towards the ongoing creation of unexpected and unpredictable elements of diversity which are not, however, understood as endemic to the system as such but, in fact, promote its greater flourishing and health by preserving a fundamental diversity in form and actual production. These are some of the theoretical considerations at stake for my overall thesis in this book. Indeed, they are the most salient issues at stake in bringing Rosenzweig and Heidegger into the kind of phenomenological orbit that I construct in these pages. A Rosenzweigian perspective is a *midrashic* one that demands concentrated attentive justice, and ultimately, concerted action.

While the meaning of existence results in tragic but autonomous defiance in the development of the human in Part I, seen through the prism of the *midrash* on the Song of Songs, the meaning of existence crystallizes in the passionate sacrifice of one's defiant independence to listen and respond to the desires of the loved one, fracturing one's wholeness for the sake of the other. But Rosenzweig turns to again re-figure that wholeness and does so through considering the "drama" of life. Unlike the tragic hero of Greek drama who is visible but ineffective, or the self-enclosed figure of the mystic saint who can only wait for god to come again to him in a mysteriously divine enrapture, Rosenzweig looks to establish connections between the loved human-become-lover and the world. He seeks to establish connections of actual, historical effectiveness and in order to do so, the human has to become whole (*der Mensch zun ganzen Menschen erschließt*) by doing one's own effective (*wirksam*) acts in the world. In the modern era, the human was thrown into the world as a "whole human" similar to the aesthetic phenomenon of the new tragic hero in modern tragic drama, and is thus "very human and all his limbs quiver with the sound of mortality."[7] But what is very new in the modern tragic drama is that the human on the stage compels the spectator in the audience into a dialogue, into a "feeling of being his occasional-partner-in-speech" (*das Gefühl seines Mitunterredner*). Unlike in Greek tragedy, the spectator does not identify with the actor in an Aristotelian catharsis of fear and compassion but rather, is drawn into contradiction and a sense of being torn out of their bond with the other. This breaking of the bond, so to speak, becomes a critical moment in Rosenzweig's explanation of the process of redemption, since the word redemption in German, *Erlösung*, means "to release (from)," which literally means a loosening of a bond. As part of a general theory of aesthetics, this moment of loosening is important because it marks a departure from classical Aristotelian aesthetics that relies on his substance ontology of a stable character with fixed attributes. The consequence for ethics of this sort of ontology is that one remains fixed in their character and always only on the verge of engaging in life with merely informed premonitions of changes that are ontologically impossible, whereas in modern tragic drama the spectator's volition is aroused and becomes engaged in a fluid world order of change and becoming.

Perhaps even more importantly for Rosenzweig is that this "new" development — that the spectator's "will" is aroused and not their mere cognition

ails an ethical imperative to act out of the two-alone-ness and momen-
ess of the love relationship. Without the sense of being-torn-out-of (one's
s~ iusion) and arousing of one's will, or drive, there could be no turning to the
next one "beyond" the chosen one. Precisely here, Rosenzweig's "messianic
aesthetics" come into view, that is, the "next one" is chosen in the same form as
a messiah is singled out — which is what I call Rosenzweig's messianic politics.
A few years later, and with the benefit of having read Rosenzweig's *Star*, Walter
Benjamin would refer to this form of treating the other by caring for their material needs and spiritual desires and by a sighting-through-attentive-singling-out
of the coming generation. He called this a "weak messianism."[8] Discerning the
cues of my social relations along Rosenzweigian lines, I learn to treat the next
one as I have been messianically chosen — each next other who comes along
becomes the sole object, for that transitory moment of attentive loving, of my
creative love. S/he is singled out and chosen from the crowd in a play of choosing and being chosen in an asymmetrical, anachronic, and dynamic process of
caring for needs and desires. In anticipation of the Heidegger section of my
text that follows, having recourse to such a messianic aesthetic that includes an
ethical dimension of historical effectiveness undermines Heidegger's setting of
the problem of the meaning of existence in terms of an implicit ethical dialectic
of authenticity and inauthenticity.[9] To preempt my conclusion, Rosenzweig's
position undermines Heidegger's primarily on a normative level because of its
resistance to being reduced to an ontological play of categories that, on the one
hand, is inevitably and necessarily self-aggrandizing and, on the other hand,
contributes to a totalizing philosophy.[10]

Their ethical divergence again comes into anticipatory focus here by
considering how Rosenzweig treats the tragic hero versus the saint — the holy
one, in the first sections of Part III of *The Star*. As we will see, the difference
between tragedy and celebrating holiness plays an important role in Heidegger's
philosophy as well. Relying on his analysis of the solitary self, Rosenzweig
explores this difference through implementing various forms of speech–acts
used by different actors as a way of distinguishing between the historical genres
of classical tragedy and modern tragedy. For example, the form of speech that
characterizes classical tragedy is monologue, which he characterizes as only a
momentary span of consciousness in an I-standpoint.

Considered historically, modern tragedy gives us the possibility of the
phenomenon of multi-perspectivalism. This represents an advance over
classical tragedy in structuring relationships in the world but still relies on a
monologue to express relationships of absolutes, namely, a relationship of an
absolute human to an absolute object. Rosenzweig notes that there are many
"I"s in modern tragedy, whereas, by contrast, in Antiquity there are many
actions but only the same defiant self. Monologue in classical tragedy gives us
the view of the hero mediated through the chorus, but "It is never more than
a view of the world and one's own position in it from one's specific point of

view, that is, that of the individual own I."[11] By contrast, modern tragedy, and thus modern aesthetics, creates multiple I-standpoints, differentiating it from Antique tragedy of action as a tragedy of character. Hence, the best modern tragedian is a philosopher — an absolute human relating to an absolute object who represents his characters as "absolute" heroes, such as a Hamlet, Wallenstein, or Faust. Goethe's heroic figure, Faust, is also a philosopher but one who is tragically driven to appropriate each and every experience of the world as his own to the exclusion of respecting all others. For Rosenzweig, Faust is a modern philosophical tragedy that attempts to move the hero out of his tragic isolation, but fails to do so because it maintains the defiant arrogance of absolute subjectivity.[12]

Combining historical commentary with phenomenological analysis, Rosenzweig argues that the goal of all modern tragedians is to write a drama of Faust, an absolute tragedy that replaces the multiplicity of character with one absolute character. The new "modern" hero would be one who would retain his absolute sameness of defiantly tragic self-enclosure as did the classical hero. However, he would also be the convergence point that cuts off all other tragic characters by uniting in one "absolute human" the power to not only cognitively "see" the absolute over against himself as one who has experienced the absolute, and out of this experience also lives in the absolute. But, Rosenzweig demurs. Such a character is still only a philosopher, a human, regardless of discipline and profession and even though he faces the absolute in his defiant and arrogant self-seclusion he can never live "within" the absolute. Hence, in order to break through this impasse, Rosenzweig contends that all modern artists basically attempt to "supplement Faust with Don Juan, to magnify the tragedy of *Weltanshauung* into a tragedy of life" by including the passion of thwarted and misguided "love." Rosenzweig asserts that characters such as those of the Faust-dramas can only approach but never reach beyond their tragedy and isolation because they remain stuck in a limited life, limited to their absolute subjectivity.

The one who reaches beyond this limitation and enjoys living in the absolute is the saint — the holy one, the healed one, the whole one — *der Heilige*. For Rosenzweig, only the servant of god, the holy one, is able to do so because she is that one who serves others — according to her own *Daimon* (one's particular spirit) — that is, as an expression of her own "Art" that she has learned by traveling down into the depths of the underworld of her own creative spirit. Ironically, however, even the saint needs the help of Mephistopheles and the keys of "nothing" in order to learn that her human life of character is given direction by having been loved in the first place. She needs art. But the direction that she is given and by which she is defined is the command to love one's neighbor (*Liebe zum Nächsten*), that is, to love the next other she meets in her lived world. The saint, however, lives absolutely in the absolute, in a tragedy that is only ambiguously possible for the modern tragic poet or character but is a way of life that is the antithesis of the condition of the Antique tragic hero, that is, the antithesis of tragic seclusion. The saint is the complete one who lives absolutely in the absolute and is, therefore, "disclosed to the highest [as] the disclosed human [who stands] in contrast to the hero, [who is] enclosed in the ever-same darkness of the self."[13] The "holy one" has experienced being loved and the awakening of desire, which is overpowering enough to transform tragic defiance into humility, breaking the encrusted, reified self as a movement opening towards and for the other who has turned to the self despite its own arrogant disrespect of that other.

But besides the overflowing power of love-as-desire, Rosenzweig claims that another power has to break forth from the soul in order to not only "drive" the holy healed one towards the next one, but to give constancy and structure to the ardor (*Inbrunst*) of the holy one so that the holy one does not resort to a mystic aloneness.[14] For Rosenzweig, this entails factoring in the temporal process of structural formation aimed at a redemptive future. The source for this additional structuring power comes from within the nature of the self: while desire stems from the "hotly cooking defiance" of the self, it turns into humility, the other dimension of the self which is its "calmly standing water." This latter source of calm reserve is its way of being as character, its own uniquely peculiar way of being human.[15] Such peculiarity is also what Rosenzweig means when he speaks of how the *Daimon* of each human being, after having been loved, becomes compelled to seek a way to express its inimitable uniqueness into the open, in the "face" of the public. The way that human "nature" works for the tragic hero in Anitquity is that the assertions of defiance which result in the ever-more-enclosed figure of the tragically silent self are "affirmed" by the constancy of character, a character, which is a result of a conclusive mixing of the elements. This constancy of the tragic hero is just what makes him a hero, thus eliciting sympathy from the spectators since the hero is "stuck" with his tragically flawed character and its uneven mixing, given that he is "stuck," he can only be pitied and not ethically transformed.

Upon having been loved and attended to precisely in one's uniqueness as the chosen one, the character of the modern tragically enclosed figure is stimulated to turn inward in order to *transform* the conclusive affirmation into "a source of an ever-renewed self-negation of its origin, the enclosed self, to become that which is wrestled out of itself."[16] This is the new work of what Rosenzweig calls the ensouled self which, in the terms of his theological narrative, he describes as analogously assimilating to the process of the loving, creative god by spontaneously renewing oneself in every moment through the taking on of passion while remaining true to the destiny of its own force (*die schicksalhafte Gewalt*). But the problem is that, while both processes are similar in their momentariness, destiny does not impel the human in the same way as it does the god, rather character does. There is no "must" that necessarily drives the human; a particular *Daimon* does. Early in his text, Rosenzweig differentiates personality from character, defining personality as that which emerges on the occasion of one's birth while character is a relative latecomer, suddenly overcoming the human, one day, one moment — like being chosen out of a crowd for no apparent reason whatsoever. But the distinction that Rosenzweig makes is even more important for my thesis, that is, that while personality institutes an enclosure (*Anlage*), the event of "emerging character" creates a division from the multiplicity of enclosures, from other selves. Once a human is "possessed" by her *Daimon*, she is given a direction which she then has for her entire life and that determines the path along which her "will" runs, determining each and every relationship for the rest of her life. In fact, receiving such directedness signifies an ethical orientation as well: "Since he has received direction (*Richtung*), he is already, in truth, judged (*gerichtet*). Because that which in the human underlies judgment, the essential will, is already fixed once and for all in its direction."[17] What is striking in this passage is how clearly Rosenzweig establishes the connection between the possibility of directed orientation, an ontological phenomenon, and an ethical condition, that of being judged. Rosenzweig makes the connection by way of semantically playing with the terms for direction, "*Richtung*," and judgment, "*Gericht*," which share the same etymological root. To concretize the connection, he uses the past tense form of the verb for directed, "*gerichtet*," to refer to how the will is fixed and to insure that we do not miss the double *entendre*.

The more important point is that the direction and judgment are themselves both interrupted. Rosenzweig notes that they are "broken up" (*unterbrechen*) and strengthened with the call of the other in revelation, precipitating an inner conversion. The willful direction remains willful direction but with the inner conversion it changes from being "fixed once and for all" to become "capable of renewal and of actual renewal of itself."[18] But such a re-working is neither short-lived nor arbitrary; rather, in every one of the individual acts of willfully directed character, "the whole force of the firmly directed character which has merged in it" becomes able to be applied.[19]

What breaks out of the human in this ever-new force and with one's whole will is the love that was given to the human coupled with the revelatory commandment to love. More specifically, the force takes form as a command to "love one's neighbor" (*die Liebe zum Nächsten*). It is "commanded" and not merely as a consequence of freedom, because it presupposes having already been called, having already been chosen, attended to, and loved. This is an important ethical point, since Rosenzweig points out that only in loving one's neighbor, and thus fulfilling the "command to love" one's neighbor, is the human first able to express herself. What makes Rosenzweig's claim even more compelling for an aesthetically charged ethical theory is in how he argues that such an expressive act is other than any other moral act, specifically those that are typically dictated by the normative formalism of Kantian moral law. But it is also other than the ontological ethics described in Hegel's philosophy.

What distinguishes the command to love one's neighbor from the moral law is the matter of content embodied as a matter of an "act of love" in the sense of a very concrete acting (*Handeln*) in the world. As Kant makes clear, the demand of "autonomy" entails that any act that has its origin in the will must be free and pure of any determination, of any content.[20] If there were a content, a something or a someone that determined the will, then the will would lose its absolute freedom and thus its autonomy. Kant begins his famous argument for the moral law by asserting that it is the will that is good in itself that enables us to act ethically and that the human has the ability to simply will. Consequently, every human being — as rational — stands in need of guidance by the formal and necessary guidelines of the universal and universally binding "moral" law. Rosenzweig counters that any will that acts without content necessarily results in uncertainty.[21] As Rosenzweig points out, the consequence of such logic is that, if everything in morality is uncertain then nothing is "certainly" moral. By contrast, instead of a merely formal law of morality, the command to love one's neighbor is clear and concrete and springs from the directed will of the freedom of character. The content is "to love" the other who comes into one's immediately sensual proximity and is based on having already been loved and is thus invested with the "memories" of particular, historical concretions.

II. *Growing the world — one dialogue at a time*

As Rosenzweig tells us, the speech–act of love wills the world to grow in life while the world waits for the act of love to enliven it, which is itself a compelling of the act of love.[22] For Rosenzweig, the impulse to turn to one's neighbor begins with the combined experience of fullness (*die Fülle*) and desire of the heart (a *wirken* of the *Wollen*) for another experience of being-at-one in love, of completed yet unattainable fullness, since ". . . in the heat of the overflowing heart, the soul — healed, whole, and holy — seeks the way to the next one."[23] The ensouled self "works" by turning to the next one, and thereby eternally anticipates its way in the waiting world. The process is also fundamentally temporal and entails a growing world which, by its very growing, compels the act of love to work into infinity because the drive to love is waited for and is expected to occur in every next occurring instant. Thus, the freedom of the drive to love is, like the flow of time itself, bound to the next one who holds the place for the most distant one, since "the waiting of the world binds the work of the human" in such a way that humans, as such, are unresolvable. They are bound together and cannot loosen themselves from each other: "They can not free themselves (*nicht auslösen*) from this reciprocal bond; because insofar as they attempt to unbind themselves from each other, they only bind themselves faster to each other."[24] In looking forward, Heidegger handles this specific issue by constructing an "in-the-world" conceptual complex, where the human as

Da-sein is thoroughly bound up with its care attachments to other beings in the world, primarily and for the most part as things and inauthentically. The more one attempts to be free, that is, to forget one's condition of being bound to the world, the more one gets entangled in that which is not one's own. As we shall see, Heidegger attempts to solve this problem of inauthentic reified entanglement through the spiritual phenomenon of decisiveness.

But for Rosenzweig, unlike for Heidegger, the process of "redemption" is not understood as a process of coming to a separating and resolute decisiveness. Instead, the process of awakening and enlivening, as well as the process of compelling inclusion, is one of a song of dialogue:

> The awakening of the soul happens in the dialogue (*Wechselrede*), which emerges (*anhub*) with the awakening of the root-I of its awakener. But the redemption of the soul in things, of the things that happen through the soul in the duet sung in the same breath (*gleichatmenden Zweigesang*) of the both, in the sentence, which rings out of the voices of both words. In redemption the great And closes over the rainbow of the All."[25]

And for Rosenzweig, this And of joining otherwise disparate elements into a common song does not reveal itself in one of the root-words, such as Yes or No, but in a root-sentence. Considered in this way as a speech–act, redemption reflects the process of joining two apparently separate terms into a unit of meaning, such as a sentence. It is the "sign of the process" (*Zeichen des Prozesses*) that "lets the completed structure that has emerged grow."[26] But this connection is neither the Kantian synthesizing of "given" or "dead material," which results in cognition and re-cognition, nor is it the natural bridge between logic and spirit of Hegel's three-step dialectic of thesis, antithesis, synthesis. It is, instead, a process that is inherently messy because it depends on the unpredictable particularity of an unannounced other who appears as she wills, when she wills, and in no fixed place in particular. In that way of appearing, the other is utterly singular in their particularity, or should be.

The other should be particularly other, but for Rosenzweig the other as a particular human is so bound up with the world that, between the human and world a third is needed to un-bind them, to loosen them and create some distance from one to the other, to *er-losen* the two, that is, to redeem them by freeing them from each other. This happens when the "third" interrupts the two bound together by a "process" which is unlike the two other life-courses, creation and revelation, which occur as uni-directional processes. God creates the world in order that it can grow as an organic and natural creature; and god calls the human by name so she can open her mouth as disclosed soul. But with human and world, the two are bound together from the beginning and each refers to the other in the same ways and at the same time. And so Rosenzweig says that we need to turn to that particularly contingent one next to us, our neighbor, who represents the other as such — "the neighbor is the other" — a condition that holds for all beings in the world. And the awakening of the soul in things, in any-thing, only happens in the duet of a song sung together: "But the redemption of the soul in the things, of the things through the soul, happens in the simultaneous duet of the both, in the sentence, which out of the voices of both words sounds together. The great And of the rainbow of the All concludes in redemption."[27]

Moreover, this process is unlike the instrumentalization of nature, as merely a bridge between logic and spirit that was institutionalized by Hegel's unifying three-step dialectic in his encyclopedia.[28] With this critique, that is, that the And is not the synthetic result of a conceptual series of theses and syntheses: "it comes to no dialectical process." Instead, Rosenzweig refers to a process of duality that gives equal weight to both members of the pair that work on each other. Resorting to his peculiar fusion of grammatical/theological construction, he contends that both subject and predicate have to be uttered simultaneoulsly in order for redemption to work its loosening effects on those who have engaged with each other:

> And since it must become a sentence, which must be spoken from both sides at the same time — actually two voices at one (*zweistimmig*) — thus such an I can not remain I; human and world must be able to sing with the same breath. In the place of the divine I, that only god can speak, the divine name has to emerge, which the human and world can also carry in their hearts. And of it, it is said: it is good.[29]

The root sentence is "he is good" which recalls the transitional movement from creation to revelation where the "it is very good" (*Tov meod*) judgment about creation and the creation of mortality is made that initiates the *midrash* on death and love through the centerpiece, the heart-piece, of the text. In the instance of the work of redemption, however, Rosenzweig weds the *Tov* (good) with the creation of community and the enduring condition of immortality. In the former case, the judgment was made about the impersonal beings, or things, of creation before the personalizing and enlivening event of revelation. With redemption, we move to the context of a particular and personal relationship, indicated with the third person article, but with an indeterminate referential source. This is also what Eric Santner astutely refers to as "interpellation without identification."[30]

Rosenzweig interprets this Psalmic verse in order to develop his case for the ethical intention of the choral form of group activity. The choral form is a dialogue that oscillates between two and which becomes the song of the many. Moreover, it is a song of love whose root sentence is the content of common community chant and itself expresses the development of a history in how to consider the function and the form of the sentence itself. We move from the lifelessness of a symbolic logic as the dictation of philosophical analysis, to the two-dimensionality of how individuals, as individual parts are connected in the telling of and attending to the stories of each other to, finally, how the whole rises from a *Zwiegespräch*, a dialogue of two, to an *Urgesang*, a primal song, of a plurality (*von mehreren ist*).

And the form of the song of the choral gathering has to be an indirect, dative case cohortative: "let us thank." Using the cohortative transforms the imperative of the command to love into a community instituting function. The demand (*Aufforderung*) to join in a common song of thanksgiving is an urging to express thankfulness for the gift given in ethical goodness: "Let us thank him . . . because he is good." It is a thankfulness for the gift given in love and of how to love. It takes form as thanks for fulfillment, but also as anticipation of an eternity of thanksgiving for the love of the other that happens today, that is, a thanks for the fullness which satisfies but which also awakens the desire to give love to other others in turn, from the fullness of one's own heart and home. By igniting the desire to give as one has been loved, a drive begins to love the next one who is separated in their tragic, defiant loneliness to join in the renewed bonds of a group dynamic that is non-possessive and non-coercive.

One does this by developing a community of commonality that is based on a face-to-face relationship. Because I have already been loved and have had my desires and needs met (for the time being), I am able to love another. And in the quasi-fulfillment of experienced abundance I am better able to meet the desires and needs of those lonely others who are bound to the demands and hardships of the world in their common neediness, in their hunger and their tears. And this is accomplished by transforming the plurality of things into a duality of souls that then leads to the love of the next one, but as a loving of that next only in their singularity. "In the song of the All, is added a strophe, which can only be sung by two individual voices — from mine and my neighbors (*Nächste*)." But the neighbor turns into a plurality of pairs such that, "where something or someone has become neighbor to a soul, there a piece of world has become something it was not previously, soul." As Rosenzweig notes, what occurs in the process of being loved as that being is loved, itself kindles "a brimming-over urge towards [another] act of love."[31] But, in fact, the loved one barely sees the neighbor and just loves the next "something" that comes into his proximity, no matter who or what that something might be. In this sense, love is blind and rejects the philosophical counsel of relying for certainty on the visibility of our conceptual structures. But for Rosenzweig, his transformed philosophy of language as the spokenness of speech, is never far from the surface of his text as the preferred method for explicating the intimacy of the ethical with our speech–acts. This is evident in his logical constructs of the process of how something is set into motion from the passive rigidity of its closed-within-itself subjectivity, redeemed to the possibility to act as a form of speech–act:

The verb, itself an indefinite copula, unites the sentence and thereby first provides the adjectival generality of the predicate with substantival fixity and uniqueness, while transforming the substantive into a subject. By the same token, once it has itself assumed definition as to content, the verb as word of action remains directed, by the subject, toward whatever object is placed before it, without choice in the matter yet withal delivering the object from passive rigidity to movement, the subject from self-seclusion to action.[32]

However, although loving one's neighbor through such speech–acts frees her through immediately engaging her in the sensuality of needs and desires and frees her from passive rigidity to the movement of acting, that acting is precisely uncertain. In fact, Rosenzweig maintains that "uncertainty" (*Unbestimmtheit*) is the sign of the act of love.

Although there are many points where the divergence of Rosenzweig and Heidegger can be clearly stated, perhaps no other point is more significantly distinct than where Rosenzweig elaborates what it means to bring something or someone into actuality, what he calls *Verwirklichung*, literally, to make something actual.[33] By way of explication, a short rehearsal of Rosenzweig's speech–act logic and the play of determinacy and indeterminacy in the other parts of his text is in order. When he first introduces a logic of grammar in the section of his text specifically dealing with what he calls creation, the movement is from *indefinite* article to *definite* article, that is from indefinite to definite, and the concentration is on that which is pre-substantive or pre-nominative. In the section on revelation, the movement is entirely within that which is defined, from the singular individual with her own name called in her particularity and only in her own particular — defined — way. It is all calling, all voice, all *be-stimmen*. In the realm of redemption, however, the movement is from that which is defined to the indefinite, from the *Bestimmte* to the *Unbestimmte*. Redemption is specifically directed to the next one, but the relation is not to some indefinite something or someone that is subordinated to one's certainty. Rather, one sets oneself in a relation to which one gives priority, to one within which there is a definite that is *übergeordnet* and not *untergeordnet*, that is, I do not subordinate myself to that which is superior or more powerful, but prioritize myself to an order of what Rosenzweig calls the "entirety of the defined ones, the All."[34] Finally, from the fragmentation of the Hegelian All that Rosenzweig announces at the end of his introduction, our guide has led us to the re-membered (re-constructed) All, the All of all those who have been called by and into the activity of loving one's neighbor, one's indeterminate "next one" — the *Irgendeiner*. But there is a certainty to which it relates, and that is a certainty that is not underneath it (*untergeordnet*) but, rather, since it is "completely undetermined (unbestimmte — uncalled)" it relates to that which is "completely determined (bestimmte — called)" which is not the individual, but the totality of all that is determined or called — the "all." And this reconstituted All is what Rosenzweig calls "The absolute factuality." Earlier in his analysis in this text, and in his essay "The New Thinking," Rosenzweig calls this condition "absolute empiricism."[35]

The goal of this duet-become-choral phenomenon is to actualize a community that can sing together in unison as a "We-all" who are all together with each other. This brings to mind the kind of community that Levinas would refer to as the community of all those who could see each other face-to-face.[36] For Rosenzweig, the dual has become the We of the newly developed allness — mysteriously prefigured by the structuring of the sexes, by the pairing together of male and female, of man and woman — which bring together the first visible ordering of the world. But in general, the new community consists of all those who have been called to sing together, each in their own way but according to the same rhythm and harmony of the indefinite determinism of the dative: "All voices have here become independent, each sings the words according to the way of their own soul, yet all of the ways coordinate themselves according to (*sich fügen*) the same rhythm and bind themselves to the one harmony."[37] As I noted in the Introduction and will elaborate below, Heidegger's sense of *sich fügen* has to do with subordinating oneself to one's destiny, one's fate as one's *Geschick*, in the sense of obedience to the dominating order, rather than being called to sing in one's own voice in the company of particularized others, despite his logic of authenticity — or perhaps precisely because of it.

One of the consequences of forming such a particularized-yet-communal structure, and is a consequence that Heidegger deals with as well in *The Origin of the Work of Art*, is that in coming to an inclusive/exclusive self-definition of a community, a community that sings according to the same harmony and rhythm, a judgment has to be a made, by a *Gericht*, which both judges who is in and who is out as well as determines the direction for the community itself. But for Rosenzweig, the defining of the community in terms of its assuming the function of judgment is not a factor of its unitive accord in communal song; rather, the role of judgment is a condition that the community speaks for itself and "carries" as its own content that speaking judgment. What defines a community is that it speaks *a word* and a word is not the final note of a song, it is open-ended in the sense of its verbalization as spoken. Phenomenologically, the "essence" of the spoken word is that it is inherently multi-valent and not-final. And so, the spoken word of judgment is the content of a particular community. Besides speaking the "We" that unites, the community speaks the "You-all" (*Ihr*) that separates and divides. This sort of judging speech–act is its content. The content (*Inhalt*) is that which particularizes this or that community over any other, which is not particular in the way of the community that comes together to sing but, instead, comes together to speak its defining word of judgment. A community achieves its identity and grows together insofar as it engages in ongoing speech–acts that defines itself as given to this or that particular historical task. Particularity is simultaneously a separation in the sense of the German word for particularity, *Besonderheit*, which plays off the root word *sonder*. To *sonder* something is to "separate it off" but which also means that which is "peculiar, special, odd, or strange." The word is also used conjunctively to raise a question in the breach of separation. For Rosenzweig, the community that sings together as a We, judges those who do not share in the effectiveness of its acts with a "divorcing Judgment" (*scheidende Gericht*), through a "decisive anticipation" (*entscheidende Vorwegnahme*) that what they are doing testifies that the coming realm will be effectively actual, that eternity will be, in fact.

However, such a judging speech–act by the community is just as much a judgment of its own members as it is of others who do not take part in its peculiar and particularizing acts. In initially presenting what he means by the messianic end-days, towards which the community is directed in its speech–acts of thanksgiving and defining judgments, Rosenzweig notes that the community that believes itself chosen by god to live in the way of loving others — loving the other in the multifaceted variety of her particularities — also believes in a final judgment that is beyond separation. In the final messianic judgment in which this community believes, all separating names — all aesthetic productions that define, divide, and particularize — will be brought together in the unity of a chaotic revelatory world-day that is revealed in a final moment, a blink of an eye, an *Augenblick*, that is, in a day that belongs to the mastery, control, and command of god. Ultimately, Rosenzweig prioritizes the absolute Other-ness to characterize his vision of a time-to-come.

But he does so with a certain, peculiar logic, a logic that has political consequences and is played out as what I've been referring to as a messianic aesthetic that is ethically effective. The ethical effectiveness of such a messianic aesthetic is that at the heart of its action, what Rosenzweig refers to as its peculiar way of acting (*Handeln*), is a practical way that members of its community are commanded to comport themselves with and towards others in the world. That way is to love others, but not in such a way that they deny themselves. Rosenzweig quite pointedly intones that "Rather, the human should love his neighbor as himself. As himself. Your neighbor [the next one] is 'as you.' The human should not deny itself. His self will in fact, in the command to love the neighbor, be definitely confirmed in its place."[38] Rosenzweig's point is a holistic one, similar to how Buber developed his own logic of wholeness with respect to the I-You encounter, namely, that an actual encounter can only occur as the members' integrity as individual selves is preserved in its own right.[39] What differentiates him from Buber, however, and clearly situates Rosenzweig's ethical theory as a forerunner for Levinas's understanding of how our subjectivity is defined by its unique assignation by an other, is that Rosenzweig defines this integrity as the "soul" that each self assumes in their wholeness as self.[40] Love, after all, works its magic by en-souling the other, that is, by messianically choosing the other out of the chaos of particulars and passionately attending to that other.

Attending to the other is an intentional act, but not in the sense of domination; rather, I attend to the other by breathing with her — paradoxically, through holding my own breath, as Levinas would say — that is, through listening and responding to the call of their needs and desires, as their own and not as those tyrannically impressed upon her or him by me. And so I turn to each other, indeterminately, without a plan to manipulate him or her, just to love that one that comes along in whatever guise or surprise the encounter may bring. My task is to bring the breath of the "love of the next one" to the encounter, thereby effecting the factuality of eternity — through the performance of en-souling — one breathless responsible step at a time.

But Rosenzweig assures us again that these acts that are to be taken are not primarily done for the sake of individuality or for some kind of individual redemption. Instead, the institutional model, rather, the institutional exemplar that he calls upon, is the relation of marriage. All relations, he says, are rooted in creation, but what he means in that saying is that they are rooted in a blood-community. What he means by "blood," moreover, is a twofold assertion of both organic rootedness in the earth and in the land of our origins, but also the "blood" of the en-souled community life that is "instituted" by marriage. Rosenzweig refers to marriage as a "great analogy" (*großen Gleichnis*) but uses analogy in the sense of sensual/trans-sensual that I have already elaborated above. The organically created blood-community is transcended by the en-souled blood community that is marriage, which is more than destiny since it is the publicly existing Gestalt of the secret relationship of a love of two souls with each other. Redemption of the world occurs initially as marriage. At the heart of Rosenzweig's ethically intended messianic aesthetics is the freeing of selves to become united as souls in marriages of love, which sets into motion a growth of creation that forms a new kind of blood community of en-souling love, a blooming, fruit-bearing tree, renewing itself in revolutions that spring from the origin of a love that urges us to free each other for the timelessness of eternity.

But this eternity, contends Rosenzweig, is a fact, a *Tatsache*, an act that matters in the world. And thus, as a fact, or act that matters, we need to talk about power and politics. And that discourse entails a discussion of art, of an aesthetics that fuels Rosenzweig's messianism. In order for any of this en-souling activity to matter, to matter in actually changing the world, there needs to be public effectiveness, public even beyond the publicness of marriage. The aesthetic effects of the acts of redemption are that the en-souled particulars are able to unite themselves in completed communities of interconnected particulars that constitute units, or sets, in themselves. The wholes that are thus formed are what Rosenzweig refers to as constituting a "content-filled, ensouled connection" that "in an aesthetic sense, comes to finished and complete condition (*Zustand*)."[41] In other words, in the aesthetic sense of *Zu-stand* implied by Rosenzweig, such a community "takes its stand" or it "stands toward"

others as a material embodiment with an evaluative content (*Gehalt*) that is
its command to love others, irrespective of their particular origin. That is not
to say that enemies are not identified; on the contrary, identifying and judging
others who do not love in the way that the loving community has experienced
and is commanded to love is an integral element of its "task" — its *Aufgabe*,
what a community gives to itself to do. However, that task is just as much an
injunction to "perform" for each and any and all others. Thus, in the final
sections of his text, Rosenzweig develops an aesthetic of public performance
that is specifically associated with redemption, the logic of which he sets forth
as a concluding theory of art.

III. *From redemptive art to a "messianic aesthetics" as performance art: the poetics of responsibility*

What is the case is that the history of humans in the world has been demytholo-
gized and needs remythologization in order for our lives to become full, factual,
and have meaningful existence. And while such a remythologization cannot
occur on the basis of a rejection of history, to have the possibility of deep-rooted
public effectiveness by reaching into how humans live with each other by
creating home spaces, it has to occur as an aesthetic structure. Thus, the only
way to make sense of the connection of work and author is to consider the role
of the spectator. To review Rosenzweig's moments of aesthetic development:
the And is what earlier brought the elements to their own factual completion
through an inner self-creation, self-revelation, and self-redemption. But it is
only through the categories of art that we can see how the courses are brought
to completion: creation categories projected the first rainbow (*Bogen*) as the
arc of the totality of a multitude of details; revelation categories project the
second rainbow as the arc of how the totality of details is transformed into the
content-full, colorful en-souled individuals (*gehaltvollen beseelten Einzelnen*),
while redemption projects the third rainbow, namely, an aesthetic sense of
structural (three-dimensional) completion through connecting the content-full,
en-souled individuals, one with the other.

But, to repeat, these latter kinds of connection can only happen through
the participation of a third one, the viewer (spectator), implying as well the
important factor that justice only takes place when the distribution of resources
and the effects of an action are judged by an impartial third. Putting this in the
context of the relationship of a work of an artist to his production, his work
of art reveals that, in fact, the artist only becomes artist-author and the work
only becomes work through the extent of its actual affects on and in the public,
that is, insofar as the work aesthetically en-souls the viewer. Only through the
viewer does the work first speak: "In the viewer the empty humanity of the
author grows together with the content-rich, soul-full strangeness of the work

(*Unheimlichkeit des Werkes*)." Without the viewer, the work remains without ongoing effectiveness in reality and remains estranged and alienated from reality: "In order to go over into reality, art has to recreate the human."[42] The work only itself becomes a reality, becomes actually effective in reality, when "it draws humans as viewers to itself and itself creates a public."[43] And once it has created a public for itself, the work can never be eliminated from the world. How is such non-elimination envisioned, and what is the relevance for a messianic aesthetic?

The author is both creator and artist, both of which are unable to live without the other and unable to live without public effectiveness. The question for determining a messianic aesthetics is: how do the fantastic productions created by an artist effect lasting social change?

To revisit Rosenzweig's logic, such lasting social change can only be effected in an aesthetic context where the artist recognizes the meaningfulness of the content of a single instant in bringing a work to "conscious" visibility, that is, in bringing the instant into the work of a whole that can be "known" — and here Rosenzweig means "experienced" — by a spectator. This means that Rosenzweig undermines the phenomenon of "art for art's sake" which superficially is associated with Romantic poets and even the artists of the German *Sturm und Drang* movement, such as Goethe, Schiller, and the Schlegel brothers.[44] Rather, Rosenzweig broadens the applicability of art to extend to the total area of the creative fantasy of the poet, namely, the fantasy which includes a creator/author's sexual life, political choices, and mundane daily activities — such as eating, sleeping and dreaming. Such an extension lends symbolic weight (*symbolischem Gewicht*) to all of the contents of an aesthetic creation. In this way, the work of art becomes the work of a whole human.

Rosenzweig claims that what binds epic breadth with lyric immediacy in a work can be said to be its dramatic dimension. The performative "drama" of a work provides the epic dimension — its unity, breadth and depth of material form — with lyrical immediacy and intensity. The quantity is cathected with quality in the dramatic presentation, which applies to every art form but in different ways. Indeed, Rosenzweig contends that poetry is more closely associated to the dramatic than either the fine arts or music because, while the fine arts (*bildende Kunst*) primarily have to do with *space* and breadth of the epical, and music primarily has to do with *time* expressed as the depth and intensity of the lyrical, that is, the fulfillment of the individual moment, poetry has to do with neither but, rather, with the inner origin (*inneren Ursprung*) of both. This is so because poetry gives us a concrete figure as speech (*Gestalt wie Rede*) because it is *more than* both in themselves. It is a form of "representational thinking" (*vorstellenden Denken*) that has to do with inner and outer views and so is "the actual living art."[45] The fine arts and music are always a little abstract, the former is dumb and the latter is blind, so that Moses, who had trouble seeing others, mistrusted the fine arts while Plato, who had trouble listening to others and loved visual forms, mistrusted music. Poetry gives us both visual Gestalt and audible music and, according to Rosenzweig, a human can still be human without having painted or sung a song, but "every full human must have a sense for poetry . . . at the least, he must have one time in his life poeticized."⁴⁶

What Rosenzweig understands as the *Gestalt* is that which primarily configures the fine or constructive and plastic arts, namely, that figure which is given material form and that assumes an exteriority in such a way that it can be something that is established or set up (*eingerichtet*) and thus be seen by others. It has a character of presenting a "face" to the outside. But what is presented as Gestalt in the work of art has two dangers in the fine arts. The dangers derive from the actual structuring of the work itself which depends not only the spiritual vision of the artist herself, her overview of the whole work, but also of the artist's investment of the intensity of connection of each individual in their relationship to nature. The former is an act of vision, the latter an act of the loving will, such that: "with loving and elective attention the artist focuses on each individual in drawing the relationships of each defined individual to its rootedness in nature. And only when each loved particular is 'immersed in feeling' can the individual be brought into a lawfully ordered direction and thus a visual Gestalt."⁴⁷ However, if there is a surplus of vision over form then what results is the extremity of ornamentation, such as the Rococo development in Baroque. And where there is too much intensity of will at the expense of vision, the work only ever remains in outline and structure and never comes together as a whole, completed work. Too much vision, no depth; too much feeling, no coherence.

Similarly in music there is rhythm and harmony; rhythm is what soundlessly moves the whole piece (vision in the visual arts), while harmony is what soundfully ensouls each individual note by investing details with passion. Melody, however, is what both moves and sounds and is thus what is *living* in the musical work of art. Rhythm, the *character* of a piece, and harmony, its *voice*, are only respectively confirmed for their respective roles with their retention in a specific melody, which is what constitutes the *essence* of a song, such that any borrowing of a melody constitutes plagiarism. Consequently, what particularizes a work, what separates it out from others is both its visible Gestalt and its irreplaceable, non-substitutable melody.

These aspects of performing a work of art come together for Rosenzweig in the performance of a poem. The corresponding fundamental characteristic to the occurrences of the totalities of vision and rhythm is the tone of a poem, which can initially be measured by its meter. But meter taken in itself is too restrictive and formal, since that measurement cannot adequately account for the breadth and depth of the primal conception of the work as a whole. The tone is what holds the whole work together and permeates the movement of the work just as much as rhythm or color does in their respective works of art.

In poetry, this is evident in the intimate relationship of vocalic to consonantal soundings, of, for example, how the same sentence is expressed differently in a work by Kleist as it would be in a work by Goethe. It takes a finely trained ear and sensitivity to the particularity of verbalizations in the familial body of the work of any one author in order to attend to such differences from one to another. Tone provides a sense of the whole (*der Ganze*) and the differences of the inter-relatedness of wholes.

The final two characteristics that Rosenzweig presents to fill out his theory are the speech of the poet and the idea in poetry. What the speech of the poet refers to is the "immersion in the individual" in the fine arts that would be "attention to the detail" of a work and in music to the lyric. In poetry it is the *individual* speech of the poet, namely, which words the poet normally takes as the heart of her poetic art. But neither beautiful tones nor beautiful speeches or phrases constitute what makes a poem an effective poem. Rather, "the idea is what first gives life to the poem," which corresponds to the Gestalt in the fine arts and melody in music. The idea in poetry is that which does not "hide behind the work" but rather is that which is "aesthetically-sensually percep-tible, the authentically actual and the working effectiveness of the work."[48] The idea has the same effect for thinking as the eye does for the fine arts and the ear for music and is that which *speaks* out of the poem to the reader/listener, just as the melody speaks to the ear and the constructed Gestalt to the eye. But poetry is that art which has the most market value without diminishing its value since its *currency* is the idea within which life most usually dwells. This is the case since prose is the language of life more often than the heights of hymns or visual gestures since life *speaks* mostly in the prose of thinking as its peculiar speech–act.[49]

The connection to life is most practically accomplished through the redemp-tive capabilities of art, in how the sense (*Sinn*) of what is immersed in the work of art by the author is *excited* in the public, the spectators, and thereby flows into life. I should note at this point that the word that Rosenzweig uses for "spectator" is *Betrachter* which connotes not only "one who views" but also "one who considers," or one who by observing takes something into consideration or "carries" a question within themselves. This excitation in the *Betrachter* happens insofar as the soul of the viewer becomes grounded in and filled with "the sum of presentations which art excited in him." Like the cre-ative author, the viewer becomes "filled with inner figure" insofar as when he turns to the individual detail (the neighbor) he becomes a "knower" (a *Kenner*), that is, he wins or is awoken to consciousness. What the viewer does is to order the unordered presentations of the artist by measuring them in consciousness in such a way that such measuring occurs as an assessment of what is "precious in a long-life of gathering-up and lovingfully ordered [as] inner possession and treasure of the soul."[50] This can fruitfully be associated with what Walter Benjamin means by the work of the collector taking up something neglected or forgotten, some remnant or fragment, and reordering it or renewing it in a new whole of a personal collection.[51] This constitutes for Rosenzweig the acts which serve as the transition from art to the greater world of life.

Creative art lays the natural groundwork for the work of revelation that provides the specific aesthetic of joining the sensuality of the natural with the relationality of trans-sensuality, that is, the communal, cooperative and fruitful joining of the one with the other in the concrete responsibility of the one for and with the other. Redemptive aesthetics, redemptive art, provides the structures of completion, of the anticipatory ideality of a healing wholeness. Creative art provides the basic rhythm and vision of the history of the story of humanity as an epic work given as a received tradition but able to be changed. It is able to be changed through the active engagement of a particular author who acts according to her peculiar genius of vision, rhythm and tone. Such engagement is revelatory and specifically lyrical since her engagement enlivens every detail and individual with which she engages and with that which is most inward, namely, the soul. Therefore, in order to engage in the work of aesthetically transforming reality, we "must learn the music of the soul, which is the most difficult because it is the most highly developed, but then is that which is the most teachable as a theoretical discipline" as form, harmony and speech. While redemptive art provides, through Gestalt, melody and idea, the completion of art leads to the joining together of author-as-artist, viewer and work in a passage to a fuller, more complete, meaningful living in the world.

Rosenzweig calls his completed theory of art an "episode" and qualifies what he means by stating that art is the episode of the "final wisdom" of life which cannot remain episodic. The finality of life, that towards which an aesthetic messianic work points, is the enlivening of the actual other who demands an "actual" kiss of life. Without the actual other, our work remains mute, dumb, blind and lifeless: "Pygmalion can not by himself imagine (*einbilden*) life into his work, no matter how hard he tries; only when he lays down the sculptor's chisel and, as a poor human, sinks to his knees, does the goddess herself bend down towards him."[52]

IV. *The word of god*

From the standpoint of redemption, creation is the content of revelation, but then so is redemption the content of revelation — only from a different temporal perspective. Creation is revealed as temporal in already-having-happened and redemption is revealed as temporal in a yet-to-become-happening. Another difference is that in redemption, what happened in the revelatory invisible experience of the soul-become-living goes out into the public world of the third, that is, redemption makes historical change possible.

Rosenzweig uses the language of the biblical Psalms to exemplify what he means by the happening of historical change because the Psalms, as a form of art, bridge the gap between the "hidden" experience of a revelatory love experience and that which makes redemption a content of revelation. In other words, the language of the not-yet of redemptive completeness, the not-yet of messianic fullness, is bound up with the yet-already-happened, the language of trust, that already occurred between the lover and the beloved. Such a song is a song of thanks for an experience of fullness that hopes for, and even anticipates, an even greater fullness for the rest of the world. Rosenzweig says that this expression of thanks for a gift of love already received combined with an anticipatory fullness can only be sung as a community because of its particular character, namely its unity as a We and its simultaneous judgment of the you-all. However, the community established on the basis of love of the neighbor does not include "all" that exists — Rosenzweig is quick to point out that that would mean the end of history, absolute rest, and the end of suffering and loneliness. Instead, the community sings Psalms of thanksgiving that are, withal, the songs of a lonely heart, a heart which has "God for its comfort" (Ps. 73.1), which Rosenzweig notes is the "guiding-saying" (*Leitspruch*) of the Psalms.

What Rosenzweig sees in the communal form of chorally singing the Psalms is that kind of ritual activity that transforms the lonely individual into a supported member of a community. This is historical change. Although the soul enters the community still chained "in the depths of his loneliness," he is able to descend from those lonely heights or rise out of the depths because, when he says "I" in the midst of community he is speaking *for* the community, as its representative. The move is from one's own soul to the soul of the community, which emboldens the soul because she no longer just speaks out of her own origins; rather, after having "given up [her] own will, friendship, house and home" because she perceived the command of god in the event of revelation, she took on the exhilic burden of being chosen to go into whatever land was shown to her and to love the next one who comes along, whoever that may be.[53] But at the moment of leaving the magic circle of revelation and entering the public realm of the new We, "the all that was one's own is returned but now [as] more than merely one's own possession," that is, not as merely one's own home, friendships or relatives, rather, one's personal property is transformed to the "ownness" (*Eigene*) of the socialist property of the community.[54] This is the case since now her own concerns are the concerns of the community to which she is called and for which she commits her life and her property, a property that now is given in community.

Rosenzweig turns to the Psalms which are especially formed as what he calls the Awe-Psalms and which are characterized by the root-sentence of redemption. Those Psalms are 111–18 and that which is most representative is the Psalm of the most middle, 115. It is the only Psalm that begins and ends with an "I" and the first is redemptively dative, dependent on the verb "to give."

What is prayed for is for the "coming of the realm" accomplished through honoring the divine name. What is prayed is that honor is not given to oneself but to the Other, not to one's own name but to the Name and in so praising, the community is drawn within immediate nearness (*Nähe*) which Rosenzweig tells us is "nearness of god." This nearness is not the same as that which was already founded by the trust that holds between two in the love-event of revelation. Rather, this is the nearness of public objectivity and, therefore, has to do with truth, namely that which is self-evident and visible to the eyes of all.

But this praise is also a "not yet" and so is not yet fulfillable in time. As not fulfillable, the "not-yet" of the end is drawn back into the present because the We is not yet We-All. What also happens is that the We divides itself from those who are not already with god, namely the "you-there" (*Ihr*). But since the We of the Psalm-singers anticipates their eventual union with the god-believing community, the "you-there" becomes a "them" (*Sie*). Moreover, their non-communal standing is further defined by establishing a combative attitude towards those who do not honor the Name as idol-worshipers, namely, those who stand outside the circle of divine love and thus are blind, rigid and unable to act. But again, the ridicule fades with the assertion of the eventual triumph of trust. Throughout the Psalms, and what appears as the defining characteristic of redemption, is the tone of "hopeful trust" which runs throughout as an anticipation of a future that occurs in the eternity of the moment.

Against the betrayal of the idol-worshipers, the anticipation is uttered in light of the hope of three communities which have already entered into the trusting We of those who praise God: (a) Israel — the actual community of the We (the Jews), the House of Aaron; (b) those who have been consecrated as priests which ministers to the "them" through space and time (the Christians); and (c) the (secular) Proselytes, namely those who "fear the Eternal" and who constitute the rest of the messianic community, the "We-All." The choir sings the song of fulfillment, which is a song of growth and increase of blessing from one to the next one, from generation to generation, step by step, to each other and their children because continual growth is the secret of creation, a growth and a secret which are both necessary. But the love-act of the human for and in the earth is free from this necessity since it acts "as if" there were not a creator and no creation that grows over against her. "Heaven is eternal but the earth was given to the children of humans."[55] It was not given to the community of Israel, but simply to the children of humans in order that the next one, simply, could be turned to in the act of love. The final cry is a We which does not conquer individual death, since that indeed is the capstone of creation, but the living whose praises do indeed become immortal as the cohortative, unitive community — but only as community. What remains outstanding as the work of a messianic aesthetics is that all things have to become redeemed to sounded soul.

However, at this point, the question has to be raised specifically to

Rosenzweig's visionary song as a theory and the possibility of a praxis that could grow from singing such a theory, about whether or not even such a song of thanks, comfort and hope can still be sung after Auschwitz? The answer to that question depends on what one thinks about Auschwitz and whether that event constitutes a unique event. Was Auschwitz and the attempt to annihilate the Jews a founding event in the sense of the event of Exodus that resulted in the historical phenomenon of exile and wandering, a phenomenon which I contend is at the very heart of Rosenzweig's project? The question is: can we believe at all in a kind of community such as Rosenzweig's that is based on a song of hope for the future, given what has happened in the decades since Rosenzweig published *The Star*? What public could be drawn to such a work of art? What hope is there in maintaining or growing a community of thanks and praise? Perhaps the question needs to be redirected: is the judgment of "You-all" ethically strong enough? With these questions in mind, some consideration of Rosenzweig's social theory are in order for how it exemplifies the theoretical structures of his messianic aesthetic which I have laid out, and in anticipation of distinguishing how his ideas about art and responsibility diverge from Heidegger's. Philosophically and ethically, these considerations are especially pertinent given the history of Heidegger's conflicted but firm commitment to Nazism in his lifetime.

V. *Configuring a messianic aesthetic in the socio-historical realm*

Up until now, I have spent a great deal of energy and textual space elaborating how I think that Rosenzweig's *The Star of Redemption* presents a phenomenology of a "philosophical" work of art written with ethical intention. Along the way, I have provided an exegesis of Rosenzweig's text in order to articulate my claim. I could do the same for Part III of *The Star*, which in some ways corroborates my case even more concretely, given what Rosenzweig says in those sections about what constitutes aesthetics and its social role in the everyday life of humans. But I will not do that since my intent is to read Rosenzweig's work with Heidegger's in order to highlight their divergence, specifically by way of developing a phenomenology of the ethical consequences of their philosophies of art. So I limit my remarks to some general observations about how the philosophy of art developed by Rosenzweig in Parts I and II of his work provides the basis for the messianic aesthetics of Part III.

While I will focus on some details of why Rosenzweig maintains that Book 2 of Part III is specifically aesthetic, I will begin by pointing out that if ritual is at all to be understood as a kind of art-form, then Book 1 of Part III is also highly aesthetic in nature, since the core of that Book explores the practical significance of socio-historical Jewish rituals. Additionally, Book Three deals with the Gestalt of the Star itself and draws everything together in a final aesthetic vision with which Rosenzweig presents not only his gathering of the many threads he spun out in the earlier structures of the work, but leaves his reader/viewer with a striking *image* of the face of the Other — the sight of the countenance of the human face, as the next one to whom we turn in loving attention after we ourselves have been in-formed and become full of figure in Rosenzweig's intentional turning to us, the individual reader via his text.

Rosenzweig calls the Part III of his work "The Figure or The Eternal Overworld" (*Die Gestalt oder die ewige Überwelt*), which is intended to elicit a reader's response on several levels. My first impression was that his title refers to the logical conclusion of the rest of the work, the way that his social theory, with its relevance for philosophies of history and politics, simply makes sense given the logic of his earlier development. It seems self-evident that if we want to influence the course of history and how we live on and with this world, with other sentient beings, we need to be intimately part-itive. That is, just as the "parts" of a sentence are helpless fragments without the role they play in the flux of spoken and written sentences, so we have no sentence, no wholes without those elemental parts wedded one to the other. Thus his *midrash* on love and marriage and the formation of communities of song and judgment. But, secondly, marriage is precisely *not* a blood-community — marriages of lovers and beloveds are unions of strangers, of members who come from distinctly separate families, often from distinct "other" blood communities but who join together and institute new spiritual and genetic blood-communities. Rosenzweig's "vision" is of a spiritual embodiment that happens via ethical relations of distinct others, joining together *despite* their otherness, or even more significantly, precisely *because of* their otherness. I desire the other in her (or his or its) very otherness and because the other is infinitely incomprehensible, in the sense of being incomparable. She is beyond the analogies of comparison, and yet serves as the standard for comparing all others, and thus I am committed to building a life with just this one particular other. Wherever I journey throughout the world, in whatever exile, my desire is ever to build a home with just this particular other regardless of time or space. But even more, building a life means celebrating my love of and with this other in the eyes of the rest of the world by entering into the very drama of life and having "our" life together confirmed by "impartial"' observers, spectators, friends, and enemies. Thus, Rosenzweig implicates the ineluctability of the social, political, and historical dimensions of life in the structures of his Star. And language enlivens the very movements of those structures.

The intention of any speech–act is to communicate, to embody a communicative performance. But for Rosenzweig, that communication has to be done with the right kind of ethical intent, that is, without intending violence or to tyrannize the other. This is why Rosenzweig subtitles his Introduction to Part III of his text with the phrase *in tyrannos!* — a reference to the phrase exuberantly used by the students Hegel, Schelling, and Hölderlin in their communications with each other in referring to the possibilities of revolutionary social change as a consequence of the French Revolution.[56] Additionally, Part III is also called the Gestalt, which recalls the visuality of the fine arts because of Rosenzweig's apparent intention to signify the construct of a verbally originated, three-dimensional image of the Star — a logical star, an emblematic star, an actual star that signifies a life or relational dialogue. And because the Star is actual, it is rooted in actual historical developments, namely, the lives and works of actual persons, not just figures, although figures as well. And thus references are made to the development of actual historical communities and to a vision (of a face) proposed for how history can actually be changed, how the messianic age is not the waiting for a messiah to come or return and save us from our sins and mis-actions. Rather, a messianic aesthetics prefigures a vision of an ideal end-time that can only come about through daily walking and acting in trust with each other, with one's god, with one's partner/companion, and with one's neighbors — in order to make the world a better place with each act of love.

Since the last part of Rosenzweig's text is his peculiar fusion of aesthetic presentation and historical assessment, Goethe is named as an emblematic historical figure in order to bring the effects of his work into historical account. The time for judgment has come. It is the final part of the text, the context of redemption out of which and from which judgments of others are made. And it is time to judge Goethe. The mask of Mephistopheles is revealed to be just that, a mask, and now we know just what it means to love another, to speak words of love to another and not to pray "that the work of one's own hands" be brought to fulfillment, Goethe's prayer to himself. Goethe is sovereign of his own work, autonomous and self-fulfilling, but to whom does Goethe pray? Who does Goethe love? Rosenzweig's dictum, about Goethe's self-assessment as perhaps the first and only Christian is a measured but resounding rejection of Goethe's choice of resigned autonomy. The arrogant "tone" of Goethe's superiority sounds with ethical hollowness as Rosenzweig writes with ironic and irenic understatement. Destiny is not a matter that can be accomplished on one's own; destiny is a matter of commitment to community, of trust in the living and practicing of love relations with others. The growing of the historical "realm" of inter-personal relations is relational and emerges from intra-, and inter-personal community relations.

Rosenzweig rejects Goethe, and rejects Goethe as his guide, precisely because Goethe's prayer is a prayer to himself and to the strength of his own art.[57] This is a judgment on that form of contemporary society that results in lives of utter isolation, of isolated modern humans willing the destiny of the work of their own hands as self-appointed tasks to somehow save themselves from despairing of their isolation and of committing one of the many forms of modern suicide. In other words, they are, paraphrasing Rosenzweig, trapped in the tragic silences of their meta-ethical selves. And Rosenzweig demonstrates his historical acuity by lining up a series of tortured, meta-ethical selves: Augustine loved but was fixated on his ascetic self-absorption; Luther hoped for the destruction of the Jews in their continued choice to embody lives of chosenness; while Goethe, as the "great pagan and Christian," hoped for a completion, which comes with trust in himself and himself alone. They are all prayers to one's ownmost destiny, self-directed and self-reflective prayers to complete the creation of one's own hands. Goethe represents for us this desire for sheer worldly fulfillment of an individual, and of bodies of monadically unrelated individuals, to have "their day in history" in complete vitality.[58] And redemption really is a matter of judging social completions. For Rosenzweig, Dostoyevski was inclined towards the right path, combining art with responsibility in his great cultural tale of Russian family life, the history of Christianity, and the suffering of innocent ones. Representative of the "Johanine Completion," Alyosha renews the strength of love and belief, but that is also the greatest danger since it represents the attempt by the Orthodox Church of Russia to renew the "old Christianity" from within itself.[59] Hence, Rosenzweig measures even this inclination as another historical attempt to come to a position of social hope in a future that would really care for others, but is incapable because of how it is based on the same tautological inadequacy of earlier historical attempts, that is, the inadequacy of trusting merely in the resources of oneself alone without turning to others.

In this case, Rosenzweig's earliest and most faithful modern guides, Goethe and Nietzsche, while having done good service to get us to the point of self-integrity, of integral vitality — of how to become true "sons of the earth" — fail with respect to their ability to come up with a form of a social aesthetic that provides for the possibility of the kind of community of lovers and believers that Rosenzweig has in mind.[60] The limits of Goethe are that he provides an aesthetic of temporality that, in contrast, builds another totalization of life. What is missing is the unpredictability of the other in a community of exile, built precisely on questioning the stability of all socio-political structures, a community that is both open to providing enjoyment for family, friends and strangers, while retaining a critical a-political stance within existing political conditions that tend toward domination by demanding the sacrifice of the individual to its social regime.

To whom do we then *turn* for a guide if, in fact, we cannot merely trust in ourselves alone? Rosenzweig's *midrashic* response to this modern, historical problem is to *turn* to the others in our historically founded and historically mediated communities, others who make up the cult of my believing community, with whom in our very differences we come together to sing a communal prayer that is based on "the love of the next one (the neighbor) *as* the love of the eternal." Only in so singing, can the eternal be "set loose" in historical time. Instead of singing for the completion of one's own (*das Eigene*), redeeming completion does not demand the work of mine, yours, his, or hers but *ours*. The work of redemption takes two hands, not one, and introduces the farthest distance of eternity into temporality and not merely the present vitalization of life. Only through the work of "*our* hands" can love be gifted to the next individual, a vitalizing piece of life, presenting a horizon of light that remains in the other as "a seed of eternal life."[61]

But how are such "seeds" planted? They are planted through taking part in the aesthetically unnatural, or supernatural, cycle of rituals and festivals that mark and divide time into the "right time" for acting. And the "right time" for acting is that which, out of the determined and predictable rituals of the past, directs our present attention to the indeterminate and unpredictable horizon of the future. Said otherwise, out of the determined and predictable relations with those who have already been named and are known and with whom we receive initial guidance and direction, we engage in the present in such a way that we remain open to the other who will come along and who will have their own particular needs and desires, an unpredictable set of needs and desires that can only be answered with my speech–acts of responsibility. And I will only be able to meet the unfulfillable desires and tangible needs of the other through performing aesthetically ethical acts of responsibility.

The final *aesthetic* movement is the move to the *silence* of gesture and liturgy, the movements of a community that does not have to verbally express itself to make its intentions known. Rosenzweig turns in his concluding textual movements to present an interpretation of the liturgies and gestures that identify and signify the historical belief communities of Judaism and Christianity. Through such communal gestures the world can be re-mythologized in the sense of winning back an enchantment and sense of the possibilities of getting along with each other, of sharing the "possessions" of the earth and the very land of our homes, without resorting to violence. Indeed, the "aesthetic response" by members of these two communities can be an ethical, messianic one that, by its very nature, can resist the violence that is the ultimate warrant for justifying the political order of the state. The aesthetic function is precisely the liturgy itself, a performative form of art that sets the stage, so to speak, for an actualization of the sensual/trans-sensual revelatory moment established at the heart of the revelatory event. Rosenzweig notes that, "Between humans who speak a common language, a glance suffices in order for them to understand each other."[62] The glance, indirect and discrete, enlivens the ritual of our daily lives by ensuring that those very rituals do not become transformed into mindless, state-sanctioned violence.

The final three sections of Rosenzweig's text present, then, his social theory that is bound up with an applied philosophy of art as well as rounding out an aesthetic textual performance in itself. It is also the way that Rosenzweig draws our attention to the ethical theme of his work, that is, the move from the affirmation of the mortality of our bodies and the inevitability of death that is "built into" the biology of creation, to the transformation of the tragedy and defiance of the lonely self-that-dies, through the revelatory duet of love, into the communal "body" of those who bear the fruits of love that thus ensure the material perdurance, the immortality, of the body. In fact, for Rosenzweig "truth" turns out to be a language-event that takes the form of confessing oneself to be, in the sense of claiming responsibility for, a "member of [an] immortal body."[63]

To conclude this part of my text, and to enunciate as clearly as possible Rosenzweig's messianic aesthetics, I will refer to three examples out of the last three Books of Part III of *The Star*. Book 1 of Part III is entitled "The Fire or The Eternal Life." This chapter presents Rosenzweig's sociology of Judaism and is primarily about how the Jewish People separate themselves off as a people of exile for the threefold reason of maintaining their own identity as a belief community of lovers, roughly analogous to the choral community of redemption. However, matters are not quite as simple as correlating the Jewish community with the community of those who are already "fully" redeemed. They burn with love for each other, renewing the names of their ancestors from one generation to another, from grandparent to parent to grandchild: "Testifying happens in producing."[64] In other words, the fertility of producing actual heirs, of begetting children, is a testimony to the love-life of the members of this community and to the fulfillment of the promise that the seeds of this community will be as infinitely countless as the heavenly stars. However, there are two other moments in this community structure. The second moment is that of the celebration of ritual feasts according to the ritual calendar, the historical movements of renewing an integrating communal life, and the third is the "judgment" of standing in critical separation from the violence of any existing political order.

There is a wealth of aesthetic references throughout Part III that bear out these examples, but three instances could suffice to make my point about messianic aesthetics: namely, the festival of Pesach, or the feast of Passover in Book 1; the festival of Christmas for the Christians in Book Two; and the event of encountering "the face" in Book Three. According to Rosenzweig, both of the communal feasts are feasts of revelation which have consequences for the process of redemption; hence, their occurrence in the final book of his text. For the Jews, Pesach is that festival that is celebrated by recounting the story of the beginning of a people as a people, freed from slavery through the call to liberation and to the task of ethical "carriers" on the one hand, and their ongoing condition of exile, and thus the condition of ongoing critical political distancing on the other hand. For the Christians, the festival of Christmas signifies their status in the world of always beginning anew and that, importantly, recognizes and celebrates a pagan incarnation of god. In what follows, I will first focus on explicating Rosenzweig's interpretation of Pesach and then turn to consider Christian and pagan phenomena.

Rosenzweig says that, "The creation of a people to their status as a People, happens in their liberation." And the Sabbath itself reminds Jews of their

withdrawal from Egypt (from the realm of the political). But Pesach is that
feast that celebrates and continues to institute the liberation of the Jewish
People and, at the same time, their institution as a People itself. In its mythic
function, it has historically defined and continues to define (*bestimmt* — based
on a calling-as-defining) the Jews as eternal wanderers through the deserts of
the world, destined in their status as ever-in-exile and thus always involved in
the redemptive work of bringing on the messianic age. The Jews celebrate the
festival not only to remember their deliverance from forced labor and slavery,
but "as though they themselves [in the act of telling the story] were the ones liberated from Egypt." For this reason, it seems as though they are only concerned
with the past in a romantic sort of longing, but "in truth their historicality (*das
Geschichtliche*) is, for them, entirely present."[65] By telling the story *as though*
they were the liberated ones, they become *in a sense* the liberated ones. The
process of inner identification creates a self-image that transforms their other
daily routines, lending the character of historical continuity and relevance
to the other actions. Precisely because the story is a myth, a *ficcione*, can the
retelling continue to provide the possibilities for ongoing *midrashic* adaptations
to extant political orders, or disorders. In fact, the word *Seder* means "order"
and the narrations and elaboration of this story, as historical myth, continues
to effectively reorder actuality.[66]

In addition to the story telling, however, Pesach is also a ritual feast and,
therefore, another kind of artistic performance. It is a ritual performance that
dramatizes one of the most basic events in our human lives, that is, sharing
food. This festive meal is meant to "perform" the condition that not only
has the work of "our" hands provided enough food to enjoy with family and
friends, but even more significantly, there should be enough food to share
with others, with strangers who may be hungry and on their own chaotically
unpredictable journeys. In order to emphasize the drama of "ethical liberation"
that is involved in this kind of performance, consider Rosenzweig's description
of the meal itself:

> The dinner, to which the father of the house gathers together all of his [family]
> is, out of the many meals of the spiritual year, *the meal* of meals. It is the only
> one which from beginning to end presents [*darstellt* — performs!] a liturgical act
> and so, from beginning to end — as in truth, we have named it, "Order" [*Seder*
> in Hebrew] — it is liturgically regulated. From the very beginning, the word
> "freedom" sheds its light upon it. The freedom of this meal, at which everyone is
> equally free, shows itself among many other ways how "this night is distinguished
> from all other nights": including the reclining of those seated. The vitality [of this
> gathering] is shown to be even greater than that which is recalled from Antiquity
> of guests lying at the table at the Symposium, in how the youngest child speaks
> [first] and that afterwards, the father directs the discussion at the table according
> to the personality and maturity of that one. In contrast to all other instruction,

which is dominating and never a matter of equality, the sign of a truly free society is that the law (*Gesetz*) for the relative level of the discussion [its relative measure] is given by those who stand on the outermost edge of the circle. The conversation has to draw him in. No one who is bodily present is permitted to remain spiritually excluded. The freedom of the "cooperative" (*Genossenschaft*) is always the freedom of everyone who belongs to it. So, this meal is a sign of the calling of this people to freedom.[67]

Rosenzweig goes on to say how the discussion is instructive, since while it is begun by the youngest child it is none the less led by the father (as the head of the household) in the presence of all those seated and joined at the common table and attentive in their "present" listening. However, the instructive tone of the discussion results in more and more talking by those bodily present until all autocracy is gone and is replaced by singing, praising, and a strangely chaotic mixture of divine mystery and jesting, brought on by wine and the fellowship of community. As you can tell, this examplar indicates how Rosenzweig's projection of the possible horizons of this empirical, sociological structure — as a thoroughly aesthetic performance — enables its participants to not only reenact the "story" of liberation, but to further enact the structures of freedom in its current social context. Every level of society is included and valued, and eventually brought to speech, in their turn — but from the least developed to the most developed. The emphasis of the circle is on the freedom of those bodily present but includes not only strangers invited from outside the circle to join in as guests, but a welcoming cup of wine is poured, providing spatial place by reserving a seat for the potential guest. Indeed, a door is left open for "Elijah" who may return at any moment, embodying the actual anticipation of the unaccounted-for guest who would complete the messianic work of redemption. In fact, the readings during this festival include not only the founding myth, the *Hagaddah* of liberation, but also readings of the Song of Songs, which indicate the work of love that is at the heart of the "wandering," as well as readings from Isaiah's prophecy about the fruition of the chosen people, the judgment of those set against them, and the messianic vision of the day when "the wolf shall dwell together with the lamb and the world shall be as full of the recognition of the Lord as the sea is of water." In other words, readings are read to engender a hope for enacting an ideal social order, set in a future time and a transformed world, when peace and justice shall reign.

But the most important point that Rosenzweig makes in this part of his work has to do with the role that Jews play with respect to politics, which is precisely their messianic role. Messianism is a particularly Jewish phenomenon that has to do with control of land, destiny of a people and sovereignty. It ultimately has to do with *not* being governed by a tryrannical ruler and being able to make one's own way in the world. During the Second Temple period, during the period after the Jews had enjoyed some measure of sovereignty in the land of Israel, the land they had wandered to after their liberation from slavery in Egypt, first the Greeks and then the Romans dominated their life as a people. In this climate, messianism as a phenomenon began to grow as a phenomenon in response to oppression and lack of freedom. Among other significations, it was primarily born out of suffering and expressed a desire for a better future for one's children. This phenomenon took many forms, both political — with an emphasis on militarized violence — and cultural, with an emphasis on revolutionizing the ethical conditions of one's life practices. Both major emphases drew from historical sources in the collective psyche of the Jewish people themselves, that is, from their former successes as conquerors and colonizers of other people and from their prophetic tradition that emphasized living better ethical lives. Hence, under the oppression of Roman occupation, some Jews variously hoped for a redeeming political figure who would reestablish their right to sovereignty in governing themselves, their possessions and their land. Other Jews, however, cultivated a form of messianism that emphasized a change in the very conditions of the political and social order such that the chain of political oppression would be interrupted. These dual phenomena can be roughly correlated with political and cultural Zionisms of the early twentieth century, simultaneous with the time Rosenzweig was conceiving *The Star*, exemplified by the divergent Zionist agendas of Theodor Herzl and Ahad HaAm. More or less, Zionism is just another form of messianism, that is, an expressed desire of the Jewish people that is based on their collective memory that was formed around a body of teachings based on a return to the land in which their ancestors once lived and that included living lives of ethical responsibility as a precondition for such a return. It seems to me that Rosenzweig clearly understood this heritage and also just as clearly made a choice to remain in exile and work for that version of messianism that would effect changes in the greater world-order from within that world-order. And this is why he aligned the political with the a-political stance of the Jewish people.[68]

In short, what Rosenzweig says is that Jews both eschew art while paradoxically maintaining alternative art-forms precisely for the sake of maintaining their a-political stance. What this means is that in maintaining their a-political stance they actually embody a quintessential aesthetic way of life: their entire life praxis is structured according to a way of life that is entirely aesthetic and that embodies the best of what we humans have come to associate with an art that creates joy, provides comfort, sustenance, and is open to a variety of perspectives. The ideal Jewish way of life is one that from top to bottom is an ideal one embodied in aesthetic experience, from the clothes that are worn and how they are worn, to the meals that are eaten and how they are eaten, to the songs that are sung to and with each other and the prayers that are prayed around the family table or on the journey in one's Sukkoth. Moreover, while Rosenzweig talks about the exclusivity of the Jewish community and its sole concentration on its own inner development, his subtext belies the language of exclusivity. Given my analysis of the central role that the Song of Songs plays and my interpretation of how he understands the Psalms as a textual source for redemption, it should be clear that the primary role of Jewish community is to live that sort of aesthetically embodied life — a life of shared song, shared meals, and the singing of love songs to a beloved other — that, given the best possible reading, should be taken with some sense of irony. What is most telling is in how he concludes his chapter on the Jewish people with specific reference to the political realm. In this regard, Eric Santner does a fine job of elaborating the political significance of Rosenzweig's stance, especially regarding Rosenzweig's remarks about messianic politics, by associating him with similar critical tendencies in Benjamin and Derrida.[69] The whole point of Rosenzweig setting up the Jewish community the way that he does is to set up an alternative community structure that would work for peace and justice and use peaceful means towards that goal, a community that sets itself against politics and the state because the state only knows violence.

But the Jews can not do such work of resistance and ethical transformation on their own. They need help and Rosenzweig looks for help in what seems to be the most unlikely of sources, that is, in the traditional enemies of the Jewish people, the Christians and pagans. In fact, the role of the Jewish people is to assert their difference from the political order whose final mandate is death, a socio-political order that executes its "order" with violence. The a-political order of the Jews, by contrast, has at its heart the song of love and a vision of peace and justice. But since their stance is a-political, the Jews need other communities to help accomplish such a goal, and that would be the Christian and pagan communities. While the Jews represent the burning fire of the Star in Rosenzweig's image, the Christians represent the streaming rays of light of that same Star, coursing over the world in a task to convert the un-enlightened ones of the of the world who have not known love, who are lonely and self-centered, who think that what constitutes a full and meaningful life is that they accomplish the work of their own hands and only their own hands and for their own sake. What Rosenzweig says about the Christians is that, due to their peculiar way of drawing from their original source in Judaism *and* their commitment to engagement in the pagan, non-Jewish, non-believing world, they are best suited for engaging in the aesthetic work of welcoming outsiders, strangers, into the warmth of their churches and their places of worship. Hence, Rosenzweig says that the quintessential material work of art is the architecture used by Christians for just this purpose, namely, of welcoming others into their dwellings to join in their teaching and speaking the words of their holy scriptures, scriptures that are in any case based on the Torah.[70] In fact, Rosenzweig says that it is the task of Christians to engage in political activism in order to ensure that the world-order remains minimally on course with respect to justice and the ethical command to love one's neighbor. This means that Christians have to engage in the violent, pagan activities of governing the world. Christians are, after all, modified pagans.

But I would argue that Rosenzweig does not really mean what he seems to be saying in this case either. In fact, Christian art, as incarnational, tends towards the idolatrous and too easily succumbs to the dangers of fanaticism and the aestheticization of the political that has resulted in the fascist political movements of the twentieth century and the horrors of the Holocaust. Rather, Christians are much more politically engaged and less aesthetically adept than their Jewish counterparts, even in Rosenzweig's own estimation of how their liturgical years compare.

To momentarily grant Rosenzweig his point, however, for Christians, Christmas is that festival which most closely parallels Pesach for the Jews. It stands at the beginning of the Church year and is therefore also a festival of the beginning. But it is so in the way that the "becoming free" of the "first born of god's sons" corresponds to the becoming of a people and the incarnation of the "native" (ethnically indigenous) corresponds to becoming a human. The parallelism to the Jews is that the people and the individual correspond exactly in the way that the world and human do and thereby both festivals celebrate "the beginning of the visible procession of revelation over the earth."[71] And similar to the Jewish festival, the reading of holy scriptures is very much at the center of the liturgical activity, even more so than any other festival of the Christian ritual year. Additionally, the narration of how the Christian cult was founded through an act of being called, and that they too are on a kind of a journey of exile involved in embodying a creative act (the incarnation) is, as with the Jewish festival, connected to a ritual meal. In fact, the acts are so broad and central for the identity formation of Christians that the myth is simply referred to as history itself. Likewise, for the Jews, it's simply the "*Haggadah*." Also, as for the Jews, Christians place "the reading of the history at the center of the festival celebration," thereby showing how a common and communal listening grounds a people as a people. It is also a festival of the present because the time of Advent renews its ground in the creation of the "Old" covenant of the prophets, directing attention to the past. Analogously, the associated festival of the Three Kings resounds as a festival of future-oriented redemption, since: "the offerings of the Kings out of the East intimates the future offerings of the kings of all lands."[72] This is clearly a political reference entailing an ongoing engagement with the political order.

But Rosenzweig further says that neither Pesach nor Christmas are actually festivals of revelation, since Easter for the Christians and the giving of the Tora for the Jews signifies the presentness of the eternal life for the Jews and the eternal way of the Christians. Once more, according to Rosenzweig:

Not the stall of Bethlehem but Golgotha and the empty grave count for Christianity as the beginning of their way. The cross, in any case, and nothing previous in the "life of Jesus," which remains always equally near and visible from the countless middle-points of its eternal way. In the same way for us, the meaning of revelation is the miracle of Sinai, the giving of the Torah, and not the withdrawal from Egypt, and is that which always accompanies us in the present. We need to first remember the withdrawal, and do so as if we were presently and bodily there, but we do not need to remember the Torah: it is present. So too for the Christians, it is not the manger but rather the cross that is always present: the latter and not the former is what he always has before his eyes. As it is said about us and the Torah, so it could be said about the Christian: that if "it is in his heart, from that his steps will not slip away."[73]

And so Rosenzweig envisions that in celebrating such festivals, the members of each community bind their sensual lives to the life of the community through ritually ordering their historically founded beliefs. But they do so through how they perform aesthetic practices that are wed to an ethical intentionality set into the world through the blood community of the one and the blood and wounds of the flesh of the other. Together, according to Rosenzweig, these communities have already embodied, but could continue to embody, an alternative Gestalt for being-in-the-world than the usual functioning of political power based on force and violence.

Finally, what makes his work a messianic aesthetic is his assumption of revitalizing through remythologizing existing historical communities in order to develop a cooperative form of federative alliances that do not rely on the traditional organs of power politics in order to provide both an ethical social critique and an alternative social vision. Ultimately, his "vision" is messianic since, while relying on transforming existing social structures in order to actively engage in creating more vital and more just social practices, Rosenzweig contends that in order to have a credible and compelling warrant for his alternative vision, a warrant that is *as* strong as death, he has to ground that vision in a hope for a future completion, a hope for a redeemed world, that is non-confessional, non-sectarian, and non-divisive. In other words, there are good grounds for why a pagan love song is at the heart of Rosenzweig's work, because ultimately a redeemed world has to be a redeemed paganism, a paganism that is rooted in the earth, which is good, very good. To make the point as clear as possible, Rosenzweig presents us with one final vision at the end of his text, namely, the description of the Star as the Gestalt of a human face. The penultimate events are that Jews will have to work to overcome their danger of introversion, of merely growing within themselves and concerning themselves only with their own "kind" as a form of political-social critique. Christians need to overcome the danger of extroversion and of identifying themselves over against the others, of believing that everyone else needs conversion and of aestheticizing the other, of converting the other into its own categories, via art for art's sake. In the end, what remains is the "face of the gestalt" or the "gestalt as face."[74] This is the "vision" of a transformed nature, of a future time when the "truth" of the possibility of living in peace with each other will triumph in the "eternal battle of state and art," a battle waged against Christians and Jews but, ultimately, as Jews against Christians. What Rosenzweig means by this is precisely that the political, with which Jewish community primarily contends, will be transformed into a system of cooperative community federation that guarantees freedom and justice for each and every one. And art will likewise be transformed from a vehicle for ultimately fascist ends to the beauty of configuring the natural world, and allowing for its incomparable beauty without dominating that beauty for one's own instrumental ends.

But until that end, we still have to handle our relations with others through an aesthetic structuring of our lives. For Jews this means engaging in the messianic aesthetic of political resistance by forming an aesthetic community that, through ritual relations, provides for the ongoing possibility of revelatory love-events that are chaotic and unpredictable, and thus avoids the specter of violence and war. For Christians this means engaging in the messianic aesthetic that validates the political order but only through sacrificing and suffering at the very hands of political management. This is why the cross, for them, is the ultimate form of art — it structures (as *Gestaltung*) the suffering of this particular human, this particular Jew whom Christians believe is the messiah. In both cases, the goal is to enlighten pagans, but only insofar as pagans are unaware of this dimension of self-sacrifice and the enjoyment of love relationships. What pagans retain is their rootedness in the vitality of the earth, a sensual earthiness that is just as much a *part* of the complete truth as are politics, art, faith, hope, and love. Indeed, the Song of Songs is the most sensually earthy *pagan* love song, which Rosenzweig situates at the very heart of all community life.

Ultimately, Rosenzweig maintains that until the very end we still have to wear our masks, and that mask is one which is the final image of the *Star*, as the living image of god, as the living image of the human face. What do we "see" when we encounter another *as other* in our revelatory events? As a process of coming to know truly, we see the face of the other, etched with the history of their particular lives in the lines and wrinkles of their countenance, the histories that result in the furrows of one's brow, the flickering smile or trembling reserve. From the bland stare of the marks of suffering, alienation, and oppression to the flash of recognition, joy, and delight that illuminates an other's face, we *read our relations with each other* in the masks that we perceive, the faces that listen, speak, and express otherness. The face is the final "analogy" (*gleichnis*) of god, but in keeping with Rosenzweig's revelatory assertions, the face is the site/sight of what Rosenzweig means by the *sinnlich–übersinnlich* relation. The face directs us beyond the between towards the absolutely other, but we remain with and "true" to this other as long as their utterly human face remains utterly human for us.

Indeed, the face is the *Gestalt* and the face *as* the star is what Rosenzweig's entire book prepares us to meet and is the proper work of redemption. But the depiction of the face is not what is last; rather, we are provided with an injunction, with imperative words to carry with us away from and out of the book, out of and away from any text into the context of life itself — "aesthetic" words to live with in actual living encounters with others. Our lives are crafted works and without the art that we produce we would be incapable of communicating our passions and desires as urgently as we do, and without the political structures which we erect we would be incapable of ordering our lives in the forms of continuity and nurturance that we do. But without our actual, enlivening engagements with others we have no life at all. And thus we must continue to be taught how to walk and talk in coming to know in truth in the process of ever-renewing our speech–acts with the many others in our lives. In doing so, we learn how to trust in others.

Notes

1   Exceptions are Costa Rica, Lichtenstein and a few others that depend on entities such as the United States or The Regional Security System.

2   Such ethical questioning is taken up in *Salvaging the Fragments*. See Simon 2009.

3   See Lyotard 1984.

4   For contrasting views on Cohen and Rosenzweig, see the excellent studies in Batnitzky 2009 and Bienenstock 2009.

5   See Arendt 1973.

6   See Luhmann 2004.

7   Ibid.

8   See "Über den Begriff der Geschichte" in Benjamin 1977: 252: "*Dann ist uns wie jedem Geschlecht, das vor uns war, eine* schwache *messianische Kraft mitgegeben, an welche die Vergangenheit Anspruch hat.*"

9   It is also other than a Gadamerian *Wirkungsgeschichte* which itself entails an ethical enframing.

10 Where Heidegger develops a totalizing metaphysics based on founding a new world order on one fundamental difference, that between Being and beings, and that resulted in his unfortunate onto-theological support for fascist Nazism in 1933, Rosenzweig provides the structure for accepting multiple differences but not in the unraveling form of a Derridean deconstructive play of dissemination. For support of my position, see Zimmerman 1990: 261. As contestation, see Thomson 2005.

11 GS2: 234; SR: 210.

12 Ibid.

13 Ibid: 236; 211.

14 Ibid.

15 Ibid. I contend that Levinas may have appropriated Rosenzweig's concept of "reserve" and use of the term *Daimon* to develop his ideas of the independence of

the interior life of the self in enjoyment and dwelling. See Levinas 1969, 109–121 and 152–174.

16 Ibid: 237; 212.
17 Ibid: 238; 213.
18 Ibid.
19 Ibid.
20 See Kant 1959: 43: "For in morals, the proper and inestimable worth of an absolutely good will consists precisely in the freedom of the principle of action from all influences from contingent grounds which only experience can furnish."
21 GS2: 239; SR: 214.
22 Book 3, II.
23 GS2: 254; SR: 228.
24 Ibid.
25 Ibid: 255; 229.
26 Ibid: 256; 229.
27 Ibid: 255; 229.
28 Incidentally, written while he was the director of a gymnasium and meant to institutionalize the logicization of nature as the educational model to be adopted across all of Germany. Hegel comes closer to this goal at the height of his career when he assumed more authoritarian control over Prussian educational policy making in his appointment to a position of Professor of Philosophy and then in his office as Rector of Berlin University. See Althaus 2000: 146–154.
29 As Samuelson points out, this refers to Psalm 136, I, to the "Tov" as a one-word, original root-sentence (*Stammsatz*) that unites creation and revelation. See Samuelson 1999.
30 See Santner 2001: 39ff. Santner also refers to Scholem's phrase, "validity without meaning" and the development of fantasy in Kafka as a response to the "surplus of validity over meaning" and is that which holds our lives together in a kind of structural torsion.
31 GS2: 262; SR: 235. At first, the Husserlian notions of "pairing" and "association" come to mind. But one is also reminded here of a Maimonidean concept of "overflowing" from Maimonides 1963.
32 Ibid.
33 See below, Chapter 6, for Heidegger's development of subordination and *sichfugen*.
34 GS2: 263; SR: 236.
35 Ibid. See also "Das neue Denken" in GS3: 161: "*Am ehesten würde ich mir noch die Bezeichnung als absoluter Empirisimus gefallen lassen müssen . . .*"
36 See "The Pact" in Levinas 2001: 217.
37 GS2: 264; SR: 237. cf. Heidegger's use of "*sich fügen*" as obedience or submission to one's destiny discussed below in Chapter 6 and referred to in footnote #33 above.
38 Ibid: 267; SR: 239. The significant difference between this imperative and the standard form of the Golden Rule is Rosenzweig's emphasis on loving the neighbor not as oneself "but as a *you*." In other words, Rosenzweig emphasizes loving the neighbor as other, just as I am a neighbor to the other.

39 See Buber 1985: 32: "*Der Mensch wird am Du zum Ich.*" Of course, Buber published his seminal work, *Ich und Du*, in 1923, already two years after Rosenzweig had published his work and several years after Rosenzweig's formulation. More importantly, though, is that Rosenzweig took issue with Buber's formulation, equating Buber's "relation" roughly with Cohen's "correlation" and that, for Buber, the "Ich-Du" and "Ich-Es" pairs are never spoken, they are merely thought-constructs. For an analysis, see Von Dániel Biró, "Franz Rosenzweigs Krtik an Martin Bubers 'Ich und Du'" in Schmied-Kowarzik 1988b: 689–96.

40 See Levinas 2000: 102–109, for his discussion of "recurrence."

41 GS2: 270; SR: 242.

42 Ibid: 271; 243.

43 Ibid: 272; 244.

44 For this reading see Schaeffer 2000, which I analyze in Chapter 7.

45 GS2: 273; SR: 245.

46 Ibid: 274; 246.

47 Ibid.

48 Ibid: 275; 247.

49 Ibid: 276; 248.

50 Ibid.

51 See "Unpacking My Library" in Benjamin 1977: 596–7.

52 GS2: 278; SR: 250.

53 Ibid: 279; 251.

54 Ibid.

55 Ibid: 281; 252.

56 Ibid: 295; 265. Also note Schiller's undertitle to his play, "*Die Räuber*" — *in tyrannos* that Schiller added to the second edition of his play, in Schiller 1806. View an image of the original Frontspiece at: http://www.teachsam.de/deutsch/d_literatur/d_aut/sci/sci_dram/raeuber/sci_raeub_2_2.htm. Schiller was responding to existing social class exploitation in Schwaden, an intervention that Rosenzweig must have known when he chose to use *in tyrannos* as the undertitle for his own Part III of the *The Star*. This accords with my interpretation of Rosenzweig's ethical critique of a segregated political system and his proposal for creating and supporting alternative, pluralist communities, viz. his "idealist" constellation of Jewish, Christian, and pagan communities.

57 GS2: 315; SR: 284.

58 Ibid.

59 GS2: 317; SR: 285.

60 Ibid: 318–319; 286–287.

61 Ibid: 326; 294.

62 Ibid: 328; 295.

63 Ibid: 329; 296.

64 Ibid: 331: 298.

65 Ibid: 352; 299.

66 See, for example, the *midrashic* retelling of the *Haggadah* by Liora Gubkin, "ReReading Redemption: The Warsaw Gehtto Uprising in Passover Haggodot" in Simon 2000a: 71–82.

67 GS: 352; SR: 317.

68 "Most discussions of Rosenzweig's anti-Zionsim, including Gordon's, stick to
    the jejune position staked out in "Atheistic Theology" and *The Star*. They usu-
    ally neglect the very favorable and even pro-Zionist letters to Benno Jacob, an
    oversight which, given their inclusion in the Glatzer anthology, is really rather
    bizzare. See the Zion chapter in the Halevy commentary, in GS4₁: 201ff. Clearly,
    there is a transition at work after the appearance of *The Star* that most of the
    diasporist readings of Rosenzweig intentionally obscure." I owe this observation
    to Zachary Braiterman from the *Journal of Textual Reading* tr-list, March 5,
    2004: http://etext.lib.virginia.edu/journals/tr/volume3/braiterman.html (accessed
    18 November 2010).

69 GS2: 364ff; SR: 328ff. See also Santner 2001, who does an excellent job of tracing
    connections of Rosenzweig's political stance with those on Benjamin and Derrida.
    However, his ultimate conclusions about Rosenzweig and Hölderlin remain
    incompatible with that analysis. This will become clear with what I have to say
    about Heidegger and Hölderlin in Chapter 7.

70 See also in this regard Benjamin's comments about architecture being the most
    fundamental kind of work of art in his remarks on the architecture of cities,
    especially of Paris, and the ongoing need for human shelter: "Architecture has
    never had fallow periods. Its history is longer than that of any other art, and its
    effect ought to be recognized in any attempt to account for the relationship of the
    masses to the work of art." See "The Work of Art in the Age of Reproducibility"
    in Benjamin 2003: 268.

71 GS2: 404; SR: 364.

72 Ibid: 405; 364.

73 Ibid.

74 For contemporary interpretations of what Rosenzweig means by the face, see:
    Mosès 1982: 2832–85; "The Face of Truth and Jewish Mysticism" in Cohen 1994:
    2412–73; and Samuelson 1999: 329–330. My interpretation of Rosenzweig's face
    is quite different from each of these, as noted, and has to do with what I contend
    is Rosenzweig's abiding interest in an ethically informed aesthetic engagement.

CHAPTER 5

HEIDEGGER'S HAMMER: FROM THE WORKSHOP OF *BEING AND TIME* TO THE WORK OF ART

I now turn to interpret the ethical consequences of Heidegger's philosophy of art by following the thread of the development of his sense of the ethical through distinct phases of his philosophy, which I do in the next three chapters of this book. First, I analyze how Heidegger's philosophy of art originated in what is inadequately developed in *Being and Time*. I then work through his formal philosophy of art out of *The Origin of the Work of Art*, which likewise remained unsatisfactory. And finally, in Chapter 7, I focus on Heidegger's thinking about the poetry of Friedrich Hölderlin, specifically, his philosophy of Hölderlin's poeticizing the origin and destiny of the German people. In that effort, I focus on Heidegger's presentation of "The Ister." What should become clear as I work through the next three chapters is the extent to which Heidegger's body of work exhibits a coherent conceptual development with troubling ethical implications. The first part of my task is to explicate parts of *Being and Time* in order to trace the continuity of a development towards a philosophy of art out of the ontological framework of *Being and Time* through his later works. I contend that Heidegger's "turn" to considerations of art and language is already at work in this text is what is missing from the phenomenological project he lays out as a guidebook towards becoming a more authentic human being, that is, a project that he begins but never finishes of becoming more authentically Da-sein.

I. Out of the "things themselves" — sighting the historical horizons of Da-sein

Against Hubert Dreyfuss's contention that Heidegger's project is somehow stanceless, I argue that Heidegger carefully constructs his workshop by means of a hermeneutic activity that takes shape as a philosophy of language derived from a clearly defined phenomenological stance.[1] That stance presupposes a condition of fallenness of human beings from their original or most authentic way of being-in-the-world, which takes place in the space of concernful engage-ments in the contextual environments historically set out by how humans have continued to raise, or to not raise, the question of the meaning of the being of beings. The "temporal-spatial" context for the possibility of original authenticity, which is determined by the relationship of Da-sein with things in the world, is what Heidegger sets up in the first stages of *Being and Time*, and is that which becomes the platform from which all of his subsequent teaching and writing performances occur.

At the end of the Introduction to *Being and Time*, Heidegger tells us that the theme of his work, an investigation into the question of the meaning of being (*Sein*), entails focusing on his interpretation of the particular being (*Seiend*), named Da-sein, whose being is already historic, thus further entailing an investigation into the genetic history of that particular being. But how does Heidegger guide us on such a journey into the historical origins and parameters of Da-sein? For that we must turn our attention to how Heidegger prepares us for this journey in the earlier parts of his Introduction by invoking not only the method of phenomenology but, by the end of the Introduction, the name of Husserl is also invoked in order to move beyond [his] beginning to philosophize from already pre-determined actualities as possibility:

> The following investigations would not have been possible without the foundation laid by Edmund Husserl; with his *Logical Investigations* phenomenology achieved a breakthrough. Our elucidations of the preliminary concept of phenomenology show that its essential character does not consist in its *actuality* as a philosophical "movement." Higher than actuality stands *possibility*. We can understand phenomenology solely by seizing upon it as a possibility.[2]

Indeed, instead of setting us off to follow a Mephistophelan thread into the underworld of negation as a preliminary pursuit of self-introspection, as Rosenzweig does, Heidegger echoes Husserl's imperative by turning our attention "to the things themselves" in order to guide us in how to initially recall the forgotten question of being as a first move towards his version of coming to a certain, carefully defined kind of self-knowledge. In fact, what Heidegger ascertains by referring to the "things themselves" becomes the critical point of access for making our way into what he later asserts about an art-thing as the work of art, and the consequences of such assertions for situating his philosophy of art within ethical horizons.

But does he turn our attention to the "things themselves?" Indeed he does and how he does so is an important methodological issue, since he begins his directive task from the very opening pages of *Being and Time*. Heidegger follows Husserl's heuristic directive by adopting the method of phenomenology from his teacher but does so by taking a cue from another reverberating thread of the many used by Husserl to weave his phenomenological web. The primary thread that Heidegger pulls out for us to follow is the intentionality structures of the subject, reformulated by Heidegger as the questioning attitude of any and every Da-sein. Moreover, and again from Husserl, that intentional attitude occurs on the horizon of possibilities established according to the parameters of temporality, but a temporality other than that developed by Kant. However, what is other than both Husserl and Kant is that Heidegger also turns our attention to that typical being, which he claims is the non-arbitrary starting point for formulating and elaborating the question of being. If the meaning of the being of beings is to be ascertained, the being that inheres in all things, the only way to do so is to be guided by the very intentionality of the inquiry itself, and thus, to that particular being that inquires about the being of itself — Da-sein:

> Thus to work out the question of being means to make a being — one who questions — transparent in its being. Asking this question, as a mode of *being* of a being, is itself essentially determined by what is asked about in it — being. This being which we ourselves in each case are and which includes inquiry among the possibilities of its being we formulate terminologically as Da-sein.[3]

Raising for himself the problem of the hermeneutic circle, Heidegger defends what is obviously a case of "circular reasoning" in how he presupposes coming to the question of being out of asserting that being is the issue to be sought and which therefore determines the line of inquiry in advance. However, he attempts to sidestep any criticism by initially appealing to a traditional logic of implicit/explicit determination. But this appeal clearly indicates Heidegger's peculiar methodological choice that begins just prior to his formulation of the term Da-sein as that being which is transparently self-reflective. The move begins when Heidegger attempts to distinguish an inquiry into the meaning of being as uniquely different from any other kind of inquiry and that results in rejecting traditional forms of narrative justification. Not content with simple negation, though, Heidegger refers to Plato's counsel in the *Sophist* that, in addressing an inquiry into what being means, we need to avoid the "*mython tina diēgeisthai*," that is, we should avoid determining beings by relying on "telling a story" based on tracing the origins of a being in another being, thereby fixing being as merely a link to be discovered in the causal chain of all that already is. Rather, the "circular reasoning" that Heidegger develops as a logic of an implicit/explicit, "backwards and forwards" mode of logical inquiry is, in itself, a traditional methodological choice. But in Heidegger's hands the obvious candidate for elaborating such a choice, axiomatic deductive logic, is declined in favor of his contention that what is at work is a "laying bare and exhibiting the ground."[4] In this case, the exhibiting has to do with laying bare the distinctive relation (*Bezug*) between that being which is Da-sein and that which is questioned about, the question of being itself. In fact, Heidegger asserts, "The way what is questioned essentially engages our questioning belongs to the innermost meaning of the question of being."[5] And this means that the way in which we question is by beginning with that particular being that is Da-sein.

By setting himself on the path of reestablishing the question of the meaning of being to its place as "the" question which orients one's way of being human, Heidegger provides us with a radically new task for doing philosophy in the lived-world of particular beings. Specifically, that human existence, which Heidegger calls Da-sein, is, as Da-sein, the unavoidable and undeniable

starting point for any endeavor to philosophically think through that way of
being. As this new sort of starting point, what makes Da-sein different than
any other particular being is that it understands itself *as* an existing being in
its way of being and its expressions to itself and to others of that way of being:
"Being-as-understanding is itself a being-as-determination of Da-sein."[6] As
Heidegger goes on to explicate, what he means by how Da-sein understands
and expresses itself as being, is that Da-sein already exists in certain ways in the
world before it makes its own existence explicitly (or theoretically) a theme for
itself, and an analysis of that way of existing is the preliminary task that needs
to be done before an analysis of being can adequately take place. This latter
form of explicit theorizing is what Heidegger proposes inevitably becomes our
ontological task, because, "The ontical sketching out of Da-sein lies in that it
is ontological."[7] What being ontological entails is that Da-sein constructs its
ontology, its study of or way of accounting for being. The phrase Heidegger
uses to convey this constructive activity is *"Ontologie ausbilden"* which
connotes not only construction as developing but also cultivating, training,
and educating. Denoted as *Logos*, giving an account of being is a matter of
becoming educated in one's culture and of cultivating one's education about
such a way of being in the world. But Heidegger tells us that it is not just any
being that commands our attention; rather, we are primarily concerned with
Da-sein because it is that being that is peculiarly characterized by explicating its
implicit concern for its own being. Therefore, what is called for is an analysis
of the fundamental structures of Da-sein.

The first step in carrying out such an analytic of Da-sein is to sufficiently
work out the ground-structures of *how* Da-sein is oriented to the problem of
being. As I will point out later, this orientation to the problem of being becomes
the issue of how the phenomenon of art orients us. Indeed, this issue of orientation to the particularity of our way of being as a particular kind of being, leads
us to not only engage with our own concrete and material situatedness in the
world, as we find ourselves in and among other beings, but also determines the
very fate of ourselves as a people. But that determination will only become clear
by working through how Heidegger sets up his framework for dealing with
the problem of being and why he establishes Da-sein as that central figure with
which to address the problem. Thus, in the opening sections of *Being and Time*,
Heidegger addresses the issue of how we gain access to Da-sein and concludes
that the way that access is gained is through better understanding how Da-sein
orients itself as it "generally and for the most part [is] in its everydayness."[8] By
coming to grips with how Da-sein orients itself in its everydayness, the essential
structures that factically and enduringly determine Da-sein will come to light
and, thus, the "Being of this being will awaken and spread up and out."[9] But
those structures will only come to light by accomplishing the preparatory
analysis of Da-sein and then repeating that analysis on the higher and more
authentic ontological level.

However, the process of coming to light, of spreading up and out, is not merely a spatial occurrence. It is primarily, and ultimately for the most part, a temporal occurrence. Heidegger makes this important conceptual move early in his text by telling us that the meaning (or sense: *Sinn*) of the Being of this being named Da-sein will be shown to be temporality.[10] Moreover, the proof that the meaning of the Being of the being named Da-sein is temporality will be tested and validated (*bewährt*) by repeating that analysis of its structures through exercising an ontological analysis. In other words, like Rosenzweig, Heidegger analyzes our being in and with other beings in the world in alignment with an analysis of how we understand existence through categories of time and temporality. However, he diverges from Rosenzweig's approach in how that analysis is practically and historically applied. In fact, Heidegger claims that insofar as Da-sein understands and expresses itself in and as being, it *is* time. And this connection of *being and time* becomes, for Heidegger, the horizon of all understanding of being. Significantly, what Heidegger contends is that by coming to understand the connection of being and time through analyzing the structures of the temporality of Da-sein, we will become more aware of the difference between this new and genuine grasp of time and the traditional, vulgar concept of time, set down originally by Aristotle and maintained up until Bergson. In fact, it is with Bergson's confusion of time with space that Heidegger takes issue.

In a crucial passage, Heidegger points out that "time" has long functioned as a way to establish what he considers are "naïve differences between different regions of being."[11] What began as developing a border between the so-called temporal beings, like the processes of nature and the happenings of history on the one hand and the so-called "untemporal" beings like spatial and countable things or conditions on the other hand, led to dividing the "timeless" meaning of sentences from the "temporal" utterance of those sentences. This then led to the occurrence of separating "temporal" being from a "trans-temporal" eternity and the history of attempts to bridge this gap resulted in merely accepting the statement that "time is" without noting how claims using temporal categories have actually and historically functioned to separate realms of beings. As is well known, for Heidegger, the unspoken discourse of the problem of time is deeply rooted in the forgotten problem of the meaning of being. But well before Heidegger thought through the opening passages of *Being and Time*, Rosenzweig took up this very same problematic in the Introduction to *The Star of Redemption* but in a significantly different manner. For Rosenzweig, the division between the "here" and the "beyond" is marked by calling on the personal exemplar of the actual philosopher Nietzsche, who negates the division of regions of being into this-worldly and other-worldly while simultaneously establishing a new realm for the ethical.[12] By contrast, Heidegger stays with explicating the impersonal, ontological structures of Da-sein to address this problem of demarcation.

In order to explicate those structures, Heidegger further argues that we need to conceive being out of the modes of time such that temporality is no longer merely understood as somehow meaning being in a kind of eternal and unchangeable vessel called "time." Instead, only by working out the temporality of being and specifically the problem of temporality itself, will we arrive at the first concrete answer to the question about the meaning of being. What such a claim entails is that the question of the meaning of being is not able to be drawn out of some kind of isolated realm of logical deductions; rather, we must research the context of the history of questions that have already served to constitute the horizons of our own task. This move, in effect, is similar to the move that Rosenzweig makes in Part I of *The Star* when he asserts that the only way forward to develop meaningful alternatives to totalizing systematic intellectual and socio-political frameworks is to wrestle with those empirically existing philosophies, those sciences that developed around the names of metaphysics, metalogic, and meta-ethics. Rosenzweig then turns to the actual, historical figures who, in exemplary fashion, founded such regions of thought and ways of thinking. And while Heidegger remains with the ontological figure of Da-sein by claiming, in Section 6, "The Task of a Destruction of the History of Ontology," that all research, and especially any research into ontology, "is an ontical possibility of Da-sein,"[13] like Rosenzweig, Heidegger inevitably turns towards history for understanding the structures of existence. It seems clear, however, that such a turn is based upon a transformed notion of history and contradicts his earlier disclaimer.

And while Rosenzweig turns to the empirical accounts out of the history of philosophy of particular figures from that history in order to develop his peculiar form of narrative philosophizing, Heidegger maintains that any research into the way of being of Da-sein is research into *its* historicity (*Geshichtlichkeit*). Heidegger differentiates this latter sense from what he says is the usual meaning of the world "history," namely, an enumeration of the happenings of world-history. Historicity, rather than a mimetic recounting of a readily available sequence of events, should be set in the context of an analysis of Da-sein, a context that has to do with the "conditions of being" (*Seinsverfassung*) of the "happenings" (*Geschehens*) of Da-sein as such, and only upon such conditions is anything like world-history possible. Da-sein "is" its history:

> Da-sein is in every sense of its factical being, how and "what" it already was. Whether expressly or not, it *is* its past. And not only insofar as its past is "behind" it, shoving it onward and as a past "thing" that it still possesses as some kind of at-hand possession which occasionally worked its effects on it. Da-sein "is" its past in the way of its being, that, roughly said, "happens" in each case out of its future.[14]

The historicity of Da-sein is the way in which Da-sein understands itself in its ways of being and insofar as it is woken up to that environment of understanding does it find itself standing within that environment and oriented in a certain temporal way. Indeed, "This understanding discloses and orders the possibilities of its being."[15] Since Da-sein's very future possibilities of being are determined by its past, Heidegger can then say that its past does not *follow* Da-sein, but its past precedes it. This historicity of Da-sein can often be hidden from itself, but it can also be discovered and revealed to itself and, thus, lead to the preservation and the following of this or that tradition. In that case, the way of being of Da-sein is its way of historical questioning and researching, a task that it is able to take up only because it is already determined by its historicity.

However, if Da-sein grasps the possibilities that lie within it, not just its own existence but the meaning of existing itself, then its own historicity will become evident by way of the necessary showing of its ontic-ontological character. To get at the question of the meaning of being entails questioning after one's own history — to become historical, such that one is positively so inclined towards the past that the questions about possibility become one's own possession. In other words, in order to get at the meaning of being Da-sein must do so by explicating its own historicity and temporality; it must understand itself as historical. But how does that happen?

To begin with, Heidegger turns us away from our conventional approach to "doing" history, possibly taking a cue from Nietzsche's own project from *On the Use and Abuse of History*.[16] Heidegger asserts that when Da-sein becomes aware of itself as it enters into the kind of interpretation of its fundamental structures of being, it is not merely inclined to understand itself in terms of its "nearest and ordinary way of being,"[17] that is, out of the way of the world into which it has fallen and is reluctantly being drawn out. Rather, Da-sein has fallen and become entangled in traditions that have taken away its own leading role in questioning and choosing. What the "tradition" has done is to cause Da-sein to look away from itself towards foreign cultures and interests, away from its own roots and origins, away from its own historicity. The critique that Heidegger employs is by now a familiar one, namely, he questions the dominating intellectual traditions of modern institutional hegemonies, in this case, the hegemony of the metaphysical tradition that no longer allows for a philological and "material" investigation of its own elementary conditions. This critique should sound familiar because Rosenzweig likewise criticized what he considered a dominating metaphysical tradition in his attack on Hegelian Idealism and, like Rosenzweig, Heidegger claims that Hegel carried on the kinds of encrusted metaphysical dogmatizing set in place by Scholastics such as Thomas Aquinas and solidified in the Modern period by the transcendental metaphysics of Descartes. But for Heidegger, and not for Rosenzweig, what is formulaically and systematically forgotten, and that precisely remains unquestioned, is the question of being and the structures of the being of those substances taken for granted by Descartes, such as the subject, the I, reason, spirit, and person, or even the dialectical substantialization of the subject by Hegel.

So what Heidegger calls for is a loosening up of the hardened and dogmatic tradition (*Auflockerung der verhärteten Tradition*), a loosening, however, that does not entail doing away with the tradition itself. Rather, approaching the tradition with the tools of deconstruction, we can also look for the positive aspects of the tradition and how its boundaries can best be set. In a generally similar way, Rosenzweig notes with Nietzsche in the Introduction to *The Star* that critically considering the past is done precisely so that the past will not be destroyed in a riot of destructiveness, assuming a critical standpoint beyond traditional ethics that he calls the meta-ethical.[18] But unlike Rosenzweig, Heidegger's intent is to let the destructuring of the history of ontology be guided by the question of being, that is, by the very task of questioning the historical development of the tradition of ontology itself. It should be clear by my previous discussion of Rosenzweig's deontological treatment of that very history that Heidegger's approach to the meaning of being is quite different than Rosenzweig's. Rather than looking for what about being is hidden within the tradition, Rosenzweig contested traditional metaphysics for the way that conceptualizing being could lead to structures of totality, and thus of dominance and war, beginning, however, not with raising the question of the meaning of being, but raising the question of the meaning of nothing as the necessary complementary conceptualization from beginning thinking with being, specifically, in his presentation of the three-fold nothings of knowledge. Thus, Rosenzweig's path is forged by deconstructing inherited philosophical traditions before any reconstruction of any possible order of thinking the whole can take shape.

But the deconstruction Heidegger has in mind is not merely a shaking up of the traditional dogmatic and typological character of our intellectual patterns of categorization. Instead, what he has in mind is the positive and productive task of defining the limits of past ontological tradition in order to de-limit the possible field for investigation. In fact, instead of a destruction of the past, Heidegger calls for a critique of the way that past categories are used to dogmatically cover up the question of the meaning of being and how that question is tied up with the problem of time. And in order to carry out such an investigation into the history of ontology and the problem of time, Heidegger states that we have to work through the "fundamentally decisive stations of that history" and points out that the first and only philosopher who made any headway in addressing the correlation of being and time was Kant.[19] Now we seem to be back in familiar Rosenzweigian territory, considering the empirical "histories" of this or that philosopher who has influenced the very thinking projects by which any self-reflection is carried on whatsoever. But in fact, one of the first signs indicating how Heidegger sets himself on a philosophical path diverging from that taken by Rosenzweig is in his remarks about the obscurity of Kant's schematism, an obscurity that he reads as an inability to deal with phenomena on the one hand and temporality on the other hand. Recall, by contrast, Rosenzweig's reliance on Kant to guide us into our critical reflections on the traditional pathways of doing philosophy, which Rosenzweig sets up as the meta-sciences of the elements in Part 1 of *The Star*.[20] Rosenzweig does not take substantive issue with Kant until Book 3 of Part I where the issue at hand is Kant's reduction of epistemology to an Idealist monism which, for Rosenzweig, inevitably problematizes the possibilities of the ethical-based responsibility for the other, and his own move away from a traditional, deontological ethics of duty.[21]

In Heidegger's case, however, we find significantly embedded in the quote used to demonstrate how Kant was unable to "schematize" the "appearances," Heidegger's first oblique reference to art (*Kunst*) in *Being and Time*:

> Kant himself knew that he was venturing forth into a dark area: "This schematism of our understanding as regards appearances and their mere form is an *art* hidden in the depths of the human soul, the true manipulation of which we hardly ever are able to divine from nature, laid uncovered before our eyes." What it is that Kant shrinks back from here, as it were, must be brought to light thematically and fundamentally if the expression "being" is to otherwise have a demonstrable meaning.[22]

The meaning that Heidegger assigns to "art" in this passage, one of his first significant references to art in his entire corpus, is the pejorative designation of obscurity aimed at Kant's employment of schematism to investigate phenomena with respect to temporality and vice versa. Clearly, Heidegger's judgment is that Kant failed miserably in his attempt, a failure that Heidegger intends to resolve. Moreover, that "art" stands for obscurity and darkness is an early indicator of how Heidegger will continue to work at elaborating the relationality of the fourfold "elements" in terms of art, that is, the relationship of things (as phenomena), temporality, being (eventually referred to *as* god), and Da-sein. For such an elaboration, Kant was woefully ill-equipped precisely because of his own deontological stance.

From the very beginning, then, Heidegger contests Kant's analytic by claiming that what Kant shrank back from (*zurückweicht*) is just what must be brought to light if the expression "being" is to have an identifiable (*ausweisbare*) meaning. What Heidegger does is to contest Kant's work as a philosopher by purporting to elaborate those phenomena that are judged to be the most secret judgments of common sense, judgments that for Kant constitute the very business of philosophy. Where Kant fails is that, precisely through relying on the formality of his schematism, he misunderstands temporality entirely and adds to the problem by not dealing with the question of being at all. However, as is already fairly common knowledge, we know from the *Critique of Pure Reason*, and as Rosenzweig pointed out even earlier than Heidegger, Kant does deal with the "problem of being" by dismissing it as a grammatical category mistake, that is, that "being" cannot be an essence or substance but is always only and ever a verbal construction, a way that humans have devised to account for identity claims or subject/predicate relations. However, for Heidegger, such dismissiveness is a failure on Kant's part to account for an important phenomenon of how humans live in the world. Heidegger implies that the "shrinking back" occurs through Kant hiding behind his formalism. In fact, Heidegger contends that because Kant's analysis of temporality and being is so woefully inadequate, he is incapable of accounting for Da-sein, namely, the subjectivity of the subject ontologically understood as the structures of existence of human beings. What Kant *does* do is to merely take over, in dogmatic fashion, Descartes's position, that relies on a relatively vulgar understanding of temporality and which results in an inadequate analysis of the relationship of time and the "I think."

For Heidegger, the problem that Kant repeats that began with Descartes was the indefinite way that he dealt with the *sum* of the *cogito sum*, and so working out the ontology of the *cogito sum* becomes the second station along the way (after Kant) towards deconstructing the history of ontology. Heidegger's initial protestation is that since Descartes was so certain about the *cogito* he felt that he had no need to question the *sum*. What Descartes does do, however, is not merely neglect an ontological analysis but, instead, in his *Meditations* he uncritically carries along a medieval ontology which he posits as a fundamental and radical new beginning. Of course, for Heidegger, there is nothing radical in that beginning by Descartes since Descartes merely adopted the medieval meaning of "being" by identifying "body" and "soul" (or mind) as "created beings" and god as "uncreated being." In passing, note how differently the treatment of Descartes is in *The Star*, where Rosenzweig relies on negating the positive consequences of Descartes' method of doubt as a way to establish the logic, as the accounting of *logos*, for thinking the biological, cause and effect structures of an environing world.

But what is more important for my thesis about the origin of a philosophy of art in *Being and Time* is in how Heidegger moves his reader's attention to what he considers to be the more salient problem of Descartes's philosophy, which is in how he misinterpreted the meaning of the *res cogitans* by not defining it ontologically. What Heidegger points out, is that Descartes's reliance on what he dogmatically carries on from the medieval tradition of ontology is most evident by looking beyond medieval thinkers to the Ancient Greeks who focused on their interpretations of the being of beings in-the-"world," understood in its broadest sense as "nature." And from there, we know that their interpretations interpreted being out of "time" because of how they employed the word παρουςιά (parousia) or ουςιά (ousia) which, as Heidegger asserts, means presence (*Anwesenheit*) in German. Importantly, Heidegger's employment of the word "presence" entails the definite temporal mode of the "present" which means that, in order to best understand the being of beings, the being of things of the world, we need to attend to how those things present themselves as presencing beings that make their being present and tangibly known to those beings that are concerned about other being(s)-in-the-world.

This is a critical point in Heidegger's analysis since it is not simply other beings in the world that first and primarily demand the attention of we human beings, those beings named Da-sein by Heidegger. In fact, the third station on the way of interpreting the history of ontology becomes occupied by those very Greek philosophers who, with their peculiar Greek ontology, likewise looked to Da-sein, "the being of the human," to define their philosophizing as that kind of being that, in its way of living, is essentially determined as being-able-to-read (*Redenkönnen*).[23] Moreover, Heidegger argues that the Greeks used the term *legein* (λεδειν) as a guiding thread to characterize the being-structure of humans insofar as they "encounter" beings defined by relationships of speaking and being-spoken-to.[24] Such usage led to Plato's development of ancient ontology into his form of the dialectic and its eventual permutation into a hermeneutic of the λογον, that is, his various presentations of dialectical interpretations on how to give an account of that which is. For Heidegger, though, the attention Plato came to pay to the dialectic made it superfluous for any engagement with beings as such, a development Aristotle took note of in his redefinition of *legein* as *noein* (νοειν), what Heidegger interprets as "the simple perception of something at-hand in its pure being-at-hand,"[25] a guiding methodological thread for philosophizing that, Heidegger claims, Parmenides used in his approach to being.[26] Furthermore, that kind of being that is characterized as presence is that kind of being which is present in the sense of the German hyphenated work *Gegen-wart* meaning, "against-waiting."

But the Greek's grasp of this meaning of being as "presence" was only implicitly and not explicitly worked out for its fundamental ontological implications. Heidegger takes as his task to work out these implications drawing especially on the way that Aristotle handled time and being as subjects of knowledge, and which, he contends, defined all hitherto attempts, including Bergson's and Kant's. But such insights can only be gained through carrying out the kind of deconstruction of the ontological tradition that Heidegger undertakes in order to show how the question of being is unavoidable and must be repeated. Moreover, the only way to deconstruct that tradition is by following Heidegger's guidance in adopting the phenomenological method for the investigation (at least, according to Heidegger).

Heidegger explicates what he means by phenomenology as that method which should be used to elaborate the question of being. In fact, he says, phenomenology is primarily a concept used to refer to a method, not to that which is investigated but to how the investigation proceeds. Heidegger claims to carry out his "method" by proceeding not along any predetermined or established discipline called ontology, or whatever. Rather, what determines the course of his analysis is "the objective necessity of particular questions and procedures demanded by the 'things themselves.'" That means that we have to in some way come to terms with the "things themselves" and do so despite his disclaimer that he proceeds "neither from an established standpoint nor direction."[27] That is, that his project is somehow stanceless.

Heidegger claims that we need to understand the meaning of the word and that the word is a combined one. That means that we first need to understand what we mean by the term "phenomenon" and then what we mean by the term "logos." After that, we can then become clearer about how the two verbal constructions combine to form the method of phenomenology. Heidegger begins his etymological analysis by referring to the way that the term was used in its original Greek context:

> The Greek expression φαινόμενον, from which the term "phenomenon" is derived, comes from the verb φαόνεσθαι, which means "to show itself"; φαινόμενον thus means, that which shows itself, the self-showing (*das Sichzeigende*), the revelatory (*das Offenbare*). Φαίνοθα itself is a *mediale* construction from φαίνω, to bring into the day, to place in brightness. Φαίνω belongs to the root φα-, like φως, the light or the brightness, that means, that within which something can be revealed, can become visible in itself. The meaning of the expression "phenomenon" is captured as "that-which-shows-itself-in-itself" (*Sich-an-ihm-selbst-zeigende*), the revelatory. The φαινόμενα, the "phenomena," are thus the totality of that which lies in the day (*was am Tage liegt*) or that which can be brought to light.[28]

What Heidegger tells us, however, is that this original meaning contains already within it another possibility, that of "semblance" (*Scheinen*), such that insofar as something can claim to show itself as revealed it is also able to show itself as that which it is not. This other possibility of "phenomenon" is, however, not what Kant means by appearance (*Erscheinung*).

Heidegger argues that what Kant means by appearance has to do with that which precisely does not show itself in the sense of "sickness-symptoms (appearances)" (*Krankheiterscheinungen*). What Kant means by appearance as that which shows itself, in his elaboration of the function of intuition (*Anschauung*), is precisely that which does not show itself in the sense that a symptom is not the disease itself, but is rather something that does not show itself. Thus, empirically, the disease makes itself known through something that does not show itself, but is rather an indication of that which it is not. For example, vomiting is *not* the human immunodeficiency virus, but is merely an indication of that which is at its origin a self-showing phenomenon in itself, but simply does not appear. Heidegger spells out the difference by noting that

> *Phenomenon* — the self-showing in itself — means a distinctive way something can be encountered. On the other hand, *appearance* means a referential relation

in beings themselves such that what does the *referring* (the making known) can fulfill its possible function only if it shows itself in itself — only if it is a "phenomenon."[29]

In choosing phenomenology as his method, Heidegger contends that, rather than returning to Kant, he must continue to follow, at least in part, the guidelines set forth by Husserl. This means that, only insofar as the "beings" which Kant intends to apprehend through empirical intuition — time and space — are understood as phenomena of phenomenology can they be shown to be the kind of beings that show themselves in and of themselves. This becomes especially pertinent for Heidegger since Kant desires to found an "order" for the thinking "subject" by claiming space as its indwelling *a priori* condition, an illegitimate order because of its misunderstanding of the kind of "space" within and with which Da-sein dwells. But that is getting a bit ahead of my own analysis.

II. *The function of logos as relational speech and truth as aesthetics*

Besides the issue of what beings are referred to when we speak of phenomena, Heidegger says that in order to determine to what extent phenomenology is a science, we must become clear about what *logos* (λόγος) means. Briefly, and in general epistemological terms, how Heidegger understands *logos* is that it does not merely mean speech (its primary meaning), concept, reason, or even judgment. Rather, drawing on Aristotle, Heidegger contends that *logos*, essentially, has the original meaning of "to reveal that about which is being talked about in speech."[30] Again, specifically drawing from Aristotle,[31] Heidegger elaborates *logos* as *apophantic*, that is: "*logos* lets something be seen (φαίνοθαι), namely, that about which the speech is and *for* the speaker (the medium) or for those who speak with each other."[32] Genuine speech reveals that about which speech itself is talking and makes it accessible (*zugänglich*) to another being. And in order to be concrete, genuine speech accomplishes this kind of accessibility in words such that something can be sighted (*etwas gesichtet ist*). In short, *logos* is letting something be seen by indicating it, and thus has the synthetic function of letting something be seen *as* something, not as a corresponding of the duality of inside and outside "somethings" but, rather, *logos* is that way of speaking to another, and thus already presupposes a relation of Da-seins (emphasis on the plural), that brings to light a way of "being-together" (*beisammen*) of a being as it is in itself. Thus, in speaking, Da-sein already presupposes the presence of the other with whom it speaks and a way of speaking that is a kind of accessible showing.

In this context, and as one of the most critical passages supporting my thesis that Heidegger's philosophy of art is already "at hand" in *Being and Time*, is that section of his Introduction where he initiates a discourse on truth. As with Rosenzweig, and keeping to his orientation towards a philosophy of speech initiated with his reflections on *logos*, Heidegger insists that truth, understood from the perspective of letting-something-be-seen, is not a matter of correspondence or even of finding truth primarily in the "place" (*Ort*) of *logos*. What Heidegger claims is that when we speak about what is "true" (*Wahr*) according to a Greek, Aristotelian concept of truth, we must turn to an expression that is even more original (*ursprünglicher*) than *logos* and that would be *aisthesis* (αἴσθησις). What I contend is that in this remarkable claim we can discern Heidegger's oft-cited "turn" already prefigured in the opening pages of *Being and Time*. To begin with, we should ask: what does Heidegger precisely mean by this "turn" from a conventional understanding of *logos* to a phenomenological understanding of *logos*? It is a turn from relying on the occurrence of speech and analysis to what he notes as "the simple sense perception of something."[33] This entails that what counts for measuring the extent to which something is true or not is a matter of measuring the extent to which that which functions in a bodily, sensual sense occurs in accordance with the organs involved in whatever perceptual occurrence is in play. Heidegger makes this functional dimension of the aesthetic experience clear with his assertion that,

> To the extent that an αἴσθησις aims at its ἴδια ["idia" — what is its own] — the beings genuinely accessible only *through* it and *for* it, for example, looking at colors — perception is always true. This means that looking always discovers colors, hearing always discovers tones. What is in the purest and most original sense "true" — that is, what only discovers in such a way that it can never cover up anything, is the pure νοεῖν (noein), the simple, observing perception of the simplest determination of the being of beings as such.[34]

What makes this claim for *aisthesis* so commanding is that Heidegger further argues that such a "noetic" experience can never be false, in the way of covering something up, but, at its worst can only misperceive, in a privative sense, and not provide "simple, appropriate access" to the being of beings.[35]

Finally, at the end of his considerations of truth, perception, aesthetics, and judgment, Heidegger comes back to his guide Husserl by drawing in his revised construction of the relational structures of intentionality.[36] This contrasts with a theory of judgment as the intellectual form which should lie at the basis of our theory of knowledge — and here, I suggest that Heidegger has an attack on Kant's later work in synthesizing aesthetics, ethics, and epistemology in his sights, namely Kant's *Critique of Judgment*. In that penultimate work, Kant works through a critique of aesthetic experience as essential to determining the kinds of ethical judgments which provide the possibilities of building ethical, responsible communities of rational, autonomous individuals. Although this task is based on Kant's idealism of the *sensus communis*, it is nonetheless a relational task that takes into account the ultimate unaccountability of aesthetic experiences which lets the experience of an other stand as the basis of their own meaningful, sensually founded judgments. What compels us to continue to draw from this "critique" lies precisely in how Kant attempts to enliven a sense for communal responsibility. What dampens such enthusiasm, however, is that Kant's idealism and teleological metaphysics dictate what we are to make of an aesthetic experience.[37] Additionally, there is Kant's seminal assertions about defending the centrality of free and spontaneous autonomy as the primary foundation for ethical decision-making. But to his endless credit, Kant does maintain an orientation towards a community that is shaped by its ethical concerns, that is, by the responsibility of its members for themselves and towards others.

By contrast, what Heidegger has in mind with his method of ontological phenomenology is to proceed "To the things themselves!" by bringing to account (*legein*) the material content of whatever is "intended" through allowing that "whatever" to show itself in itself. That means that the phenomenon is such that it does not reveal itself, or show itself, since it at first explicitly remains concealed while nonetheless being, in itself, that which essentially is that kind of thing that shows itself. As Heidegger notes, ". . . what remains *concealed* in an exceptional sense, or what falls back and is *covered up* again, or shows itself only in a distorted way, is not this or that being but rather, as we have shown in our foregoing observations, the *being* of beings."[38] Besides concealment, the other two ways of covering up beings are that beings can be undiscovered or buried over, the last being the most pernicious and common, entailing semblance and distortion. The concepts that more or less correspond to this or that being are respectively integrated into a system taking on the "semblance" of clarity and thus do not need any further justification. What Heidegger seems to have in mind with such a line of thought is best exemplified by arguments made by positivists which rely upon the "self-evidence" of their foundations, distorting their original premises and covering up what was initially "grasped." But that is another pathway that would lead to a different thesis than that which I am developing here.

In order to begin clarifying my thesis, that Heidegger already lays down the foundation for his philosophy of art in *Being and Time*, the following passage exemplifies an important point about how we should stand in meaningful relation to the things in our environment:

> The way of encountering being and the structures of being in the mode of phenomenon must first be *wrested* from the objects of phenomenology. Thus the *point of departure* of the analysis, the *access* to the phenomenon, and *passage through* the prevalent coverings must secure their own method. The idea of an "originary" and "intuitive" grasp and explication of phenomena must be opposed to the naïveté of an accidental, "immediate," and unreflective "beholding."[39]

What Heidegger has in mind with this "wresting" is a fundamental way of approaching being, a form of covert violence connected with his understanding of deconstruction and that becomes an essential moment in what constitutes an authentic event called "the work of art." Without getting too far ahead of myself, the event of "wresting" is itself built into what Heidegger will eventually depict as the battle to wrest meaning out of the ongoing work of constructing and erecting works, as worlds, out of the earth. It will also become the battle of the new gods against the old gods for determining what counts as holy and worthy of being preserved and maintained.

Early on in *Being and Time*, however, Heidegger must establish the priority of Da-sein as that univocal kind of being that interprets being in such a way that it allows beings, beginning with itself, to show themselves in themselves. Discovering the hermeneutic structures of Da-sein through elaborating "the historicity of Da-sein ontologically as the ontic condition of the possibility of the discipline of history,"[40] is the *sine qua non* for establishing the horizon of interpretation for any other phenomenal being, and the methodological basis for all of the other historical humanistic disciplines, including the philosophy of art. Curiously, though, Heidegger weds these assertions with his claim that "*Being is the transcendens pure and simple.* [and that] The transcendence of the being of Da-sein is a distinctive one since in it lies the possibility and necessity of the most radical individuation."[41] In a footnote to this assertion, Heidegger glosses his use of the term "*transcendens*" by noting that his appropriation does not derive from a scholastic etymology but, rather, transcendence should be understood [preliminarily, of course] as: "the ecstatic-temporal (*Zeitlichkeit*) — temporality (*Temporalität*); but 'horizon'! Being has 'thought beyond' (*überdacht*) beings. However, transcendence from the truth of being: the event (*das Ereignis*)."[42] The importance of this "hedging" only becomes clear with the later development of Heidegger's thoughts about art and *Ereignis*, built upon the centrality of the autonomous figure of Da-sein that he establishes in *Being and Time*.

But what becomes clear in Heidegger's presentation of the phenomenological method is that by developing a method in the way that he does in order to focus on the being of beings, and not merely on the being of Da-sein, is that Da-sein appears as that particular kind of being that is set in the context of being-in-the-world that consists of other kinds of beings, preliminarily beings called things. What then becomes crucial for Heidegger is to differentiate Da-sein from those other kinds of beings, those things, as having an existentially determinate relationship to and with those things. Phenomenologically, this means that in order for Da-sein to discover its own orientation it has to come to terms with how it deals with those very things and how it is not itself essentially a thing. Its characteristics are precisely not thing-like in how they are determined by the way in which Da-sein's temporality emerges from and defines its own kind of being.

In the section where Heidegger elucidates his phrase "being-in-the-world," and as a way to clarify the "integration of the existential analytic," Heidegger raises the issue of "things" in distinguishing the analytic of Da-sein from the descriptions of anthropology, psychology, biology, and theology.[43] Specifically, the first mention of things as such occurs in a paragraph that has to do with the historiographical, in which Heidegger raises what he considers to be Descartes's putative founding of modern philosophy with the principle *cogito ergo sum*. For Heidegger, Descartes resorts to his founding principle in order to come to terms with the question that is not raised when distinguishing between the being of things and their thingliness and the being of spirit or subject. By considering Descartes in this way, Heidegger indicates that he chooses not to focus on the "things themselves" as a Husserlian phenomenologist might but, rather, to disclose the method of his own analytic that is structured around the usability or servicability of things by *a* Da-sein, in general. The point of his discussion and rejection of Descartes, Bergson, and Dilthey is that each of them, without realizing their limitations, contribute to the conclusion that, "The person is not a thing-like substantial being." Furthermore, they also contribute to the insight that "the being of the person . . . [can not] . . . consist in being a subject of rational acts that have a certain lawfulness."[44] Through Christian dogma, the teaching of transcendence — of humans being created in the image of god and thus being *drawn* to god, takes over the ancient Aristotelian definition of the human as a "thinking animal." However, both definitions, in their attempt to determine the essence of the human, have forgotten the question of the meaning of its being.

In such a metaphysical understanding, because human being has self-evident *objective* presence as a *thing* among other created things, it's a "given" and no longer a matter of question. That is, as created, human being is "given" and thus no longer the source of question, it is no longer a self-referential question for itself. By contrast, Heidegger draws our attention to a distinction that he makes between things as objectively and locatively related to other things, a relationship Heidegger calls *categorial*, and the kind of being that constitutionally belongs to Da-sein, what Heidegger calls *existential*. However, Heidegger makes this move specifically not in order to get at a way of differentiating between the being of things and the being of Da-sein, in such a way that Da-sein can be understood non-spatially. Rather, he notes that insofar as we can say that Da-sein is located, we should say that it dwells (*wohnt*) in-the-world in a care-full and familiar way:

> "In" stems from *innan-*, to live, *habitare*, to dwell. "*An*" means I am used to, familiar with, I take care of something. It has the meaning of *colo* in the sense of *habito* and *diligo*. We characterized this being to whom being-in belongs in this meaning as the being which I myself always am. The expression "*bin*" is connected with "*bei*." "*Ich bin*" (I am) means dwell, I stay near . . . the world as

something familiar in such and such a way. Being as the infinitive of "I am": that is, understood as an existential, means to dwell near . . ., to be familiar with . . . *Being-in is thus the formal existential expression of the being of Da-sein* which has the essential constitution of being-in-the-world.[45]

What Heidegger seeks to dispel is what he claims is the naive metaphysical, and theologically constructed understanding that Da-sein is at first some kind of created "spiritual thing which is then subsequently placed 'in' space."[46] The problem that Heidegger seeks to diagnose in these passages is the problem of how Da-sein, as traditionally informed, "skips over the phenomenon of worldliness ontically and ontologically in its way of knowing the world."[47] In order to dispel the possibility of "skipping over," Heidegger claims that we need the correct point of phenomenological access as our point of departure for a methodological directive in bringing the world into view. Thus, the importance of determining the care relationships of Da-sein with how it relates with the things that surround it in-the-world, how it *dwells* as being-in, reveals that the spatiality of the horizons that are opened up by an analytic of the average everydayness of Da-sein is the *nearest* kind of spatiality whereby the being of Da-sein is disclosed.

However, Da-sein's primordial project in the world is one that has to do with its history and its destiny, its *Geshichte* and its *Geschick*. And since that project is primarily constituted as care, complemented by the horizons of possibility, Da-sein only becomes authentically aware of itself as fallen and already thrown into a world in various ways of being toward the world by way of a referential totality of "care relations" understood as "use relations" — of producing, using, undertaking, accomplishing, observing, speaking, and determining. In other words, Da-sein relevantly relates to other beings in the world primarily via use-relationships signified as "cares" about the world but cares in such a way that Da-sein also always fundamentally misunderstands itself. It misunderstands itself since, by its very nature, Da-sein interprets itself through those very things in the world which it is not, namely, "things," traditionally taken for objective presences. However, while it interprets itself through those things which it is not, and thus always misunderstands itself, Da-sein also always is implicitly familiar with itself. Heidegger sets the phenomenological task, then, as addressing that problematic of vague misunderstandings and forgetfulness of the most important question(s) about being. What phenomenology, and thus philosophy, should then do is to prescriptively encourage an explicit understanding of Da-sein which is not limited to the misguided epistemological distortions of self-definition through definition by the other things in one's environment which are not one's ownmost way of being. Rather, we should concern ourselves with the discovery of a referential totality denoted as spatiality, through circumspective heedfulness, that is, we need to attend to how we care in the sense of attending to the serviceability of things in Da-sein's environment.

So, very early on in this text (and his career!), Heidegger already introduces us to a reformulated dualism of the clarity and transparency of the mode of authenticity versus the vague forgetfulness and superficiality of inauthenticity, with the thinly veiled agenda that we should affirm one over the other. Specifically, this understanding of Da-sein's "agenda" for being in the world "can become a task, and as scientific knowledge can take over the guidance for being-in-the-world."[48] But such a guiding way of knowing is based upon the more primordial structure of being-in-the-world and is thus conditioned by worldhood as such, which entails an even more fundamental, or prior interpretation of the being of the beings of the world. That interpretation occurs under the rubric of the thingliness of the things that constitute the environment Heidegger calls world.

In the section entitled "The Analysis of Environmentality and Worldliness in General," Heidegger tells us that in order to gain phenomenological access to beings we need to do away with the interpretational tendencies which cover over the ways that we take care of things. In other words, we need to do away with the overwrought methods of analysis foisted on us by the various sciences that instruct us in their limited ways of knowing the being of beings. The way to commence such a phenomenological explication (*Auslegen*) of the beings that we encounter in the world, the theme of which is being, is to proceed by way of appropriately considering *things*.[49]

III. *The hammer as tool and work as a function of totality*

What we find, through taking care of things, is a myriad dispersal of associations. But the kinds of associations that Heidegger argues are the closest, and thus of primary concern for providing a foundation for his ontological analysis, are not associations of mere perceptual cognition that one might find in the behavioral sciences, but, rather, "a handling, using, and taking care of things which has its own kind of 'knowledge.'"[50] What is most "lively" (*lebendig*) for Da-sein is what is used and produced (*Gebrauchte, Herstellung Befindliche*), not in the sense of artificially putting ourselves in some kind of experimental situation that would only distort the actuality of my lived situation. Rather, what Heidegger points us toward are those everyday and average kind of situations within which we find ourselves already situated. And in order to gain phenomenal access to such a realm, we need only look around us to determine what we take care of on a daily basis; that is, our preliminary theme for investigating the spatiality of our environment focuses on the *things* that surround us.

The problem that immediately presents itself, however, is that the *things* that we address are not self-evidently at hand. By presupposing that we simply need to address things we already apply traditional methodological tactics, such as those employed by Descartes and Kant or even Husserl, and come up against the traditional issues of attempting to determine *thingliness* (*Dinglichkeit*) and reality (*Realität*). This is a conundrum that Heidegger seeks to avoid by resorting to his now-famous distinction of *Vorhandenheit* and *Zuhandenheit*, or presence-at-hand and handiness. It is precisely in establishing these distinctions that we come across that area in Heidegger's ontology, which presents him with the problems with which he grapples for the rest of his philosophical career, namely, how best to account for the relationships that Da-sein maintains with those *things* in the world which are either "used and produced" or "natural" in such a way that the ultimate destiny of Da-sein, both individually and communally, is not predetermined as merely a pragmatic function of being reduced to the forces of material production established by the "world" of industrialization and technologization. Ultimately, Heidegger *must* turn to art. But as preparation, in *Being and Time* he *must* turn to the hammer.

Not unsurprisingly, in *Being and Time* Heidegger introduces us to things by way of an etymological reference to the term the Greeks used for things, namely, *pragmata* (πράγματα). By doing so, we are already inclined towards the construction that follows his analysis because of how he convinces us that the originary "pragmatic" character of things was left in the dark and which historically led to considering things as "mere things," that is, to the distorting and forgetting way of isolating something in order to understand its function. For Heidegger, that beginning began centuries of misunderstanding what things are and what "directives" are possible to find in our relationships with those things that surround us. What Heidegger establishes is that any thing that we encounter in "care" relationships should be called a "*tool*" (*Zeug*).[51] The usual translation for *Zeug* has been "useful thing" but it seems clear to me by the context in which Heidegger introduces the term and how he continues to use the term both in this text and the texts to follow, entails that we translate the term as "tool." In fact, Heidegger goes on to explicate the phenomena of "things" by way of analyzing the environment of the totality of references involved in "work" relationships, even going so far as to call what he constructs a "workshop."

To begin with, Heidegger points out that "Strictly speaking, *a* tool 'is' nothing."[52] What he means by this is that we can not "have" a singular tool but, rather, any single tool already occurs in the context of a relevant web of references, signifying relational structures to not only other tools, but to the process of work itself. What is at stake is the construction of the workshop, which Heidegger begins by introducing the term, "in order to" (*um-zu*) as that intentional structure, revising Husserl's elaboration of the structure of "intention,"[53] which already "contains a *reference* of something to something."[54] A tool is essentially something that "has" the characteristic of "in order to" that reveals various kinds of use-relations — such as serviceability, helpfulness, usability, and handiness — with which we find references to a variety of other tools, such as: pen, ink, paper, deskblotter, table, lamp, furniture, windows, doors, room, etc. All such things do not merely "show" themselves in some way as they are "in-themselves," but their very way of being in-themselves is already defined by their characteristic ways of being tools, of demonstrating "toolishness" (*Zeughaftigkeit*). Moreover, though, "What we encounter as nearest to us, although we do not [understand] it thematically, is the room, not as what is "between the four walls" in a geometrical, spatial sense, but rather as material for living."[55] Through this exposition, Heidegger develops the modes of caring defined through "distancing" and "nearness" as a way for determining what constitutes our spatial aroundedness as we discover ourselves surrounded by a world characterized by its "tool-totality."

By the time we come to one of the few "hands-on" examples of a thing that Heidegger provides for us in this text — the "hammer" — we are already prepared for the move from the abstract conceptualization of a thing, removed from its context of associations, which is the crux of the problem of traditional ontologies such as Descartes's and Kant's. In fact, as Heidegger notes, this distorted removal of "things" from their context of functional usefulness eventually leads to compounding the problem of "skipping over" by distorting the relationship of practice to theory. What is at stake in this important section of the text is determining the way that we *grasp* things at all which Heidegger denotes as an act of "*erfassen*," meaning: to seize, fasten on, or lay hold of. The nominalization of the word as "*Erfassung*" means: registration or recording. So the phenomenological task of grasping something means actually grasping something in one's hand with the sense that such an act is recordable and able to be maintained by documented registration. With respect to the "hammer," the act of grasping is sensually apprehensible. But the connections to the constitution of Da-sein are even more complex because of how Heidegger considers that Da-sein is that kind of being that is distinguished from other kinds of beings by its ability to be-able-to-read (its *redden-können*), as I noted above. As such a being, not only does Da-sein identify itself and move in the world as a sign-reader, but it is also a sign-maker, using tools to make signs and a referential world of signification.

But Heidegger has an even more nuanced point to make that has far-reaching consequences for his philosophy, a point that ultimately plays a determinative role for his philosophy of art as well. Heidegger points out that in taking up a hammer *as a tool*, the very process of using the hammer, of "hammering with the hammer," provides me with a special kind of knowledge. What I do *not* do is to grasp the hammer as a thing in terms of an object of cognition, nor do I even grasp the structure of useful things as such. The act of hammering does not provide me with any knowledge of the useful character of the tool itself or of the character of toolishness. Rather, what happens is that the act of hammering "has appropriated this useful thing in the most adequate way possible."[56] With such an assertion Heidegger is able to forge a novel term to refer to what happens when we become subordinate to the in-order-to care of whatever tool we are using at the time, in this case the hammer. To get the "in-order-to," Heidegger notes that:

> The less we just stare at the thing called the hammer, the more actively we use it, the more original our relation to it becomes and the more undisguisedly it is encountered as what it is, as tool. The act of hammering itself discovers the specific "handiness" of the hammer.[57]

Heidegger identifies this "handiness" as the specific essence of a tool that is unavailable for us by just looking at something, that is, the essential characteristic is not an object for disinterested theorizing. Rather, as I use something in its context of association I am guided by a specific kind of sight, what Heidegger calls circumspection (*Umsicht*), which guides our doings with tools and enables us to subordinate ourselves in a kind of "accommodation" (*Sichfügens*) to the "manifold of references of the in-order-to" (*Verweisungsmanigfaltigkeit*). The importance of this kind of subordination as accommodation has the ultimately long-term consequences of conditioning Heidegger's understanding of how Da-sein, humans as such, must subordinate themselves to the decisive directives provided by the referential totality of significant relevance within and with which they find themselves. Additionally, *Sichfügen* has the clear connotation of complying and resigning oneself to that which happens, in essence, submitting to one's history as destiny, to one's *Geschichte* as *Geschick*. And in what way does such resignation and submission occur? By attuning oneself to the *Fugue* of being, by attuning oneself to the power of art in one's midst, in the world.

But where are we to find such art? We certainly do not find explicit reference to art or works of art in *Being and Time*. Instead, we find an analysis of work-tools themselves and, ultimately of work itself and those tools, as the referential structure of that which exists for-the-sake-of: "The work [as a process] bears the totality of references in which tools are encountered."[58] It is only because of the process of work that we are even able to discover something like referential-totality in the first place, which enables us to come upon an even more startling discovery, an element that remains unaccounted for in Heidegger's ontology for several years until his so-called "turn" through the turmoil of his political involvement with the Nazi party as Rector of Freiburg University. That is, his occupation with not merely the work of the referential-totality of work-tools, but with the work of art. What emerges at this critical juncture in *Being and Time* that remains unresolved for so long and only emerges when such political events exert their crucible-like forces? This question will have to wait until more work is done in the next two chapters but, preliminarily, it has to do with working out the fate of Da-sein decisively concentrated in a polis as one *Volk* among other historically and politically determined peoples in-the-world.

As Heidegger notes, the referential-totality of the work-world remains hidden from "objective" or theoretical investigation, ever more so as the tools that are used and the work that is done is engaged in with appropriate adequacy. What emerges is the world of production, of not only work-things but, dependent upon the work itself as a product, the so-called "material" of nature as the stuff of which hammers, tongs, and nails are made: steel, iron, metal, stone, and wood. "Nature" is discovered in the use of tools in the sense of "products of nature" as the wind which "fills the sails" or the river which "produces water power" or the rock from a quarry. We discover "nature" in the using of tools but only insofar as "nature" itself is understood from the context of the work-world itself as well. However, this understanding of the being of the beings of "nature" becomes problematic for Heidegger, given his ultimate orientation towards understanding Da-sein in terms of possibility and as a potentiality-for-being-whole. It is problematic because, given that Da-sein must be able to function in a decisive way in choosing its own authenticity after being called to integrate itself from its fallen and alienated inauthentic state as they-self, Heidegger needs to be able to call upon a constitutional structure that would enable the possibility of making an original decision at all. But what are the conditions that allow for such an original decision? It seems that, at least preliminarily, a decision necessarily arises in the context of conflict, in the context of violence. How does Heidegger lead us into accepting such a state of affairs, that is, that at the heart of decision-making is an unavoidable act of violence? It is important to note for my general thesis that this conflictual process is at the heart of Heidegger's philosophy, but makes its first appearance in how he sets up the problematic in *Being and Time* through his elaboration of the constitutional structures of Da-sein.

In Part II of *Being and Time*, Heidegger turns to an ontological analysis of the temporality of Da-sein based on the preliminary results of the ontical analysis of Part I, an analysis that provided us with both the existential structures that constitute Da-sein, but also with the open-ended task of working towards clarifying how Da-sein comes to understand, accomplished through how Da-sein comes to an original, free decision, through understanding itself and its environment in terms of the totalizing "wholeness" of its own being. Coming to such an understanding, however, entails deconstructing vulgar time, time experienced as a succession of isolated points as from a calendar or clock in favor of temporalizing time authentically as ecstatic. What Heidegger means by "ecstatic" is that way of standing in the world which lets us encounter other beings in the way that they are, in themselves, in-the-world. Only by taking such a decisive stand is Da-sein able to understand its way of experiencing its time in a different sense than the vulgar way of being dispersed (or alienated) in the time and occupations, and the way of handling beings, with which "they" (*das Man*: "the others") determines Da-sein. Rather, in taking a decisive stand, Da-sein exercises a resolute anticipatory raptness which projects out of its own possibilities its own way of being-in-the-world as caring for things out of the context of its own thrownness:

> In resoluteness, the present is not only brought back from the dispersion in what is taken care of nearest at hand, but is held in the future and having-been. We call the *present* that which is held in authentic temporality, and is thus *authentic*, the *Moment*. This term must be understood in the active sense as an ecstasy. It means the resolute raptness of Da-sein, which is yet *held* in resoluteness, in what is encountered as possibilities and circumstances to be taken care of in the situation.[59]

Heidegger clarifies this phenomenon of "moment" by renaming it as the "now," noting that it "belongs to time as within-time-ness: the now 'in which' something comes into being, passes away, or is objectively present."[60] Since Heidegger's interpretation draws from Aristotle's account for how things come into being and pass out of being as an account based on a stable substratum,[61] it is easier for us to understand his claim that the phenomenon of "In the Moment" does not entail that something extraordinary "happens." On the contrary, he says, "'In the Moment' nothing can happen, but as an authentic present it clears a space from attachment to things in order to let us *encounter for the first time* what can be 'in time' as something at hand or objectively present."[62]

But how does one distinguish between the different ecstatic modes of being authentically "in the Moment" and the inauthenticity of "making present?" The way that Heidegger distinguishes between these two kinds of ecstatic modes is based on how Da-sein handles "things." In the inauthentic mode, Da-sein is irresolute, oriented towards the "having-been" of things and, thus, towards the fixity of the past, crafting its projects according to a care structure that takes care of available things at hand, retaining and holding onto them because, in a way, they constitute the security of the already accomplished productions of beings "like" Da-sein, they constitute already formed, and thus certain, traditions of beings "like" Da-sein in which Da-sein can flee from the authentic certainty of its ownmost possible uncertain future. In other words, the authentic mode of temporalizing oneself "in the Moment" on the basis of futural possibility, can only occur as Da-sein temporalizes itself within an environment, within a situation, in terms of the resolute kind of anticipatoriness that comes back to its own self as thrown in a process of individuation having been accomplished as its own. As Heidegger notes, such a way of standing in-the-world of things allows for an authentic way of retrieving oneself: "This ecstasy makes it possible for Da-sein to be able to take over resolutely the being that it already is."[63]

But instead of being in resolute ecstasy in-the-world, Da-sein primarily forgets itself in its dispersion in the they-self as it is immersed in its mode of

"having-been" and losing itself in its superficial care of the things that surround it. In this ek-stasis of retaining beings unlike itself, surrounding itself
with things, Da-sein inauthentically understands its temporality and turns
away from itself in various modes of fear, primarily heeding the condition of
its "past" throwness. As Da-sein then becomes attuned in the mood of fear,
it becomes attuned to the thingliness of being-in-the-world because fear as a
mode of attunement in-the-world always occurs as the fear *of* some*thing* that
threatens from out of the things of my environment at hand, some*thing* with
objective presence. Da-sein does so because, "Taking care of things which fears
for itself leaps from one thing to the other, because it forgets itself and thus
cannot *grasp* any *definite* possibility."[64] What happens is that when one cannot
grasp any possibility, then — since the constitution of Da-sein is to actualize
itself as possibility — any and every possibility is blindly grasped at, including
impossible possibilities. One is "lost" in the surrounding world, confused at
the myriad possibilities that surround oneself in a jumbled confusion of unat-
tachment, characterized by confusion and a depressed mood of awaiting. The
example Heidegger gives is that inhabitants of a burning house usually save
the most trivial things lying nearest to them as they flee the impending fire in
confusion.

The difference between *Angst* and fear is likewise understood with respect
to how Da-sein handles the things around itself:

> In particular, that in the face of which one has *Angst* is not encountered as
> something definite to be taken care of; the threat does not come from something
> at hand and objectively present, but rather from the fact that everything at hand
> and objectively present absolutely has nothing more to "say" to us. Beings in the
> surrounding world are no longer relevant.[65]

Note the emphasis on what the "things" can or cannot "say" to us. This is
significant in how Heidegger goes on to develop his ideas about language and
poetry in the years that follow. While discourse is not the specific theme in
Being and Time, it is the underlying phenomenon without which the entirety
would sink into obscurity. The only way that Da-sein is able to make sense of
itself to itself is in and through language in the way that it distinguishes itself
from the context of useful things that surrounds it, initially and primarily. In
Angst, the understanding of Da-sein is brought to the state of confronting
its own condition of being "thrust toward the world"[66] of things. And what
takes the place of the *fear* of things at hand and as objective presence in
one's immediate environment is the *Angst* that Da-sein has of and for itself
in its futural anticipation, that is, in resolutely anticipating its own destiny as
thrown being-toward-death. One's potentiality of being cannot be fulfilled by
superficially taking care of the things at hand; rather, only in being brought
back to oneself in an act of remembering the wholeness of one's own self, as a

being "stretched" in possibilities between a beginning and an end, is one then brought into the mood of resoluteness in readiness to freely decide for oneself: "He who is resolute knows no fear, but understands the possibility of *Angst* as *the* mood that does not hinder and confuse him. *Angst* frees him from 'null' possibilities and lets him become free *for* authentic ones."[67]

Simply put, this freedom to choose for oneself out of the context of a world of things at hand is the task of remembering the question of the meaning of being. But what is it that one chooses for oneself? As I will elaborate in the next chapter, one chooses one's destiny as a way to live close to the origin of one's own land and to live among one's own people. One also chooses a way of living accomplished as "dwelling" with one's art as a way to linger with things and not to merely use them; but such living with things is done as a way to have control over the world. Those developments will only become clear after working through the path Heidegger forges with *The Origin of the Work of Art* whereas, in *Being and Time*, the two "paths" of authenticity or inauthenticity can best be described in the limited terms of either looking forward towards an "evil" future — actually, a broken future — which is determined by fear conditioned by the "broken" tool or the loss of the tool, or one can look towards a "good" future as that which is hoped for and, in that hoping, accomplishes the task of bringing oneself wholly and fully into the future. By choosing this latter path: "He who hopes takes himself, so to speak, *along* in the hope and brings himself toward what is hoped for . . ."[68] and is that one who freely decides for oneself. In this way, hope brings relief from depressing anxiety about an evil future or brings one out of the pallid, gray mood of indifference where nothing matters and where one is not urged on towards anything. In giving oneself over to throwness and forgetting, one is barely living, or frantically living by busying oneself with every*thing* with equanimity, and thus with nothing. Instead, out of the resoluteness in the Moment of being-toward-death, of being-toward-end, one has a "view of possible situations of the potentiality-of-being-a-whole disclosed in the anticipation of death."[69]

IV. *Constituting the transcendent world and deciding freely for oneself*

By articulating Da-sein in terms of the possible unity of its structure as a totality, Heidegger can consider the intrinsically related issues of "how . . . something like world [is] possible at all, in what sense *is* world, what and how does the world transcend, how are 'independent' innerworldly beings 'connected' with the transcending world?"[70] These are issues that, Heidegger notes, need to be articulated in order to raise a question about transcendence at all. In other words, articulating the constitution of Da-sein in how it takes care of things at hand, as tools or as objects for scientific investigation or as mere objective presences (as things of "nature"), entails considering not only the phenomenon of taking care of things, but of determining the meaning of the possible theoretical knowledge of things that are objectively present as well as the temporal problem of the transcendence of the world as such. And all of these "articulations" are done in the context of a discourse on the temporality of the being of beings.

With that in mind, some final remarks about how we are oriented to "useful things" and the "work world" are in order. As Heidegger notes, we are never able to "grasp" an isolated "tool" but, rather, any useful thing can only be grasped from the referential relevance of the work-world as a whole, a world that has "already always been disclosed." Furthermore, he argues that, "If in our analysis of having to do with things, we aim at what we have to do with, our existent being together with beings taken care of must be given an orientation not toward an isolated useful thing at hand, but rather toward the totality of useful things."[71] That is, insofar as we understand *a thing*, we only ever understand it in a relationship of relevance to a structural totality of a work-world of *things* constituted by care that is grounded in temporality. Heidegger elaborates this point by pointing out that the relevance of structural unity is characterized by intentionality that takes the form of awaiting and retaining. While getting "lost" in the absorption in taking care of the world in the work-world of tools entails a forgetting of the self, such taking care is nonetheless "guided" by the ownmost potentiality-of-being of Da-sein. The familiarity that is the condition of forgetfully making one's way around in the work-world of tools entails "letting things be in relevance" or simply, "letting-be." Only in this way are things encountered for the *beings* that they are. This becomes Heidegger's opening towards an analytic of *Gelassenheit* as a revised way to relate to things.

What consideration of this phenomenon leads to, however, is the issue of how we can "let things be" in order to attend to them in a conspicuous manner, but not as the object of a thematic, scientific investigation. Rather, with Heidegger we are compelled to ask: how do things provide the occasion for directing our orientation to act or decide in one way or another? In working with a tool, when it becomes damaged and un-useful, the "what-for" and the "how-to" are encountered for the first time. The usefulness of making something present is "held-up" and our attention is shifted to the "ecstatic unity of the making present that awaits and retains." This simply means that my attention is not fixed merely on the broken hammer as such, although I do attend to that as well; rather, my attention shifts to the overall horizon of the project of work with which I am engaged in the world. I could never find out that something is missing or broken unless that something was already set in a context of a referential totality of relevance, the "end" of which I await with some expectation given my involvement in using the tool and in "having" a project. Only because I am already situated in the context of a work-world that is characterized by my expectation of some sort of fulfillment of a project can I be surprised by the interruption of the everydayness of that world. Moreover, in taking care of things in the context of the overall project, Da-sein accepts that something breaks in its "insurmountability," considering it as inconvenient, hindering, disturbing, etc. However, in its unsuitability for the work at hand, the broken thing is "retained" and "not forgotten" precisely in its unsuitability.

This problem of unsuitability remains with Heidegger, reformulated in his later work on the "work of art" in the context of reliability. But in *Being and Time*, the concept of unsuitability is used to develop the issue of taking control and mastery of the world, since, "Only because things offering resistance are disclosed on the basis of the ecstatic temporality of taking care, can factical Da-sein understand itself in its abandonment to a 'world' of which it never becomes master."[72] This raises for us the problem of control of one's environment and to what extent Da-sein is subject to a world that is beyond its control, namely, to what extent Da-sein is ever able to determine its ownmost-potentiality-for-being a whole. At this point, the possibility of making a "free decision" is still open for Heidegger, but conditioned by how one chooses to use this or that tool or by how one deals with the way that things are brought to a standstill and of assessing the operations of the tools that make up one's workshop.

V. *Deciding freely for oneself? An enduring problem*

What Heidegger gains for his argument in asserting this "thematic" point has to do with determining with greater certainty the region and perspective of a possible subject-area for the methodical questioning of any discipline of science. The more appropriately and adequately "the being of beings to be investigated is understood in the guiding understanding of being" in the context of a totality of beings having this or that fundamental determination, this or that "as-structure" of objective presence, then the more assured we will be in our questioning. But if thematizing is possible, Da-sein must then transcend the beings that are thematized, and indeed does so because a world is already disclosed to Da-sein by way of temporality. Why is it important to define thematizing? It is important because that process is the way that we articulate to ourselves (and to each other) an understanding of the being of beings:

> It aims at freeing beings encountered within the world in such a way that they can "project" themselves back upon pure discovery, that is, they can become objects. Thematization objectifies. It does not first "posit" beings, but frees them in such a way that they become "objectively" subject to questioning and definition.[73]

This *is* the project of scientific theorizing about any *thing* whatsoever and, Heidegger claims, such a project of "being-in-the-truth" is possible only because it constitutes a determination of existence of Da-sein. This is the under-standing of the origin of any scientific activity about things as objects of nature. But what remains to be done, however, is to determine in what way Da-sein, as that being which thematizes, already transcends the practical work-world of things that constitute its region of taking-care. In fact, it is questionable whether Heidegger succeeds in adequately elaborating this phenomenon of transcending, a lacuna already intimated in Rosenzweig's work and one that Emmanuel Levinas would later focus upon by addressing the "neutrality" of Heidegger's stance and his neglect of the "other" and of responsibility.[74]

Not suprisingly, in light of the problem of transcendence, Heidegger notes that "This understanding of being can remain neutral. Then handiness and objective presence are not yet differentiated and still less are they grasped ontologically."[75] Determining such neutrality allows Heidegger to establish that, for Da-sein to have anything whatsoever to do with a context of useful things, it must already have a world of relevance (transcendently) disclosed for it. And since Da-sein exists essentially *as* being-in-the-world and that existence is completely grounded in temporality, then the temporality of Da-sein must make the transcendence of the world, and thus the beings that constitute that world, possible. The significance of this move for Heidegger's philosophy of art is that having a world at all entails that Da-sein exists in an intentional structure of a totality of relevant relations in such a way that its choices determine its factical place in that world. As Heidegger notes, we live grounded in a world of taking care that is structured by the relations of "in-order-to, what-for, for-that, and for-the-sake-of-which" the connections of which are referred to as "significance" and whose total unity is referred to as "world." How then does Da-sein exist as that being whose essential facticity consists of being-in-the-world?

Recall Rosenzweig's clear conviction that what it means for me to live my life as fully human means answering the call of the other and forming communities of trust. And I do that, at least once in my life, by performing poetically with others in the world. What becomes critically important for dis-tinguishing the diverging ethical paths of Rosenzweig and Heidegger becomes clear in Heidegger's contention about what defines the essential intentional structure of Da-sein *as* being-in-the-world: "Da-sein exists for the sake of a potentiality-of-being of itself. Existing, it is thrown, and as thrown, delivered over to beings that it needs *in order* to be able to be as it is, namely *for the sake of* itself."[76] Already intimating my conclusion, how is Heidegger's stance, his ontologically grounded philosophy of words, that much different from the Spinozistic/Hegelian ethical position attacked by Rosenzweig? Rather than concerning himself with the ethical quandary that emerges with understanding human being-in-the-world as Da-sein, Heidegger deepens the quandary by pointing us in the direction of the task that is outstanding for us: determining the horizonal direction of Da-sein in-the-world by establishing its condition of "being-*there*" as ecstatical unity. Guidance and direction is what is at stake, and each temporal "ecstasy" of Da-sein, that is, the differing directives of the ecstasies of past-present-future, provide the "horizonal schema" for Da-sein. In the "whereto" of each "ecstasy" belongs the motivating directedness that leads back to the self, whether authentically or inauthentically. Fundamentally, Da-sein is *futural* and thus comes back to itself. It comes back as thrown, whereby Da-sein becomes disclosed to itself as "that *in the face of which* it has been thrown and that to which it has been delivered over," while at the same time it "makes present" in the sense of being-together-with (beings it needs in-the-world). The *for-the-sake-of-itself* as the having-been of Da-sein complements the *in-order-to* of the present as moments of the predominantly futural horizonal schema. It is predominantly futural because, as potentiality-of-being, Da-sein is always already projected *towards* an end, *towards* its own end, in understanding its having-been thrown and its taking-care-of things in order to fulfill its project.

What is the extent of Da-sein's free decision? Of its possible act in fulfilling its potentiality-of-being? Heidegger tells us, given that the world is presupposed in one's being-together with things in the world, one's thematizations of those very things that are discovered and spoken of as objective presences are the only possible modes of being-in-the-world and, therefore, constitute the *transcendent world* as horizonal unity of ecstatic temporality. It is only in and with such a world that innerworldly beings can be encountered as such and that Da-sein can "come back to itself" in temporalizing itself in the There. These are the parameters of authenticity and limit what Da-sein is capable of: "That such beings are discovered in the There of its own existence is not under the control of Da-sein. Only *what*, in *which* direction, *to what extent*, and *how* it actually discovers and discloses is a matter of freedom, although always within the limits of its throwness."[77]

So what it means to become "authentic" is to act freely within that realm of beings in which Da-sein finds itself thrown and existing. But the actual "matter of freedom" is the process of discovery of the transcendent world of innerworldly things, a process of discovery that is not controlled by Da-sein. Hence, the fundamental constitution of Da-sein turns out to be the factical way that Da-sein ecstatically understands itself as the unity of itself with other beings of its world in the unity of the There and how it "comes back from these horizons to the beings encountered in them. Coming back to these beings understandingly is the existential meaning of letting them be encountered in making them present . . ." of letting them be as innerworldly beings of a transcendent world.[78] In order to determine the motivation out of *Being and Time* for a philosophy of art, the unanswered and perhaps unanswerable question emerges: how do we communicate the objectivity of those innerworldly beings, the things that constitute that transcendent world? As I already noted in my Introduction, the related question also arises: what does such communication matter except that it is for the sake of fulfilling my ownmost potentiality for being?

What Heidegger does by prioritizing the temporality of Da-sein as opposed to following the Kantian epistemological tradition of prioritizing spatiality, is to complicate how we go about understanding sensibility. By way of comparison, the "heart" of Rosenzweig's project is his peculiar understanding of the fused occurence of sensibility, the "*Sinnlich*," and the trans-sensible, the "*Übersinnlich*," that occurs in the dynamic of a poetic dialogue of love sung between two lovers, bound there and then to each other in the revelatory moment. For Heidegger, there is no such dynamically binding or situating dialogue because, as he says, Da-sein can only be spatial as care, that is, as "factically entangled existing" and never as a bounded kind of "thing" such as a tool. Rather, as temporally existing, Da-sein, ". . . makes room for the play-of-space. It determines its own location in such a way that it comes back from the space made room for, to a 'place' that it has taken over." Da-sein does not just occur "in space" but, rather, "takes space in," a phenomenon that is to be interpreted not as some kind of fatal consequence of the connection of the body with the spirit. "Rather, because Da-sein is 'spiritual' (*geistig*), *and only because it is spiritual*, [can it] be spatial in a way that essentially remains impossible for an extended thing."[79] Remarks such as these in *Being and Time* became critical preparations for Heidegger's turn to art that occurred several years later.

Curiously, with *Being and Time*, Heidegger works out the issue of the existence and temporality of Da-sein in such a way that the issue of space and the productive relationship of Da-sein to things, insofar as these two constituents determine Da-sein's historical destiny, remains problematic. It remains problematic because, I contend, between the time when Heidegger composed *Being and Time*, and his engagement in the political process by assuming a leadership role at Freiburg University and thus in the Nazi Party, the world had become a different place. It is to that problematic that he "turns" in taking up the issue of creation and the work of art and it is in that turn that the question of "art *and* responsibility" becomes a problem.

Notes

1 See Dreyfus 1991: 7.
2 SZ: 38; BT: 34. Heidegger most likely refers to Husserl's critique of the over-extension of psychologism in the early sections of the *Logical Investigations*. See Husserl 1980 for his critique of Mill's and Spencer's empirical psychologism as vague and arbitrary: 78–101.
3 SZ: 7; BT: 6.
4 Ibid.

5   Ibid: 8; 7.
6   Ibid: 12; 10.
7   Ibid.
8   Ibid: 16; 15. Everydayness = *Alltäglichkeit*.
9   Ibid: 17; 15.
10   Ibid.
11   Ibid: 18; 16.
12   GS2: 9–10; SR: 9–10.
13   SZ: 19; BT: 17.
14   Ibid: 20; 17.
15   Ibid.
16   See Nietzsche 1980c: 10ff. for Nietzsche's ideas on the creative making of history, as opposed to the rote learning of the same, by the use of the unhistorical and the ability to forget. Heidegger's lengthy engagement with Nietzsche's philosophy is well known: "We call Nietzsche's thought of the will to power his *sole* thought." See Ne3: 10.
17   SZ: 21; BT: 18.
18   GS2: 11; SR: 10.
19   The point that Heidegger contests is that such an investigation entails an historio-graphical approach, an insight Kant only comes to late in his career, if at all, with his turn towards aesthetics, history, religion, and politics. That is, for Heidegger, his concerns were merely ontic. See Kant 1963.
20   Rosenzweig criticizes Kant's epistemology, that is, for conflating the Elements into one "world" rather than allowing for the possibility of distinct starting points for knowing things — the three "Nothings" of knowledge. "*Der Vergleich, der das Selbst in eine Welt einordnet, verführt schon bei Kant selbst und ganz offen bei seinen Nachfolgern zur Verwechslung dieser 'Welt' des Selbst mit der vorhandenen Welt.*" (GS2: 76).
21   See GS2: 72ff; SR: 67ff.
22   SZ: 23; BT: 21.
23   Ibid: 25; BT: 22.
24   Ibid.
25   Ibid.
26   See Pd and Pe.
27   SZ: 27; BT: 24.
28   Ibid: 28; 25.
29   Ibid: 31; 27.
30   Ibid: 32; 28.
31   See: "De interpretatione" chapters 1–6; "Metaphysics" VII.4; and "Nichomachean Ethics" VII in Aristotle 1941.
32   SZ: 32; BT: 28.
33   Ibid: 33; 29.
34   Ibid.
35   Ibid.
36   The return to Husserl should not be surprising given the context of Heidegger's assertions about the terms of *noein* and *noetic* and Husserl's overwhelming

predilection for an analysis that figures "intentionality" as its central concern. See Husserl 1931, esp. "Theory of the Noetic-Noematic Structures: Elaboration of the Problems": 2603–30.

37 This point, about Kant's idealism, is left out of the otherwise excellent analysis of the modern German philosophy of art by Jean-Marie Schaeffer that I deal with in Chapter 7. See Schaeffer 2000.

38 SZ: 35; BT: 31.

39 Ibid: 36; 32.

40 Ibid: 37; 33.

41 Ibid: 38, 33.

42 Ibid: 39; 34.

43 Ibid: 48; 44.

44 Ibid: 51; 47.

45 Ibid: 54; 51.

46 Ibid.

47 SZ: 66; 62.

48 Ibid.

49 Ibid: 67; 63. In elaborating the structural characteristics of worldliness, Heidegger explicitly directs us to reconsider how we conceptualize "things" as those "beings" which "are to be our preliminary theme and established as a preliminary basis."

50 Ibid: 68; 63. For an alternative argument contesting my interpretation of the functional role of *Zeuge* as tools, see Benso 2000. Benso argues for synthesizing Levinas's primacy of ethics with Heidegger's attention to the things-themselves in order to revitalize an ethical sensitivity to non-human beings.

51 Ibid. "*Wir nennen das im Besorgen begegnende Seinede das* Zeug." Although the usual German word for tool is *Werkzeug*, shortening the term to *Zeug* provides greater comprehensives and, given the etymological association, is not an unreasonable interpretation.

52 Ibid: 68; 64. For an interpretation of the history of the *Zeug* as it occurs in three stages — craftsmanship, the industrial age, and cybernetical plannification, see Dreyfus 1984: 233–5.

53 See Husserl 1931: 223: ". . . this *wakeful* intercourse with the correlate-object, this directedness towards it (or indeed away from it, though with the glance upon it all the same) . . ."

54 SZ: 68: BT: 64.

55 Ibid.

56 Ibid: 69; 65.

57 Ibid.

58 Ibid: 70; 65.

59 Ibid: 338; 311.

60 Ibid.

61 See *De Generatione et Corruptione* in Aristotle 1941: 470ff.

62 SZ: 338; BT: 311.

63 Ibid: 339; 311.

64 Ibid: 342; 314.

65   Ibid: 343; 315.
66   Ibid.
67   Ibid: 344, 316.
68   Ibid: 345; 317.
69   Ibid.
70   Ibid: 351, 321.
71   Ibid: 353, 323.
72   Ibid: 356; 326.
73   Ibid: 363; 332.
74   See "Against the Philosophy of the Neuter" in Levinas 1969: 2982–99.
75   SZ: 364; BT: 333.
76   Ibid: 365; 333. How is this any different than Spinoza's *conatus*? See Spinoza 1992, 108; Part III. Proposition 7: "The conatus with which each thing endeavours to persist in its own being is nothing but the actual essence of the thing itself."
77   Ibid: 366; 334.
78   Ibid.
79   Ibid: 368; 336.

CHAPTER 6

TURNING THROUGH PHENOMENOLOGY TO ART AND ETHOS: AN ANALYSIS OF THE *ORIGIN OF THE WORK OF ART*

In *The Origin of the Work of Art* we follow the trajectory that Heidegger established with his phenomenological analysis of the "hammer" in *Being and Time* to its transformation into a tool in a constellation that comes to include the "thing" and the "work of art." In that trajectory, the hammer-as-tool occupies a mediate position vis à vis the "natural" thing (or thing *simpliciter*) and the work of art. While the "natural" thing is that which is unworked-upon, the tool is that which is worked-upon and which retains a connection to thingliness; the work of art is that which stands in some way alone. We are already familiar with this character of "standing alone" with Rosenzweig's handling of works of art. Moreover, and despite Gadamer's observation about how often Heidegger talks about the distance between poetry and thinking,[1] like Rosenzweig Heidegger privileges poetry as that art activity that most closely correlates with the task of thinking, but unlike Rosenzweig he situates poetry with politics and philosophy as fundamental cornerstones in establishing the polis.[2] Thus, along with philosophy and politics, art occurs as one of the three directing human activities without which humans would be less than human. This latter point roughly correlates with Rosenzweig's position on art but, as we shall see, the similarity is superficial.

For Heidegger, the move from the workshop of *Being and Time* to a more diversified world that includes natural things and art-works is no simple matter of phenomenological description of some arbitrary state of affairs to another. Rather, constructing such a "world" entails also establishing an overriding structure that houses the origin of meaningful existence. Indeed, discovering such an origin further entails having already been prepared by having already understood — and thus experienced — the kind of authentic/inauthentic choices offered to our circumspection through the hermeneutic of disclosure presented in *Being and Time*. One must already have been confronted with the existential structures of one's temporal, historical existence and how that existence is itself embedded in the ontological structures of being-in-the-world, of one's determination by the they-self and of Da-sein-with. From these structures, however, Heidegger moves us to consider the necessity involved in discovering the destiny of a people, a discovery that is only possible through coming to terms with the work of art as it is relationally situated in and grounds the very understanding of the being-in-the-world of Da-sein as an aesthetically grounded and oriented, politically destined people. In discovering the ground and orientation that destines a people, we then learn how and what decisions should be made for the sake of maintaining not only the authentic existence of a people, but what decisions are made to establish a holy existence. In fact, as I will indicate, Heidegger makes use of an onto-theological framework, adapted from the very metaphysical tradition from which he so insistently attempts to distance his work, in such a way as to ground the political, poetical and philosophical choices that he contends co-determine the appropriating ek-static event of being as presence-of-the-world.[3] Such a grounding, however, must be established by way of the opening of the presencing act of the work of art.

I. *Establishing the connections*

The work of this and the next chapter considers the completing part of the phase in Heidegger's career initiated by what even he called the "turn," a move that is essential for better understanding his constellation of philosopher-poet-politician. Specifically, my contention is that Heidegger's involvement in the Nazi party and his failed role in assuming the leadership of Freiburg University significantly precipitated his definitive "turn" from his project of ontological phenomenology begun with *Being and Time*. But in fact, his "turn" was really a two-step process: at first he turned to direct political involvement and administrative control, and then turned away in concealment to a more "distanced" concern for and explication of the role of philosopher as intellectual provocateur, rather than as administrating governor. That is, Heidegger re-turned to his academic role in the university as a professional philosopher in order to influence the course of history in ways that he found he was incapable of doing as Rector of the University of Freiburg. But understanding his "turn" in philosophical terms of his earlier phenomenological project — a "turn" that clearly assumed political significance — becomes more evident when I consider Heidegger's work with Hölderlin's poetry in the next chapter and with my remarks on his *Letter on Humanism* in the conclusion. For now, those constructive connections can only be offered as proleptic presentiments and must await an interpretation of his profound and seminal text, *The Origin of the Work of Art*.

In the first few passages of *The Origin of the Work of Art*, Heidegger intimates that the primary focus for our activity as thinking beings should be the nature of art itself which is, at least preliminarily for us, the origin of both philosopher and artist. In other words, the process of experiencing the work *as* a work of art becomes a question of determining not only the essence of art, but by extension, determining the essence of both philosopher and artist. Such a strategy, however, apparently leads into the kind of circular thinking with which Heidegger began *Being and Time*: in order to define a work of art, the artist and spectator have to be posited, while in order to have an artist and spectator there must already be an existing work of art. Taking up the logical challenge of the hermeneutic in this text, Heidegger launches an entirely different strategy by claiming that all thinking is already a kind of "handwork."[4] Such a strategy enables Heidegger to align at the very start the analysis of art, the work of the poet, with the work of the thinker, the work of the philosopher. He then adds the important qualification that each and every work — and thus all thinking — refers to a kind of thingliness.[5] In addition to these two characteristics, Heidegger abides by the phenomenological method that he already established in *Being and Time*, which is that the work itself has to be taken in the context in which it is encountered and as it is experienced and enjoyed.[6]

Heidegger goes on to further contend that the thingly character of the work prevails, despite the confusion that the philosophical tradition has produced in devising various theories of aesthetics, each of which has collapsed because of understanding the work of art either via an epistemological correspondence theory of truth or via an utterly irrational theory of beauty. For example, Heidegger calls attention to the terms "allegory" and "symbol," referring to their etymological origins in Greek language as evidence of the long history of the aesthetic theory that has to do with art. He contends that what is most particular about the work of art is not that it expresses a theoretical relationship projected upon it by this or that metaphysical variation but that it publicly expresses an otherness: "The work joins with otherness by making it public, it reveals otherness."[7] On the one hand, this propensity to express an otherness makes the work more than a simple thing, while on the other hand the thingliness of the work is what the artist works with: "And is it not this very thingliness of the work that the artist with his hand-work really deals?"[8] That is, the very physiological hand-work of the artist entails working with the thingliness of that with which he works. This dealing with the thinglinness of the work is part of Heidegger's goal, which is to encounter the actuality of the work of art as it is actually worked: "We want to meet the immediate and full actuality of the work of art; because, only by doing so do we also find through it actual art."[9] In order to get at this "worked" or "actual" quality — which is what is meant in the root-form of the German word *Wirklichkeit*,[10] we have to be clear about what a thing is in order to determine whether the artwork brings forth something other which is never a thing. Hence, Heidegger sets himself the task of more closely defining what a thing is, a task left unfinished from *Being and Time*.

II. *The thing and the work*

Heidegger takes up this unfinished task by asking: "What in truth is the thing, insofar as it is a thing?" in order to position us to accept that we have to pursue the issue out of whatever the work-"thing" itself stands for. To pursue that issue means that we have to examine our "vicinity" (*Umkreis*) for all those "beings" (*Seiende*) that we call things which he lists as natural things, such as clouds and leaves, as well as Kantian objects such as the *Ding an sich* and god, airplanes and radios and even those words which we use to refer to things that are "totally other," namely, events such as death and the Last Judgment. In total, with the word "thing" Heidegger could be said to name that domain of referents which Rosenzweig referred to as the *nicht Nichts* in developing his symbolic logic: "In totality, the work thing names everything that simply is not."[11] In other words, the term "thing" is used as a parameter to refer to everything that is not absolutely nothing. And while the discussion of nothing is significant, as he indicated in his lecture, *An Introduction to Metaphysics*,[12] his real task is to delimit "beings" in the general form of "the way-of-being of the thing" from "beings" in the general form of "the way-of-being of the work (of art)" — "to delimit the being of the way of being of the thing over against the way of being of the work."[13] In order to accomplish such a delimitation, Heidegger relies on distinctions already established in *Being and Time*, such as the understanding established in his analysis of Descartes's metaphysics that "The human is not a thing."[14]

His conclusion is that: "Nature-, and use-things are those which we usually name things." In a significant modification, however, he relies on common-use language to make his point, claiming that: "The simple things, even excluding the use-things, count as the authentic things." This is much different than what Heidegger presents in *Being and Time*, where the hammer as a "use-thing" was the only kind of thing that really mattered in the task of establishing the platform of the existential analytic of Da-sein. In considering the work of art, however, we must look for the thingliness of things themselves in order to also determine where the "otherness" (*Anderes*) of the work hides. In other words, the characteristic of usefulness which orients Da-sein to things in the ontological workshop of *Being and Time* is displaced by a search for something other, as other. But that something other has to do with the phenomenological question of "what beings are at all."[15] And whenever such a question as "what beings are at all" arises, the question of "things as the measure of beings arises" as well. With such a question of the "measure" of things in mind, Heidegger provides three examples from the tradition of the history of philosophy of what constitutes a thing.

a. *The thing as the bearer of attributes*

What the thing is, is a "core" or "nucleus" — in German *Kern*, in Greek, το ὑποχείμενον — with its "peculiarities" or "marks" — in German its *Merkmale* or *Eigenschaften*, in Greek, τα συμβεβηχότα. As Heidegger notes, what is important is not the one or the other but that the one always goes with the other. Moreover, Heidegger extends his etymological analysis by further pointing out that these Greek names are not merely arbitrary, but indicate the originary Greek experience of the presencing of the Being of beings. Moreover, "These namings are not optional names. What speaks in them is that which is no longer shown: the Greek ground-experience of the being of beings in the sense of presence."[16] In fact, Heidegger claims that it was the translation of these words from Greek to Latin that resulted in a different kind of thinking that initiated the groundlessness of Western thinking: "Roman thinking took over the Greek words without the corresponding experience of those words, without what they say, without the Greek word. The groundlessness of Western thinking begins with this translation."[17] What Heidegger implies is that there exists privileged words that emerge from experiencing a holy language, Greek, without which one does not have access to the grounding experience of the being of beings. However, what the case actually is, is that there are words for the experience of the presencing of the being of beings for each epoch that are concentrated into a characteristic "rule" or law for each respective epoch. Therefore, there can be words for such a presencing experience in German — *Anwesenheit* — as the significant example.

For Heidegger, however, the decisive moment is that the rootlessness of Western thought begins with the translation of Greek names into Latin, namely, from the linguistic practices that refer to presence and a core with assembled properties to those linguistic practices that refer to substance and accident. So the first move in the translation resulted in the substance/accident mode that also resulted in the corollary attempt to explain/mirror the structure of things according to the subject/predicate structure of a sentence. But neither one of those attempts is natural enough and is just the result of a long habituation which merely relied on something foreign that had astonished us: "What occurs naturally to us, is probably only the habituation of a long habit, which, however, the unusual at one time attacked humans as a foreigner and brought thinking to astonishment."[18] In short, philosophy *was* born of wonder — in a kind of an "attack" on human sensibility. But such a current confidence is only illusory because, as Heidegger maintains, such propensity to astonishment can apply to any kind of being. Alternatively, Heidegger looks for a standard that "grows out of its own [self] and rests in itself" (*Eigenwüchsige und Insichruhende*), instead of the kind of standard which does not get at the essence of what a thing is because it holds it too far from the body in abstraction, attacks it and thus lets a thing disappear. The problem with this "attack" standard is that it pushes the thing away with its "assault" mode of being. Additionally, a significant association in Heidegger's use of the term *Bodenlosigkeit* in this context, to argue for "groundlessness," is a clear reference that the word has to the earth as land or soil, a reference that will become the actual "source" in Heidegger's later thinking, especially in his Hölderlin interpretations. But as with *Being and Time* Heidegger finds it necessary and helpful to continue his deconstruction

of how the Western philosophical tradition has covered over the word "thing'
in such a way that it has lost touch with the "ground."

b. *The thing as the unity of the manifold perceptions*

The second option in thinking about the work of art is not the substance/
accident option, but occurs in the way of taking a thing to be a collection of
perceptible attributes, a philosophical model preferred by such empiricists as
Locke, Berkeley, and Hume. However, notes Heidegger, as opposed to assault-
ing us and being distanced from our body by abstraction, this option is too
body-oriented because it holds a thing too close to the body, thus also letting
the thing disappear. The problem is that by bringing the thing too close, we are
not allowed to account for how the thing rests in itself or stands on its own.
Rather, Heidegger insists that "The thing must be allowed to remain resting
in itself. It is in that [resting within itself] that its own steadfastness is to be
taken."[19] As subtext, the word for "steadfastness" that Heidegger uses in this
quote, *Standhaftigkeit*, also connotes "resoluteness" and carries with it the kind
of decisiveness for which Heidegger had been seeking since the incompletion
of *Being and Time* and the apparent irresoluteness of the Germans during the
early period of the success of National Socialism.

c. *The thing as form-stuff*

The third option sees the thing as a combination of form and material, of
material as form (*hyle*) and matter (*Stoff*). Heidegger notes that, in fact, the differentiation of matter and form is the conceptual scheme for all contemporary
theories of art and aesthetics, that is, for categorizing the thing according to
form and content. But he then asks if the form/material categorization holds
for all things, how do we go about differentiating things from other beings?
This raises the question of what is primary — the thingliness of the thing or
the workliness of the artist? By looking at some examples of some material,
like shoes or axes, one sees that the form/content issue works itself out as a
product for service of some sort and thus, Heidegger concludes, such a way of
thinking things consigns them to be only made for a pre-determined purpose.
In other words, the question that is raised regarding "for what purpose is
a thing made," is answered with Heidegger's claim that things are readily
regarded as a "Product of a making. The product becomes made as a tool for
something."[20] Clearly Heidegger has in mind here the development of "tool"
earlier established in *Being and Time*, but what is different in his development
in this later interpretation is that, while taking the earlier contextual analysis
for granted, Heidegger places the tool "between" the thing and the work of art

in a kind of a continuum. Not only does the tool (*das Zeug*) reveal what stands around us as our circumstances, it also reveals its own place — and thus how we should situate it — in the continuum of thing-tool-artwork.

"Generally, the things around us are the nearest and most authentic things." Interestingly, the word he uses in this phrase for "generally" (*durchgängig*) is rooted in the German word for passage, "*Durchgang*," which literally means "a going through." So we "go through" the "use-things" or tools, in order to get at "things" and "artworks."[21] In other words, the tool has a "between" status, between the thing as simple natural thing and the work as a stand-alone sort of thing. Heidegger even rejects a Thomistic teaching of creation out of the unity of material and form, which, as a projected belief in a believed world loses the knowledge of being in the whole, because it is only a foreign philosophy that is loaned to us to explicate beings according to the form/content strategy.[22] Heidegger rejects this because, in reducing the thing to the class of merely simple things, the thing is relegated to just another kind of tool.

Rather, we cannot take any one option on its own; rather, all three options have to be taken together because all three have grown together to form the ruling and general ways by which we think about all of our experiences with beings. However, they have also formed a blockade to our way to thinking the thingliness of things, the toolishness of tools, and the workliness of works because of the boundless arrogance and apparent self-evidence of our metaphysical projections elaborated through the history of philosophy, an arrogance of systematic projection which obstructs us from bringing the three thinking-ways to word.[23] This blockade of metaphysical projection is also an assault mode because it can only account for equipmental things and not a *mere* thing; in fact, all three are presumptive and dissembling in their pretension to self-evidence.

Rather, says Heidegger, we must first turn to beings and, by letting them rest in themselves (as we think them) we will be able to think being in the way that beings rest in their own essence.[24] But the attempt to do such a turning and thinking comes up hard against the thingliness of the thing, because, "The unappearing thing draws itself away from thinking in the most hard-necked way."[25] However, this very way that a simple thing holds itself back in the way that it rests in itself, is its way of resting in itself so as not to be forced, and thus the very essence of the thing remains essentially estranged and enclosed. If such foreignness and concealedness constitutes the very essence of the thing then we cannot force our way into the thingliness of the thing.

The problem now is that the history of the interpretation of the thingliness of the thing has taken on an unbearable veneer of infallibility which Western thinking has associated with the being of beings. But even in this history Heidegger sees a sign of the being of beings which is in the relationship of form and content as it appears as the toolishness of tools. The very toolishness of tools is connected to our own human generation in being, such that, in thinking of how the tool has a middle function between its own being and being, we can then think how the tool has a "between" function for the thing and the work.[26] As a consequence of that line of logic, Heidegger leads us to consider our own "generation in being," namely, how we handle the being of beings as such. In short, we do so through understanding the "work" of tools, at least at first.

But what is the tool in truth, that is, at first? Heidegger assures us that he approaches the tool "simply descriptively, without a philosophical theory."[27] The phenomenological description that he provides is the well-known example of Van Gogh's farmer's shoes and how they do or do not exemplify the category of service. Heidegger posits that the shoes do not reveal to us their serviceability; instead, they are just a picture of shoes without context. With an elliptical "And yet . . ." (*Und dennoch*), Heidegger sets his own context and provides a hermeneutic to go along with the shoes — a valorizing myth of the hardened and hard-working peasant woman:

> Out of the dark opening of the interior of the heavily worn workshoes (*Schuhzeug*: shoe-tools), stares the toil of the footsteps of work. In the genuine solidity of the heaviness (seriousness) of the workshoes is stored up the toughness of the long passage through the wide stretches and ever-uniform furrows of the field, over which a raw wind blows. On the leather lays the moisture and seeds of the ground. Under the soles slide the loneliness of the field-paths as they make their way through the sinking evening. In the workshoes vibrates the silent call of the earth, its still bestowal of ripe corns and its inexplicable self-failure in the deserted fallow lands of the winter fields. Through this tool is drawn the uncomplaining anxiety about the certainty of bread, the wordless joy of the repeated success over need, the trembling in the arrival of birth and the quaking in the threat of death. This tool belongs to the earth and in the world of the farmwoman it is guarded. Out of this guarded belonging-to arises the tool itself to its resting-in-itself.[28]

As Heidegger continues, such a scenario only occurs to us as a picture-story, but the hypothetical farmwoman who simply wears the shoes knows such a scenario as self-evident insofar as she continues in her routine of wearing them or not wearing them. In fact, as we have already learned from *Being and Time*, the being of the tool is constituted by its service, that is, by its involvement in the relational web of our concern, known, however, by its breakdown from or dysfunction in that usual service. While such a "breakdown" in the line of service is broadly connected by Heidegger to the metaphysical breakdown of Western civilization and philosophy, at that place — German and global culture in the 1930s — and with this textual agenda — *The Origin of the Work of Art* — the breakdown refers to things in general and works of art in particular. Heidegger renames that relational web of concern and calls it reliability (*Verlässlichkeit*) rather than serviceability.[29] The strength of the peasant woman's tool is the strength of the "quiet call of the earth" and in the strength of her tool she is sure of her world.[30] Extending the web of reliability, Heidegger contends that the "reliability of the tool first gives the simple world its hiddenness and secures for the earth the freedom of its constant press (thrust)."[31] The point that Heidegger makes is that the very *toolishness* of the tool, its reliability, is that which *holds* all things in how they are. But usefulness, as opposed to reliability, degenerates into a commonplace usualness of seviceability which itself even fades away into the mere relation of form to matter as productivity. This degeneration, characteristic for Heidegger of the metaphysical tradition of Western thinking, leaves us with the form/matter distinction and the unresolved problem of the thingliness of the thing.

Shifting our attention, Heidegger goes on to ask: "What is at work in the work?"[32] The "work" of Van Gogh's painting is the opening (*Eröffnung*) of what the tool, in this case the pair of farm shoes, "*is* in truth." This "opening" allows Heidegger to introduce the conceptual complex of "truth" and his claims regarding the Greek origin of truth: "This being steps out of its unconcealedness into its being. The Greeks named the unconcealedness of beings truth, *aleithea* (αληθεια)."[33] Consistently, Heidegger maintains that the opening of a being, "in what and how it is," is truth happening in the work.

> In the work, art as the truth of beings has set itself in the work. "To set" says here: to bring to a standing. In the work, a being, a pair of farmer's shoes, comes to stand in the light of its being. The being of the beings comes to its shining in the constancy [of the reliability of its "standing" forth].[34]

Heidegger contrasts what he refers to as his "discovery" to the traditional notion of aesthetics that art has to do with the beautiful. His contrast takes shape in opposition to the view of art out of the Middles Ages that has to do with agreement with reality, with an *adaequatio*, and with Aritstotle's *homoiosis*, namely, agreement (*Übereinstimmung*). These are the views that we have come to associate with modern aesthetics and the theory of representation, namely, that the work copies reality in its production, a theory that Heidegger situates not with modernity but rather with ancient Greek ways of thinking. But even with such a resituating, this correspondence theory based on representation is unsatisfactory for Heidegger because the work does not merely depict the individual being at hand. For example, of what is a Greek temple a copy? The temple is not a "copy" but rather, he insists, truth is set to work in the work of art. But what is the nature of this setting-to-work of truth? Is it not something timeless and a-temporal or is it historical and something that happens? Heidegger claims that in order to get at what art is, we have to raise the question of truth anew with regard to the tool-character of a thing and attempt to avoid current interpretations. This means getting to what it means for truth to be set forth in the work of art.

His phenomenological claim is that, "We are told what the tool should be through a work itself," which turns out to be the opening of a being in its being and the happening of truth.[35] His two conclusions are that: (a) we cannot get at the thingliness of the work itself with the current thing-concepts; and (b) that the attempt to present thingliness as the real substructure of the work does not even belong to the work. This is the case because such a line of thinking only leads to conceiving the work in terms of a tool-structure that in fact does not capture what the work is. What Heidegger maintains is that looking at the thingliness of a work and at its tool-function is a traditional aesthetic issue and diverts our attention from looking at the work itself. By getting caught up in the usual way of questioning we miss what is essential about the work itself. Rather, all of the characteristics of a work/thing only become open to our view (*Blick*) when we first think the "being of Beings (*Sein des Seienden*)."[36] Moreover, because the thingliness of the work is nonetheless essential to it we need to think that thingliness out of the perspective of the work itself to which it belongs. Thinking from such a perspective means that to get at what happens in the work entails thinking of "art as the truth setting-itself-[to work]-in-the-work." Given that the correspondence theory of truth leads to a *reductio ad absurdum*, the next step is to delimit what truth entails in this case of focusing on the work itself.

Heidegger continues by pointing out that art is the origin of the work of art and that art is real in the artwork, entailing that we define "reality," a task he already deconstructed as superficial in *Being and Time* — although failing to come to a satisfactory revision of the term in that context. That failure had to do with the inadequacy of his working out the issues of control, decisiveness, and destiny, which entail working through the phenomenon of the work of art. This is what Heidegger undertakes in the text at hand by taking up the issue of origins. In doing so, turning to the question of origin, Heidegger contends that reality — as that which is worked — is grounded in thingliness but, as he already noted, the traditional categories of thingliness, that is, describing "reality" from the perspective of individual things — the method of the traditional sciences — we fail in our attempt to get at the being of a thing in its originality. Likewise in this case, we are not allowed to force the thingly character of a work on it from the onset; instead, the thingly character of the work can only be found when the pure standing-within-itself of the work has been clearly, or outspokenly, pointed out (*deutlich gezeigt*).

But is the work even able to be seen on its own? According to Heidegger, the work is able to be seen on its own through how the artist releases the work to its "pure standing-within-itself" (*Insichselbststehen*), acting as a mere channel for a "self-destroying passage for the emergence of the work."[37] In a very complex and subtle way, Heidegger builds a suppression of responsibility into his new metaphysics in how he argues that an artist gives himself up to the happening of art. Given that surrender to the process, the inevitable consequence is that as an artist, I am ultimately not responsible for what I produce but am merely the channel for some greater, not to be identified source or *"Ursprung."* What this source, or origin, *is* must remain for Heidegger an undetermined mystery. But as I indicated earlier, the issue of responsibility for any work is, for someone like Rosenzweig, critical. This also became an issue for Derrida as we know from the contradictory assertions about his relationship with the works that he produced.[38]

Heidegger notes that artworks are usually handled as pieces of art collections, in a business, in museums, or as part of the art industry: "The art-business cares only for the market."[39] Setting a post-modern tone for the next half century of art criticism, Heidegger claims that art has been reduced to the function of commodity answering to the demands of consumerism and the for-profit forces of market economics.[40] The work of art, as embedded in its contextual origin, has been ripped out of its own essential space and displaced (*Versetzung*) in a collection of works which has drawn it away from its own world. Not only is the work of art displaced but we are also unable to reconstruct the world in which it first arose in itself because that world has decayed and is removed. Instead, we only find the work in the traditions with which they have been handed down to us, traditions, which Heidegger has attempted to point out are no longer helpful at getting to authentic truth and the being and essence of things as they are in themselves. The self-subsistence of the work has fled from the work in the decay of the tradition. All the business of the market-driven art-world now handles works of art as mere objects, as commodities, and does not allow us any access to their instantiation as works.

III. *Standing on the ground of decision*

Heidegger pursues the consequences of this state of affairs by posing the question: is it still a work if it stands outside of all relations? If not essentially financial, within what relations does the work still stand? Where does the work belong? The etymology of the German word for "belong," "*gehören*," is the word "*hören*," which means "to hear." By phrasing his question in the way that he does, Heidegger also implies the related language-based question: "Where can the work be heard?"[41] The response is "that the work belongs to that area which it itself has opened up and which is the happening of truth in the work." This reply leads to the question of how truth happens in the work. With respect to this issue of relations and assessing the originality of creating determinative connections between beings, Heidegger provides us with his second example of a work of art, the Greek temple, which he says is more than just a mimetic or representational form of art as a painting would be, that is, something that is not merely a copy of something else:

A building, a Greek temple, copies nothing. It simply stands there in the middle of a rugged, rocky valley. The building closes itself around the figure of the god and in this concealment lets the god stand out through the open portico into the holy surrounding area (*Bezirk*). Through the temple the god is present in the temple. This presence of the god is in itself the spreading-out and outer-limits of the surrounding area as a holy area. But, the temple and its surrounding area are not suspended into the indefinite. The temple-work submits to and gathers at the same time around itself the unity of those courses and relations in which birth and death, victory and disgrace, endurance and decline — the human-essence, gains the shape of its destiny. The governing expanse (*waltende Weite*) of these open relations is the world of this historical people. Out of and in this expanse the people first returns to itself for the completion of its definitive calling.[42]

It is clear from this critically important passage that, for Heidegger, the fundamental defining of the destiny of a nation, of a people, is determined by the "ruling (or *working*) expanse" — its "*waltende Weite*" — of the holy circle constituted by the god, which makes its presence known only in and through the work of art. But what is constituted by such a "ruling/working expanse?" What appears are the thingly materials out of which the work of art is made, but they appear in such a way that "adjectival occurrence" displays what it is they are as occurrences. For example, note the descriptive modifications of the nouns in the following passage: "It is only through the splendor and the lighting of the stones, illuminated only by the grace of the sun, that the light of the day, the expanse of the heavens and the dark of the night are brought forward and seen. The certain towering [of the temple] makes the invisible space of the air visible."[43] Heidegger contends that what occurs in the working of a work of art is that the products which constitute the work itself are only able to radiantly show themselves in the unity of the work itself in its happening as a work, and only through that radiant showing are we able to see how they are related to the ground of the earth out of which and upon which the work takes form. Moreover, "This emergence and arising itself and in totality the Greeks initially named *physis* (Φυσιζ). It lights at the same time, that on which and in which the human grounds his dwelling. Continuing his vocabulary lesson, Heidegger says that we have named it the *earth*."[44] The earth is also the place where the arising of all that which arises occurs and is brought back to safe concealment. What the temple does, then, is to open up a world while at the same time grounding a people on the earth, the earth which then emerges as the people's "native ground" (*heimatliche Grund*). With these moves, Heidegger has begun to establish the "ground" as *Boden*, or earth/soil/land which had been lost and forgotten through the confusing settlements of traditional habituations.

But having a ground is not enough. What Heidegger is after is the *work* of human activity and how that is situated and structured. In the very standing of the temple where it is at, things are able to be sighted and given their face

(*Gesicht*) and the human is given its outlook (*Aussicht*) on itself. While his bias for vision and sight situates Heidegger's own hermeneutic clearly within the visually oriented tradition of Western philosophy (although recall the indirect reference to hearing above), it is as directional an assertion as his phenomenological account of "circumspection" (*Umsicht*) in *Being and Time*. Only here, the stakes are much higher since he maintains that this sighting (*Sicht*) remains open only so long as the god within has not fled out of the work and, in fact, the work as work not only occasions the presence of god but *is* god (*der Gott selbst ist*). I will return to this remarkable claim in the next chapter in considering how "god" or the "absent gods" plays into the decision-making of a people through their "art" and what that means for their political destiny. For now, though, suffice to say that the assertion works as a sort of transcendental or concentrated rallying point for unifying the effective and forceful acts of a people.

In fact, the same sort of "rallying" is true for works of speech in how they become occasions for the battle of new gods against the old, and where even the sayings of the people lead forth the essential word of the battle but in a changed form, namely, as decision.[45] What Heidegger means by decision (*Entscheidung*) is a dividing of one from the other, a division made on the basis of bringing one to "the decision for what is holy or unholy, what is small or big, what is precious or fleeting, what is master or slave."[46] For support, Heidegger cites Heraclitus's Fragment 53 in order to draw upon one of the earliest "fiery" proponents of conflict as the essential mode of philosophizing, and indeed, of living. This matter of "conflict" remains central for Heidegger, from his earliest works up until the end of his career. Recall, for example, Heidegger's development of the polar structures of authenticity and inauthenticty and decisiveness/resoluteness in *Being and Time* as well as the prevalent modes of concealing/unconcealing (*behren/entbehren*) in his later philosophy.[47] But again, this issue of conflict has to be laid temporarily aside, but not forgotten.

What is the work-being of the work, Heidegger asks? He leads us to consider how we view the work, of how it is "set up" — its *Aufstellung*, and asks us to consider two different kinds of setting up. On the one hand we have the bringing in of an artwork into a collection, which is what is done in the art industry, or on the other hand, the setting up of an artwork in the midst of a people as part of their religious identification, say as a temple for a god or as a theatrical presentation in a festival. In this latter case, setting up has to do with dedication and praise and what occurs is a "working emplacement of the holy as the holy."[48] In this latter case, the god is called into the openness of his presence and, withal, serves as the source of "presencing" for the decision-making of the people within whose midst the presencing occurs. Dignity and splendor are not adjectives appended to the presencing god but in dignity and splendor (or brightness) (*Glanz*) the god is shown. Following his hermeneutical method introduced in *Being and Time*, Heidegger substitutes another word for the one at hand in order to transform our vocabulary: "In the reflection of this brightness shines, that means, lightens there itself, what we name the world."[49] What we see, in other words, is not the prescencing god, but the object that appears in the radiating light of that presencing, namely, the world.

But perhaps even more significant is his next move: "To e-rect (*Er-richten*) says: open the right (*Rechte*) in the sense of the guiding-along measure, as that which gives guidance to what is most essential."[50] Here we have the source from which Heidegger suggests we draw for the guidance for our decisions and the assurance that we are "in the right" in following that essential guidance. And we get this "rightful" guidance from the originary working of the work of art as the site of the holy presencing radiance of a god, dedicated and praised by the people, and significantly not from the kind of art hanging in art museums or other industry associated uses. Moreover, this guiding activity is one based on sight, since in the working of art, in its towering-up-of-itself (*in-sich-aufragend*) the work opens up a *world* with all of the interconnections that such an opening-up implies; because in this way of opening-up of a world, the work of art — and the world it founds — achieves their endurance.

To be a work means, then, to give indications (*Anzeigen*) or signs of the right way to proceed along the way and to prescribe limits to avoid distorting our view of the nature of the world. What is the authentic world for Heidegger? It should be clear by now that it is not a collection of individual things; rather, drawing on the form of phrasing phenomenological processes begun in *Being and Time*, Heidegger asserts that the *world worlds* (*die Welt weltet*) and is more tangible and graspable than where we believe ourselves to be at home. As Heidegger challenges traditional theories of knowledge, he also challenges common-sense beliefs about the objectivity of the world. He continues to build on what our relationship to this kind of world "worlding" should be when he claims that the world is "ever-nonobjective, to which we are subject, as long as the courses from birth to death, from blessing to curse hold us removed [from] being."[51] What it means for the world to world is that humans are questioningly involved in their historical course of decision-making, involved in a process of determining the signs of blessings and cursings emanating from the reflected radiance of the presencing god. While animals and rocks and plants have no world, humans do because they dwell in the openness of the beings that only caringly take on their relational spatial status in a world and of a world that worlds.[52] But not only the presencing god accomplishes such a worlding process. Such a process is also accomplished by an absenting god: "That spaciousness is gathered in the worlding, out of which the protective grace of the gods is given or denied. Also the doom of the god that remains away is a way in which the world worlds."[53]

The result of this process is that the *Aufstellung* work of the work accomplishes a holding-in-openness of a world freely open. Open means here the possibility of displaying the guiding measures of the work which enable a people to continue authentically along their way of being a people. It is an essential part of their "home-work." This *Aufstellung* activity is one of the twofold characteristics of that which constitutes what happens in a work. The other characteristic activity Heidegger names *Herstellung* (from the verb *herstellen*: to place, to produce, to bring about) which has to do with the *Stoff* out of which a work is produced, the *Werkstoff*. However, keeping in mind Heidegger's reworking of traditional form/matter distinctions, he twists the relationship of work to stuff and says that: "The work as work is, in its essence, a producing."[54] What does the work produce? What is "placed-here" (*stellt-her*) in the work? In the analysis of the tool above, Heidegger demonstrates how the stuff of which something is made disappears in the functionality of the tool; the best kind of peasant shoes are those that remain in the stream of their use. However, with a work of art, the case is that the stuff out of which the work is made is shown forth for what and how it is, namely, the rocks of the temple support and allow the building to rest upon the earth, and so for the first time become the rocks which they are [for us]; only in the reflection of the iron do we see light and dark and color, etc. Heidegger develops this line of thought further by adding, "The place where the work returns to and that which is enabled to come forth in this returning-to-itself-place, we name the earth. It is the coming-forth — sheltering . . . Upon the earth, the historical human grounds his dwelling in the world."[55]

Heidegger then puts both functions together: "While the work sets up a world, it sets forth the earth."[56] And then he concludes by saying that the work allows the earth to be earth. Why is this the case though? It is so because any exercise in analyzing any particular stuff of the earth, which is done with conventional sciences, rips it out of its originary environment. He claims that the earth "shows itself only if it remains undisclosed and inexplicable" and any attempt at forcing one's way into it shatters in failure.[57] According to Heidegger, the appearance of mastery by proponents of progress that results in the kind of objectification of nature done by the technical sciences is really just the indication of an impotent will. Taking this evaluative stance against a historicist form of faith in the progressive science of the Enlightenment enables Heidegger to highlight the connected realms of "will" and "power." But what follows this judgment is critically important for understanding the underlying difficulties and entanglements that lead to Heidegger's later ethical obfuscations and their direct connection to his predilection for distorting the human effects of "will" and "power." While the earth has to remain undisclosable (*Unerschlössbare*) and essentially closed up, all the things of the earth nonetheless stream together in a back and forth accord. Heidegger plays out this "back and forth accord" in his later analysis of Hölderlin's reference to the Ister at its origin, which is also a twofold movement which I will attend to in the next chapter. In the *Origin* work, however, this pairing is a strange accord since in such a stream bounds are also set, delimiting each thing from the other, each presence from every other presence; since, "in each self-secluded thing there is the same not-knowing-each-other."[58] This is because the earth, and everything in and of it, is essentially self-secluding such that what it means for the earth to be "set-forth (*her-stellen*)" through the work is to bring it into the open as essentially self-hiding (*Sichverschliessende*). The obvious consequence of this development of thought is that in accepting such a setting forth as the nature of things as they are, we are likewise presented with a radical irrational inexplicability that entails that we also accept a radical irrelationality of things in the world. Significantly, and conservatively, we are later told by Heidegger that the authentic response to such a state of affairs is to leave things in their isolated aloneness, to "let things be" as an exercise in *Verlassenheit*. The contradiction that emerges with this new emphasis on "letting things be" arises with Heidegger's thought complex developed around the acts of resolute decisiveness in coming to one's ownmost appropriation of one's self, spelled out in *Being and Time*. However, this horn of the dilemma will only be worked out later, with Hölderlin, and Heidegger's estimation of the significance of Hölderlin's poetry for the German people.

IV. *The work of art as the place of conflict*

The setting forth of the earth is achieved by the work itself as it itself returns itself, and our attention, to the earth. To repeat, in this enclosing/revealing activity of the work, the earth unfolds itself in a myriad of simple forms and shapes which only then allows colors, metals, stone, and even words to become what they truly are. In fact, in a work there is no trace of work material remaining since what happens is that the stuff is allowed to be seen as it is. This happening occurs as the unity of the work in the combined process Heidegger names "setting-up" and "setting-forth" and in what Heidegger calls the "enclosed rest of that which rests upon itself."[59] But, he continues, this is not a usual rest; instead, it is a kind of enclosed movement — an "en-framing" of movement — and the closed frame of the work just represents the limit of the movement which is displayed in the work. What is this movement that is displayed? The answer is significant for determining the unique function that art plays in Heidegger's philosophy.

The movement is a *conflict*. However, this is no simple, abstract, conflict. What art presents is the conflict between earth and world. The world, as Heidegger tells us, is the "self-opening openness of the wide course of the simple and essential decisions in the destiny of an historical people." While the earth, on the other hand, is the "unforced emergence of that which is continually self-secluded and thereby concealed." Both combine yet separate from each other, the "world grounds itself on the earth, and earth towers through world."[60] In this battle of forces, the world has no patience for a secluded earth and attempts forcefully to open it up, while the earth, which is all patience, tends towards concealment and attempts, therefore, to draw the work into itself and to keep it there. This issue of patience is likewise very important for evaluating the stance Heidegger takes in the entire body of his work, since "letting be" is a "waiting," which remains at odds with political decisiveness.[61] Note that these variations on patience radically depart from the patience that Rosenzweig counsels that we should cultivate in our relationship to others in redeeming the world, one "patient" step at a time.

Possibly drawing from Heraclitus's idea of conflict as a kind of striving, the relationship of the members involved in the conflict that Heidegger articulates are even more concretely established when he asserts that in this kind of essential conflictual striving, which he counters is no mere discord nor malcontent, we find the combatants raise each other to the "self-assertion of the nature of each."[62] Moreover, such a "self-assertion" is never a kind of dogmatic adherence to some kind of contingency, but rather it results in the "self-surrender to the hidden originality of the source of one's own being"[63] Could this be the preparatory grounds for the kind of philosophical conditioning which Heidegger needed for a speech such as his Rektorat speech, "The Self-Assertion of the German University?" In that speech he called for Germans to join in the battle for one's own German identity and surrender oneself to the secret original source of one's own being. But what or who leads one to these original sources of one's own being? Who is the Führer? As Heidegger's former student (and current editor of Heidegger's collected writings) von Hermann notes, this was written in the winter Semester of 1932 just before the Nazis seized national power and just prior to Heidegger's own assumption to administrative power in Freiburg. Hence, the argument can and perhaps should be more strongly made for the rootedness of Heidegger's own political actions very deeply in his philosophy and, especially, in his "turn" to a philosophy of art. That is the argument I make here.

The conflictual struggle of "setting-up" and "setting-forth" becomes ever more intense, more authentic, and more their own the harder each combatant battles and the more they carry each other beyond itself (*über sich hinaus*). With a strong resemblance to the contestation that eventually results in the binding of the *Aufhebung* of Hegel's dialectic, Heidegger notes that the more each struggles the more each combatant realizes that they need each other.[64] The earth needs the world to appear in its secludedness while the world needs the earth as a ground for the essential destiny of its decisiveness, that is, the earth grounds the decisions of its worldly people. The role of the work is to allow for the conflict to take place in the antagonistic intimacy of the setting-up of the world and the setting-forth of the earth. Moreover, the work does its work not with the goal of resolving the conflict, but precisely in order that the conflict is able to be carried on: "The work-being of the work consists in the conflicting of the conflict between world and earth."[65] The work not only instigates the battle but gathers the movements within itself which is the movement within rest that results in that which constitutes its own essence.

As resting, and only as resting, are we thus capable of seeing what is at work in a work. This setting to work of the truth and the setting to work of truth entails, for Heidegger, a closer analysis of what truth means. He points out that the usual meaning is to refer to some specific thing to which the word corresponds, in reality. But this is just a logical *Teufelskreis*. Hence, Heidegger leads his reader through a word-play from the essence of what is true to what a being *is* in truth. He leads us to an abyss of reasoning only to reintroduce his earlier etymological claim that truth is derived from the Greek word, *aletheia*, which means to unconceal beings, in the etymological sense of a non-forgetting. As Heiddeger points out, this is really just a play on words unless we first *experience*, in the sense of *erfahren*, as a "going over something," and that entails the necessity of what has to happen.[66] Such experiencing has to happen in order to be able to equate the word truth with unconcealedness.

Heidegger makes the additional startling claim that it is not necessary or even possible to go back to the Greeks to make sense of the process of *aletheia* as unconcealedness, although this happening of truth has "from early on been that which determines the presence of everything present."[67] Despite such a far-reaching claim, it is the case, Heidegger insists, that Greek philosophy itself is hidden, within which the enlightening essence of *aletheia* did not conform and, in fact, becomes ever more derivative and concealed in the philosophy which follows. Of course, what Heidegger refers to here is the forgotten question of being with which he begins *Being and Time* and which carries him through the analysis of the work of art to the "history of being" in the last stages of his career. According to his method, the traditional handling of such an important question is inadequate and inauthentic, on the grounds of the nature of experience and in order to facilitate the binding hold of conformity of knowledge with fact. In order that the stuff with which we are dealing conforms to the propositional sentences of our cognition, the stuff itself has to show itself as such,"[68] otherwise the proposition will not be binding. Furthermore, the proposition, while still concealed, shows itself as true if it *directs itself to* (*richtet*) the unconcealed. It is in this directiveness, or correction (*Richtigkeit*) that Heidegger redefines traditional theories of truth as certainty, departing from Descartes's theory of representation.

Even more comprehensively, Heidegger claims that in our thoughts as representational (*Vorstellen*), that is, in the sense of a displacing function, we are already determined by the very nature of the unconcealedness of beings to be in and directed toward unconcealedness. Not only that, the entire realm of unconcealedness as a whole has to come into the lighting (*Gelichtete*) as uncon- cealed beings in order for us to measure the conformity of our propositions of truth about any particular cognition of a particular being. But what is the concealed? All beings — things, humans, gifts, plants, animals, *stand* in being.

But, "through the being goes a veiled fate (doom, disaster — *Verhängnis*)," which hangs between that which is godly and that which is against god.[69] This is one of the strangest lines in a body of work that is full of strange lines because it constitutes that definitive line for Heidegger which is irrefutable, establishing "destiny" as a dividing curtain. It is an assertion that lies at the very core of his later anti-technological rhetoric and conservative, even mystical tendencies.[70] He goes on to claim that there is much about beings that humans are permitted to overpower. What humans know is, in fact, only approximation, that is, what is mastered is only uncertain and never do we ever have beings within our power.

And yet, Heidegger redirects us to what he calls the "happening of an other" in the middle of beings.[71] There occurs "an open place. A lighting is. Thought from out of beings, it is more being than being itself (*seiender als das Seiende*). This open middle is therefore not excluded from beings, but rather as lighted middle encircles like the nothing, which we hardly know, everything that is."[72] Moreover, this lighted clearing guarantees the very existence of beings as beings since only what is lighted within this lighted circle of being *is* and stands out. In fact, "Only this lighting grants and guarantees humans a passage to beings which we ourselves are not, and the access to the beings which we ourselves are."[73] These are very strong, categorical claims on Heidegger's part and all in the context of the working of a work of art. They are strong because it is only through this lighted clearing provided by art can beings be revealed or concealed according to different degrees. That is, art provides the *measure* for determining our judgments about the very nature of beings with and within which we move and direct our own being. Furthermore, all beings are both revealed in this lighting as well as concealed, and concealed in a twofold way. In fact, what it means to reveal is to conceal, and denial (*Versagen*) is the very beginning of the lighting while, at the same time, as one being is revealed another is shoved to the side, covered over, etc. Heidegger names this process *Verstellen* — understood at this point as dissembling (misplacing/disguising?). As readers of Heidegger's text, however, we have reached a crisis in philosophical responsibility because at the heart of the clearing of truth that Heidegger sets up is also situated a remarkable ontological justification for deceit and subterfuge; there is no possibility for judgment because of the built-in necessity of ambiguity and uncertainty. The play that Heidegger sets into motion, in the name of descriptive phenomenology, is a play of light and mirrors where the lighting of the clearing in the midst of beings only occurs via these two forms of concealedness — of denial and/or dissembling.

What results from these musings on Heidegger's part is the insight that we are "at home" in the usualness of things but the core of things is that they are quite unusual and that what it means to reveal is to conceal, and that the nature of truth is denial, or untruth. The simplistic ground for such an apparently inconsistent or at best ambiguous assertion is, of course, the recourse to a

very familiar solution which Heidegger himself names, that is, the dialectic.[74]
Dialectical opposition as the primal conflict is the nature of truth and is that
which happens in the midst of beings and is that which constitutes their very
being. More importantly, Heidegger turns our attention back to the conflict
between world and earth when he asserts that "the world is the clearing of
the courses of the essential guiding directions in which all decision submits."[75]
Earth towers freely through the world and the world grounds itself decisively
on the earth only insofar as this conflict is allowed to occur. And this is the
conflict of truth as *aletheia*, which happens in many ways, but fundamentally
includes its happening in the working of the work of art. Heidegger makes
the strong claim that the "work is the fighting of the conflict in which the
unconcealedness of beings in the whole, or in the truth, will be fought out."[76]
What are we to make of such a claim, especially since it was conceived during
the very period that Heidegger is "fighting out" what he considers the destiny
of the German people in the context of the emergence of the National Socialist
German Worker's Party?

The final point Heidegger makes in this regard is that in a work, such as
in the mere "standing-there" of the temple referred to earlier, truth happens,
which means that beings in their totality are brought into unconcealedness and
held there. And, Heidegger adds, what it originally means to "hold" something
in its totality is to "tend or guard" it.[77] Furthermore, what is at stake in the
working of the work of art is to show the being of things as they essentially
are and the purer and more unadorned the more purely and immediately will
they be perceived in their being set off against the other beings in which they
are in relation. Insofar as such "holding" and "guarding" as a "setting off"
occurs is the self-concealedness of being (itself) lighted. And it is this light
which shines on the work and is called beauty: "Beauty is a way that truth as
unconcealedness shows itself."[78]

The transition to the next major development in the work of this text is
made by determining the thingly nature of the work. In his attempt to grasp
the work's independence (its *Insichstehen*) as purely as possible, and with
some affinity with Rosenzweig's conceptualization of creation, Heidegger
considers how the work is always something "worked" (*Gewirktes*), namely,
its "having-been-created." For Rosenzweig, this createdness as a work endows
the work with a kind of organicity. But for Heidegger, what is important is
that since the work is something created the work needs some kind of medium
out of which and in which it creates, which entails the thingly element in the
work (the *Dinghafte*). This leads to two questions: (a) how does being created
differ from being produced and made; and (b) what is the inmost essence of
the work to which the work as created belongs and which defines the work?

What Heidegger needs to show is how the createdness of the work "bright-
ens" what truth is as unconcealedness even more originally. But in doing so, he
wants also to avoid merely asserting what is or is not the essence of truth. Thus,

he needs to determine just what is the nature of truth that must be set to work in a work of art in order for truth *to be* truth. This means that the more essential pursuit of setting-into-the-work of truth can only be determined by analyzing the essence of art. So the last question is: what is truth that it can happen as art, or that it *has* to happen as art? And, to what extent is there any art at all?

V. *Truth and art*

Heidegger claims that the origin of the work of art is art itself and that the origin is the source of the essence of the being of something, initiating a line of thought into the problematic nature of thinking about causes, sources, and origins. So to ask about what something is, is to ask about its essence, which Heidegger says we must seek in an actual work. Moreover, the actuality (*Wirklichkeit*) of the working of the work of art is the happening of truth at work which is the rest-full showing of the conflict between world and earth. He goes on to say that not only does the truth happen *at* the work but also *in* the work, such that it presupposes that the actual (*wirkliche*) work is the carrier (*Träger*) of the happening. These word choices set up the possibility for us to accept Heidegger's additional assertion, which shortly follows, that humans are carriers of the question of the being of beings. But at first he reminds us that in our concern for the independence of the work, we cannot forget that the work is something that "has been worked" (*Gewirktes*) and therefore has the character of thingliness, when he says, "*in* the work we *hear* the worked."[79] Note the etymological connection Heidegger makes of *Gewirktes* to *Wirklichkeit* and *wirkliche* which connotes effectiveness as well as actuality. Thus, the work is effectively actual in that it not only is the place where truth happens as a conflict of earth and world, but it is such that the work has an effect *for us*. Not only does the work have an effect for and therefore on us, but also, Heidegger points out, in the very word "work" we *hear* "worked," namely, that something was created *through* an artist, that it was created by *one of us*. The emphasis on the word "through" is important because in what follows, Heidegger attempts to explain what it means to create a work of art by, or "through," a human being.

   Guided by his hermeneutic phenomenology, Heidegger claims we have to look purely at the stuff itself, in this case, at the creative process so as to determine just what the essence of the process of work is. In order to come to such a determination, however, he has to return to exemplars, transgressing his own aversion to the employment of "actual" particulars in his phenomenological explication of a pure process. In this case, we are impelled to ask about the role of the few exemplars Heidegger mentions, namely, van Gogh's picture of the peasant's shoes and the Greek temple of the god. Both are *used* to remind us that a creative work is a process of emergence, which is also, paradoxically, the case with the production of a tool. In both cases, the works of art and the works of tools are primarily the activities of "hand-work," both of which the Greeks referred to with the same word: τεχνη (techne) and the artists and handworkers with: τεχνιτηζ (technitez). However, what Heidegger contends, that is, the conflict that he sets forth, is that even that application by the Greeks is a misunderstanding, because *techne* is better understood as a way of knowing and that "to know means to have seen . . . to perceive the presence of something as such." Where the essence of knowledge for the Greeks is truth as *aletheia*, that is, the uncovering of beings — which carries and produces every attitude (*Verhalten*) towards beings, "*techne*," as knowledge for the Greeks, is the *experience* (in the sense of *erfahren*) of bringing forth something out of hiddenness into the unconcealedness of how something *appears*.

Both the artist and the handworker, therefore, bring something forth into the presence of its appearance, whereas all the while what goes on is that these kinds of bringing-forths occur in the middle of the process of the earth-earthing, "growing-on-its-own going-up beings, the φυσιζ." But there is something else going on with the work which does not happen with the tool, namely, creation. Heidegger tells us that to create is to "let-something-go-forth into something-that-is-brought-forth." And that bringing forth is a way of "becoming" which is also the happening of truth. But despite claiming that that is all there is to it, Heidegger goes on to say that we still do not know what truth is. If truth is the letting-something-be-brought-forth of creation, how is the truth grounded in the work of art? In order to get at this groundedness, its origin, truth has to be redefined not to include the actuality of creating. To recapitulate, truth is shown as the dialectical opposition of a twofold concealing and a lighting, that is, the truth as the primal conflict in which every being shows itself and returns, stands forth and holds back. What occurs in the space of this conflict Heidegger calls the open (*Offenheit*) and the open, the truth, can only happen if "a"' being stands in "this" open and the openness itself takes possession of "this" being and takes a stand in its constancy.[80] Note the heavy emphasis on possession, since, Heidegger says, only insofar as the openness "possesses (*besetzt*)" this open space can it be held open and perceptible. "To set" and "to possess," Heidegger claims, should be understood from the Greek word *thesis*, which means to "set up in the unconcealedness."[81]

Heidegger says that this is a "setting-up of openness in the open" which creates an area, the *Bezirk*, which is similar to what is created around the holy temple.[82] Insofar as this particular being relates to being in some way, then being, "out of its essence lets the free playing space (*Spielraum*) of the clearing (*die Lichtung des Da-*) happen, and the particular being as such is brought in and arises [in this clearing] in its own way."[83] The arising of the being in its own way, is the happening of truth setting itself up which happens in a series of steps: through setting itself in work; through the founding of a state; through the nearness of the beingness of beings; through essential sacrifice;

and through the questioning of the questioner as the one named who questions being. Against all of this, science is not a happening of truth but merely a realm of extrapolations of an already open truth. In fact, questioning the arrogant claims to the absoluteness of "the" truth typically posited by practitioners of the natural sciences, Heidegger contends that if it is the case that a particular science in the directions which it takes happens to arrive at a truth, that is, the uncovering of a particular being, then it is called philosophy. And because it is the case that what truth does is to set up the being-in-self, it is therefore a possibility that the pulling process towards the work, its draw (*Zug*), is one of the possibilities of truth in action as letting the being of beings, as such, happen.

Moreover, what happens in the work is the bringing forth of a singular being that never was before and never will happen again. But in order to be brought forth in the clearing the work has to allow for the openness of beings, which is truth. Heidegger renames this process of "bringing forth in the clearing," as a receiving/welcoming (*Empfangen*) and "gathering-inferring from" (*Entnehmen*) dual process that occurs in a relationship (*Bezuge*) to unconcealedness.[84] Being-created occurs as truth executes or directs (*richtet*) itself in the conflict which occurs between world and earth in the work which is opened up on its own account and not by some outside process or train of events where the unity of the world is conflicted and fought out. As the work opens a space, it places such conflicts as wars and defeat, blessing and curse, and master and slave, before a historical humanity for decision. In the face of the conflict of ambiguity referred to above, the work itself opens up the moment of resolute decisiveness that determines the direction, as destiny, of a people.

But as world opens, earth towers up — it actually *rages* up — in a process which, in the act of arising, shows itself as that which carries all in its law and is nonetheless self-closed. But world demands decisiveness as divisiveness — an *Ent-scheidenheit*, and so lets the particular being go its way while the world attempts to entrust everything to its inexorable law, to what is set down (*Gesetz*). The rupture is not a simple cleft but rather shows itself as the origin of the unity of the two — it is a ground-rupture as basic outline (*Grundriss*) and a tearing-open as "sketch" (*Aufriss*) which shows the arising of the lighting of beings. It does not let the opponents break apart but keeps them together by bringing in the opposition of measure and boundary into a common ground-rupture in the form of a united divisiveness retained in sketch.

The truth as *aleithia* directs and erects itself in the being brought forth only as the rupture occurs as the "unified" drawing-together-in-relation (*Gezuge*) of: *Aufriss* — something torn open and elevated; *Grundriss* — something torn out from the "ground" as a plan; *Durchriss* — something torn in half; and *Umriss* — something torn down. Heidegger sets these processes in the context of the fundamental conflict of earth and world by noting that the truth is erected in the being as the being *possesses* the light of opening, but the being can only possess such a lighted opening if the rupture is entrusted to the self-closed earth. The heaviness of the stone, hardness of the wood, etc., sink back into the setting and ground of the earth. The earth has to take the rupture of world worlding as created work back into itself and only then is the rupture capable of being open as both self-secluding and sheltering.

Heidegger names this whole process *Gestalt* (figure/shape). What it means for a work to be created is for truth to be placed fast and is thereby enabled to stand as figure or *Gestalt*. That is, the composition (*Gefüge*) is that to which the rupture resigns (submits) or to which it fits, understood as *sich fügen* — as a joining-together-with. In other words, the particular being (a *Seiend*) submits to being fit into a large, compositional structure. In contrast to how Rosenzweig depicted the way that an artist infuses life into a particular detail of a total work by sacrificing their totality for the sake of enlivening that particular "other," Heidegger implies that the artist resigns or submits to one's work as to one's own fate, to one's own throwness, to one's own death. The rupture which is submitted to is the *Fügue*, which occurs as a song of joining, as composition of the appearance of truth. Again, note the difference: Rosenzweig considers the "song of truth" that occurs as the ethical heartbeat of his philosophy of art, the Song of Songs. In that song sung between lover and beloved, the convergence of singular individuals does not proceed by way of a conflict of opposites or of one in violent battle with the other but occurs, rather, as a call to respond to the other in a sensual/trans-sensual answering to the needs and desires of the other. For Rosenzweig, that poetic call-and-response is the heartbeat of his *Gestalt*, the figure of *The Star* and is essentially non-conflictual. If anything, it could be said to be sacrificial. For Heidegger, however, what is called Gestalt is always to be thought of as that particular act of fixing or placing a work in its context, as a frame or framing which the work shows insofar as it sets up and emerges (*auf- und her-stellt*) as the conflict of worlding and earthing activities.[85]

The created process of the work entails that the conflict of the rupture has to be set back into the earth so that the earth itself can be brought forth and used as that which is self-closed. While in this case the earth provides the shelter, Heidegger maintains that such a use does not misuse the earth; instead, it liberates it to be its own self. This use of the earth as self-closed can also be confused with the use of the earth in a handwork thing or a tool. But the difference is that the production of a tool is not the immediate happening of truth, a happening which is ultimately meant to show the event of the unique loneliness of beings as constitutive of the history of being. In fact, the use of the earth with respect to a tool is that the earth disappears in the serviceability of the tool and the more serviceable it is the more the earth disappears. With the work of art, on the other hand, the stuff is never used up but, nonetheless, Heidegger adds, the earth is still used and needed by the work of art — or needed to be used, or used as needed. For the tool, the use of the earth lies precisely in its being made *for use*, an ontological condition familiar to readers of *Being and Time*.

What further differentiates the work of art from the tool is that its created-ness itself stands out as its most essential characteristic, because that nature of self-referential createdness is what is created in and with the work of art itself as a work of art. It is this createdness which emerges as the distinguishing sign of the work *which we experience*.[86] Significantly, Heidegger clearly parts ways with Rosenzweig's development of an artist as genius/author whose works constitute a family of works when he claims that the emergence of the work of art out of its being created does not signify that it was made by a great artist. This is so because the work of art is not made by the artist having the work within his *power*, that is, as having power over the work. Rather, the authentic artist is merely a channel or placeholder for the happening of truth as the happening of the being of beings and thus is not responsible, as such, for the work she produces. The authentic artist is not one whose work is *seen* as the *production* or *achievement* of an *ability* (of someone who is able, of a *Könners*) and thus placed in public view. Instead, Heidegger claims, what is given to us to know as spectators and thus "knowers" of the work of art, is not the "N.N. *fecit*," namely, the origin of the making, but rather the *factum est* that is, the facticity that this particular being is at all — the "that it is.' This "that it is" is what is held open in the work of art, namely, "that the unconcealedness of the [particular] being happens here and first happens as this [kind of] happening."[87] Insisting on the facticity of the work of art enables Heidegger to resurrect the Greek metaphysical question which played so important a role for Schelling and the Idealists, namely: why is there something at all rather than nothing? Set within Heidegger's purview of the conflict of earth and world, however, this question becomes an issue of what constitutes the work, that is, what gives it existence and standing. What makes it stand?[88] The work is simply the ongoing (*ständig*) thrust of its "that" — it is.[89] And neither the particular artist nor the process of the circumstances of the *Enstehung* of the work matter, which is radically different than Rosenzweig's sense of taking responsibility for creation through the historicizing call and answer of personal responses of one for and to the other, as taking responsibility for the work one produces. For Heidegger, in contrast, the purest characteristic of what constitutes the work is the "that" of its having been created, and thus we are confronted with the brute fact of the isolated character of an existent being.

In order to more clearly define this sense of isolatedness of the work, Heidegger briefly turns our attention back to the relationship of the thingliness to the tool. Again basing his comments on the structures established in *Being and Time*, Heidegger reminds us that the more the thing character disappears into the tool, the more it is a tool and the more it is ready-to-hand to be used in its usual way. And, he notes, "what's more usual than this: that being is?"[90] But in a work, insofar as it is a work of art *as such*, it is the unusual that is remarkable, that is, it stands out from the usual. Imperceptibly, Heidegger strongly links this conception of the work of art with the individuating process

established earlier in *Being and Time*, as a correlation with the individuation
that occurs with the appropriative authenticating process of experiencing
Angst in the face of understanding one's existence as being-towards-death. The
occurrence of an authentic work of art is likewise associated with the isolating
event of *Ereignis*:

> The event of its being-created does not simply reverberate, rather the work casts
> itself out as eventful (*Ereignishafte*). The more essentially the work opens itself,
> the more lighted it becomes as that peculiar that it is and much more that it is
> not. The more this stuff [material] comes into the open, the more strange and
> *lonely* the work becomes.[91]

Again, the emergence of the work is simply the presentation *that it is*. What the
work puts out into the open is the "that" it is. What Heidegger goes on to say is
that "the more solitary the work" the more all of its connections to the human
seem to be dissolved."[92] The consequence is that if we submit to the process
at work in a work of art, if we come under its "un-usual" and individuating
influence, it becomes the vehicle for *changing* the "usual" and traditional,
everyday relations we have to world and earth, which includes all doing,
estimating, knowing and seeing. In essence, in order to dwell *in* the happening
truth in the work, one's relationships undergo a change in the way we *dwell*
or shelter with the work. And, Heidegger adds, it is only with the "attitude of
dwelling" that the work is allowed to be what it is, stipulating that such an
attitude occurs as, "preservation of the work."[93] And only in the preservation
of the work does the work take effect, that is, work effects presence (*werkhaft
anwesende*). So, by preserving this or that work of art, an effective presencing
occurs in the world, a presencing that one knows is authentic in the way that
it enables one to come to one's isolated condition of being-in-the-world.

But even if the work has no preservers it is inconsequential because it is
directed to the preservers and waits and hopes for them. Even the forgetfulness
of being into which a work falls is a kind of preservation because the forgetfulness itself "lives from the work."[94] To preserve a work means to stand in the
openness of the being created by the work (*Inständigkeit der Bewahrung*)
— which Heidegger calls a way of knowing, as opposed to mere cognition
or a representational form of knowing, and thus is set against representative
art. Moreover, he ties this way of knowing to *volition*: "Whoever truly knows
the being, knows, from within the being, what he wants."[95] And this kind of
volition is what was already explicated in *Being and Time* as the identity of
knowledge and volition and which is, precisely, "ek-static self-engagement
of the existing human in the unconcealedness of Being."[96] This resolution or
decisiveness — the *Entscheidenheit* that cuts oneself off from others — is not
an act of a subject but the "opening of Da-sein out of its fallenness in beings to
the openness of being."[97] Volition — willing, is connected to the disclosedness

(*Ent-schlossenheit*) of the existent process of what emerges from the openness
of being in the work — an "existing going over and out of itself."[98] This "going
over and out of itself' is a kind of submission which, standing-within, is a sober
kind of law (*Gesetz*) that includes an awesome kind of wonderment.

This kind of "knowing" which is at home as "wanting" in the truth of the
work thus becomes a kind of law that elicits wonderment. And as a kind of
knowing that becomes a kind of law, it is not a simple stimulant for experience
(*Erlebnis*), but rather individualizes the human not in *its* experiences but in her
relation to the work, which grounds its status as "being-with-another" and the
historical standing-out of humans in history, that is, how the "standing-out"
of humans refers to the unconcealed. So, *as* humans "stand toward" or in
relation to their work, their stand will determine the judgment of the work,
in the sense that *how* we preserve a work determines the standard — as a
law — for judgment. Heidegger asks: do we preserve a work as connoisseurs
of merely formal qualities and charms, as with Kant and therefore in keeping
with traditional aesthetics and a dogmatic formalism, or do we preserve a work
as one who *knows* that the *I have seen* (*Gesehen-haben*), which occurs as a
resolute decisiveness that sets one off from others? Such a resolute and decisive
"having-seen" occurs in the in-dwelling of the *Fugue* structure of the rupture
of the work, entailing that how the work itself is created *also* co-creates its
possibilities for preservation. In other words, only because I have seen a work
can I judge whether the work was created simply for pleasure or for the sake
of providing more brightness, in the sense that the most authentic actuality of
the work only occurs insofar as the happening truth can only happen as it is
brought to the light of day.

Against those who would maintain that, in some way, Heidegger's "turn"
somehow signified a radical break with the direction of his earlier work,
Heidegger himself points out that, "The reality of the work is defined out of
the essence of the fundamentals (*Grundzügen*) of the being of the work."[99] And
those fundamentals have to do with the thingliness first sought for from the
beginning, which *we cannot ask* about lest we repeat the old errors of making
the work an *object* and us a subject. Rather, from the perspective of the work,
"thingliness" appears as the earthliness that shows itself as towering up, which
as "that which is enclosed within itself by essence" occurs as that where truth
occurs — which is only applied to a particular thing.[100] But as it is applied it
becomes that which meets with the most *resistance* and is thus becomes a case
of an "enduring stand" (*ständigen Standes*), whereby we find the figure, the
Gestalt. In short, the "enduring stand" of *Being and Time* happens through
the *Origin of the Work of Art*.

But asking about thingliness was none the less essential since it brought us
on the right way away from the old ways of thinking, namely, away from trying
to master the totality of the ways of all beings, which is unfit to understand
tools and works and is *blind* to the truth. Rather, Heidegger contends that the

only way to get to the truth of things is to see how they belong to the earth, a belonging which only shows itself as a conflict with world in the earth's attempt to *rage* through the world. Moreover, such a conflict is only revealed through the work because, in fact, we do not even get what a tool *authentically is* except through the work, nor do we get what the thingliness of a thing is because it is through the work that the truth of beings happens.

VI. *Founding art as poetry*

The work is the in-setting of truth — as an establishment of truth — done by creating but also bringing it into *happening*, done by preserving; therefore, it is a creative preservation — and a becoming and happening of truth. It is created "out of nothing" in the sense that it is not created out of usualness or beings-at-hand but is only as "outlined in [the] throwness of on-coming openness."[101] Again, Heidegger has in mind the kind of openness to what is oncoming that reminds us of Da-sein as that being which becomes open towards its ownmost possibility of being-toward-death. But the difference in this work, which has for its task determining the origin of the work of art, is that "Truth as clearing and concealment of beings, happens in that it becomes poeticized. *All art* is as the letting-happen (*Geschehenlassen*) of the advent of truth of beings and is, as such, in essence poetry."[102] What is retained from *Being and Time* is the conceptualization of the non-possibility of being. Regarding truth in the context of the work of art, Heidegger notes that, as the truth is set in-work in the work of art, in the outline of what is set, all that is usual becomes unbeing. What Heidegger means by "unbeing" is a rejection of "normal language" in the sense that the normal use of language by Da-sein takes the form of a kind of unbeing that has *lost* the power to *measure* being, that is, true being. Hence, Da-sein, in resorting to poetry, no longer has an effect on previous beings because its existence is not in the effects that it works, and so has no connection to so-called normal reality but, rather, it rests in changing the unconcealedness of being into the light and clearing of actuality.

But poetry is neither whimsical nor fanciful [in its non-effectiveness]; it does not sink into irreality. Instead, through the work of art that is poetry — *what is* unfolds from the rupture as clearing outline, as the openness that "lets happen" *a being as a work of art* in the midst of beings and lets them light up and sound out. To accomplish this process, imagination is inadequate because it is connected with representation and is thus too sensual (i.e. *Sinnlich*). And although Heidegger rejects the notion that the thinking of poetry as the pure essence of art makes all other arts derivative, he nonetheless does say that poetry as a "work of speech . . . has a privileged place in the totality of art."[103] This privileging of poetry is important not only for the priority that Heidegger accords Hölderlin, but also for Heidegger's later claims about language being the "house of being" and for the irreplaceable role that language plays in the "history of being."[104] What he means by the work of speech is that art *as* speech *as* poetry is not just *used* for verbal and written communication but its primary function is to bring "being as being" (*Seiende als ein Seiendes*) into the open where there is no speech. This is the case with the kinds of beings such as plants, rocks and animals where there is no openness of beings and no emptiness. Truth precisely has to do with these kinds of beings insofar as truth happens "as clearing and concealment of beings as it is poeticized."[105] In fact, since poetry in particular is a way of speaking that happens through the *dichten* of poetry, in the etymological sense of a thickening and bringing together of our thoughts and expressions, Heidegger contends that: "*All art* is as a letting-happen of the advent of the truth of beings [which] is as such the *essence of poetry*."[106] But what is this "letting happen" as a thickening of our speech?

The "letting happen" occurs in the way that language *names beings* for the first time — in this poeticized happening of truth. It does so because it *sees* them in their relations: "This naming names beings *to* their being *out* of their being."[107] And this kind of naming speech is an outlining of the lighted clearing wherein what is announced (an *Ansage*) is the being that comes into the clearing. It is a *projective announcement* as a release of a throw.[108] What Heidegger means by the "release of a throw" is that speech, analogous to Rosenzweig's act of redemptive "loosening," releases the throw of the rupture. The analogy is a weak one, however, since for Rosenzweig the "release" is more akin to the loosening up of a boundedness to enable a spontaneous response to the other in their "chaotic" difference and otherness, whereas for Heidegger, the release is precisely meant to divide and separate one from the other, to "thicken" and cohere out of the many the singularity of the determined certainty of one's own. In fact, Heidegger says that the release releases Da-sein to the unconcealedness where it can resign itself — in the sense of being sent (*sich schicken*) — to beings, to that which is. The *Ansage* then becomes the denial (*Versagen*) of all the dim confusion in which beings are veiled and withdrawn. This is how we have the judgment of authenticity in Heidegger, namely, that speaking enables a division to become actual and effective in the world — it introduces the rupture into the play-room (*Spielraum*) of its conflict within and from beings. In other words, speaking happens as the saying of the earth/world conflict, which is also the nearness or absence of the gods as the granting of that holy *Bezirk* where the thickening of a coherence can take place. Speech is the happening of the saying where an historical people *arises* into their world *and thereby preserves* the closed-off earth in the place and on the soil where that rising occurred.

Projected saying is an event of the sayable bringing or inflicting upon the unsayable a simultaneity of "being" being brought to the world. Such sayings are what impress a historical people with its essence, namely, the saying of their ownmost way of *belonging* to world history.

"Language itself is poetry in the essential sense" and is a happening which discloses beings as beings.[109] Here we have the fruition of what is established in *Being and Time* as talk, the analysis of which makes clearer sense with Heidegger's elaboration through art, that is, art that in its most originary sense is poetry. But not all speech is poetry; rather, "poetry eventuates itself (*ereignet sich*) in speech," that is, it comes into its own in how it functions as a form of proto-typical speech.[110] What Heidegger means by proto-typical relates to what he developed as the dialectic of the usual and the unusual, but here in the sense of historicality. Speech becomes historical as poetry in the sense that the eventuation that occurs is one that *must* be in-human in historical resolution, that is, in making decisions historically, speech eventuates as poetry because the preservation of one's own way of being is ultimately at stake. In the *dichten* of one's sayings one creates a rupture and preserves the earth and its authentic beings in such historical decisiveness that one's own part of the earth, and one's standing on and emerging from that part is established. For historical example, by naming the land that was encountered by European colonists "America," that saying divides — or sets off — the land from whoever may have had a previous claim to it. Hence, such a dividing saying, such a primal *Ur-teil*, partitions what is authentic and inauthentic and has the consequence that it determines that which is for a people *is* truly, that is, is in truth as historical. In short, the world *is* theirs because the beings are formed according to its laws of appropriation, effected by heeding the call of its happening via the work of art as the work of naming and thus grounding. And only by such saying-as-naming and thus as grounding work, can building and forming (*Bauen und Bilden*) happen as *derivatives* of the opening of such original saying in naming from the clearing-as-dividing of beings. Again, we are familiar with one line of the logic that Heidegger uses in these complex constructions through Rosenzweig's similar contention that the actuality of a love event (an *Ereignis*) needs publicity in order to "count" as actuality, that is, to become historically effective. In other words, for Heidegger, a work is only actual insofar as it has historical effects. In this case, insofar as we reject the "usualness" of what is found or inherited from tradition and stand within the new light of being established by the throwing rupture of poetic saying, we are working to actualize a saying that establishes a decisive conflict in that which is. In this sense, art as poetry is foundational.

In fact, Heidegger claims that the founding function of art as poetry works as an "Institution of truth."[111] And art "institutes truth" as foundation in a threefold way, as: giving, grounding, and beginning. As giving/gifting, the setting-into-work of truth is unprecedented and rejects all that is past.[112] This constitutes a critique of dogmatic tradition, of tradition overall and entails that a work of the origin, and thus an original work of art, is not possible from what is ready-to-hand or at one's habitual or usual disposal. Rather, it is an overflow that comes up against the unfamiliar (*Ungeheure*). What Heidegger means by the *Ungeheure* as unfamiliar can be understood through its etymological association with *Heimlich*, or better yet with *unheimlich*. The word *Ungeheur* is used to express the feeling that one gets as shock or dislocation that one feels when not at home with, or comfortable with this or that, or encrusted in usualness. Its normal usage is to refer to something monstrous.

In order to clarify Heidegger's use of the term, consider how Leora Batnitzky makes her case that we should read Rosenzweig's passages on revelation as inciting just this sense of the *unheimlich* as a not-being-at-home in a Heideggarian sense.[113] In some ways, this works for Rosenzweig, given the subtext of exile that plays thoughout his work, a thread that Batnizky follows in her reading of Rosenzweig's work as essentially the kind of anti-idolatry that emerges out of Hermann Cohen's ethical monotheisim. I find that reading problematic precisely because of how that situates Rosenzweig more closely with Heidegger than he actually is and misreads Rosenzweig's philosophy of art. In fact, such a reading is not true to Rosenzweig: to be awoken may happen as a shock but that does not mean that we should interpret Rosenzweig as rejecting in some way the ordinariness of our everyday lives. In fact, only if one presents Rosenzweig's presentation of revelation as awakening as a conflict — a *Reißung* or a rub, as an irritation, then perhaps can we get irritated enough to respond ethically to act and change the world out of a perceived injustice of incongruity. But does Rosenzweig prioritize the *Reißung* or the eros/desire of the experience of love in his phenomenology of a sensual/trans-sensual experience? We could also ask, generally, if Rosenzweig's ethics are more Stoic or Epicurean, body affirming or denying? Further yet, is the celebration of Sabbath truly a celebration of the sensual and sexual, of all levels of aesthetic enjoyment, or is it an ascetic denial of the world as such? From what do we celebrate rest? In what way is the Sabbath, for example, *unheimlich*? These issues are not readily resolved in Batnizky's interpretation in part because it lacks what I have been calling a messianic aesthetic.

The second way that poetry institutes truth, for Heidegger, is as "grounding" and has to do with the historicality of a people. This means that what is thrown from the work is not done arbitrarily; it is always done to an historical people as historical Da-sein, which already belongs to the earth. This earth, moreover, is that upon which this historical people rests and already has contained within it everything that already is, but just hidden. This seems, at first glance, to be Aristotelian and compatibilist, that is, *determinist* in a way that affirms the necessary causal chain of bio-physical events, yet allows for a voluntarist account of free will.[114] Indeed, in some important ways, this claim is at odds with the first "moment" of shock and unfamiliarity. Instead, Heidegger contends that this sort of grounding is what is needed for the support of the unusual in the sense that everything given to humans in outline and projection has to be *set* on this ground to *show* that this ground is supportive as a bearing ground and that it not only can carry something but has in fact already done so. Said otherwise, Heidegger defines the original work of art as drawing from a spring and not as the production of a free gift of a self-mastered genius — it is a "ground-laying grounding" and is that which can never be gifted *from* the ordinary or traditional. In a short work entitled *Gesunde Menschenverstand* (*Understanding the Sick and the Healthy*) that he wrote to explicate *The Star* (but never published), Rosenzweig diagnoses this sort of rejection of "common sense" thinking as precisely the sickness of philosophy, from which it needs to be healed.

The third moment in the institution of truth through the art of poetry is how the work of art is also a beginning. Heidegger notes that "gifting" and "grounding" also have the unmediated character of a *beginning* as the institution of the conflict of truth. As beginning, it both sets the work of conflict going and establishes the process at the same time. It is a *spring* into the peculiar (*Eigentumliche*), a spring insofar as it is a pre-spring into that which is coming. As springing into that which is coming, the work entails a prophetic character that again, and despite Heidegger's assertions to the contrary, implicates an Aristotelian logic of the teleological.[115] He even notes that, "The beginning contains already the end hidden within itself."[116] The beginning contains the undisclosed fullness of the unfamiliar so it is always in conflict with what is familiar — the work of art does not allow one to be comfortable or at home since it must be a disturbing of the commonplace. It is such a "disturbing of the commonplace" because it is essentially the giving of conflict. This perspective entails that whenever beings come together as a group, as a people, and demand a foundation in openness, in the public, then art *acts* as instituting as historical essence. For Heidegger, the prime example of when this happened for the first time in the West was in Greece, when the word "being" was *named* and was instituted as a future task. But it was not until the Middle Ages that that realm of beings changed into an entity created by god. In modernity this being changed again into a realm of transparent objects controllable by calculation and quantification. In short, a new world broke through as the setting-in of the figure of truth which happened via art. In fact, for Heidegger, whenever art happens, history changes; it begins again or just begins. History is the removal of a people from their usual place in history and happens in their submission to their task as an entry into what they have been given as task. Said otherwise, they submit to the destiny given to them in their constitution as a people, shocked out of their habitual everydayness in order to stand in conflict with that everydayness.

Heidegger finishes this tour-de-force, which is the critical turning point in his career, by constructing what I would consider the "turn" as a dividing line. He claims that such a "dividing line' (as a turn) is called for by arguing that the historical and destining nature of art functions as the creative preserving of truth in the work itself. "Art happens as poetry" as founding, which is the tri-fold giving, grounding, and beginning and thus is also historical because it appears along with what Heidegger calls "many others." In fact, Heidegger definitively asserts that "art is history in the essential sense, in that it grounds history."[117] It grounds history because it lets truth spring out as the founding preservation in the work of art in its essential origin in being, that is, out of its origin. "The origin of the work of art, that is, simultaneously the creating and preserving, that means the historical existence (*Dasein*) of a people, is art."[118] That is so because the creation of art originates, itself is an origin, and is thus an excellent way for truth to happen historically. In this regard, Heidegger approvingly quotes Albrecht Dürer as support: "For in truth, art lies hidden within nature; he who can wrest it from her, has it."[119] But *wresting* is understood by Heidegger as presupposing the rupture of conflict between world and earth already in nature, and what shows that rupture is *art*, and indeed is *only* revealed in the work of art.

By reflecting on art as origin, Heidegger claims to be preparing for the *space* of art, a preparing of the space of the way for the creators and the location for the preservers. Such preparation has to do with establishing and maintaining community, working with language, and holding a special relationship to the land. This takes a special kind of knowledge of how a people maintains itself in their identity, namely, how they grow within themselves and determine their own destiny vis à vis other peoples, vis à vis other communities who lay claim to the land, the production and distribution of things, and who speak other languages. These are the many instances against which the one people assert their identity and destiny. And for Heidegger, as for Rosenzweig, in the many ways a people creates art for themselves there occurs a decisive kind of knowledge that separates kinds of art as either the prophetic pre-spring or just as "merely usual appearances of culture." For both philosophers, where we come from determines how we walk the pathways of this world with each other and with other peoples. For Rosenzweig, that walk is determined in trust relationships developed with unpredictable and unanticipated neighbors, based on both traditional forms of community structure and revelatory experiences of worldly humans with each other and based on ritual communities that are grounded on experiences of what they call their god(s). As I noted in the Rosenzweig section of this book, these communities are political only in the sense of referring to their development as critically independent, a-political entities. Heidegger, on the other hand, writing in 1932 on the threshold of the Nazi assumption of power and his own installment as Rector of Freiburg University, cryptically asks: are we historically at the origin or are we just reacting to old forms of culture? For Heidegger, the answer lies in poetry itself, in the poet Hölderlin's work, which Heidegger claims "still stands before the Germans as a work to be withstood."[120] For Heidegger, at that time and place, Germans were faced with a challenge that *had to be encountered, engaged, and mastered*. And to more closely define that task, it is to Heidegger's Hölderlin that we also now must turn.

Schwer verlaßt
Was nahe dem Ursprung, den Ort.

Only with great reluctance does
What is near to the origin, abandon the place.
                              Hölderlin "The Journey" (v. 181–9)

Notes

1 See Hans-Georg Gadamer, "Thinking and Poeticizing in Heidegger and in Hölderlin's 'Andenken,'" in Risser 1999: 1451–62.
2 On "polis" and the political, see: http://www.wsu.edu:8080/~dee/GLOSSARY/POLIS.HTM (accessed 20 November 2010).
3 By contrast, see Thomson 2005.
4 HW: 3; PLT: 18.
5 Ibid.
6 Ibid.
7 Ibid.
8 HW: 4; PLT: 20.
9 Ibid.
10 The etymological root of *Wirklichkeit* was formed in the Middle Ages and has to do with that which has factual existence or reality, that which has activity, effectiveness and creativity. See Etymologisches 1993: 1572. Also, recall from Chapter 5 the importance that the terms *wirken* and *Wirklichkeit* already assumed for Heidegger in *Being and Time*.
11 HW: 5; PLT: 20.
12 Much has been made about Heidegger's references to *Nichts* in this text and for mostly the wrong reasons. Phrases such as, "He who speaks of nothing does not know what he is doing. IN speaking of nothing he makes into a something." (IM: 23) especially raised the ire of many Analytic philosophers such as Carnap. See: "The Elimination of Metaphysics Through the Logical Analysis of Language" ("Überwindung der Metaphyik durch Logische Analyse der Sprache"), translated by Arthur Pap, in Ayer 1959: 60–81. Contra Carnap, Heidegger develops a philosophy of language and ontology related to the phenomenon of experiencing "nothing" out of *Being and Time* that has to do with the existential structure of *Angst* and the neglect of the sense of our creaturely finitude that arises with respect to how we find ourselves involved in projects of possibilities in-the-world.
13 HW: 5; PLT: 20.
14 HW: 6; PLT: 21.
15 Ibid.
16 HW: 7; PLT: 23.
17 HW: 8; PLT: 23. The key terms are *Denkungsart* for that "way of thinking" and *Bodenlosigkeit* for "groundlessness."
18 HW: 9; PLT: 24.

19   HW: 11; PLT: 26.
20   Ibid.
21   HW: 14; PLT: 29.
22   HW: 15; PLT: 30.
23   Ibid. *Dinghaften des Dinges*. Heidegger also means the toolishness of tools here, *Zeughaften des Zeugs*, and the workliness of works, *Werkhaften des Werkes*.
24   HW: 16; PLT: 31.
25   HW: 17; PLT: 32.
26   Ibid.
27   HW: 19; PLT: 34.
28   Ibid.
29   Note my discussion of the referential structure of the relevant signification from *Being and Time*. See Chapter 5.
30   HW: 19; PLT: 34.
31   HW: 20; PLT: 34.
32   HW: 21; PLT: 36.
33   Ibid. Note also my discussion above about *aleitheia* in Chapter 5.
34   Ibid.
35   HW: 23; PLT: 38.
36   HW: 24; PLT39.
37   HW: 26; PLT: 40.
38   See Wolin 1992: ix–xx.
39   HW: 26; PLT: 40. This stance, critical of the death of art in its necrophiliac entombment on the walls and in the halls of private and public museums, is shared by Rosenzweig as well. See GS2, Part III, Book 2.
40   This is also a theme that occupies Benjamin around the time that Heidegger was developing his theses. Benjamin, however, specifically raises the issue of the aestheticization of politics and the politicization of aesthetics as an issue of a fascist manipulation of art as commodity, varying not only from Heidegger but also from other members of the Frankfurt School such as Adorno. For Benjamin, the "ripping out" of context that Heidegger refers to in the following analysis is part of a materialist, dialectical process of messianic redemption that is accomplished through the efforts and effects of collecting, such as book collecting, and thus the ongoing formation of ever-new, alternative communities — a process of renewal and regeneration. See, for example, Benjamin's "Ich Packe Meine Bibliothek Aus" in Benjamin 1977. For a fundamentally "conservative" misunderstanding of the importance of aesthetics for determining and grounding the political process, see Best 1997.
41   Supporting my thesis that Heidegger's work should be read as a continuum without radical break, that is, that the questions raised in *Being and Time* continue in the broader context of the phenomenon of *Ereignis* and in terms of a musical fugue, see BP. As the editor, von Hermann points out: "Nach der ersten, der fundamentalontologischen Ansetzung der Seinsfrage in *Sein und Ziet* sind die *Beiträge zur Philosophie*, der erste umfassende Versuch 'einer zweiten, der seyns-geschichtlichen und zugleich ,ursprünglicheren' Ansetzung und Ausarbeitung derselben Frage, in der nach dem Sinn als der Wahrheit und

dem Wesen, d.h., der Wesend des Seyns, gefragt und diese als das Ereignis gedacht wird" (511). Significantly, one of the final meditations included in this text is #278, "Ursprung des Kunstwerks" (506). The final meditation is #281, "Die Sprache (ihr Ursprung)" (510).

42 HW: 27; PLT: 41.
43 HW: 28; PLT: 42.
44 Ibid.
45 Almost 25 years later, in 1957, Heidegger would accentuate this point of "rupture" and division in his lecture "Der Weg zur Sprache" in UWS: 251–52: "Die gesuchte Einheit des Sprachwesens heiße der Aufriß . . . Der Aufriß ist die Zeichnung des Sprachwesens, das Gefüge eines Zeigens, darein die Sprechenden und ihr Sprechen, das Gesprochene und sein Ungesprochenes aus dem Zugesrpochenen verfugt sind."
46 HW: 29; PLT: 43.
47 See Sections 243–47 "Die Wesung der Wahrheit als Bergung" in BP: 389–94 and Section 131 "Verbergung" in GSh: 144.
48 HW: 30; PLT: 44.
49 Ibid.
50 Ibid.
51 Ibid.
52 Again, note the connection to the "Care" structure of Da-sein Heidegger developed in *Being and Time*. See Chapter 5.
53 HW: 31; PLT: 45.
54 Ibid.
55 HW: 32; PLT: 46.
56 Ibid.
57 Ibid. As an aside, this is also the case with the question of being, which is meant to remain inexplicable.
58 HW: 33; PLT: 43.
59 HW: 34; PLT: 48.
60 HW: 35; PLT: 49.
61 Looking forward already to the conclusion, the importance of waiting for the god to come looms in retrospect over the emergence of this position. By contrast, compare what Levinas has to say about the importance of "patience" for his elaboration of the role of suffering in the face of the other. See Levinas 1969: 238–40: "This situation where the consciousness deprived of all freedom of movement maintains a minimal distance from the present, this ultimate passivity which nonetheless desperately turns into action and into hope, is *patience* — the passivity of undergoing, and yet mastery itself."
62 HW: 34; PLT: 49.
63 Ibid.
64 As Heidegger analyzes Hegel's concept of experience, the progress of Spirit as an historical process in its inversion from "natural consciousness" to its phenomenal presentation to itself of its own appearance, namely, a presentation of a *parousia* in the realm of representation. The movement is from "natural consciousness" to "real consciousness," but as a conflictual tension within the oneness of consciousness. See "Hegels Begriff der Erfahrung" in HW: 158.

65 Ibid: 36.

66 Recall the distinction made already in Rosenzweig: *Erfahren* has the sense of traveling or going or moving over something, a more denoting empirical interface with one's environment that the more qualitative sense of experience denoted by *Erlebnis*.

67 HW: 38; PLT: 51.

68 Ibid.

69 Ibid.

70 See Caputo 1978 for an argument bridging Eckhart's religious mysticism with Heidegger's ontology. Although intriguing, I disagree with the extent to which Caputo reduces Heidegger to a modern-day mystic because that seems to relieve Heidegger of the onus of responsibility for his work. In this respect, I would respond with the contention that Heidegger's inclusion of the *Sichfügen* complex, taken up by Caputo in its guise as *Gelassenheit*, as an inclination towards, and even prescription for, subordination to a politically supplied world-order, is closer to the mark.

71 HW: 39; PLT: 53.

72 HW: 40; PLT: 53.

73 Ibid.

74 HW: 41; PLT: 55.

75 HW: 42; HW: 55.

76 Ibid.

77 Presciently providing us with a signpost towards his later assertion in "The Letter on Humanism" regarding our role as speakers functioning, most authentically, as "shepherd[s] of being." The word used for "to hold" is *halten* and the word for "to guard" is *huten*. See WM: 361: "'Halt' bedeutet in unserer Sprache die 'Hut.' Das Sein ist die Hut, die den Menschen in seinem ek-sistenten Wesen dergestalt zu ihrer Wahrheit behütet, dass sie die Ek-sistenz in der Sprache behaust. Darum ist die Sprache zumal das Haus des Seins und die Behausung des Menschenwesens."

78 HW: 43; PLT: 56.

79 HW: 45; PLT: 58. (My emphasis.)

80 HW: 48; PLT: 60.

81 Ibid.

82 Ibid. Also, see SZ/BT, section 44.

83 HW: 49; PLT: 61.

84 He uses the term *Empfangen* for what I understand to be receiving/welcoming; the term *Entnehmen* for "gathering-inferring from"; and in this instance the term *Bezuge* for relationship, connotes "being drawn towards."

85 HW: 51; PLT: 64.

86 *Kennzeichnung.* Note the divergence on this point from Rosenzweig's notion of *die Erkenntnis* that occurs consequent to a revelatory love experience. After the revelatory love encounter, god — as subject, "kann . . . sich auch seinerseits zu erkennen geben, ohne Gefahr für die Unmittelbarkeit und reine Gegenwärtigkeit des Erlebens" (GS2: 203). This is a process that radically diverges from Heidegger's sense of hiddenness and disclosure of being. For Rosenzweig, the presentness of the experience of the love relationship demonstrates or makes evident the actual ground of the experience itself.

87   HW: 53; PLT: 65.
88   Heidegger plays on the German word, *Beständigkeit*, which has as its etymological root in the word "stand," but which is used in German to variously denote "enduring existence" as well "origin" and "success." Hence, something successfully exists by coming to stand in the world.
89   The word for "thrust" that Heidegger uses is "*Anstoss*," which can mean: offense, stumbling block, impulse, or even starting point.
90   HW: 53; PLT: 65.
91   Ibid.
92   Ibid: 54; PLT: 66.
93   Ibid.
94   Ibid.
95   Ibid: 55; PLT: 67.
96   Ibid.
97   Ibid. The word Heidegger uses for "fallenness" is *Befangenheit*, which means not only "the state of being caught" but also "embarrassment."
98   Ibid.
99   HW: 56; PLT: 68.
100 HW: 57; PLT: 69.
101 HW: 59, PLT: 71.
102 Ibid.
103 HW: 61; PLT: 73.
104 See footnote 77 above.
105 HW: 59; PLT: 71.
106 HW: 60; PLT: 72.
107 Ibid.
108 Ibid.
109 HW: 62; PLT: 74.
110 Ibid.
111 HW: 63; PLT: 75.
112 Giving: "Schenken"; all that is past: "Bisherige."
113 See Batnitzky 2009: 90–93.
114 See Book III of the Nichomachean Ethics in Aristotle 1941, for his argument that humans are responsible for the actions they freely choose to do; i.e. for their voluntary actions.
115 See Hatab 2000, esp. Chapter 4: 109ff.: "Heidegger and Aristotle" for a relatively comprehensive overview of Aristotle's influence on constructing a Heideggarian ethics: "In a way we can understand Heidegger's ontology as a radicalization of Aristotelian teleology that inscribes creative openness into temporal development."
116 HW: 64.
117 Ibid: 65.
118 Ibid: 66.
119 Ibid: 70.
120 Ibid.

CHAPTER 7

PHILOSOPHY, POETRY, AND THE ABSENT GOD: INTERLOCUTIONS ON HEIDEGGER, HÖLDERLIN, AND THE POLITICAL

I. *Interlocutions and the Heidegger controversy*

The battle to preserve one's own origin, as the battle rages forth in Heidegger's philosophy, comes into clearer relief in his controversial and important interpretations of Hölderlin's poetry. As I noted in my introduction, I reflect on three determinative phases of Heidegger's work in order to accomplish what I do in focusing on the three-tiered text of Rosenzweig's. This is partly because Rosenzweig's peculiar systematicity allows for an interpretation of *The Star* as a philosophical work of art that, as I have argued, includes a radical moment of chaotic unpredictability figured in the star-like radiance of the face of the other. This enables Rosenzweig to provide a certain kind of ethical impetus towards responsibility for the other, as other. Moreover, Heidegger's three works roughly correspond to the three parts of Rosenzweig's *Star*: Part I of *The Star* to Heidegger's *Being and Time* (oriented towards phenomenologies of knowledge); Part II of *The Star* to Heidegger's *The Origin of the Work of Art* (both focused on phenomenologies of aesthetics); and finally, Rosenzweig's Part III of *The Star* to Heidegger's interpretations of Hölderlin's poetry, with their respective ethical and political implications.

As I also pointed out in the previous chapter, Heidegger's philosophy of art entails a moment of radical ambiguity at its heart, a heart that beats with conflict. But in fact, with respect to the issue of systematicity, just as Heidegger was unable or unwilling to finish the project begun with *Being and Time*, he was likewise unable or unwilling to finish the project begun with *The Origin of the Work of Art*.[1] This was so because he needed a concrete particular in order to actualize his theoretical projections. As he himself noted, even more urgently than other works the work of art needs actual historical effects to "count" as a work. It has to demonstrate what Gadamer referred to as a *Wirkungsgeschichte*, in the sense that a work proves its enduring and transformative staying power through the record of its actual effects in history.[2] I believe that my treatment of the first two major phases of Heidegger's philosophy corroborate my judgment about the rootedness of his political choices deep within the lines of his philosophy and its origins in his self-estimation. In short, Heidegger's dalliance with political power was no arbitrary mis-adventure. Rather, his actions should be judged as calculative and measured, decisive even, although irresponsibly thought through. But clearly crass political considerations are not all that matters since there is the very complex issue of how best to understand Heidegger's reading of Hölderlin's poetry. Because Heidegger considered his philosophy to be a re-origination of the political that somehow was to be both beyond and thoughtfully enacted from one's own political situation, Heidegger's reading of Hölderlin played a definitive role in that re-origination.

For this last chapter, I take up a Levinasian phenomenological-ethical challenge by considering three relatively recent commentators who have measured Heidegger's Hölderlin, in order to raise questions about what could be considered an ethical shortfall of his philosophy, namely (and in rather vulgar terms), that his methodological choices are dictated by his proclivity to promote his own agenda at the cost of doing violence to others, as others. I present their perspectives, however, *as* perspectives in a phenomenological and thus critical sense. That means that I do not merely re-present their perspectives, but do so with the awareness that I translate them by bracketing my own agenda. Only by allowing others to speak for themselves can we hope to minimize the possibility of violating them. Thus, in this experimental attempt to perform in writing the multivocality of a cacophonous chorus, such as that which Rosenzweig envisions, I briefly introduce three different voices, each with their own agenda about Heidegger's philosophy of art in general and Hölderlin's role in that philosophy in particular. The three are: Jean Marie Schaeffer, Julian Young, and Veronique Fóti. After listening to their voices, I conclude by presenting my own reading of Heidegger's lecture course on "Hölderlin's Hymn, 'The Ister.'"

II. *Jean-Marie Schaeffer on Heidegger's role as a traditionalist*

In his book, *Art of the Modern Age: Philosophy of Art from Kant to Heidegger*, the French philosopher and aesthetician Jean-Marie Schaeffer presents his claim that the German intellectuals that he chooses: Kant, Novalis, Schlegel, Hegel, Nietzsche, and Heidegger constitute a coherent philosophical tradition that developed a unified, metaphysical theory of philosophy of art, which he calls "The Speculative Theory of Art," a theory that provides a "philosophical legitimation of the ontological cognitive function of art."[3] He points out that the recent so-called crisis in contemporary art is a result of what he calls a myth of the legitimation of the arts that occurred mainly because of the loss of traditional legitimating institutions, namely, religious, didactic, and ethical institutions, and a delegitimizing process initiated by these German philosophers which created a breach filled by philosophy itself as a compensation for the very loss of art. Hence, what Schaeffer refers to as a kind of sacralization of art emerged that served as a constitutive means for the past 200 years to determine the Western world's aesthetic horizon of expectations. The penultimate chapter of his text is entitled, "Art as the Thought of Being (Heidegger)" that situates Heidegger as the apogee of that coherent philosophical tradition and the chief protagonist of "The Speculative Theory of Art."

As Arthur Danto points out in his lengthy Preface to the text, Schaeffer is a contemporary French thinker who departs from the pantheon of other, more noted French philosophers — whom Danto identifies as "villains" — such as Derrida, Foucault, and Baudrillard, in deconstructing the very Germanic philosophical tradition that largely informs their works. What Schaeffer calls the "sacralization of art" developed as a philosophy of art out of this German tradition and produced a horizon of expectations that was motivated by a cult-like historical movement that took the form of a utopian messianism and whose processes of quasi-religious determinations led not only through Hegel's initiation of a discourse of exclusion and marginalization of non-essential works of art, but also to the slow but inevitable social transformations of artistic practices that integrated the arts as they developed into autonomous commodity products of the market economy. Thus, under the philosophical tutelage of a stream of Germanic philosophers, the arts were reduced to "Art" with an ontological revelatory function, namely, to ecstatically reveal Being as the "essence" of Art, with the necessary corollary that, then, the variety and plurality of works (of art) reveal "Art." He argues that what has been lost in the reduction of art works to such metaphysical hieroglyphs is our personal sense for the changing reality of the arts and of works of art. These are the major lineaments upon which Schaeffer bases his critical analysis of the story of the Germans' Speculative Theory of Art.

In Part One of his text, Schaeffer situates the birth of modern philosophical aesthetics with Baumgarten and then Kant whose Critical Aesthetic Philosophy functions as a heroic kind of analytic theory over against the anti-heroes that follow. With his *Critique of Judgment*, Kant attempted to construct a sort of meta-aesthetic contemplation, specifically, "an inquiry into the status and legitimacy of judgments of taste," which essentially referred to an inquiry into an analysis of acts of judgment. According to Schaeffer, Kant did not propose a specific theory of art but instead proposed a transcendental theory of the aesthetic Subject and the aesthetic experience as such. Kant's inquiry, then, results in an analysis of the judgments of any subject's aesthetic experience that can be translated into socially transformative discourse. As Schaeffer goes on to elaborate, Kant's inquiry, however, disappeared in the Speculative Theory of Art, which, interestingly, Kant's very critique helped stimulate by way of the negative response to his conclusion that any doctrine of Art was *a priori* impossible. For Kant, the only issue at stake was the development of a theory of individuality and of inter-human communication. Schaeffer points out that the Romantics, especially Novalis and Schlegel, rejected these conclusions of Kant's philosophy but exploited other elements, namely, the Kantian theory of genius, in order to provide a psychology of the artist that would support their definition of Art as ecstatic knowledge. In addition, the Kantian thesis of finality without a goal would support a thesis of the artwork as autotelic and organic, elements that the Romantics would use to solidify their project of the sacralization of art.

Schaeffer sums up his initial analysis of Kant's role by stating that "The speculative theory of Art seeks to establish the *excellence* of Art, its ecstatic character *qua Art*, in contrast to other human activities." Now this is precisely the kind of definition that Kant's aesthetics declares to be impossible, since it asserts that the criterium of excellence could not be a universal criterium, grounded "objectally" and objectively, but only via subjective criteria, "valid for an individual subject confronted by a particular object, and incapable of leading to a definition of universalization."[4] As Schaeffer succinctly notes, Kantian meta-aesthetics depends on separating "feeling" from "concept," which results, with the Romantics, in a doctrine of art based on a category error, namely, confusing art as an ontic, phenomenal object while valorizing it definitively and evaluatively as an exclusionary value. Schaeffer elaborates this thesis as the speculative theory of art in the way that it legitimated such art practices as a doctrine of exclusionary sacralization, through his analysis of the Romantics, then Hegel's, Nietzsche's, and finally Heidegger's contributions to a German philosophy of art.

In his concluding remarks, Shaeffer confesses that some of the distinctions that he introduces are simplistic, but they suffice to demonstrate his point that the Speculative Theory of Art established, and continues to establish, oppositions that exclude popular art from so-called "high art." Works of art are separated from the artist and, in the case of Heidegger, for example, are no longer part of the domain of equipment, the domain of the common folk. What a German-inspired philosophy of art neglects is that aestheticization as a human way of encoding aesthetic pleasure in general, takes place across all domains of human activity from the pleasure taken in the "worked" quality of tools such as plowshares to the mundane rituals of Japanese tea ceremonies, the everyday fashioning of Chinese pottery, the ubiquitous presence of Arabic calligraphy, or Zen Buddhist sand gardens. Schaeffer's point is that valorizing art via the process of enshrining works in the sacralization process instituted by the Speculative Theory of Art, has lead to a hierarchy of arts that privileges mediocre art works just because they belong to the canon of intentionally produced works of art. Shaeffer opposes that theory with broader considerations that include taking into account the "singularity of each aesthetic experience." Proceeding from such singularity will enable us to begin to evaluate aesthetic pleasure according to the individual object, regardless of category, and the sensibility of the unpredictable individual who may be approaching the object from any number of unforeseeable aesthetic points of view. Keep in mind Schaeffer's point about "singularity" since that is also the issue that Fóti takes up with Heidegger in her critical assessment that I introduce below.

Turning our attention to how Schaeffer deals specifically with Heidegger, we find, not unexpectedly, that Heidegger turns out to be the chief villain and provides us with the most recent attempt at reducing art, and poetry in particular, to a philosophical presupposition — a substance, by not respecting the specificity of the poem itself. This phenomenong of "specificity" is precisely what indicated was outstanding, in the sense of missing, in Heidegger's philosophy of art, and is that which drove him to take up Hölderlin's poetry in the first place. However, Schaeffer uses Heidegger's analyses of Hölderlin's later poetry as his case in point that Heidegger ignores the fragmented incompleteness of the work at hand (the analysis of Hölderlin's *Hyperion*) and, instead, unilaterally injects his own theoretical program into his interpretation as interpreter of the poem, distilling the poem down into a preordained function, as one might do with any other document. Schaeffer argues that, in the case of Hölderlin, the philosopher (Heidegger) reduces the poet to the role of revived spokesman for the Speculative Theory of Art. In Schaeffer's hands, Heidegger is shown to be not only trapped in the tradition of the Speculative Theory of Art but serves as its conclusive apogee and self-fulfillment. What that means is that poetry, which comes to stand for all of the arts (as it does with Hegel), is reflective only of its impersonal, non-specific self-reflection. In consequence, artistic and aesthetic specificities are sacrificed to the rigors of onto-logical coherence.

The gist of Schaeffer's analysis of Heidegger's work is that Heidegger is simply a poor interpreter of poetry, that he not only focuses on just one poet, Hölderlin, but that he only focuses on a few poems and only on a few words in each of those poems. Thus, Schaeffer argues that the "Heideggarian interpretation creates a philosophical metapoem to which he devotes the majority of his 'clarifications.'"[5] As an example, Schaeffer, rightly I would say, considers Heidegger's analysis of Hölderlin's poem, "*Andenken*," for the way in which Heidegger insists on reading into, or out of, the poem Heidegger's pre-established and autonomous philosophical theme on the nature of poetry itself as occupied with the fundamental term *An-denken* as it has to do with instituting the future thought of being and a thanking (Andenken) that is a peculiar kind of thinking (An-denken). Schaeffer notes that reducing the poem to merely its biographical referents, that is, reading the poem as merely an expression of the personal, psychological and emotional situatedness of Hölderlin as a concrete social individual, would be impoverishing. However, Heidegger commits an error that is just as egregious by intentionally neglecting the lived situation of Hölderlin. This is a point that even Gadamer makes in his noteworthy analysis of this same work by Heidegger, although Gadamer responds much more sympathetically.[6] As Schaeffer points out, "'Andenken' *was* written by the tutor Hölderlin and describes the landscapes of southern France that he *did* pass through . . . it is hard to see just how one could deny that 'Andenken' refers to events in Hölderlin's life."[7] More or less, Schaeffer contends that Heidegger's analysis simply dismisses the unavoidable, and very

Kantian consideration, that any interpretation of any poem must necessarily refer, in some way and on some level, to the private events of its author.

Perhaps even more incisive are Schaeffer's remarks regarding what he takes to be Heidegger's incompetency in analyzing the mechanics of the poem as a poem in itself, which should include some attention paid to poetic techniques. This is a serious methodological critique since what characterizes phenomenology most clearly as a peculiar discipline is in its practitioners' claims to get at the essence of the things themselves or the matter at hand. In the case of poetry, then, a phenomenological analysis, such as Heidegger's, should attend to issues such as rhyme, meter, versification, and poetic form in general. If Heidegger cannot even come to terms with what makes a poem a poem, then why should anyone turn to his analyses of poetry? Again, keep this critique in mind, because Fóti makes similar claims about the "violence" that Heidegger exerts in his interpretations. A more sympathetic Heideggarian would respond that one turns to Heidegger's interpretations (and not his "analyses") for what he has to say about translation, sound, and meaning. But these areas are precisely what draw the ire of Schaeffer, as he lists Heidegger's "sins": "Paraphrase, translation, dismantling of syntax, making the text autonomous with regard to the concrete subject who utters it, absolute silence regarding poetic form [and] . . . hermeneutic authoritarianism."[8] What Schaeffer means by this last term has to do with the argument he proposes about how Heidegger postulates oppositions between what the poem seems to say and what it really means, reminiscent of the pattern he sets forth in *Being and Time* between authentic and inauthentic modes of being-in-the-world, polar oppositions to which I referred in the last chapter for their ongoing logical functions in Heidegger's work.

In analyzing Hölderlin's poetry, however, Schaeffer argues that whatever runs counter to his onto-logical agenda is dismissed as merely the "apparent" contextual and commonly accepted meaning, which is replaced by the more "authentic" meaning that accords with the theme of the thinker of being. To briefly sum up Schaeffer's thesis, for Heidegger the work of art happens as that unique phenomenon that provides the occasion for the explication of being as the saying of being.

What I found most insightful in Schaeffer's analyses is in how he understands Heidegger's commitment to interpreting things, such as poems and poets, in order to make sense for his presentation of the "unified phenomenon" of the totally relevant, referential structure he calls "world" in *Being and Time*. This is related to the point that I highlight below in my own interpretation, namely, that the question of the meaning of being *is* answered with the sayings of the philosopher-poet and poet-philosopher by way of establishing definitive directional guidance for the destiny of the people of the *polis*. However, what Heidegger does best, by drawing attention to the utterly relevant and unavoidable effectiveness of his conceptualization of truth as *aiesthesis*, is also what should cause us to hesitate in adopting his phenomenological perspective. The hesitation is warranted, since what I would argue is overlooked by Schaeffer is precisely the implied normativity involved in an ethical element in Heidegger's work that goes hand-in-hand with his philosophy of art. For this critique, I turn to Rosenzweig and his version of what Schaeffer specifically targets: a messianic and utopian philosophy of art.

III. *Julian Young: rehabilitating the fallen master*

There are many supporters of Heidegger's entire project, including his philosophy of art, who read his philosophy as an enduring antidote for the crisis of modernity, namely, a crisis in traditional hegemonies of all sorts, including Western forms of capitalism, the totalitarian regimentations of communisms, global technologizations, and even as a measured critique of the tyranny of National Socialism. Such is the work of Julian Young, among others. This valorization of Heidegger's critical stance is a valorization of his philosophy *as* taking a stand and precisely for a judgment that can be made for the relative worth of philosophy and art for maintaining and renewing the political life as it originates out of the *polis*. Young enters the Heidegger wars on these grounds, namely, assessing Heidegger's philosophy of art for what it says about the contributions to philosophy of art from a great philosopher. His work is a monograph that, in his own words, is

> a history of intellectual development and personal integration; of how a great thinker, starting from an account of art that condemned him, *qua* philosopher, to a stance of complete alienation from the art of his own times, thought his way out of a position which, as a passionate lover of, in the event, a great deal of modern art, and himself a poet of no mean ability, he had always known to be an error. The hero of my story — or rather the other hero — is Hölderlin. For Heidegger, I shall argue, it was Hölderlin who was, in the poet's own language, the "saving power," not only with respect to art but also, as we will see, with respect to politics.[9]

In other words, it is a story of political heroes, and Heidegger is, for Young, clearly such a hero. And, most tellingly, a footnote early on in the text reveals Young's strategic preferences when he notes:

> Already in 1935, in the *Introduction to Metaphysics*, Heidegger had abandoned many of his illusions about Nazism, criticizing its racism, militarism, and totalitarianism as well as the crassness of the Nuremburg rallies. Though it is hard to doubt that a reference to Hitler is intended here, it should be thought of as to the Hitler of Heidegger's 1933 hopes and dreams rather than to the reality of Nazism as it stood before his eyes at the end of 1936.[10]

What becomes clear by these two early references is that Young proceeds in his interpretation with giving Heidegger the benefit of the doubt. Although I am not as generous, I do follow Young's reading and find his analyses generally helpful for understanding Heidegger's development. But I also find very troubling that Young lauds him as a political hero.

Besides his obvious sympathy for Heidegger, the primary reason that I include Young in my admittedly very small pantheon of dialogue partners is for how he provides a relatively comprehensive overview of Heidegger's philosophy of art. In fact, Young proceeds along remarkably similar interpretive lines as I do in my approach to Heidegger; it is just that we come to very different conclusions. In fact, as I noted in the quote above, Young contends that Hölderlin is the "other" hero in his writing about Heidegger's philosophy. Again, I am troubled that anyone could consider either figure as a hero, but I am convinced that there are many people in the world, including me at one time in my life, who have held either one or both of these German intellectuals as standard-bearers for human excellence.

Young begins his overview of Heidegger's philosophy of art where he says most other commentators do as well, with *The Origin of the Work of Art*. He notes that this work has assumed an almost cult-like status for Heidegger aficionados, who have gone so far as to obsess about it. However, Young spends a good deal of time with it himself, and I would say that he even devotes an obsessive amount of textual space to that work, but for good reason. More or less, Young develops the initial lines of his thesis on exploring the extent to which Heidegger raised the problem of the phenomenon of art as great, and therefore able to exert extensive social transformation, or as elitist, or as trivial and thus able to exert only limited social effect. This strikes me as a helpful way to interpret Heidegger's intentions and plays a role in my own judgments about Heidegger's philosophy, as well as my comparative concerns for the ethical consequences of both Rosenzweig's and Heidegger's philosophies of art.

Young sets up the general parameters of his interpretation by noting that in raising the issue of the greatness of art, Heidegger was raising a question about whether or not modern art has degenerated into an aesthetics that results, merely, in the "experience" of the beautiful, which is a titillating sensation that makes everyone homogenously alike and not distinctive. In modern art, there is no temple or cathedral that could correspond to the *Bezirk* of holiness, the individuating capability of the Greek occurrence of art, to encourage the production of heros. If so, if there is no corresponding *Bezirk*, no *place* for such holiness to eventuate, then all of modern art is decadent triviality; that is, Young contends that with *The Origin of the Work of Art*, Heidegger presents a relatively rigid dualism between the Greek and modern phenomena of art. Supporting this approach, Young points to Heidegger's comments from the *Introduction to Metaphysics* where he derisively notes that the sort of art that merely "reposes and relaxes . . . [is] . . . a matter for pastry cooks."[11] Not incidentally, this supports Schaeffer's thesis that Heidegger belittles the normal, everyday arts, the art of ritual, of garden planning, of cooking, the art of the everyday, and that, for Heidegger there can only be great art or the Modern sort of decadent, dying art. But Young provides a much more nuanced reading of Heidegger's position, going deeper into Heidegger's concerns about how in fact artists such as Klee and Cezanne, artists Heidegger treasures and turned to for inspiration, could exercise determinate historical effects. In other words, Young maintains that it is simply simplistic to say that Heidegger was in the business of validating the "great ones" of history, a point that has considerable merit. As Young notes, this complex of sorting through "great" from "mediocre" art was tied up precisely with how Heidegger came to terms with Hölderlin's poetry. With Hölderlin, Heidegger finds an art that can, on the one hand, validate artists such as Klee and Cezanne and call into question as well the "tyranny" of the Greek paradigm and a degenerate "aesthetics."

In short, Young notes how Heidegger demands communal and rejects private art, but still valorizes Van Gogh in *The Origin* as great art when, in fact, the access to Van Gogh's art is limited and elitist. Such a contradiction is compounded when he notes that for Heidegger the *polis* should be considered not as the city-state but as "the place and scene of history" when in fact Heidegger's interpretations of Hölderlin's poetry belie such an a-politicization.[12] For Heidegger, Hölderlin was both great and a peculiar source for communal-political origination. In the 1966 Spiegel interview, Heidegger says how Hölderlin was the single most important influence on his thinking: "My thinking," he says, "stands in a definitive relation to the poetry of Hölderlin."[13] Given the duality set up in *The Origin*, the problem for Heidegger with Hölderlin was that Hölderlin was neither Greek, and therefore not paradigmatically "great," nor were there any "communal" readings of his poetry, no gathering of a people, thus disqualifying him as a poet of the people. Rather, Hölderlin did not write for the community at large, but for a small group of "elites" or "initiates" and yet is read by Heidegger as the poet of the source for the gathering of the *polis*. So the question becomes, how is he great and how does his poetry "gather?"

To answer these questions, Young at first notes that Heidegger was occupied with Hölderlin's poetry from the mid-1930s to the mid-1940s and so the problem was a serious one for Heidegger. But the key to sorting out the paradoxes of "greatness" and "gathering" turns out to be Klee and dividing Heidegger's preoccupation with Hölderlin into early and latter periods. To begin with, there was the 1934/1935 — lectures on "Germania" and "The Rhine" and the 1936 lecture series compiled as *Hölderlin and the Essence of Poetry*,[14] as well as the extended references to Sophocle's *Antigone* which occur in the *Introduction to Metaphysics* of 1935, references which become so important for Heidegger's seminal and, I would argue definitive, interpretation of Hölderlin in *Hölderlin's Hymn "The Ister."*

Young, however, argues that these earlier works don't initiate an "escape from the tyranny of the Greek paradigm" because, though he treats Hölderlin as a poet who is of the utmost importance, he does not treat him, at least at first, as being important *as a poet*.

> Without being properly alive to the fact that this is what he is doing, he treats the work of the "thinking poet" as the work of a thinker who happens to express his thoughts in verse but might just as well have done so in prose.[15]

The later texts, however, address the inadequacy of this early treatment of Hölderlin and address him specifically as a poet, capable of "valid" art, and Hölderlin as a "great" poet. So, Young's argument is that through art, Heidegger moves away from interpretive tyranny, and thus from political tyranny, to pluralism, and is able to include, thereby, the visual art of Klee or Cezanne, or even Rilke, but especially Hölderlin. In fact, Young argues that Hölderlin *educated* Heidegger in the sense of leading him away from his intellectual and political positions of the mid 1930s to the serenity of the *Gelassenheit* of his later thought, that is, to the poetic language of the fourfold of earth, sky, gods, and mortals.[16] As Young notes, this "serenity" was differently expressed than in *The Origin* which Heidegger says he took directly from Hölderlin, and thus, because of this debt, considers Hölderlin as an "origin" for his thought and can say that his relationship to Hölderlin was decisive.[17]

According to Young, in Heidegger's earlier analyses of Hölderlin's poetry, Hölderlin, as a thinker rather than as a poet, is indistinguishable from the philosopher thinker because he thinks the "essence" of poetry, which is to think of what endures, and what endures is what the poet "founds," namely, a world. This world which he thinks is also only one world and one "essence," a correlation that is important because with the seriousness of our having only to do with "one" world, if it were otherwise poetry would be merely play. Rather, poetry is in fact taken seriously and is not relegated to mere dream status or ineffectuality. In short, either poetry is effectual, and thus "ethical," or else it is the stuff of pastry cooks and, therefore, Holderlin's "essence" is a continuation of *The Origin* and the tyranny of Greek art.

For Heidegger, notes Young, modernity is the age of spiritual decline and the "flight of the gods" because only the gods found authentic community — only by dwelling in the charismatic presence of the "divine destining" can the human become historical, that is, a people.[18] Since individuals only find integration in a community and meaning in commitment to communal "destiny" modernity is an age of alienation and meaninglessness, of Nietzschean nihilism. But most modern people are insensible to the decayed condition of their times because they are sleeping the sound sleep of a Zarathustrian decay and are unaware of the godless night; they are, as in *Being and Time*, dwelling with inauthentic temporality, forgetting the past and thus unable to project into the future. They not only are unable to project into the future, but they forget the past because their horizons are limited to their busyness and curiosities of the present.

Poets, however, have climbed out of the valleys of inauthenticity and stand on the mountain peaks of authentic time, able to survey past and present and thus have the power of temporality, of historicity in their works. As Young points out, what makes Hölderlin alive to the spiritual poverty of the present age, for Heidegger, is his poem, *Andenken*, in German — *Remembrance* — the poem and the thought that Young considers is the heart of all his poetry. The poem, and the thought memory, is the memory of the Greek festival, the celebration of humans betrothed to the gods, the memory of the richness of *our* Greek origin which, by its richness established the poverty of our age.[19] What makes Hölderlin great despite his elitism is this ability to survey historicality as a way to measure the condition of our current epoch. And because of this awareness of past and present, Hölderlin's poetry is deeply sad, with a sense of loss and absence, and which constitutes the *Grundstimmung* of his work, that is, the "holy mourning" (*heilige Trauer*) for the departure of the gods which is a mood that is not a psychological state, but a spiritual–intellectual condition of how the modern world is disclosed as permeated by absence.[20]

However, this sort of "holy mourning" is not, notes Young, "ineffectual melancholy" but is "creative and productive."[21] It is creative because it is a remembering as a communicative kind of thinking of the gods that has been definitive and productive because it is a projective founding of the "future historical being of the Germans."[22] In this sense, Heidegger turns to Hölderlin as the means to recover our endowment, that is, Hölderlin shows us that task that must still be withstood, referred to by Heidegger at the end of *The Origin of the Work of Art*.[23] Specifically, what Hölderlin discloses as our task is to restore the Greek artwork by diagnosing the sickness of our present age, providing in the poetic process, as well, a prescription for the cure: the need to create a new artwork.[24] Even more, in analyzing Hölderlin's poem, "As when on a holiday . . ." Heidegger claims that

> What is coming is said in its coming through a calling. Beginning with this poem, Hölderlin's word is not the calling word . . . Hölderlin's word conveys the holy thereby naming the space of time that is only once, time of the primordial decision for the essential order of the future history of gods and humanities. This word, though still unheard, is preserved in the Occidental language of the Germans.[25]

We create the new artwork through world-disclosure rather than some sort of vague inner feeling, that is, we create through the fundamental mood, which is the truth of the existence of a people, originally founded by the poet. But this disclosed being of beings is first grasped and ordered by the thinker, which is given its first seriousness among beings, a seriousness which means to be formed into a definite (called for, *be-stimmt*) historical truth so that the people is brought to itself as a people. This happens through the creation of the state — which in its essence has already been determined — by the state-creator.[26]

According to Young, Heidegger clearly refers in this context to his involvement with Hitler and the Nazis, outlining a plan for the spiritual rebirth of the German people, for the self-collection of the German *Volk*, which is also a rebirth of not only Germany, as the most metaphysical of the peoples of the world, but of the entire West. Germans, called to their task, must seize their destiny to lead the way, to restore "the history of the West to the primordial realm of the powers of Being" by means of "new spiritual energies unfolding historically from out of the [German] center."[27]

The beginning of this new self-collection activity begins with the poet Hölderlin, who founds the truth of beings, while the thinker — Heidegger, articulates this truth more clearly and thus more accessibly for the political leader — Hitler, who puts into practical effect the poetically founded and philosophically disclosed truth. As Young correctly notes, Heidegger is thus the thinker who mediates between poetry and politics in order to facilitate the political order and, thus, Heidegger can say that he has replaced the philosopher-king by the poet-king and that poetry is "politics in the highest and most authentic sense."[28] But what is the highest politics of the poet, aided by the thinker, and effectuated by the politician? Specifically, the work is the founding of the people through "remembering" (*Andenken*) the Greek origin. But because the poet is so obscure about this task of remembering, he needs the philosopher to "translate" his work from the educated elite to the masses, that is, to make him more accessible, via exemplars, as in Heidegger's "*Elucidations of Holderlin's Poetry.*"[29] The issue is that Greek art is essentially "popular" art, and a work is never able to gather a community as a whole unless it can be accessible to the whole community, and so Hölderlin can never be popular in this sense.

Since the poet, Hölderlin, can never be popular it is up to the politician to sponsor artworks that will appeal to the popular idiom, namely,

> artworks which will gather together a whole community in a reaffirmation of classical values. The films of Leni Riefenstall — *Triumph of the Will and Olympiad*, in particular — something like the architectural programme of Albert Speer, a revised version of the Wagner-Nietzsche conception of Bayreuth, and something perhaps not completely unlike a Nuremberg rally seem to be examples of the kind of thing Heidegger had in mind.[30]

But, Young observes that Hölderlin would not be among these types of artists. Rather he points out that Heidegger intentionally misreads Hölderlin, classifying him as only a thinker and not as a poet, a classification that makes him indistinguishable from Heidegger himself and Heidegger's agenda for the renewal of the German people. As I noted above, this type of intentional misreading echoes Schaeffer's analysis of Heidegger's works as agenda-driven and oblivious to "popular" considerations. However, Young is much more circumspect regarding Heidegger's actual intentions because of his ability to consider the breadth of Heidegger's works, especially the range and development of his interpretations of Hölderlin.

For example, with Heidegger's teaching on "The Ister" of 1942, seven years later than *Andenken*, he leaves behind his proclivity for identifying himself with Hölderlin by saying that thinking is not poeticizing, a point not lost on Gadamer as well.[31] The problem is that even though in *Germania* Heidegger characterizes Hölderlin as "the poet of the Germans, he only allows him to provide the task for poetry in the present age, which has to be accomplished by other poets and, perhaps most importantly, by the political leader."[32] In fact, Young argues that Hölderlin is still just a great "thinker" who understands temporality in Heidegger's sense of understanding the past out of its Greek origin and projecting that past as a present task into the future horizon. In other words, the problem is in measuring Hölderlin as a poet according to the categories of *Being and Time*, that is, according to the standards of authentic temporality, as well as the standards of *The Origin*, namely, that poetry is a kind of "projective saying."[33]

Thus far, Julian Young. Both Rosenzweig and Heidegger rely on a concept of createdness and both emphasized a notion of creation that entails making history happen, creating through human endeavors alone founds new historical epochs, new cultural evaluations of value. But Heidegger ultimately rejects this possibility because, he says, due to the post-war and post-victory "success" of the two dangerous superpowers, humans must go into a mode of waiting rather than creating, since the world is destined to be the self-disclosure of the self-concealing of the being that has no equal and that never allows itself to be mastered by human doing founded solely on itself.[34] Such creating, as a technological mastering of that which should remain one's ownmost, would essentially equate to a return to the "forgetfulness" of being, once again. Moreover, out of Hölderlin's poetry, creation is unnecessary because we are destined by a world given to us in graciousness — our lives are in gift-giving hands and so the attempt to "force" the return of the gods through the festival, is an attempt to force that which is already coming, the messiah.[35]

Modernity is night and Hölderlin's poetry is an absolute and unredeemed blackness; the darkening of the world is the flight of the gods, which stands for the demonic and absolute evil. But from references in "Bread and Wine" — the "wine-god's priests" journey through the "holy" night, as well as references out of the work "Homecoming," night is experienced as "serenely cheerful" and "joyful" because our age is the age of "god's default" which is not a mere absence but is the time of "stored-up" treasure. Therefore, Heidegger concludes, god's default is not a deficiency, a *Mangel*, but rather, a time for a "destinal" letting-be. And so Young concludes that with Hölderlin Heidegger rejects artifice — and art! — as, for example, in the "Poet's Calling," when he maintains that the citizens are not to strive through artifice to make their own god and so, by force, to do away with the supposed deficiency.[36] In fact, in elaborating the process of "dwelling" in "Building, Dwelling, Thinking," Heidegger claims that mortals "dwell" by allowing the divinities to appear as divinities, which means that mortals do not "make their gods for themselves and do not worship idols. In the very depths of misfortune, they wait for the weal that has been withdrawn."[37]

In the end, Young provides what he argues is Heidegger's philosophy of art as a critique of Hitler and the tyranny of hegemony, precisely in the way that Heidegger draws on Hölderlin to present a view of nature that is based on the natural, beautiful cycles of nature. Accordingly, Young's Heidegger sees the graciousness of being in the beauty of the world's design, in its embracing of opposites, both synchronic — of mountains and valleys, and diachronic opposites — of seasons. With such a view, a new understanding of the crisis of modernity is possible, namely, the "default" of god only appears to be absolute when we "forget" the cyclical, seasonal nature of Being, the self-collection of winter for the coming of spring and the self-collection of spring for the coming of summer, etc. Thus, for Young, Heidegger's "turn" is a turning that is understood as cyclical, with dawn beginning at the darkest hour:

> But where the danger is, grows
> The saving power also.[38]

According to Young, rather than progressive or apocalyptic, Heidegger's philosophy of art becomes a cyclical, seasonal philosophy of history that has for its "task" to facilitate dwelling and to recreate authentic community.[39]

IV. *Veronique Fóti: on dissembling, violence, and feminism*

For Fóti, Heidegger as community builder would be oxymoronic. Indeed, by contrast, he is simply a dissembler — and a violent one at that. But he is also a master at doing what he does. In order to make her case, she explores in some detail Heidegger's way of handling the poetry of the several poets whose works so deeply influenced Heidegger's own turn to art and language in his later philosophy. This is no easy task and in the constellation of my small cabinet of dialogue partners, deserves special notice. Schaeffer's work allows me to consider Heidegger as a philosopher in a particular tradition of philosophy which neglects everyday forms of aestheticization and results in a utopian messianism.

This has important consequences for what I say about Rosenzweig's messianic aesthetics vis à vis Heidegger's implicit messianism. Young's work gives me an overall view of Heidegger's philosophy of art and serves as a support for how I consider Heidegger's Hölderlin as a key to understanding his ideas about the possibilities of festival and celebration and as a way to "accept" Heidegger's diagnosis of the technologization of modernity as having some considerable and relevant merit. Fóti, however, brings Heidegger most sharply and critically into an ethical dialogue with the others with whom he was presumably already in dialogue. For both Schaeffer and Young, Hölderlin is that poet who fundamentally determined Heidegger's view on art and poetry, on Heidegger's own admission. And indeed, they each consider Heidegger's work on Hölderlin's poem "*Andenken*" as constitutive of that relationship. Fóti recognizes these relationships as well but reads the poems of the poets herself and, especially, given their French focus, reads them in French, in their own language. My point is that despite what Fóti says in her preface of her book, *Heidegger and the Poets: poēsis/sophia/technē*, that she wrote in relatively complete isolation, she nonetheless entered into a remarkable dialogue with the poets, Mörike, Trakl, Rilke, Hölderlin, and most especially Celan, in order to sound the depths of what she considers Heidegger's dissembling and violence.[40] For me and for the thesis of this book, and pointedly for the focus of this final chapter, although her last two chapters are dedicated to Celan and appropriately entitled "A Missed Interlocution" and "Meridians of Encounter," her chapter that addresses Heidegger's treatment of the two poems already at hand in the last several pages of my own text, namely, "*Andenken*" and "*The Ister*" is what interests me most.[41] I will consider that and a more recent essay of hers, "Heidegger, Hölderlin, and Sophoclean Tragedy"[42] in this section. But perhaps more significantly, much of her reading of these poets that deal with Heidegger's interlocutions are similar to my own that I acquired through exploring the place of the ethical in the philosophies of art in Rosenzweig and Heidegger over the last several years.

Fóti begins her argument by pointing out that, after resigning from his position as Rector, Heidegger contended that his teaching and writing immediately after his resignation should have been characterized as a confrontation with National Socialism. Since this was the time that he was working on the history of metaphysics, Nietzsche, and Hölderlin's poetry, that response re-problematized the issues that led to his political engagement in the first place, namely, historicality and technologization, and was, in Fóti's assessment, typically "displaced and cryptic."[43] She notes further that,

> It remains somewhat strange that an intellectual confrontation with a genocidal ideology and regime should proceed through Greek tragedy with its focus on the undoing of an individual; and it is also rather ironic that Sophocles, who won his first public distinction when Cimon and his fellow-commanders, acting as

judges at the Greater Dionysia in 468 BCE, awarded him first prize with a view
to his political conservatism, should be the Greek poet whose work mediates the
confrontation.[44]

Fóti claims that her intent in focusing on this reading is to develop the
deeper import of the relationship of Heidegger's readings of Sophocles in
An Introduction to Metaphysics and his later work, but her actual readings
say otherwise. In her earlier work, she notes that she intentionally leaves
Heidegger's readings unexplored and on another level she focuses on the figure
of Antigone in order to strike a deeper blow to what she takes to be Heidegger's
barely concealed philosophical sexism. Fóti condemns Heidegger at several
points for his gendered readings and eventually draws on Hannah Arendt's
philosophy of natality as an alternative to Heidegger's philosophy of mortality
to provide a clear alternative. The question becomes: does Heidegger's turn to
Hölderlin sufficiently account for "ultimate difference," an issue that abides
with Fóti from her early judgment about Heidegger's failure as an interlocutor
with Celan?

A telling indication of Fóti's interpretation is that she commences by
situating Heidegger's reading of Sophocles vis à vis Hegel's well-known
debt to *Antigone* as an inspirational source and paradigm for his dialectical
phenomenology. The difference is that while for Hegel the conflict plays out
between divine law and ethical self-consciousness, for Heidegger, the conflict
plays out between the ontological role of *poiēsis* and *technē*, that is, between a
historical legitimizing of the poetic task and the "aesthetization and glorifica-
tion of technology in the writings of Ernst Jünger."[45] He works through that
distinction in what he determines to be the task of the German people set for
the Germans by Hölderlin.

Fóti points out that only the 1935 reading focuses on the ontological,
Promethean character of the power of the human and that the human creates
as "confrontation," a theme that Heidegger was working out in how to found
something new and originary with respect to the beings with which the human
finds himself confronted. Fóti recounts Heidegger's interpretation of Hölderlin's
poetry in how it presents the form-giver, the human, in the way that he enters
into a disclosive relationship with beings that is essentially transgressive and,
thus, violent. Human creation as *poiēsis* is fundamentally a violent act that
is bound up with the *to deinon* — "the awe-inspiring" grounding word of
Greek tragedy. For Heidegger, *to deinon* refers to the character of man (as
masculine gender, notes Fóti) as "the unhomelike (*das Unheimische*)" connot-
ing "strange" and "out of place." That is, the one who is subject to *to deinon*
is that one who is cast out of "every context of familiarity, ease, protection,
or assured interpretation. This outcasting into exposure prevails over, 'over-
whelms' (*über-wältigt*), any order or economy of presencing."[46] Fóti points out
that this overwhelming is not subject to man's disposal, but in the historicality

of being's unconcealment, man is overwhelmed by the configurations that bring beings to their presencing. Recall, at this point, the conceptual development of *sich fugen*, or subordination, from *The Origin* work that Heidegger develops in this context and that I outlined in the last chapter. Fóti cites that work as well, pointing out that it is the exercise of *poiēsis* and *technē* to represent the "human enactment of power that pits itself against the over-powering sway of being's enigma."[47] But the problem is that the human is "thrown back upon his own resourcefulness" becoming enraptured in his own inventions, in the semblance (*Schein*) of being — which is the temptation of technology, thus precluding himself from being confronted with the actuality of being. In this way, the work of technology becomes ontically reified, establishing hegemonic structures that are even more dangerous than works of art. Consequently, the essential strife turns out to be between *technē* and *dikē*, but a *dikē* that is not understood as a distributive justice between equals, which is its normal definition, but rather as an exceeding of the phenomenal presencing, the *Schein*, that assigns presencing as that which presences its appropriate role. Again, this analysis of Heidegger's reading of "the tragic conflict" still "fits" with my own contentions about Heidegger's development of control with respect to destiny and history, but now only much more elaborately. That is, the context is more complex but the discourse is still on the dialectic of human power and the over-powering of being as the context of the totality of relational significance.

As Fóti goes on to note, the power of being shatters human creations as they attempt to control the enigma in various forms of challenge and sacrifice. *Technē* is a form of defiant knowing set over against the necessarily static figure of *anangkē* as being figures forth as historicality and temporality. His promethean creation is set over against being but is shattered by being and thus becomes the manifestation of being entering history. She notes: "Man, the creator, disappears into the created work which mesmerizes by its compelling and imprevisible singularity, while effacing the singularity of the creator."[48] Fóti sets up her critique of Heidegger, which I find compelling and supportive of my own thesis, with the following comparison: "Whereas Schelling saw in the perishing of the tragic hero(ine) an exaltation of human freedom, Heidegger perceives in tragedy an erasure of the face of man in favor of a revelation of being's self-concealment through the work of *technē*."[49] If I broke with Fóti at this point, her work would still provide enough assistance for my thesis about the divergence of Rosenzweig and Heidegger merely on the level of the erasure of the face. Recall, for example, how Rosenzweig leaves us with the "face" as the penultimate figuring of the star and of the other as Other at the end of *The Star*.

But I would like to follow Fóti a bit further for what she has to say about Heidegger's treatment of homecoming and singularization because of how they contribute to my own reading of Heidegger's Hölderlin. In the section of her essay entitled "Homecoming to the Unhomelike," Fóti works through

Heidegger's passages on how one deals with the alien other, with coming to the passion necessary to be able to live from one's own, because one needs to come into one's own in order to relate to the future, to relate to what is to come. As Fóti explicates Heidegger's intentions, she notes that:

> The itinerary of *essential* appropriation and the historical distention of the dwelling place that Heidegger explores through the Hölderlinian figure of the stream concern Occidental man's homecoming, out of long alienation, to his true identity as the being who responds to and safeguards being's enigma. To point out to Occidental humanity the need for a path to this homecoming is, in Heidegger's view, Germany's destinal mission (particularly that of her poets and thinkers) . . . For a historical people to grasp its true identity requires, for Hölderlin, a passage through what is alien without being either random or multiple; the alien is rather called for by the ownmost itself.[50]

In other words, the call comes from the own and not the other, as opposed to Rosenzweig's order of priority, affirming Heidegger's point of departure established in *Being and Time*, namely, that Da-sein calls to itself from itself to integrate itself out of its alienation in the they. In her interpretation, Fóti carries on the mode of analysis begun in her earlier work of examining the way that Heidegger unsuccessfully carries out the role of interlocutor, but this time with especial attention on his interlocutions with Hölderlin rather than with the more easily marked failure of Heidegger's lack of response to Celan.

Fóti notes how Heidegger renames *to deinon* "the unhomelike" in order to name being's enigma as a way to refer to the inflexible reduction of everything to a common denominator, that is, to the reductive totalization of technology. But in moving to the figure of Antigone he moves from the rhetoric of power to a dialectic of alienation. Fóti points out that the first form of homecoming is one that rejects any concern for the enigma of being and "seeks its abode among beings in their familiar and fully interprable interrelationships, rejecting any concern with being's enigma as pointless and incomprehensible."[51] Although she does not draw the connection, these are the same structures out of *Being and Time*, where Heidegger likewise says that there is a forgetfulness of being, while an "inchoate awareness of being" remains. But this latter condition constitutes what Heidegger terms homelessness in the Hölderlinian context and drives the human to nihilistic despair. In the language of *Being and Time*, the condition of *Angst* similarly drives one to consider the non-possibility of Da-sein's limited horizon of possibilities. And, thus, Da-sein is confronted with its ownmost possibility based on the temporality of its mortality. With his later thinking, the complex of the they-self and the language of authenticity and inauthenticity has been replaced by the dialectic of the art-work and technology, now replaced by the dialectic of homecoming and homelessness.

Fóti notes that this latter dialectic, of an illusory being at home in the world masked by the hegemonic structures of technology, is, for Heidegger, shattered by a type of character symbolized by Antigone, a type that exposes itself to seeking its "abode in being itself. It incurs thereby an estrangement from familiar patterns of world-construal and puts one at risk of losing one's home in the polis."[52] Antigone assumes a guiding principle of *to deinon* that takes form as anarchic non-governance and a defiant unwillingness to submit to any sort of governance that would legitimate the governing status quo. Consequently, she exposes herself to an exclusionary judgment by carrying to an extreme this other extreme of the *to deinon* to the point where "she renounces earthly attachments for the sake of an ontological passion that leads to her expulsion, not only from her native city, but, so to speak, from the lighted domain of the human lifeworld." She abandons the realm of the sighted, lighted domain of "normal" humans for the "sightless" realm of the dead. Fóti glosses Heidegger's text to explicate just this point, namely, that Heidegger valorizes Antigone's choice because that means that she ultimately embraces her ownmost possibility, "The belonging to death and blood . . . the human being's relation to death itself."[53]

Fóti emphatically rejects Heidegger's interpretation at this most critical juncture, taking issue with Heidegger's reduction of the response as a sacrifice to the ontological categories of blood (with its barely concealed political overtones) and death. Rather, she argues that,

> Her passion for the family dead (or "warm heart for the cold," as Ismene calls it) is not a matter of "blood" (which a child would certainly share), or of obedience to divine law (as she earlier presents it). Neither is it a commitment to being's enigma. It is rather her singular response, inexplicable in terms of any hegemonic principles, to her particular situation as a child of the doomed house of Laius, daughter of Oedipus and Jocasta . . . Antigone responds and acts eccentrically, out of her difference and her passion for those with whom birth, fate, and love have joined her and whose importance, for her, overrides both the claims of the *polis* and the claims of erotic love (which, in its generativity, and in the open-endedness of desire, is forward-looking.) *Her difference cannot be subsumed under some aspect of the ontological Differing*, or her singularity construed in terms of the binary (if ambiguous) opposition between two modalities of estrangement and homecoming.[54]

Fóti goes on to criticize Heidgger for essentializing Antigone as an historical archetype for the political, while distancing himself from any attempt to essentialize his own choices as politically motivated. Indeed, Fóti points out, Heidegger argues that the *polis* determines the political and not vice versa, and calling it into question is "beyond" either the Greeks or the Germans.

But Fóti's point is that Heidegger commits just this error, namely, of thinking "the *polis* ontologically and alethically, rather than in terms of pluralistic *praxis*. It constitutes for him, the singular pivot and gathering pole (*polos*) around which beings gather to attain to their presencing (*pelein*)."[55] It is the place, the "state," where humans gather in their "historical abiding in the midst of beings as a whole." But even more damning, is that by prioritizing the event of the gathering to attain presence at the *polis*, Heidegger impersonally presupposes human singularity as such: "As an aletheic configuration within the history of being, it presupposes that the human being already stand[s] within the 'opening' of disclosedness of being." In addition, Fóti points out how Heidegger appropriates Hölderlin's analyses in order to relegate Greece to an instrumental way station "to be appropriated for Germany's future."[56] Basically, Fóti criticizes Heidegger for typologizing Antigone and for his general tendency to not refer to her specificity as a person and how he purposively appropriates Hölderlin's verses to promote his own agenda:

> Heidegger goes so far as to suggest that Germany might yet outdo Greece in the latter's proper domain of "the fire from heaven" and instate a dwelling place for the gods "to which the Greek temples no longer come close." He conflates the character and "law" of history with the "single history of the Germans," ignoring the multifarious complexity of history and civilizations.[57]

As such, she contends that Heidegger exercises a "willingness to countenance violence and devastation as the unavoidable but in*esse*ntial shadow-side of a supposedly salutary historical transition, revealed as such to an intellectual and spiritual elite . . ." He does so by providing a weak analogy of already standing within the already accomplished neighborhood of destruction that is natural to historicality proper.[58] Not content with the weakness of the analogy and disturbed by its subterfuge, Fóti characterizes such glossing as "sleight of hand" and, implicity, a lack of integrity. Simply speaking, Heidegger is a dissembler, and a violent one at that.

In her concluding sections, Fóti argues that, in fact, despite Heidegger's claims to the contrary, and ongoing critical support from scholars such as Schürmann,[59] Heidegger should not be turned to for guidance for ways to subvert hegemony, because his "single-minded focus not only effaces human singularity but valorizes (with an echo of Plato's discussions of the relationship of the philosopher to the *polis*) the estrangement from the political community by one who heeds being's enigma."[60] Ultimately, she takes issue with how Heidegger treats "singularizing differentiation" as revealing mortality by means of a "passion for death" (*Todeslust*) as a way to come to terms with the infinite or boundless. Instead, she turns back to a rereading of Hölderlin that emphasizes an Arendtian-inspired conceptualization of singularity, where "ultimate difference reveals itself as bound to natality, rather than as introduced by the subversive trait of mortality."[61]

In fact, a less manipulative reading of Hölderlin's emphasis on the political and historical phenomenalizations of tragedy challenges Heidegger's interpretations. Fóti concludes: "In Greek tragedy, as Hölderlin perceives [it], the fatefulness that singularizes and renders the singular obtrusive disrupts the whole (by whatever name it may be called) that seeks to integrate subversion and difference."[62]

V. *My turn*

As I noted at the beginning of this chapter, publicly putting into practice the sense of textual interlocutions, in the sense elaborated by Fóti, has been one of the tasks of this work and of this section of the work in particular. Schaeffer similarly criticizes Heidegger for his inattention to appropriate the "singularity of each aesthetic experience" and of neglecting multi-perspectival, aesthetic, points of view. But while Schaeffer maintains that Heidegger does not respect the specificity of the poem itself, Fóti is even more demanding in her judgment that Heidegger does not respect the specificity of the other, as either poet or person. There is that which touches on the powerful in Heidegger's philosophizing, though, that elicits strong, visceral reactions and which is why I include Young in my reflections as well. Young provides the opportunity to think about Heidegger's preoccupation with strong, great figures, with heroes, gods, and powerful poets, political leaders, and philosophers. This is why reading Heidegger *with others* is so important, especially with an other such as Rosenzweig, a contemporary whose aesthetics has an ethical impulse that leads us, draws us, impels us towards receiving an other as other. But first, my interpretation of Heidegger's text, "Hölderlin's Hymn, 'The Ister,'" presented as a lecture course during the Summer Semester of 1942 in the same year that the *Endlösung* was formulated at Wannsee and the systematic gassing of Jews through mobile killing units was begun.[63]

Taking up the thread from the previous chapter, but with the intervention of these other critical voices, the terms for assessing Heidegger's "turn" can be more clearly set as having to do with his self-appointed "turn" in thinking from a transcendental, that is, philosophically authoritative, analytic of the existence of Da-sein to what he would later characterize as a more adequate, non-metaphysical meditation on the ecstatic clearing of the being of the "Da-" of Da-sein.[64] That meditation takes the form of the simultaneous clearing, disclosure, and concealment of being as a whole, namely, a meditation on the revealing and the "oblivion of being," which "progresses" through what Heidegger came to refer to in his later years as "the history of being" and which, according to von Hermann, constitutes the third major development in Heidegger's thought.[65] The "turn," then, is from raising the question of the "meaning of being" to the "truth of being" which, on Heidegger's terms, is the problem of the origin and history of Western metaphysics. This history of traditional metaphysical thinking, with its mixed origins in Plato and Aristotle, has concealed being in its thinking while neglecting or forgetting the oblivion or "absence" of being.[66] Heidegger's de-structuring meditation involves a reexamination of the "history of being" which entails thinking through the primordial origins of understanding being as it was first thought by the early Greek philosophers and writers. The historical destiny of the West is bound up with just this renewal of the question and thus the question of restoring "the human's historical existence — and that always includes our own future existence in the totality of history allotted to us — to the domain of being."[67] From Heidegger's phenomenological perspective, as I have initiated an explication of that perspective here, raises the question of the truth of being by asking about the question of the hidden ground of our historical existence; this then entails comprehending the historical and cultural ground as the formation and fulfillment of a people. Specifically, Heidegger thought of that people as the German people, but generally and more importantly, as the entire people of the West, rooted in the geography of what is called in German the *Abendland* — the land of the evening, or night, or absence of being, or the absence of god. And, as Young points out in his work on Heidegger's philosophy of art, Heidegger learned about that absence from Hölderlin.

a. *Hölderlin's hymn "The Ister"*

In order to address this need for a resolute revision of the work of art as not only the originary conflict of earth and world but as a presentation of the encountering of the absence or presence of god by the human, Heidegger "turns," via a series of lectures, to Friedrich Hölderlin's poetry. With his series of lectures/texts on Hölderlin's poetry, Heidegger concerns himself with that poet's *hymns*, that is, those works that deal with the kind of poetizing work involved in preparing the German people to at first recognize and then assume the risk for their divine calling and destiny and what assuming that risk entailed.[68]

In his final and most clearly definitive lecture in this series, on "The Ister," Heidegger begins by pointing out that Hölderlin "poetizes a river" and his poem, "The Ister," commences with the calling of the poet/reader to that which is coming, namely, the "fire" of the gods.[69] Heidegger notes that the opening call of the poem "Now come, fire!" not only indicates that the coming fire would "make visible the day" and that it also "gives rise to the day" but, perhaps more importantly, "The call says: we, the ones thus calling, are ready . . . and are so only because we are called by the coming fire itself."[70] He designates this calling as a vocation and that the poet "sings" not only to the coming god but also to tell of themselves as those who are prepared to listen, or to "hearken."[71]

Heidegger further emphasizes the importance of Hölderlin's placement of the initial "'Now' — as though [to indicate that] the fire had hitherto remained absent and there had been a long night."[72] Clearly this refers to the absent god and the long night of the forgetting of being and consequent decline by those in the West. The decline takes the form of the loss of the ability to correctly "read" the signs of the world and, thus, the loss of belonging to place and people. The task set forth, then, is to explicate the work of the poet-demigod, Hölderlin, and the poetized rivers become the locus for the gathering of a people at the river in a renewed forming of a relational *polis*. How that gathering takes place decisively determines the destiny of a people, specifically the German people and generally the people of the West.

We know that Heidegger assigns great importance to this gathering/calling since the "'Now' — tells us: something has already been decided. And precisely the appropriation that has already occurred" [*sich ereignet*] alone sustains all relation to whatever is coming. The "Now" names an appropriative event (the *Ereignis*)[73] which determines the new beginning of a people after having been decisively cut off from those still mired in the undifferentiated crowd of technologically induced conformity. The new beginning for Heidegger is precisely a consequence of turning within one's own, but not one's own Da-sein, rather, the turning is a turning to the *polis* which constitutes the relations of one's own people in such a way that the people themselves are awakened to a decisiveness (*Entscheidenheit*). In contrast to Young's reading, given that the German people are his referent, at the time of Heidegger's speech and writing, the political subtext to an appropriative event that had already occurred in the history of a people necessitates the corresponding assertion that Heidegger was still firmly and deeply working within the context of National Socialism, as anyone with eyes to see and ears to hear should be able to tell.

Such a turning within can only be effected by the poet as the "besouler" who points the Germans towards experiencing their own home, their Fatherland, and the path toward commencing on their "singular" history (as if history can be "singular," as Fóti points out). What it means to be a besouler has to do with Heidegger's understanding of the role of the poet, specifically, Hölderlin, but also Heidegger's own role as a thinker. The renewed beginning has to do with a thinking-poetizing experience:

> This experience now becomes a way of learning how to freely use what is one's own, since one's own has now been freed for its determination, for the cool clarification of the fire from the heavens, and has thus become "proper." The journeying into the unhomely must go "almost" to the threshold of being annihilated in the fire in order for the locality of the homely to bestow its gladdening and rescuing.[74]

This is not quite sacrificing oneself for the sake of the other but, rather, has to do with one's journey to the "unhomely." Significantly, such a journey is accomplished without crossing the threshold into annihilation — that would be risking too much. Rather, one goes "almost" to the threshold of the fire, for the sake of "freely using one's own" in its proper application of "cool clarification" of philosophical reflection and the building of institutions, but via a higher order of utilization impassioned by the near-experience of the appropriated fire. Note the difference in this depiction of what Rosenzweig meant by his conception of "ensouling" as a revelatory, ethical process of prioritizing the other and Heidegger's hermeneutic that prioritizes the task of appropriation for the sake of "freely using one's own."

According to Heidegger, what the Germans are good at and what is therefore their own, is "the formation of projects, enclosures, and frameworks. They become carried away by the provision of frames and compartments, making divisions and structuring."[75] What Heidegger has in mind here is the historical record of German production and their skill at tasks such as maintaining feudal structures, mechanical engineering, bureaucratic organization and systematic philosophy, all important factors in establishing a world that Heidegger saw as paradigmatic of the modernity of Enlightenment-inspired metaphysics of a totalizing technological world. For Heidegger, such a modern world, which began with the Greeks, has, however, become art-less and thus god-less. It is art-less and god-less because it no longer provides the occasion for human-transformative events that allow for unbridled expressions, and therefore authentic expressions, of the being of human particularity. What Heideigger means by particularity here, though, is different than, say, a Rosenzweigian sense of particularity. As opposed to a Rosenzweigian sense of particularity as *Besonderheit*, Heidegger has in mind *Einzelheit* in the sense of individualizing from a crowd, which entails putting oneself forward, or in place, through presenting what is one's own. This sort of presenting, however, entails first "appropriating" or "seizing upon" what is foreign so as to differentiate that other from what is one's own. Thus, for Heidegger:

> What the Germans lack, what must therefore first come to be encountered by them as that which is foreign to them, is the "fire from the heavens." [Hence, they] must learn to experience so as to be struck by the fire and thereby to be impelled toward the correct appropriation of their own gift for presentation.[76]

The way to be struck by this "fire" is through learning to perform certain acts of language, specifically, those poetic acts that entail localizing and temporalizing discernible signs in the relational web of the polis. Regarding such activity, Heidegger distinguishes between representational and thus merely symbolic activity, that is, that kind of representational activity that can be studied by any of the several scientific disciplines, and the performative and determining acts of the involved poet. The poet is the one who not only can read the signs but who, in fact, en-acts the signs because he becomes the sign itself. In other words, the poet as sign is itself spirit, which is the essence of the holy, and as such is a soul "to which a mind is appropriate" and thus "bears the stars of the heavens." Such a bearing of the "stars of the heavens" occurs, moreover, as a showing, that is,

> a showing [which] is of such a kind as to first let appear that which is to be shown. Yet such a sign can, as saying, let appear that which is to be said only because it has before this already been shone upon by that which thus appears as what is to be poetized.[77]

Only such engaged, poetic activity (which purportedly is not political, economical, technological, etc.) is able to contribute to overcoming the unhomeliness, the numbing estrangement, to which humans have declined in their long and oppressive history of forgetfulness of the being of beings.

In order to institute this relational *polis* that becomes the homely dwelling as the source of gathering those who know and care about themselves in their environment, the poet "must name the gods, say them in their essence," and thus act *as* the sign, as the river, as the demigod, leading the lost and fallen ones, by practical acts, in a renewal of their holy relationships with the earth and with the gods. The poet is the founding besouler: "The sign, the demigod, the river, the poet: all these name [signify] poetically the one and singular ground of the becoming homely of human beings as historical and the founding of this ground by the poet."[78] But what does Heidegger mean when he says that the poet must "name the gods in their essence"? What is the essence of the gods and what does that have to do with the founding/naming acts of the poet?

In order to address this question, recall what Heidegger said about the fire. The essence of the gods has to do with the "fire" while naming the gods has to do with letting the fire speak. But in what way do we "let" the fire speak? Letting the fire speak is, for Heidegger and his interpretation of Hölderlin, poetizing the holy, which is that which "eventuates itself" (*ereignet sich*). For something to "eventuate itself" means that it "constantly is the source and remains the locality of its own essence."[79] It is the spirit of the river that experiences its own journeying to the unhomely (to the stranger) and returns to the homely, to its ownmost locality. In *flowing*, it experiences its own journey and issuing from its source. What is said in the poems is the *holy* which "determines the gods themselves" while at the same time it "brings the dwelling of historical human beings into its essence."[80] As such, the poet is the demigod and acts *as* the river that is likewise a demigod, but not just any river(s) or demigod(s). Rather, Heidegger claims Hölderlin specifically *names* two rivers: the Rhine and the Ister but nonetheless, means only the Ister even in naming the Rhine. He names the Ister because it is that river that issues from his blissful mother-land, Swabia, and is in fact what is meant when Hölderlin speaks his "Now."

Not only does the Ister provide fertility and shelter but it also embodies the mythic welcoming of the stranger — the Greek Hercules, as guest. He is the one from the southern land of the "fire," the land of the sun, Greece, and who remains as guest in the land of the Germans, the land of the shadow and the cool rationality of the systematizers. And it is by acknowledging the guest that the Germans "are able to acknowledge the fire from the heavens that [they] lack."[81] Significantly, Heidegger notes that this "guest-friendship" not only entails "the resolve not to mix what is one's own, as one's own with the foreign, but to let the foreign be the one he is."[82] This "not mixing" of the foreign with one's own is the "letting be" referred to earlier and constitutes a significant step in the process of self-identification. It also explains why the reading/welcoming of Antigone as unhomely other takes the central place in this lecture — one needs to journey to the foreign unhomely in order to be able to recognize and then to appropriate what is not one's own, and only thereby be able to return to one's own home.

But perhaps even more importantly is that Heidegger contends that human poetizing determines the gods themselves. This is accomplished by the poet whose own destiny is to *feel for the gods themselves* as only a mortal who can die is able to feel. Again, recall the reworking by Heidegger of the mood-full nature of human mortality so clearly enunciated in *Being and Time*, but here developed into an essential moment in the clarifying of a people's destiny by the prophetic poet. In this regard, Heidegger quotes Hölderlin's Rhine hymn:

> Es haben aber an eigner
> Unsterblichkeit die Götter genug und bedürfen eines Dings,
> So sinds Heroën und Menschen
> Und Sterblich sonst. Denn weil
> Die Seeligsten nichts fühlen von selbst,
> Muss wohl, wenn solches zu sagen
> Erlaubt ist, in der Götter Nahmen
> Theilnehmend fühlen ein Andrer,
> Den brauchen sie; jedoch ihr Gericht
> Ist, dass sein eigenes Haus
> Zerbreche der und das Liebste
> Wie den Feind schelt' und sich Vater und Kind
> Begrabe unter den Trümmern,
> Wenn einer, wie sie, sey will und nicht
> Ungleiches dulden, der Schwärmer.[83]

> There has been enough of their own
> Mortality for the gods and they need one thing,
> Of those heroes and humans
> Who are otherwise mortal. Then because
> The most soulful can not feel anything from themselves,

They have to, if such can be said
To be allowed, to partake of feeling an other
In the gods name,
Because they need them; therefore their judgment
Is, that they should let their own house
Be destroyed and the most loved one
Treat like the enemy and they themselves should bury
Father and child under the remnants of the ruins
If someone, like them, will be and not
Tolerate unequals, the fanatic.

He comments further that: "An 'other' must be, who is other than the gods and in his being other must 'tolerate unequals.'" This "other" is needed to "partake in feeling" in the name of the gods and be able to tolerate "difference" or the unequal. Partaking in feeling consists in his bearing sun and moon, the heavenly, in mind, and distributing this share of the heavenly to humans, and so, standing between gods and humans, shares the holy with them, yet without ever splitting it apart or fragmenting it. Such communicating occurs by this "other" pointing toward the holy in naming it, so that in such showing he himself *is* the sign that the heavenly needs. The poet is the one best able to take on this holy task because he is the one who best articulates the emotional experience that complements the seeing/thinking experience. The importance for Heidegger's agenda of elaborating this structure has to do with his claim that such complementary working is what best characterizes being human: for "feeling" and "bearing in mind" belong to humankind.[84]

Hence, by pointing, the sign, the poet, "besouls" everything in such an originary way that "in naming the holy" the sign lets the heavenly show itself as the holy, and the fire that enflames the poet would likewise then enflame the people to whom the poet poetizes. But, since the gods are without feeling, they are unable to comport themselves towards beings and therefore what is needed is the work of the poet who *lends* feeling to the gods thus enabling a new form of relationship to take place. In this way, the poet acts as an intermediary demigod and with his or her poetizing builds stairs for the descent of the heavenly,[85] which is thus both celebratory and a "holy mourning."[86] It is a "holy mourning" not only because of the reflection that occurs upon the absence of the gods and the forgetting of being, but also, says Heidegger, because of the necessity that the poet must continue to dwell near the enigmatic source of the river, thus enabling the surrounding land to become arable. It is celebratory, however, precisely because of this renewed arability and thereby the advent of a new relationship of humans with the gods composed through the new understanding of the relationship of earth to the historical world. What is established is "locality" and thus the relational *polis*. That new relationship is disclosed by poetic embodiment of the fourfold relationship. And it is only

through the work of art that the conflictual, in-tense relating of earth–world/
Da-sein–gods can occur, namely, through the poetic "saying," of one such
as Hölderlin. The earth becomes disclosed in its sheltering relationship to its
"onto-ethical" status (standing) of being that provides a relationship with
which humans can measure themselves, that is, a "measure" with the heavenly,
with the gods. And that is what is called beautiful.

What needs to be said, but without sufficient elaboration here, is that for
Heidegger these events are not general and universal. Rather, just as the events
initiated by the Greeks — as those people of the sun and the *Morgenland*,
disclosed a way of understanding being and established an initial relationship
of humans with gods and of earth with world — relationships of beauty, so now
the Germans — those people of the *Abendland*, must fulfill their holy destiny
to disclose a new turn to the divine as an effective force in history and genuine
transmitters of events of beauty.

In the end, Heidegger's "turn" to art, specifically to the poetry of Hölderlin
and Hölderlin's vision of German renewal, is a turn to what he claims is that
visionary one who has become ego-less and non-subjective. The problem with
modern humans, claims Heidegger, is that they are entangled in thinking in
"terms of self-consciousness and subjectivity." Whereas, Hölderlin, alone of
all modern German poets — perhaps alone of all poets (!),

> poetizes purely from out of that which, in itself, essentially prevails as that which
> is to be poetized. When Hölderlin poetizes the essence of the poet, he poetizes
> relations that do not have their ground in the "subjectivity" of human beings.
> These relations have their own essential prevailing and flowing.[87]

If the "poet is the river" and the "river is the poet" as Heidegger claims, and
they "ground the dwelling of human beings on this earth,"[88] then not only
humans and other beings but the gods and the very earth itself depend upon
what is shown through the work of art. And if that saying/showing is likewise
dependent on the poet and thinker — as the one who transforms the truth of
thinking by his own authentic experience of the sayings of the poet — then we
are, in fact, not entirely without measure as Heidegger himself claims at the end
of his lecture. The question he raises at the very end is one of authority: "If we
merely attempt, on our own authority, to set or seize upon the measure, then
it becomes measureless and disintegrates into nothingness." But if we dwell
poetically and thinkingly, with Hölderlin and Heidegger, the saint and the holy
sinner, we could very well be saved. As he claims in a penultimate conclusion:
"Yet if we are strong enough to think, then it may be sufficient for us to ponder
merely from afar, that is, scarcely, the truth of this poetry and what it poetizes,
so that we may suddenly be struck by it."[89]

Consistent to the very end, Heidegger stands on this conclusion with
the force of law, asserting imperiously that we are necessarily consigned to

subordinate ourselves to our destined, assigned roles as signifiers, as pointers, and thus to rely on the shepherds of our being from whom, and presumably only from whom — since they are the demigods, we receive our "measure." In fact, we receive that measure as Heidegger notes approvingly by quoting Hölderlin's "Rhine" hymn, from the poet or thinker who is likewise the *Schwärmer* (the fanatic). If only a god can save us, as Heidegger maintains, then perhaps only a fanatic can lead us to such a god.[90]

Notes

1 See Robert Bernasconi, "The Greatness of the Work of Art," and François Dastur, "Heidegger's Freiburg Version of the Origin of the Work of Art," in Risser 1999: 95–144. While Bernasconi's evaluation is very critical, especially on the grounds of what can only be termed his tracing of textual manipulation by Heidegger as a response to his political predicament, that is, the maintenance of a credible academic career in the aftermath of his involvement with the Nazis, Dastur is much more sympathetic in following Heidegger's philosophical journey as one of ongoing critique.

2 This is, of course, counter to what Benjamin would maintain about how "fragments" constitute the saving remnants of the products of our world, by which the world itself can and needs to be redeemed from the inexorability of consumptive progress. See, for example, his remarks about dialectical materialism and the unfinished character of our world in "Theses on the Philosophy of History" in Benjamin 1977, especially VII and IX.

3 See Schaeffer 1992: 7.

4 Ibid: 61.

5 Ibid: 267.

6 See Gadamer's "Thinking and Poetizing in Heidegger and in Hölderlin's 'Andenken'" in Risser 1999.

7 Schaeffer 1992: 267.

8 Ibid: 268.

9 See Young 2001: 2.

10 Ibid: 17.

11 Young 2004: 63. See also pp. 73, 101,102.

12 IM: 152.

13 See Heidegger, "Only a God Can Save Us" in Wolin 1992: 112. The entire quote is worth considering: "My thinking stands in a definitive relationship to the poetry of Hölderlin. I do not take Hölderlin to be just any poet whose work, among many others, has been taken as a subject by literary historians. For me Hölderlin is the poet who points to the future, who expects god and who therefore may not remain merely an object of Hölderlin research and of the kind of presentations offered by literary historians."

14 Both found in HHG.

15 Young 2004: 71; and also HHA: 197.

16 Young 2004: 72.
17 See EHD: 170.
18 Compare IM: 38 and HHG: 39, 216.
19 On the importance of festival in Heidegger, see Young 2004: 849–0, and "Festive Celebrations," in Benso 2000: 181–96. The question that needs to be asked is whether or not our age is so impoverished that we no longer can celebrate the festival — any festival, not only in the face of the Shoa, as Adorno asserted in *Negative Dialektik* (but later modified) and said otherwise by Edith Wyschogrod in Wyschogrod 2000: 1. She opens her text by asking: "What is the meaning of death in the twentieth century, when millions of lives have been extinguished and the possibility of annihilating human life altogether remains open? Is there an art of dying which is useful in this time and circumstance? Or does quantitative change, the emergence of the numberless dead, so alter our perspective on death that no interpretation is adequate to the apocalyptic character of the phenomenon except perhaps the gasp of horror, the scream, that in Greek tragedy accompanies the revelation of things unspeakable?"
20 See also HHG: 146. Could it be that because Rosenzweig had not lived through the Shoah that he is still able to elicit a profound sense of hope, a *Grundstimmung* of joy and expectation? Is Rosenzweig's sense of exile enough? Can we understand his including the ongoing possibility, even necessity, of festival other than as profanation, as perhaps even a necessary celebratory affirmation?
21 See HHG: 170 and 94.
22 Young 2004: 73–5; HHG: 39, 146.
23 See my discussion of "Der Ursprung des Kunstwerkes" in Chapter 6 and Young 2004: 75. cf. also Section 74 in SZ/BT and Nietzsche's notion of "memorializing" aspects of the past in the creation of (roughly) "role models" for the future, in Nietzsche 1980c: 19–21.
24 See HHG: 144.
25 See EHD: 77.
26 Ibid.
27 See Heidegger's speech assuming the rectorship of Freiburg University, "The Self-Assertion of the University" in Wolin 1992.
28 See Young 2004: 76. See also HHG: 39, 214.
29 See EHD: 4.
30 Young 2004: 78.
31 See HHIe: 1111–2.
32 See HHG: 214.
33 See PLT: 74.
34 See Young 2004: 113.
35 cf. my discussion of Rosenzweig's "messianic aesthetics" in Chapter 4.
36 See EHD: 28.
37 PLT: 150.
38 QCT: 42.
39 Young 2004: 173.
40 Fóti 1992.

41 See "Textuality and the Question of Origin: Heidegger's Reading of 'Andenken' and 'Der Ister,'" in Fóti 1992.
42 See Veronique Fóti, "Heidegger, Hölderlin, and Sophoclean Tragedy," in Risser 1999: 1631–86.
43 Ibid: 163.
44 Ibid: 165.
45 Ibid: 166. Fóti refers to Zimmerman's argument in Zimmerman 1990, chapters 4–6.
46 Ibid: 167.
47 Ibid: 168.
48 Ibid: 169.
49 Ibid.
50 Ibid: 171.
51 Ibid: 173.
52 Ibid: 174.
53 Ibid. Heidegger quote is from HHId: 147.
54 Ibid: 175.
55 Ibid: 176.
56 Ibid.
57 Ibid: 177. Heidegger quote is from HHId: 155.
58 Ibid.
59 Ibid: 1801–82.
60 Ibid: 180.
61 Ibid: 182.
62 Ibid: 183.
63 See HHIe and HHId.
64 See the section "The Last God," in BP.
65 See GSh. Heidegger's former student, F.W. von Hermann argued that this work fulfilled the body of Heidegger's entire work and can continue to be read as a resource for continuing to challenge the totalizing structures of, especially, American-inspired capitalism and technology. Noted in a philosophy seminar on this work taken during Summer Semester 1999 in Freiburg, Germany.
66 For a detailed discussion of Heidegger's notion of truth as disclosedness of being, see "Interrupting truth" by John Sallis, in Risser 1999: 19–30.
67 EM: 32.
68 Heidegger delivered three major courses on Hölderlin's poetry: a 1934/1935 courses on Hölderlin's hymns "Germania" and "The Rhine" (published as volume 39 of the Gesamtausgabe), and a course on the hymn "Remembrance" (Andenken), presented in 1941/1942 (published in volume 52 of the Gesmatausgabe).
69 HHIe: 6.
70 Ibid: 7.
71 cf. the analytic section of *Being and Time*. Also, in using the term "sings" Heidegger did not intend to valorize that particular aesthetic form, as I note in the Final Words of this book.
72 HHIe: 8.
73 Ibid: 9.
74 Ibid: 134.

75   Ibid: 136.

76   Ibid.

77   Ibid: 151.

78   Ibid: 154.

79   Ibid: 138.

80   Ibid: 139.

81   Ibid: 141. The implied reference is to the German tradition of "Gemütlichkeit," which affords experiences of comfort and welcome to strangers and guests. Note also that Heidegger's critique of Descartes, which serves to support his critique of Kant, includes his assessment that Deacartes's ultimate weakness was in leaving out reference to *Gemut*, a kind of thinking comfort that Germans traditionally provide for their guests.

82   Ibid.

83   Ibid: 155.

84   Ibid. Such tolerating of unequals does not have a democratic leveling — as Rosenzweig's Pesach celebration does but is, instead, a reworking of a hierarchical ordering structure — in this sense, Heidegger sets non-revolutionary and more reactionary, conservative forces in motion. Additionally, besouling in Rosenzweig is done by the lover, not the symbolizer.

85   Ibid: 158.

86   Ibid: 157, 163. For a discussion of "holy mourning" in the context of how Hölderlin's poetry relates to Heidegger's ideas on technology, see also: Zimmerman 1990: 116. Because Zimmerman primarily draws upon the two earlier Hölderlin lectures for his analysis, the critical element of "celebration" is missing, which Heidegger includes in the Ister lecture. The "homecoming" is not only a reaction to the "departure of the gods" and the "concealment of being," as Zimmerman correctly points out, but it is likewise a celebratory event of welcoming the guest, the foreigner, as intrinsic to the process of the journey from the unhomely to the homely.

87   Ibid: 165.

88   Ibid: 166.

89   Ibid: 167.

90   Since aesthetics is bound up with sensibility, then if the one who is invested to lead, either the poet, thinker or politician is an enthusiast, the danger of the fanatic is but one step away from the "spring" into the "origin" of the creative acts that initiate historical destiny. The word *Schwärmer* can be translated as "enthusiasts," with the connotation of "fanatics" and with historical reference to the sixteenth-century Inspirationists who relied on inner inspirations and visions, such as the Zwickau Prophets, Thomas Müntzer, and David Joris. See: http://www.gameo.org/encyclopedia/contents/S3863.html (accessed 20 November 2010).

FINAL WORDS

Was Heidegger really a *Schwärmer* in leading us to wait for the coming god? Perhaps, but as a phenomenologist's version of an Anabaptist fanatic.

Minimally, however, I hope to at least have made a case for considering the connection between aesthetics and ethics as a way to clearly distinguish the divergent agendas of these two philosophers, as opposed to forcing these philosophers into an affinity under the rubric of philosophers of *Existenz*. The judgment about Heidegger being a *Schwärmer* will be left in the hands of my readers, but making my case for the indirect but strong linkage of aesthetics and ethics constitutes the major work in this book and differentiates, in both perspective and judgment, my position from others such as Peter Gordon's on Rosenzweig and Heidegger, Iain Thompson's on Heidegger, or Benjamin Pollock's on Rosenzweig.[1] Without reiterating the argument or body of evidence provided in the preceding chapters, I would like to provide a few final words from my interpretation of Rosenzweig's and Heidegger's respective ideas about art and the ethical and what constitutes the role of art in our social relations. Heidegger's philosophy of art reaches its apogee with his taking up for the Germans and the rest of the Westerners what he has determined to be the *alethic* task set before us in Hölderlin's poetry. But while that task assumed its political shape for Hölderlin as a response to the democratizing forces set in motion with the French Revolution, for Heidegger the task is re-read as an imperative of remembering our mortalizing destiny, and our calling to resist the dangers of technology, capitalism, and communism. For Heidegger, that imperative became tied up with the role that he played in the machinations of National Socialism. In truth, Heidegger's Hölderlin is not the end of the story, either for him or for us. For Heidegger, after completing his talks on Hölderlin, several more decades of teaching, writing, and publishing followed which included several more revisions of his earlier projects resulting in major commentaries on the earlier pre-Socratics, German Idealism, Nietzsche's philosophy, and his own *Contributions*. Withal, Heidegger's body of work is an *Ereignis* that, however, can be brought to ethical judgment; indeed, the work calls for an ethical measure. From his early structural phase, the intervening, interpretive phases are marked with many significant pathmarks that guide us along the way, none any less significant than his exchange of letters with Sartre and the interview that he granted to *Der Spiegel* with the proviso that it not be published until after his death.

In support of that thesis, consider Heidegger's later assertions in *The Letter on Humanism* from 1956, that "language is the house of being" and that the role of the philosopher is equivalent to a caretaking shepherd of being.[2] How Heidegger comes to those assertions in his exchange with Sartre is through his work in the 1930s and 1940s on art and especially on Hölderlin's poetry. At the time when Heidegger was in the process of composing *The Origin of the Work of Art* in the early 1930s, he was also formulating his theory of history and historicity, namely, that language is always the historical language of a specific people located in a concrete land and epoch. In fact, language is the most original art, since it says and names, and therefore guides the destinies of peoples. On that basis, it is more primordial than the plastic arts, such as architecture or painting, or even music, and serves to guide and pervade the Opening cleared by the saying of being which is poetry. Poetry is the happening of the clearing of being, thus functioning as *the* art which enables Heidegger to bring other arts into a single, coherent theory.

Heidegger initiated his revision with his claim that, "According to our human experience and history, I know that everything essential and everything great originated from the fact that man had a home and was rooted in a tradition." He went on to say that present-day literature, implying present-day culture, is predominantly destructive because it contributes to a global movement leading up to an "absolute technological state."[3] To the question of whether or not an individual or philosophy as a discipline could influence or guide the world toward an adequate response to the apparently catastrophic developments of technology (which certain strands of especially contemporary environmental postmodern-influenced activism highlight),[4] Heidegger responded:

> Philosophy will not be able to effect an immediate transformation of the present condition of the world. This is not only true of philosophy, but of all merely human thought and endeavor. *Only a god can save us.* The sole possibility that is left for us is to prepare a sort of readiness, through thinking and poetizing, for the appearance of the god or for the absence of the god in the time of foundering [*Untergang*]; for in the face of the god who is absent, we founder.[5]

Apparently threatened by American-style capitalist consumer culture and Soviet–Chinese-style communist corporate control, Heidegger thought that we were (and still are) in a dire time of foundering and that in this modern age of technology we live in the absence of god. But just what Heidegger means by "god" and what he means by the "absence of the god" is not very clear and must be gleaned from his earlier works, as I have attempted to do in this text.

In the *Spiegel* interview, Heidegger denies a "causal connection" between his work as a thinker and the possibilities of initiating an "emergence of this god" that is absent/concealed because, he noted, we cannot simply "think him into being here; we can at most awaken the readiness of expectation." And in fact, the task is not a simple, autonomous task since he claimed that,

> the world cannot be what it is or the way that it is through man, but neither can it be without man. According to my view, this is connected with the fact that what I name with the word Being, — needs man for its revelation, preservation, and formation. I see the essence of technology in what I call the frame [*das Ge-stell*]-. The frame holding sway means: the essence of man is framed, claimed, and challenged by a power which manifests itself in the essence of technology, a power which man himself does not control. To help with this realization is all that one can expect of thought. Philosophy is at an end.[6]

But then Heidegger further qualified his pronouncement saying that philosophy and the individual are capable of "this preparation of the readiness, of keeping oneself open for the arrival of, or the continued absenting of, the god." Moreover, the experience of this absence is not nothing, but rather a liberation of man from what he called "fallenness amidst beings" in *Being and Time*.[7] This sort of meditating preparatory thinking was called "other thinking,"[8] by which Heidegger means a kind of thinking that would awaken, clarify, and fortify thinking as an "action which stands in dialogue with the world-destiny (*Weltgeschick*) in a way of thinking ahead."[9]

This "other thinking," however, is not directly related to the ethical, since, as Heidegger maintains, silence is perhaps better preparation than premature public utterances because "the questions are so difficult that it would be contrary to the meaning of the task of thought to step up publicly, as it were, to preach and to impose moral judgments."[10] Unlike Levinas's sense of the other in the face of whom I publicly respond by responding to their desires and needs (and thus is ever and always an ethical response), Heidegger makes it clear that he distances himself from such "moral preaching" in what he means by other-thinking and that specifically such thinking is not an ethical task.[11] Rather, that preparatory thinking entails a task of thought that is in very determined ways a mix of political, philosophical and poetic thinking, and that consists in "helping man in general within the limits allotted to thought, to achieve an adequate relationship to the essence of technology. National Socialism, to be sure, moved in this direction." This judgment is further qualified with the addition that, "But those people were far too limited in their thinking to acquire an explicit relationship to what is really happening today and has been underway for three centuries. Nonetheless, 'those people' had the potential to effect a 'free relationship to the technical world.'"[12] They merely (!) did not make their initial impulse explicit.

Heidegger was only able to reach such a judgment out of the logical development of his earlier work, which proceeded in conjunction with his involvement in what he might consider the general *polis* and what has been taken to be his political situation at the time. Those political involvements can be traced through his philosophy by way of the other works that I have included in this study that exemplify what seems to be a veiling of the political associations in his articulation of teachings on art and what Heidegger would later develop as the fourfold (*Gevierte*), namely, the relationship of humans to divinity and the earth to world. Again, as Heidegger noted, my "thinking stands in a definitive relationship to the poetry of Hölderlin"[13] whom Heidegger did not take to be just any poet. Rather, Hölderlin is that "poet who points to the future, who expects god"[14] and who, with Nietzsche, has put a "question mark" before the German people in confronting them with their task to find their being, that is, their historical destiny. For Nietzsche, this took the form of working out of the Dionysian/Apollonian opposition of sacred passion and sober presentation which Heidegger at first accepts. However, he soon rejected Nietzsche's position as the final maneuver in the history of metaphysics and science begun with the Greeks and distorted through the Romans.

His path for coming to such a preparation and for dealing with the decline of thought and culture in the West, for what I would term a hesitancy in the face of the demand of the other, is prepared precisely in his move to incorporate earth as earth and the holy and divinity in his phenomenological world-view. That task he hoped to accomplish with his analysis of art. In summary, Heidegger's problem was that he brought to wholes, to completenesses, what should remain unfinished; as Schaeffer notes, he was completing fragments of poetry that should have remained fragmentary (and should still remain fragmentary). Thus, Heidegger proved himself to be incapable of remaining open to the unpredictability of an actual other, constructing wholes and wholenesses instead, in order to secure philosophical completion and a completion of the "work of his own hands." This is especially clear in how Heidegger was unable to account for the emergence of the personal voice of the poet Hölderlin substituting, instead, Heidegger's own theoretical conclusion. Incidentally, this fundamental assertion on my part further distinguishes my conclusions from Peter Gordon's about how we should understand the relationship of Heidegger and Rosenzweig. Gordon maintains that Heidegger's and Rosenzweig's philosophies should be read as convergent precisely on this point that he identifies as "holism."[15]

Thus, in defending my thesis about the divergence of Heidegger and Rosenzweig with respect to the issue of their respective political orientation, I would also argue against Young that the continuity in Heidegger's philosophical work remains undisturbed (by the political) and that the resources for mounting a critique against political hegemony are limited. This is the case because, for Heidegger, the founding of the people connected to the land and in spirit and blood has the unwanted historical effects of also being able to be utilized to affirm a path toward political tyranny. Concretely, Heidegger himself accomplishes such guiding actions by shepherding us through his later works with the "Letter on Humanism" and *Der Spiegel* interview, waiting for a god, or another leader, to do the unifying "holistic" work that failed with Hitler and the Nazi elite, rejecting the cooperative redemptive work of joining human hands and voices in communities of difference. Instead of striving to work with other communities in interdependent cooperation, Heidegger retains and strengthens his proclivity towards independent and essential conflict, until the bitter end.

That end is a reflection on death. Heidegger leaves us with mortality, while Rosenzweig opens a horizon toward the possibilities of natality and immortality, since he situates at the heart of his text a dialogue of desire and love as the source of the ethical and the foundation for the possibility of social justice. Reading Heidegger reveals his lack of trust in others. Instead, we seem to be confronted with a closed book, a completed project even though he never could come to actual completions of his various projects. Despite his turning to the East for dialogue partners, Heidegger's is never an actual interlocution because he withholds the words of actually getting to know the history of the other. Heidegger's project takes shape as an appropriative one, out to take from the other what enables the authentic and elethic appropriation for oneself. And despite his language of risk, he withholds the words of recognition of the other as other in their particular history. In short, the "fugue" for the "history of being" is fixed.

Rosenzweig, on the other hand, does not leave us with any final words from the very grave itself. His waiting for the final god is, as I noted above, not content with letting tears remain on a single face and so continues to remain open to walking and talking with others, with trusting in others. In getting to know the actual history of the other, Rosenzweig shares words, and thus histories with others, intertwining his own with the other in constellations of complex choral fugues. But in such sharing, that means that Rosenzweig withholds words as well, but does so in order to be receptive to the other, intentionally suffering, undergoing the passion of not-speaking in order to attend to the other as other. This withholding is for the sake of the other, as a way to prioritize their desires and needs. He leaves us with a completed text but an open project because, even though it is a completed work, since he trusts in the other he leaves open the chaos of possibility, of actual anarchy in a ritualized structure of infinitizing the finite and thus continually allowing for the possibilities of criticizing the violence of political totalitarianism.

In order to better interpret Heidegger's last stand, I would like to highlight what I consider to be an ethical result of Rosenzweig's philosophy of art, namely, that art entails an ethical dimension precisely in how it takes shape as a performative messianic aesthetic that has political consequences. Historically, Heidegger's last stand does not occur with Hölderlin, but with his final interview with *Der Spiegel*, an event that haunts his heritage with an echo of the apparent arrogance and disillusion springing into the future from *"The" Master out of Germany*.[16] The ethical problem is a matter of control and of how, or whether, one is able to relinquish control of determining the course of "my" future destiny to the unpredictable needs, wants, and desires of the "other" — of my interlocutor — who, as Levinas so clearly calls to our attention, calls into question the enjoyment experienced through my own autonomous freedom and spontaneity, calls into question the very body of my work and the works of my body. This brings up the problem of Heidegger's return to redefining a traditional notion of the self as autonomously and ultimately acting for its own benefit in order to attain the certainty of ontological authenticity. This position remains true to a hallowed traditional of ontology stretching from Aristotle through Hobbes, Spinoza, and finally even to a Hegelian modified Kantian version of a self absolutely concerned with itself as its first priority. This becomes clear for us, following Fóti, with the issue of how Heidegger, despite his turn to art and language, fails to listen and thus speak "with" his interlocutors. In fact, as the chief case in point, Heidegger attempts to have the last word, and thus the last laugh, with his penultimate "dialogue" that takes place as the *Spiegel* interview.

An alternative way to interpret laughter is to eliminate the definitions that have to do with simple mirth, joy, and amusement. Instead, if we highlight the secondary, more marginal sense of laughter as a form of ridicule[17] and derision, indifference, disregard and even contempt, to have the "last laugh" means, then, to win after apparent defeat and discomfiture. Additional variations of this marginal alternative can mean: "to laugh away," which means to get rid of something unpleasant or embarrassing by laughter; "to laugh down," which means to silence or suppress by laughing; and "to laugh off," which means to scorn, avoid or reject by laughter or ridicule. Such laughter is the laugh of a scornful, self-adulating victor, the laugh which results from humiliating an opponent.

In coming to this concluding line of thought, I was inspired by an exchange of letters between Heidegger and his former student, Herbert Marcuse, when, despite Marcuse's enduring sympathies for Heidegger's philosophy, "To his credit . . . Marcuse refused to allow the "philosopher of Being" to have the last word. The reference is to how Marcuse, like many others, desperately sought a word of renunciation by Heidegger of Heidegger's sympathies for, and significant part in promoting, the Nazi agenda.[18] As is relatively well known, Heidegger not only refused to recant but went on to affirm his abiding belief in the spirit of renewal that the NSDAP represented.[19] Marcuse sent a terse reply and finally broke off the relationship, not allowing Heidegger the last word. In fact, however, Heidegger attempted to "get the last word in" and thereby the "last laugh" when he forbade publication of the March 1966 interview with *Der Spiegel*, when he defended his earlier affiliation with the Nazi party, a tenacious defense he held onto until after his death.[20] But such an exchange and choice of defining laughter alternatively still does not address clearly enough the relationship of this event with my preoccupation with Rosenzweig.

In order to take into account the heritage of their works, with these Final Words I conclude by considering Rosenzweig's concept of the pagan Christian as a way to highlight what I have been calling the Rosenzweig/Heidegger divergence.[21]

Although Goethe's ideas play a critical role throughout Rosenzweig's *The Star of Redemption*, they serve as a pivotal touchstone for the culminating third part — as crucial as Nietzsche's idea-complex is for defining the direction of the Introduction to that text. Even though the Nietzsche idea-complex occurs as a focal point in the introduction to the whole work, as the culmination and sign of the disintegration of Western, Greek philosophy, that introduction also serves as the introduction to Part I. Similarly, the Goethe idea-complex formally occurs in the introduction to Part III, namely, that part whose sub-text is ostensibly ethics and the formative forces of community structures. In the section entitled "The Life of Goethe," Rosenzweig utilizes two conceptualizations to depict Goethe as a transitional figure in how modern humans have come to realize their power to act. This is also done within Rosenzweig's structure of defining the relatedness of secular, what Rosenzweig calls pagan, Jewish and Christian marks of identity and their respective roles in his presentation of an ideal model of reality. Those two conceptualizations have to do with fundamental human self-determination and Christian mission.

The two conceptualizations that Rosenzweig uses to crystallize the role of Goethe in his context are, first of all, a line from an early Goethe poem, "*Hoffnung*" which means "Hope" — and is thus future-oriented, but which Rosenzweig identifies as a prayer.[22] The lines he includes are: "Labor of my hands that I / finish, grant oh Fortune high." Rosenzweig immediately distinguishes such a prayer to one's own fate [as fortune] from that attributed to Moses in Ps. 90.1–17 and Ps. 65.3. In Psalm 90, Moses prays to God a prayer based on his belief in the redemptive power of god to change the human condition, which begins:

Lord you have been
our refuge age after age.

Before the mountains were born,
before the earth or the world came to birth,
you were god from all eternity and for ever.

and which ends:

May the sweetness of the Lord be on us! / Make all we do succeed.

While Ps. 65.3 is a hymn of thanksgiving it is also based on the power of god. It reads:

All flesh must come to you / with all its sins; / though our faults overpower us, / you blot them out.

However, Goethe's prayer is a petitional one which offers the "work of his own hands" at the "feet of his own good fortune." Furthermore, Goethe's prayer is one of *hope*, that he be able to complete this work himself. In other words, it is a prayer of hope by Goethe directed to his own fate and is one, notes Rosenzweig, that Goethe continually repeated over the course of his lifetime until he achieved a visible and concrete fulfillment in the corpus of his work.

Significantly, however, it is not a prayer prayed to represent all of humanity, which Rosenzweig, following Psalm 65, refers to as "all flesh." Rather, it is a prayer *of* one solitary, isolated individual *to* himself, alone, that is, to his own personal fate. As Rosenzweig more specifically points out, it is a prayer *in* one's own fate — a self-enclosed prayer prayed to no one else than to one's own self and to one's own fate: "He is concerned only that whatever comes should merge in his life, that he be privileged to offer up all in the sanctuary of his own fate, own as well as alien, alien as well as own."[23] Such a prayer, moreover, is one that does not consider the other, i.e. a prayer that results from an egotism like that of Faust's in Goethe's revival of the old, Germanic folk tale. Furthermore, it is very similar to Heidegger's notion of appropriation *in* one's own ethos, as I will briefly discuss below.[24]

In other words, Goethe's prayer is in a sense radically exclusionistic, which was also the meta-ethical conclusion of Nietzsche and which pushes that philosopher beyond the conventional limits of good and evil. In Rosenzweig's framework, Nietzsche, in the guise of Zoroaster, stands for the sinner and fanatic — that one who not only smashes all the old tablets, thereby breaking all traditional ethical rules, but also represents he who also acts as a tyrant in over-powering one's neighbor (as an over-coming) to be eternally reaching for the next-but-one.

Rosenzweig tells us that, like Nietzsche, Goethe had no faith in the past, as he had no love for the neighbor in the present. After rejecting love for Gretchen in the present, Faust does not consummate a relationship with Helen and beauty, in the past. But like Faust, Goethe does successfully trust, and thereby hope, in his own feet, succeeding thereby in becoming a "pure son of the earth." What it means to be a "pure son of the earth" (Rosenzweig refers to him as an *Erdensohn*) is to become one with the processes of the world and, consequently, to be able to identify with the "pagan," or "unredeemed" element(s) of the world, which is likewise to be beyond good and evil. For Rosenzweig, to redeem means to vitalize, to bring to life, which Goethe does on one level with his pagan vitality, but fails to do on another level; namely, that of freeing the human from the bonds of earth structures to relate freely, that is, to relate responsibly, with other humans.

In an earlier writing, the "Germ-cell,"[25] Rosenzweig claimed that Goethe's union with Fichte and Schelling enabled universal philosophy to become reconciled with national culture that then is exemplified in the professorial fusion of human culture, national spirit, and academics in Hegel. With Goethe, the speech of the poet embodied the thought of such professorial thinkers. Indeed, after Schiller and Goethe, Germany becomes a world power, as German spirit is united in the German professor who viewed himself as the mediator between the world-spirit and their own folk. Significantly, Heidegger consciously adopted such a public, mediator role in his assumption of the Freiburg Rektorat, evidenced by his Rektorat speech, "The self-assertion of the German University."[26] This inflammatory speech also includes his much-debated and problematic association of education with labor and military.[27]

The other conceptualization that Rosenzweig attributes to Goethe is Goethe's own assessment of the course of his own life, as that life neared completion, by claiming "to be, in his time, perhaps the only remaining Christian as Christ himself would have had a Christian be."[28] According to Rosenzweig, by uttering such a dictum, Goethe was fusing the mark of Christianity — total submission and subjection to the life of Christ, an other, with Goethe's apparent, and complete, pagan vitality. Rosenzweig goes on to claim that the imitation of the life of Christ is inexorably tied to the creation and redemption of the whole world as the core of Trinitarian dogma. Briefly, what it means to be a Christian, then, is to be involved as an individual in redemptive activity of the world by re-creating the world or re-newing the world consonant with the work of creation. Such activity entails liberating other individuals through revelatory acts of love.

In support of Rosenzweig's contention, Goethe's life was marked by 60 years of prodigious creative activity and literary production which led to his total immersion in human social life in the world, artistically, scientifically, and politically. As I mentioned earlier, he forged himself into the first modern German literary master to attain international prestige, which, by the end of the nineteenth century, led to the formation of a certain German kind of national self-confidence.[29] In fact, at the end of his career, Goethe even attempted a globally encompassing, synthetic-poetic bridge of East and West with his collection of poems, *Der West-Östliche Divan*, poems emulating a Persian style which nonetheless remains essentially German.

To situate Goethe in his framework as the exemplary pagan-Christian, Rosenzweig utilizes a Hegelian dialectic of Christianity, in order to characterize the historical trajectory of Christianity as an ongoing confrontation with paganism. Accordingly, Christianity forms a tripartite dialectical development, whose formative structures continue to function in current Christian dynamics as missionary activity. He identifies these structures as: Petrine, Pauline, and Johanine each of which is respectfully associated with both temporal and existential characteristics, namely, body-soul-body/soul; external-internal-synthesis; present-past-future; love-faith-hope. The Petrine or Patristic structure constitutes the ongoing confrontation and missionizing activity with the *external* pagan, through a relationship of love of the external other. Scholastic Christianity constitutes the confrontation of the internal pagan, that is, of the memory of the pagan spirit whereby the soul gives up its entire content of memory and receives back faith, and consequently results in the dual truth of reason and faith. Protestantism took this confrontation with paganism a step further by overcoming the reason/faith duality and by working on the conversion of the human form within the soul itself. Such concentration on the soul itself led through German Idealism to Pietism as an answer by mainline Protestants of the logical need, in response to the Enlightenment and religious toleration/liberation, to dispense with proselytizing. This then inevitably led to the death of that form of Christianity.

The remaining problem, however, was that the body and soul were still seen to be separate entities resulting in the substance problematic which, in turn, led to the embodied spirituality of the Russian, Johanine form of Christianity. Such a form answered the need to fuse the way of the world with the life of Christ, accomplished by spiritually devout, Christian individuals immersed in the ways of the world, such as Alyosha Karamazov and Goethe. Because he represents the culmination of such dialectical forces, Rosenzweig asserts that "Goethe is truly the great heathen and the great Christian at one and the same time. He is the one by being the other."[30] He is so because, "In the prayer to his own fate, the human is at one and the same time domiciled within one's self and — by virtue of that very fact — also entirely at home in the world.[31]

However, with Goethe, all the people of the worldly orders now pray the modern prayer to their own fate, that is, they have their own unique, isolated parts to play in the process of the course of the world. For Rosenzweig, the pagan Christian is, therefore, one who has not only wed oneself to the workings of the world but is also one who is convinced of and committed to the task that such work/activity/deed is a radically individual task, achieved through transforming the world through ongoing continual acts of recreation in one's ownmost, authentic self-image, that is, through ethnic self-assertion. Consequently, Rosenzweig notes that a new tablet is erected which warns "every traveler who has ascended the ridge not to retrace Goethe's steps on Goethe's path," like Goethe, hopefully trusting in the "tread" of one's own feet — without faith in or love for any other, but nonetheless hope in one's own future.[32]

But isn't this precisely what Heidegger does? Despite, or perhaps because of Heidegger's rejection of Goethe's inheritance, both academic and philosophical, Heidegger nonetheless ascends the Goethean ridge by, in effect, rejecting all past and present — and likewise claiming that his work is of the future. In the end he confesses in the *Spiegel* interview that, "My thinking stands in a definitive relationship to the poetry of Hölderlin . . . For me Hölderlin is the poet who points to the future, who expects god . . ."[33] and continued to maintain that

National Socialism, as the contemporary reincarnation of the "ancient traditions of a 'thought,'" before its leaders fell short of its promise, pointed the way beyond the decadence of Western metaphysics, the absolutization of the subject and the power of global technology. With that 1966 interview, Heidegger persists in his attempt, even from the grave, to have the last word, and thereby the "last laugh." But is his the *best* laugh, or more ethically, a *good* laugh?

What I mean by the best has to do with a common definition of laughter, namely, that which expresses mirth, joy, merriment, gaiety, cheerfulness, pleasure and liveliness, perhaps even the kind of *joissance* Levinas claims is absent from Heidegger's entire body of work.[34] Such a primary occasion of enjoyment provides the occasion for that kind of human relationship that is able to affirm the other in their holistic development by meeting their need for expressing a desire that is other than my own. In other words, the *best* laugh is contingent upon that kind of relationship which takes the other most seriously as an other than me upon whom I have no right to exercise my will to will or to dominate, but towards whom I nonetheless stand in a responsibly responsive relationship.[35]

Rosenzweig's judgment on Goethe's limits can be effectively applied to the case of Heidegger. His judgment is that although Goethe achieves a necessary dimension, because of his pagan vitalization of the individual, of unifying body and soul, as one individual, and making it "ripe for eternity" through self-determination, the conclusion of his life remains ultimately tragic because of a skewed sense of social mission. He returns from Italy (and from the realm of the "Mothers" where he takes us earlier in *The Star*) to serve the emperor and thereby ultimately fails to help the mass of other humans by not recognizing that there is more to life than temporality, that there is eternity.[36] Karl Löwith, a former student and disciple of Heidegger, makes a similar assertion in one of the first, earliest, and sharpest critiques of Heidegger's philosophy in the twentieth century. For Rosenzweig this eternity can only be revealed in community which is demonstrated by the Jewish people who testify to the reality of eternity through their relationships with each other, expressing their faith in their god, and thereby forming a model of community that demonstrates social responsibility. Even more so than Goethe in the nineteenth century, Heidegger became the philosopher of temporality, the philosopher of "Existence," for the twentieth century. Unfortunately, Heidegger similarly yoked his philosophy to the leadership of his day, to the *Führer*, in assuming the public leadership of Freiburg University in 1933.[37] As we now know, he saw his task as a fateful one, leading the German people in a social mission to assume their ownmost, authentic, leadership position in the world.[38]

In his "Letter to the Rector of Freiburg University" seeking reinstatement to the Philosophy Faculty after the war, Heidegger defended his association with the NSDAP as motivated by spiritual and not racial concerns (explicitly rejecting Rosenberg's racist conception of spirit) and wanted to claim that he was only working to "save" the West from forces of the impossible and that the West rested on metaphysical foundations that undermined the authentic development of Da-sein, at first individual and then as a folk. However, despite claiming to work for and respect "differentiation," he saw his efforts as deploying the "power of spiritual legislation" to "transform the force of Da-sein which besieges them *into a single* spiritual world of the Volk."[39] Furthermore, in that fateful *Spiegel* interview of 31 May 1966, he reiterated his patriotic promotion of the same kind of "knowledge" which would transform students into an "organic unity" of a "people of labor to have certainty and faith in following the towering will of our Führer," that he called for in his earlier speeches as Rector.[40] And finally, with a paen to the labor of one's own hands, when asked how he could follow such an unintellectual leader as Hitler, Heidegger proclaimed: "Yes, but just look at those *hands*."[41]

There really is not very much distance connecting Rosenzweig's conception of the work of the modern pagan-Christian to what Heidegger envisioned that the work of modern National Socialism should be. And although Heidegger envisioned an individualized kind of National Socialism, he nonetheless consistently maintained that the Volk needed to be directed by a Führer. But such a Führer could not be a mere political leader; rather, the Volk need a savior to save them from their ordinariness and inability to free themselves from the evils of technology and consumerism. To the end of his life, and even beyond, Heidegger saw his unique role as that "voice crying in the wilderness," preparing for the way of the Second Coming of that savior. It seems, however, that the First Coming of the savior — in the guise of the Führer named Hitler — could not unify the Volk because they had been taught to pray the prayer to their own fate, without responsible regard for the fate of any other. What makes Heidegger's cynical voice echoing today beyond the grave any different than his political call from the podium as Rector, in 1933, to Heil Hitler?

Besides, who dares to laugh at the horrors of the Holocaust? But yet, doesn't Heidegger, with his highly nuanced philosophical revision, continue to laugh the laugh of ridicule and derision? With whom should we laugh to laugh best? Is his a good laugh?

In order not to allow Heidegger to once again have the last laugh and thus the last word, I conclude my remarks by returning to the set of questions with which I opened this book, but by way of some final reflections on the art of music and the ethical. The phenomenological difference between Rosenzweig and Heidegger is in their appreciation and lack of appreciation for music as a measure for grounding a process of communal relations that take seriously the demands of social justice. Rosenzweig presents his *midrash* on the Song of Songs as the aesthetic and ethical heart of his work. The relationship of the lover to the beloved, of the one with the other, is fraught with the unpredictable risk of unfaithfulness and spontaneous demands, but it is also the occasion for the establishment of trust, enjoyment of aroused desire, and the promise of fulfillment of needs and the continuation of unfulfilled desire. Moreover, the event is revelatory and provides the foundation for the growth not merely of the self out of its tragic self-centeredness, but of the possibility for heterogenous communities of difference, communities that, in their a-political self-identity provide the possibility for political critique. Heidegger, on the other hand, sees music as mushy and sea-like, based on his critique of Wagner's music as reducing art to just feeling and feeling as redemptive.[42] In music, art loses its function to isolate and individuate, that is, art always has to be subjected to a linguistic text, to poetry, as in *The Origin of the Work of Art*, and music, as art, is deficient in this way since it is incapable of facilitating dwelling and thus remains incapable of facilitating the *polis*. Music has to give way to a pre-existent text, to drama, but yet is ultimately incapable of giving birth to drama or to the pre-existent world.

For Rosenzweig, music is not a *Verschmelzung* of particulars and individuals but precisely depends upon cooperative practices that entail the cultivation and promotion of each member singing their own peculiar and thus *besondere* note at their own time, but in the context of a choral community. Moreover, music introduces us to the elements of social justice that depend upon answering the non-textual needs of members in this or that *polis*, in this or that actual community that dwell in houses and homes, or not, and that provide nourishment for themselves, or not. Feeding is justice, and a dwelling is the source of enjoyment and provides a horizon of opportunities to emerge to alleviate suffering. But dwelling is also insecure and exilic — a place to gather family and friends, and most importantly, to welcome strangers.[43] It is not the place to retreat in one's isolated waiting and individuality, bitter and disillusioned; rather, we dwell with others in this world and work for the sake of bringing the kind of enjoyment and nourishment that we have experienced to those suffering others who make up the greater part of the world and who are just as capable, and perhaps more so than I, to join in songs of joy and thanksgiving.

Notes

1 See Gordon 2005: 12, where he argues against situating Rosenzweig as some kind of an ethicist in order to make a political point. One of his more helpful comments is his insightful footnote detailing Rosenzweig's self-assessment of his work vis à vis Husserl's, who he met, and with a Husserlian. The salient point is Rosenzweig's comment about how Husserl "expects . . . chaos . . . [to be] a return to originality (this goes along with his 'phenomenology,' *which wants to return abstract and formalistic thinking to the simple and immediate "phenomenon.*)" [Rosenzweig's emphases]

2 See "Brief über den Humanismus," in WM: 313–65.

3 See "Only a God Can Save Us," in Wolin 1992: 7.

4 Such as Steve Best in his recent work in animal rights activism. However, he set

himself in this direction by his earlier work with Kellner in *The Postmodern Turn*. See Best 1997: 6–7, 28–9.

5 See "Only a God Can Save Us," in Wolin 1992: 9.
6 Ibid: 10.
7 Ibid: 11.
8 Ibid: 12.
9 Ibid: 13.
10 Ibid: 14.
11 Ibid: 15–16. Also, cf. Levinas's "Ethics and the Face" in Levinas 1969: 194–219.
12 Wolin 1992: 17–19.
13 Ibid: 21.
14 Ibid: 22.
15 Ibid. Also, on Gordon, see footnote 1.
16 See Safranski 1998. Of course, the italicized definite article is mine. Safranski uses the indefinite article.
17 See Wolin 1992: 159.
18 See "An Exchange of Letters: Herbert Marcuse and Martin Heidegger," in Wolin 1992: 152–64.
19 Habermas notes, "Heidegger's attitude to his own past *after* 1945 exemplifies a state of mind that persistently characterized the history of the Federal Republic until well into the sixties . . . we must inform ourselves of what Heidegger, to his death, repressed, glossed over and falsified." From Habermas, "Work and Weltanshauung," in Dreyfus 1992: 189.
20 Wolin 1992: 91–116. In the interview, Heidegger concurs that in 1933 he saw in Nazism a "new dawn" and even continued to maintain what he claimed in 1953, with the publication of *An Introduction to Metaphysics*, namely, that there was (and is!) an "inner truth and greatness of this movement" — as the "encounter between global technology and contemporary man." The interview is further significant in how it demonstrates Heidegger's unrelenting rejection of Western democracy because it creates consumerism and "tears men loose from the earth and uproots them." It creates more of the *they* and lessens the possibilities for authenticity. The only way to transform the present condition of the world is to prepare for a new "god," by thinking and poeticizing.
21 Contra Gordon 2005, Allan Udoff's "Rosenzweig's Heidegger Reception and the re-Origination of Jewish Thinking," in Schmied-Kowarzik 1988: 923–50, and Lyotard's attempt to justify Heidegger's philosophy as a philosophy of remembrance and of "difference" as a philosophy *for* the Jews as the forgotten *other* in the history of Western metaphysics, in Lyotard 1990.
22 For Rosenzweig, prayer is a relational speech–act.
23 GS2: 276.
24 For Heidegger's concept of appropriation, see esp. his essay "The Way to Language," in OWL: 111ff. Language as human activity becomes appropriating activity that becomes a monologue to reveal the isolated lonesomeness of self.
25 See "Urzelle des *Stern der Erlösung*," in GS3: 125ff.

26 See "The Self-Assertion of the German University" (delivered in 1933), in Wolin 1992: 29ff.

27 See: "Labor Service and the University" (20 June 1933), in Wolin 1992, an address published by the Freiburg Student Association, the official Nazi student organization, in the "Freiburger Studentzeitung." The opening lines read: "In the future, the *school* will no longer enjoy its exclusive position in education. With the *Labor Service*, there has arisen a new and decisive force for education [*Erziehungsmacht*]. The *work camp* is now taking its place alongside home, youth league, military service, and school" (42–3). Also, in that same issue and along similar lines, see "The Call to the Labor Service" and "National Socialist Education," (53–60).

28 GS2: 277.

29 See Gray 1967: 258.

30 GS2: 283.

31 Ibid.

32 Ibid: 286–7.

33 Wolin 1992: 110.

34 See Levinas 1969: 122–42.

35 John Haugeland evaluates Heidegger's conceptualization of Da-sein as holistic and responsible in his essay, "Da-sein's Disclosedness," in Dreyfus 1992: 27–44. However, his evaluation depends on reiterating Heidegger's own rather obvious view that responsibility is not ethical but is rather functionally oriented. The kind of responsibility that I have in mind is that which Rosenzweig initially conceptualizes in *The Star of Redemption* (Part II, Book 2) through his concept of revelation and which Levinas takes up and concentrates as the core of his own ethical philosophy (in his two central works: *Totality and Infinity* and also in *Otherwise Than Being*).

36 See "Martin Heidegger und Franz Rosenzweig. Ein Nachtrag zu *Sein und Zeit*," in Löwith 1960: 68–92.

37 See esp. Heidegger's acceptance speech of the Rectorship, "The Self-Assertion of the German University" where he yokes together "labor service, military service, and knowledge service," in Wolin 1992: 36.

38 Especially in response to the two great "pincers" of communism and capitalism, Russia and America. Even as late as his interview with *Der Spiegel*, in "Only a God Can Save Us," Heidegger still assigns a "special task to the Germans." In keeping with his "dialogue with Hölderlin" begun 30 years earlier! Heidegger saw the Germans in linguistic connection with the Greeks, against technology, consumerism, pragmatism, and rationality. He sought in the untranslatable, poetic ground of being the key for the "turn" away from "authoritative assertions" in his advocacy for the advent of the saving god. See Wolin 1992: 107.

39 "Letter to the Rector of Freiburg University," in Wolin 1992: 63.

40 Ibid: 60.

41 Ibid.

42 See Young 2001: 168.

43 My reference to Levinas's philosophy of the priority of the ethical should be evident.

BIBLIOGRAPHY

Primary Works by Martin Heidegger

BP   Heidegger, Martin. *Beiträge zur Philosophie: Vom Ereignis* (Band 65 der Gesamtausgabe). Herausgegeben von Friedrich-Wilhelm von Herman. Frankfurt am Main: Vittorio Klostermann GmBH, 1994 (erste Auflage 1989).

EHD   *Erläuterung zu Hölderlins Dichtung* (Band 4 der Gesamtausgabe). Herausgegeben von Friedrich-Wilhelm von Herman. Frankfurt am Main: Vittorio Klostermann GmBH, 1996 (erste Auflage 1944).

EM   *Einfuhrung in die Metaphysik.* Tübingen: Max Niemeyer Verlag, 1953.

GSh   *Die Geschichte des Seyns* (Band 69 der Gesamtausgabe). Herausgegeben von Peter Trawny. Frankfurt am Main: Vittorio Klostermann GmBH, 1998.

HHA   *Hölderlins Hymne "Andenken"* (Band 52 der Gesamtausgabe). Herausgegeben von Curd Ochwadt, Frankfurt am Main: Vittorio Klostermann, 1982.

HHG   *Hölderlins Hymnen "Germanien" und "Der Rhein": WS 1934/35* (Band 39 der Gesamtausgabe). Herausgegeben von Susanne Ziegler. Frankfurt am Main: Vittorio Klostermann GmBH, 1999 (erste Auflage 1980).

HHId   *Hölderlins Hymne "Der Ister": SS 1942* (Band 53 der Gesamtausgabe). Herausgegeben von Walter Biemel. Frankfurt am Main: Vittorio Klostermann GmBH, 1993 (erste Auflage 1984).

HW   *Holzwege* (Band 5 der Gesamtausgabe). Herausgegeben von Friedrich-Wilhelm von Herman. Frankfurt am Main: Vittorio Klostermann GmBH, 1994 (erste Auglage, 1950).

Nd   *Nietzsche I und II* (Band 6.1 und 6.2 der Gesamtausgabe). Stuttgart: Klett-Cotta Verlag, 2008 (7. Auflage).

Pd   *Parmenides: WS 1942/43* (Band 54 der Gesamtausgabe). Herausgegeben von Manfred S. Frings. Frankfurt am Main: Vittorio Klostermann GmBH, 1992 (erste Auflage 1982).

SZ   *Sein und Zeit.* Tübingen: Max Niemeyer Verlag, 1986 (zuerst erchienen als Sonderdruck aus *"Jahrbuch für Philosophie und phänomenologische Forschung"* Band VIII herausgegeben von Edmund Husserl, 19vxvx27).

UWS   *Unterwegs zur Sprache.* Stuttgart: Verlag Günther Neske, 1997 (erste Auflage 1959).

WM *Wegmarken* (Band 9 der Gesamtausgabe). Herausgegeben von Friedrich-Wilhelm von Herman. Frankfurt am Main: Vittorio Klostermann GmBH, 1996 (erste Auflage, 1967).

Translations of primary works of Martin Heidegger

BT *Being and Time.* Joan Stambaugh (trans.). Albany: State University of New York Press, 1996.

EHP *Elucidations of Hölderlin's Poetry.* Keith Hoeller (trans.). Amherst, NY: Humanity Books.

HHIe *Hölderlin's Hymn "The Ister."* William McNeil and Julia Davis (trans). Bloomington, IN: Indiana University Press, 1996.

IM Heidegger, Martin. *An Introduction to Metaphysics.* Ralph Manheim (trans.). New Haven and London: Yale University Press, 1987 (original publication: Tübingen: Max Niemeyer Verlag, 1953).

Ne1 *Nietzsche: Volumes One and Two.* David Farrell Krell (ed.). San Francisco, CA: HarperCollins, 1991.

Ne3 *Nietzsche: Volumes Three and Four.* David Farrell Krell (ed.). San Francisco, CA: HarperCollins, 1991.

OWL *On the Way to Language.* Peter D. Hertz (trans.). San Francisco, CA: HarperCollins, 1971.

Pe *Parmenides.* Andre Schuwer (trans.). Indianapolis, IN: Indiana University Press, 1992.

PLT *Poetry, Language, Thought.* Albert Hofstadter (trans.). New York: Harper and Row, Publishers, 1971.

QCT *The Question Concerning Technology and Other Essays.* Introduction by William Lovitt (trans.). New York: Harper & Row Publishers, 1977.

Primary Works by Franz Rosenzweig

BGK Rosenzweig, Franz. *Das Buchlein Vom Gesunden Und Kranken Menschenverstand.* Herausgegeben und Eingeleitet von Nahum Norbert Glatzer. Frankfurt am Main: Judischer Verlag, 1992 (erste Auflage, 1922).

GB *Die Gritli-Briefe: Briefe an Margrit Rosenstock-Huessy.* Herausgegeben von Inken Rühle und Reinhold Mayer. Mit einem Vorwort von Rafael Rosenzweig. Tübingen: Bilam Verlag, 2002.

GS1 *Der Mensch und sein Werk. Gesammelte Schriften 1: Briefe und Tagebücher 1.* (Band 1918–1929), 2. (Band 1918–1929). Herausgegeben von Rachel Rosenzweig und Edith Rosenzweig-Scheinman. The Hague: Martinus Nijhof, 1979.

GS2 *Der Mensch und sein Werk. Gesammelte Schriften 2: Der Stern Der Erlösung.* Herausgegeben von Annemarie Mayer und Reinhold Mayer. The Hague: Martinus Nijhof, 1976.

GS3 *Der Mensch und sein Werk. Gesammelte Schriften 3: Zweistromland,*

Kleinere Schriften zu Glauben und Denken. Herausgegeben von Annemarie Mayer und Reinhold Mayer. The Hague: Martinus Nijhof, 1984.
GS4₁   *Der Mensch und sein Werk. Gessamelte Schriften 4: Sprachdenken im Übersetzen* 1. (Band Hymnen und Gedichte des Jehuda Halevi). Herausgegeben von Rafael N. Rosenzweig. The Hague: Martinus Nijhof, 1983.
GS4₂   *Der Mensch und sein Werk. Gessamelte Schriften 4: Sprachdenken im Übersetzen* 2. (Band Arbeitspapiere zur Verdeutschung der Schrift). Herausgegeben von Rachel Bat-Adam. Dordrecht: Martinus Nijhof, 1984.
HS   *Hegel und der Staat*. Aalen: Scientia Verlag, 1982 (erste Auflage 1920).

Translations of primary works of Franz Rosenzweig

NT   *Franz Rosenzweig's "the New Thinking."* Barbara E. Galli (with an introductory essay) and Alan Udoff (with a concluding essay) (eds). Syracuse, NY: Syracuse University Press, 1999.
OJL   *On Jewish Learning*. Nahum N. Glatzer (ed.). Madison, WI: University of Wisconsin Press, 2002.
PTW   Rosenzweig, Franz. *Franz Rosenzweig: Philosophical and Theological Writings*. Paul W. Franks and Michael L. Morgan (eds). Indianapolis, IN: Hackett Publishing Company, 2000.
SR   *The Star of Redemption*. William W. Hallo (trans.). Notre Dame: University of Notre Dame Press, 1985.
USH   *Understanding the Sick and Healthy*. Nahum Glatzer (ed.) and with an Introduction by Hilary Putnam. Cambridge, MA: University of Harvard Press, 1999.

Additional References

Aczel, Amir D. *The Mystery of the Aleph: Mathematics, the Kabbalah, and the Search for Infinity*. New York and London: Four Walls Eight Windows, 2000.
Adorno, Theodor. *Negative Dialectics*. E. B. Ashton (trans.). London and New York: Routledge, 1990 (original publication: *Negative Dialektik*. Frankfurt am Main: Suhrkamp Verlag, 1966).
Althaus, Horst. *Hegel: An Intellectual Biography*. Michael Tarsh (trans.). Cambridge, UK: Polity Press, 2000 (original publication: *Hegel und die heroischen Jahre der Philosophie*. München: Carl Hanser Verlag, 1992).
Anckaert, Luc with Brasser. Martin and Samuelson, Norbert (eds). *The Legacy of Franz Rosenzweig*. Leuven: Leuven University Press, 2004.
Appiah, Kwame. *Experiments in Ethics*. Cambridge, MA: Harvard University Press, 2008.
Arendt, Hannah. *The Origins of Totalitarianism*. Orlando: Harcourt Brace, 1973.
Aristotle. *The Basic Works of Aristotle*. Richard McKeon (ed.). New York: Random House, 1941.

Austin, J. L. *Philosophical Papers*. Oxford: Oxford University Press, 1961.

Ayer, A.J., editor. *Logical Positivism*. New York: The Free Press, 1959.

Bambach, Charles R. *Heidegger, Dilthey, and the Crisis of Historicism*. Ithaca and London: Cornell University Press, 1995.

Barbour, Ian. *Religion in an Age of Science*. New York: Harper & Row, 1990.

Batnitzky, Leora. *Idolatry and Representation: The Philosophy of Franz Rosenzweig Reconsidered*. Princeton, NJ: Princeton University Press, 2009.

Bauer, Ann Elisabeth. *Rosenzweig's Sprachdenken im "Stern der Erlösung und in seiner Korrespondenz mit Martin Buber zur Verdeutschung der Schrift."* Frankfurt am Main: Peter Lang, 1992.

Benjamin, Walter. *Illuminationen: Ausgewählte Schriften 1*. Frankfurt am Main: Suhrkamp, 1977.

—*Walter Benjamin: Selected Writings, Volume 4: 1938–1940*. Howard Eiland and Michael W. Jennings (eds). Cambridge, MA and London: Belknap Press, 2003.

Benso, Silvia. *The Face of Things: A Different Side of Ethics*. Albany, NY: State University of New York Press, 2000.

Best, Steven and Kellner, Douglas. *The Postmodern Turn*. New York and London: Guilford Press, 1997.

Bienenstock, Myriam. *Cohen face à Rosenzweig: Débat sur la Pensée Allemande*. Paris: Vrin, 2009.

Buber, Martin. *I and Thou*. Walter Kaufmann (trans.). New York: Charles Scribner's Sons, 1970.

—*Das Dialogische Prinzip*. Heidelberg: Verlag Lambert Schneider, 1985.

Caputo, John D. *The Mystical Element in Heidegger's Thought*. Athens, OH: Ohio University Press, 1978.

Casper, Bernhard. *Das Dialogische Denken: Eine Untersuchung der Religionsphilosophischen Bedeutung Franz Rosenzweigs, Ferdinand Ebners und Martin Bubners*. Freiburg: Herder Verlag, 1967.

Cohen, Hermann. *Logik der reinen Erkenntnis*. Hildesheim: Georg Olms Verlag, 1977 (erste Auflage, 1914).

Cohen, Richard A. *Elevations*. Chicago: The University of Chicago Press, 1994.

Dallmayr, Fred. *The Other Heidegger*. Ithaca: Cornell University Press, 1993.

Davies, Paul. *The Cosmic Blueprint*. New York: Simon & Schuster, 1988.

Descartes, René. *Descartes' Philosophical Writings*. Norman Kemp Smith (trans.). New York: Random House, 1958.

Desmond, William (ed.). *Hegel & His Critics: Philosophy in the Aftermath of Hegel*. Albany: State University of New York Press, 1989.

Dilthey, Wilhelm. *Selected Works: Volume III: The Formation of the Historical World in the Human Sciences*. Rudolf A. Makkreel and Frithjof Rodi (eds). Princeton, NJ: Princeton University Press, 2002.

—*Selected Works, Volume IV: Hermeneutics and the Study of History*. Rudolf A. Makkreel and Frithjof Rodi (eds). Princeton, NJ: Princeton University Press, 2010.

Dreyfus, Hubert L. "Between *Techne* and Technology: The Ambiguous Place of Equipment in *Being and Time*," *Tulane Studies in Philosophy*, (1984), 32: 233–5.

—*Being-in-the-World: A Commentary on Heidegger's Being and Time, Division I*. Cambridge, MA: MIT Press, 1991.

Dreyfus, Hubert L. and Hall, Harrison. *Heidegger: A Critical Reader.* Oxford, UK: Blackwell Publishing, 1992.

Düttman, Alexander. *The Gift of Language: memory and promise in Adorno, Benjamin, Rosenzweig, and Heidegger.* New York: Continuum, 2000.

Einstein, Albert. *Relativity. The Special and General Theory.* New York: Crown Publisher, 1961.

Epictetus. *"Discourses of Epictetus" in The Stoic and Epicurean Philosophers.* Whitney J. Oates (ed.). New York: Random House, 1940.

Etymylogisches Wörterbuch des Deutschen. München: Deutschen Taschenbuch Verlag, 1993.

Euclid. *The Thirteen Books of Euclid's Elements.* Thomas L. Heath (trans.). New York: Dover Publications, 1956.

Fackenheim, Emil. *Encounters Between Judaism and Modern Philosophy.* Philadelphia, PA: Jewish Publication Society, 1973.

—*To Mend the World: Foundations of Future Jewish Thought.* Bloomington, IL and Indianapolis, IN: Indiana University Press, 1994 (first published by Schocken Books, 1982).

Falk, Marcia. *The Song of Songs: A New Translation and Interpretation.* San Francisco, CA: Harper, 1990.

Farias, Victor. *Heidegger and Nazism.* Paul Burrell and Gabriel Ricci (trans.). Forward by Joseph Margolis and Tom Rockmore (eds). Philadelphia, PA: Temple University Press, 1989.

Fichte, Johann Gottlieb. *The Science of Knowledge.* A. E. Kroeger (trans.). London: Trubner & Co., 1889.

—*Wissenschaftslehre nova methodo (1798/99).* Herausgegeben von Eric Fuchs. Hamburg: Felix Meiner Verlag, 1982.

Foti, Veronique. *Heidegger and the Poets: poēsis/sophia/technē.* Atlantic Highlands, NJ: Humanities Press, 1992.

Fox, M. V. *The Song of Songs and the Ancient Egyptian Love Songs.* Madison, WI: University of Wisconsin Press, 1985.

Frege, Gottlob. *The Foundations of Arithmetic: a logico-mathematical enquiry into the concept of number.* J. L. Austin (trans.). Oxford: Blackwell, 1950.

—*Die Grundlagen der Arithmetik: eine logisch mathematische Untersuchung.* Hamburg: Felix Meiner Verlag, 1986.

Freund, Else. *Die Existenzphilosophie Franz Rosenzweig's: Ein Beitrag zur Analyse seines Werkes Der Stern der Erlösung.* Hamburg: Felix Meiner, 1929.

—*Franz Rosenzweig's Philosophy of Existence.* The Hague: Martinus Nijhof, 1979.

Gadamer, Hans-Georg. *Hegel's Dialectic. Five Hermeneutical Studies.* Christopher P. Smith (trans.). New Haven, CT and London: Yale University Press, 1976.

—*Truth and Method.* New York: Crossroad Publishing Co., 1985.

Galli, Barbara. *Franz Rosenzweig and Judah Halevi.* Montreal, QC and Kingston: McGill-Queen's University Press, 1995.

Gibbs, Robert, *Correlations in Rosenzweig and Levinas.* Princeton, NJ: Princeton University Press, 1992.

—*Why Ethics? Signs of Responsibility.* Princeton, NJ: Princeton University Press, 2000.

Glatzer, Nahum. *Franz Rosenzweig: His Life and Thought*. Indianapolis, IN: Hackett Publishing, 1998 (first published: New York: Schocken, 1961).

Gleick, James. *Chaos. Making a New Science*. New York: Penguin Books, 1987.

Gödel, Kurt. *Gödel's Theorem in Focus*. S. G. Shanker (ed.). New York: Croom Helm, 1988.

Goethe, J. W. "Faust: Eine Tragödie": *J. W. Goethe Werke in Zwei Bänden*. München: Dromershe, 1957.

Gordis, Robert. *The Song of Songs: A Study, Modern Translation, and Commentary*. New York, Ktav, 1974.

Gordon, Peter. *Rosenzweig and Heidegger: Between Judaism and German Philosophy*. Berkeley, CA: University of California Press, 2005.

Görtz, Heinz-Jürgen. *Tod und Erfahrung: Rosenzweigs erfahrende Philosophie und Hegels Wissenschaft der Erfahrung des Bewusstsein*. Düsseldorf: Patmos, 1984.

Gray, Ronald. *Goethe: A Critical Introduction*. Cambridge, UK: Cambridge University Press, 1967.

Guerrière, Daniel. *Phenomenology of the Truth Proper to Religion*. Albany, NY: State University of New York Press, 1990.

Guttmann, Julius. *Philosophies of Judaism*. New York: Holt, Rinehart, & Winston, 1964.

Habermas, Jürgen. *Nachmetaphysisches Denken*. Frankfurt: Suhrkamp, 1988.

Harman, Graham. *Tool-Being: Heidegger and the Metaphysics of Objects*. Chicago: Open Court, 2002.

Harris, Errol, E. *Cosmos and Anthropos*. Atlantic Highlands: Humanities Press International, 1991.

—*Cosmos and Theos*. Atlantic Highlands: Humanities Press International, 1992.

Hatab, Lawrence J. *Ethics and Finitude: Heideggarian Contributions to Moral Philosophy*. Boston, MA: Rowman and Littlefield Publishers, 2000.

Hegel, Georg Wilhelm Friedrich. *Ästhetik: Band I und Band II*. Herausgegeben von Friedrich Bassenge und mit einer Einführung von Georg Lukacs. Frankfurt am Main: Europäische Verlagsanstalt GmbH, 1955 (erste Auflage, 1935).

—*Grundlinien der Philosophie des Rechts*. Stuttgart: Reclam Verlag, 1970 (erste Auflage, 1821).

—*Phenomenology of Spirit*. A. V. Miller (trans.) with analysis of the text and Foreword by J. N. Findlay. Oxford, UK and New York: Oxford University Press, 1977.

—*Phänomenologie des Geistes*. Stuttgart: Reclam Verlag, 2009 (erste Auflage, 1807).

Heintel, Erich, (ed.). *Sprachphilosophie: Ausgewählte Schriften*. Hamburg: Felix Meiner Verlag, 1960.

Heisenberg, Werner. *Physikalische Prinzipien der Quantentheorie*. Stuttgart: S. Hirzel Verlag, 1958.

—*Ordnung der Wirklichkeit*. München: Piper, 1989.

Herder, Johann Gottfried. *Lieder der Liebe*. München: Süddeutsche Zeitung Neue Produkte, 2007 (erste Auflage, Leipzig, 1778).

Hesiod. *Hesiod and Theogonis*. Tanslated by Dorothea Wender. Harmondsworth/ Middlesex: Penguin Books, 1973.

Hilbert, David. *The Foundations of Geometry*, Chicago: The Open Court Publishing Co., 1902.

Hofstadter, Douglas R. *Gödel, Escher, Bach: An Eternal Golden Braid*. New York: Vintage Press, 1980.

Holtz, Barry. *Back to the Sources. Reading the Classical Jewish Texts*. New York: Summit Books, 1984.

Houlgate, Stephen. *Hegel, Nietzsche and the Criticism of Metaphysics*. Cambridge, UK: Cambridge University Press, 1986.

Hume, David. *An Enquiry Concerning Human Understanding*. Indianapolis, IN: Hackett Press, 1976.

Husserl, Edmund. *Ideas: General Introduction to Pure Phenomenology*. W. R. Boyce Gibson (trans.). New York: Collier Books, 1931.

—*Logische Untersuchungen: Elemente einer phänomenologischen Aufklärung der Erkenntnis, II/2*. Tübingen: Max Niemeyer Verlag, 1980a (erste Auflage, 1901).

—*Logische Untersuchungen: Prolegomena zur reinen Logik I*. Tübingen: Niemeyer, 1980b (erste Auflage, 1900).

—*Logische Untersuchungen: Untersuchungen zur Phänomenolgie und Theorie der Erkenntnis*. Tübingen: Niemeyer, 1980c (erste Auflage, 1901).

—*The Essential Husserl: Basic Writings in Transcendental Philosophy*. Donn Welton (ed.). Bloomington, IL and Indianapolis, IN: Indiana University Press, 1999.

Ingram, David. *Critical Theory and Philosophy*. New York: Paragon, 1990.

Johnson, Neil. *Simply Complexity: A Clear Guide to Complexity Theory*. Oxford, UK: Oneworld Publications, 2009.

Kant, Immanuel. *Critique of Judgment*. J. H. Bernard (trans.). New York: Hafner Press, 1951.

—*On History*. Lewis White Beck, Robert E. Anchor, and Emil L. Fackenheim (trans). Indianapolis, IN: Bobbs-Merrill Educational Publishing, 1963.

—*Critique of Pure Reason*. Norman Kemp Smith (trans.). New York: St. Martin's Press, 1965.

—*Kritik der Praktischen Vernunft* and *Grundlegung zur Methaphysik der Sitten*. Frankfurt am Main: Suhrkamp Verlag, 1974a.

—*Kritik der Urteilskraft*. Frankfurt: Suhrkamp Verlag, 1974b.

—*Kritik der reinen Vernunft 1 & 2*. Frankfurt am Main: Suhrkamp Verlag, 1974c.

—*Foundations of the Methaphysics of Morals*. Lewis White Beck (trans.). Upper Saddle River, NJ: Prentice Hall, 1989 (first published 1959).

Kaplan, Lawrence and Robinson, Ira. *The Thought of Maimonides: Philosophical and Legal Studies*. Julien Bauer (ed.). Lewiston: Edwin Mellen Press, 1991.

Katz, Stephen T. *Jewish Philosophers*. New York: Bloch Publishing, 1975.

Kierkegaard, Søren. *Concluding Unscientific Postscript*. David F. Swenson and Walter Lowrie (trans). Princeton, NJ: Princeton University Press, 1941.

—*Fear and Trembling* and *The Sickness Unto Death*. Walter Lowrie (trans). Princeton, NJ and London: Princeton University Press, 1944.

Kline, Morris. *Mathematics and the Search for Knowledge*. Oxford: Oxford University Press, 1985.

Lévinas, Emmanuel. *Totality and Infinity: An Essay on Exteriority*. Alphonso Lingis

(trans.). Pittsburgh, PA: Duquesne University Press, 1969 (first published: The
Hague: Martinus Nijhoff, 1961).

—*The Theory of Intuition in Husserl's Phenomenology*. Evanston, IL: Northwestern
University Press, 1973 (original publication: *Théorie de l'intuition dans la
phénomenlologie de Husserl*. Paris: Librairie Philosophique J. Vrin, 1963).

—*Otherwise than Being or Beyond Essence*. Alphonso Lingis (trans.). Pittsburgh, PA:
Duquesne University Press, 2000 (first publication: Kluwer Academic Publishers,
1981).

—*The Levinas Reader*. Sean Hand (ed.). Hoboken, NJ: Wiley-Blackwell, 2001.

Lowe, Victor. *Understanding Whitehead*. Baltimore, MD: Johns Hopkins Press, 1962.

Löwith, Karl. "M. Heidegger and F. Rosenzweig or Temporality and Eternity,"
Philosophy and Phenomenological Research. (1942) 3, 1: 53–77.

—*Heidegger: Denker in dürftiger Zeit*. Frankfurt am Main: S. Fischer, 1953.

—*Gesammelte Abhandlungen Zur Kritik der geschichtlichen Existenz*. Stuttgart:
Kolhammer, 1960.

Luhman, Niklas. *Law as a Social System*. Klaus A. Ziegert (trans.). Oxford/New
York: Oxford University Press, 2004.

Lyotard, Jean-François. *The Postmodern Condition: A Report on Knowledge*. Geoff
Bennington and Brian Masummi (trans) with a Foreward by Fredric Jameson.
Minneapolis, MN: University of Minnesota Press, 1984.

—*Heidegger and the Jews*. Andreas Michel and Mark Roberts (trans). Minneapolis:
University of Minnesota Press, 1990.

Maimonides, Moses. *The Guide of the Perplexed. Volumes I and II*. S. Pines (trans.).
Chicago: University of Chicago Press, 1963.

—*A Maimonides Reader*. Isadore Twersky (ed.). New York: Behrman House, 1972.

Marx, Werner. *Toward a Phenomenological Ethics*. Albany, NY: State University of
New York Press, 1992.

Mendes-Flohr, Paul, (ed.). *The Philosophy of Franz Rosenzweig*. Hanover and
London: University Press of New England, 1988.

Moran, Dermott. *Introduction to Phenomenology*. New York: Routledge, 2000.

Mosès, Stephane. *Systeme et Revelation. La Philosophie de Franz Rosenzweig*. Seuil:
Collection Esprit, 1982.

—*System and Revelation: Philosophy of Franz Rosenzweig*. Catherine Tihanyi
(trans.) and Foreword by Emmanuel Levinas. Detroit, MI: Wayne State University
Press. 1992

Murdoch, Iris. *Metaphysics as a Guide to Morals*. New York: Penguin, 1993.

Murphy, R. E. *The Song of Songs: A Commentary on the Book of Canticles or the
Song of Songs*. Minneapolis, MN: Fortress Press, 1990.

Newton, Isaac. *Philosophiae Naturalis Principia Mathematica*. London:
G. Brookman, 1833.

—*Newton's Principia. A Revision of Motte's Translation*. Florian Cojori (ed.).
Berkeley, CA: University of California Press, 1946.

Nietzsche, Friedrich. *Thus Spoke Zarathustra*. Walter Kaufmann (trans.).
Harmondsworth/Middlesex: Penguin Books, 1966.

—*Twilight of the Idols and The Anti-Christ*. R. A. Hollingdale (trans.).
Harmondsworth/Middlesex: Penguin Books, 1968.

—"Götzendämmerung" (179–184) and "Umwertung Aller Werte. Vorwort und Erstes Buch: Der AntiChrist" (185–290), *Friedrich Nietzsche Werke* (Band 5). Leipzig: Alfred Kroner Verlag, 1980a.

—"Also Sprach Zarathustra," *Friedrich Nietzsche Werke* (Band 4). Leipzig: Alfred Kroner Verlag, 1980b.

—*On the Advantage and Disadvantage of History for Life*. Peter Haas (trans). Indianapolis, IN: Hackett, 1980c.

Origen. *On First Principles — Origen*. G. W. Butterworth (trans.). New York: Harper & Row, 1966.

Pappus. *The Commentary of Pappus on The Tenth Book of Euclid*. William Thomson (trans.). Cambridge, MA: Harvard University Press, 1930.

Peitgen, Heinz-Otto and Richter, Peter H. *The Beauty of Fractals*. Berlin: Springer-Verlag, 1986.

Plotinus. *The Essential Plotinus*. E. Obrien (trans.). Indianapolis, IN: Hackett Press, 1964.

Pollock, Benjamin. *Franz Rosenzweig and the Systematic Task of Philosophy*. Cambridge, UK: Cambridge University Press, 2009.

Pope, Marvin. *The Song of Songs: A New Translation with Introduction and Commentary*. New York: Doubleday, 1977.

Risser, James, (ed.). *Heidegger Toward the Turn: Essays on the Work of the 1930s*. Albany, NY: State University of New York Press, 1999.

Rosen, Michael. *Hegel's Dialectic and its Criticism*. Cambridge, UK: Cambridge University Press, 1982.

Russell, Bertrand and Whitehead, Alfred North. *Principia Mathematica*. Cambridge, UK: Cambridge University Press, 1973.

Safranski, Rüdiger. *Ein Meister aus Deutschland: Heidegger und seine Zeit*. München: Carl Hanser Verlag GmbH & Co, 1994.

—*Heidegger: Ein Meister aus Deutschland und seine Zeit*. Frankfurt am Main: Fischer Verlag, 1998.

Samuelson, Norbert M. *An Introduction to Modern Jewish Philosophy*. New York: State University of New York Press, 1989.

—"Divine Attributes as Moral Ideals in Maimonides' Theology," *The Thought of Maimonides: Philosophical and Legal Studies*. Lewiston, NY: Edwin Mellen Press, 1991: 69–76.

—*Judaism and the Doctrine of Creation*. Cambridge, UK: Cambridge University Press, 1995.

—*A User's Guide to Franz Rosenzweig's "Star of Redemption"*. Surrey: Curzon, 1999.

Santner, Eric. *On the Psychotheology of Everyday Life*. Chicago: The University of Chicago Press, 2001.

Sartre, Jean-Paul. *Being and Nothingness: an Essay on Phenomenological Ontology*. Hazel Barnes (trans.). New York: Pocket Books, 1953.

Schaeffer, Jean-Marie. *Art of the Modern Age: Philosophy of Art from Kant to Heidegger*. Steven Rendall (trans.). Princeton, NJ: Princeton University Press, 2000 (original publication: *L'Art de l'âge moderne. L'Esthetique et la philosophie de l'art du XVIIIe siècle á nous jours l'homme*. Paris: Editions Gallimard, 1992).

Schelling, F. W. J. *Die Weltalter* (1811–15). *Auswahl in drei Bänden.* Herausgegeben von Otto Weiss. Leipzig: Fritz Eckardt, 1907.

—*The Ages of the World.* Frederick de Wolfe Bolman (trans.). New York: Columbia University Press, 1967 (first published: 1942; original publication: *Weltalter. Vol. 8 of Sämmtliche Werke.* Herausgegeben von K. F. A. Schelling. Stuttgart und Augsburg, 1861).

—*Philosophische Untersuchungen über das Wesen der menschlichen Freiheit und die damit zusammenhängenden Gegenstände.* Frankfurt am Main: Suhrkamp Verlag, 1975.

—*Philosophie der Offenbarung.* Frankfurt am Main: Suhrkamp Verlag, 1977.

—*System of Transcendental Idealism (1800).* Peter Heath (trans.). Charlottesville, VA: University Press of Virginia, 1978.

—"Stuttgart Seminars" in *Idealism and the Endgame of Theory: Three Essays by F. W. J. Schelling.* Introduction by Thomas Pfau (ed. and trans.). New York: State University of New York Press, 1994.

Schiller, Friedrich. *Theater von Schiller: Die Raueber, Die Verwoerung des Fiesko, Kabale und Liebe, Der Parasit.* Tübingen: G. Cotta'sche Buchhandlung, 1806.

Schmied-Kowarzik, Wolfdietrich, (ed.). *Der Philosoph Franz Rosenzweig (1886–1929). Band II: Das neue Denken und seine Dimensionen.* Freiburg/ München: Verlag Karl Alber, 1988a.

—*Der Philosoph Franz Rosenzweig (1886–1929). Band I: Die Herausforderung jüdischen Lernens.* Schmied-Kowarzik, Wolfdietrich, (ed.). Freiburg/München: Verlag Karl Alber, 1988b.

—*Franz Rosenzweig: Existentielles Denken und gelebte Bewährung.* Freiburg/ München: Verlag Karl Alber, 1991.

Schopenhauer, Arthur. *The Works of Schopenhauer.* Will Durant (ed.). New York: Frederick Ungar Publishing, 1928.

Schwarz, Stephen P. (ed.). *Naming, Necessity, and Natural Kinds.* Ithaca, NY: Cornell University Press, 1977.

Searle, John R. *Speech Acts: An Essay in the Philosophy of Language.* Cambridge, UK: Cambridge University Press, 1970.

Serafini, Anthony. *Ethics and Social Concern.* New York: Paragon, 1989.

Simon, Jules. "Benjamin's Feast of Booths," *Philosophy Today,* Fall (2003), 47, 3: 258–65.

—*The Double Binds of Ethics after the Holocaust: Salvaging the Fragments.* Jules Simon, John K. Roth, and Jennifer L. Geddes (eds). New York: Palgrave MacMillan, 2009.

Simon, Julius. *History, Religion, and Meaning: American Reflections on the Holocaust and Israel.* Julius Simon (ed.). Westport, CT and London: Greenwood Press, 2000a.

—"The Life of Franz Rosenzweig," in *World Philosophy.* John K. Roth (ed.). Pasedena, CA: Salem Press, 2000b.

Sluga, Hans. *Heidegger's Crisis: Philosophy and Politics in Nazi Germany.* Cambridge, MA: Harvard University Press, 1995.

Smith, Leonard. *Chaos: A Very Short Introduction.* New York and London: Oxford University Press, 2007.

Spiegel, Murray and Lipschutz, Seymour. *Schaum's Outline of Vector Analysis.* Columbus, OH: McGraw-Hill, 2009.

Spinoza, Baruch. *The Ethics.* Samuel Shirley (trans.). Indianapolis, IN: Hackett Publishing Co., 1992.

Stewart, Ian. *Does God Play Dice? The New Mathematics of Chaos.* London: Penguin Books, 1990.

Tewes, Joseph. *Zum Existenzbegriff Franz Rosenzweigs.* Meisenheim am Glan: Verlag Anton Hain, 1970.

Thomson, Iain D. *Heidegger on Ontotheolog: Technology and the Politics of Education.* New York: Cambridge University Press, 2005.

Von Herrmann, Friedrich-Wilhelm. *Heideggers Philosophie der Kunst.* Frankfurt am Main: Vittorio Klostermann, 1994.

Whitehead, Alfred North. *Process and Reality.* New York: The Free Press, 1978.

Williams, Bernard. *Ethics and the Limits of Philosophy.* Cambridge, MA: Harvard University Press, 1985.

Wolin, Richard. *The Heidegger Controversy: A Critical Reader.* Cambridge, MA: The MIT Press, 1992.

Wyschogrod, Edith. *Hegel, Heidegger, and Man-Made Death.* New Haven, CT and London: Yale University Press, 1985.

—*Emmanuel Levinas: The Problem of Ethical Metaphysics.* New York: Fordham University Press, 2000.

Young, Julian. *Heidegger's Later Philosophy.* Cambridge, UK: Cambridge University Press, 2001.

—*Heidegger's Philosophy of Art.* Cambridge, UK: Cambridge University Press, 2004.

Zimmerman, Michael E. *Heidegger's Confrontation with Modernity: Technology, Politics, Art.* Bloomingtion, IN: Indiana University Press, 1990.

INDEX

CPSIA information can be obtained at www.ICGtesting.com
Printed in the USA
LVOW030356061011

249351LV00005B/11/P